Wisdom Wide and Deep

*A Practical Handbook
for Mastering Jhāna and Vipassanā*

SHAILA CATHERINE

Foreword by PA-AUK SAYADAW

WISDOM PUBLICATIONS • BOSTON

Wisdom Publications
199 Elm Street
Somerville MA 02144 USA
www.wisdompubs.org

Library of Congress Cataloging-in-Publication Data

Catherine, Shaila.
 Wisdom wide and deep : a practical handbook for mastering jhāna and vipassanā / Shaila Catherine.
    p. cm.
 Includes bibliographical references and index.
 ISBN 0-86171-623-X (pbk. : alk. paper)
 1. Meditation—Buddhism. I. Title.
 BQ5612.C39 2011
 294.3′4435—dc23

                        2011022681

ISBN 9780861716234
eBook ISBN 9780861718528

15 14 13 12 11
5 4 3 2 1

Author photo by Janet Taylor. Cover design by Pema Studios. Interior design by Gopa&Ted2. Set in Diacritical Garamond Pro 11.5/14.75.

Wisdom Publications' books are printed on acid-free paper and meet the guidelines for permanence and durability of the Production Guidelines for Book Longevity of the Council on Library Resources.

Printed in the United States of America.

This book was produced with environmental mindfulness. For more information, please visit our website, www.wisdompubs.org. This paper is also FSC® certified. For more information, please visit www.fscus.org.

TABLE OF CONTENTS

LIST OF MEDITATION INSTRUCTIONS

LIST OF TABLES

Many of these tables, plus additional, expanded, and updated tables, may be found at www.imsb.org.

PUBLISHER'S ACKNOWLEDGMENT

THE PUBLISHER gratefully acknowledges the generous help of the Hershey Family Foundation in sponsoring the publication of this book.

FOREWORD

IS IT POSSIBLE for people today to attain the deep absorption states of jhāna? Can modern meditators directly know and see ultimate realities, and personally realize the liberating fruit of vipassanā? Decades of teaching both monastics and laypeople from all over the world have demonstrated to me that the answer is *yes*.

Effective methods for practicing jhāna and vipassanā have been preserved and mastered by generations of dedicated monastic and lay practitioners, but until recently have been little known in the West. Many years ago my teacher asked me to plant the seeds of this approach in the West. Under my guidance, Shaila Catherine, one of my American lay students, has since 2006 thoroughly practiced the detailed methods of both jhāna and vipassanā. I encouraged her to write a book based on her own experience of this training, and I am very pleased with what she has done.

Wisdom Wide and Deep is a beautifully written handbook that describes an effective approach to the path of jhāna and vipassanā. This book introduces meditation practices adapted from the fifth-century meditation manual *The Visuddhimagga*, supported by the philosophical structures of Abhidhamma analysis, and securely rooted in the Buddha's teachings. This method is distinguished by its emphasis on the initial development of the meditative absorptions called jhāna, and the precise discernment of the ultimate realities of mind and matter. Once the mind is concentrated and psychophysical processes are seen clearly, insight practice becomes efficient, transformative, and exceedingly effective for realizing liberating knowledge. *Wisdom Wide and Deep* skillfully guides dedicated meditators to experience the stability of deep concentration, to recognize the subtle nature of material and mental processes, and to realize the exquisite peacefulness that arises from genuine insight knowledge.

This is a handbook that respects both the ancient tradition and the needs of contemporary lay practitioners, without compromising either. Shaila Catherine presents the Buddha's teaching by blending scriptural references, personal examples, and timeless stories with detailed meditation instructions. She writes with an authority that comes from genuine meditation experience, and a clarity that is informed by her own personal experiences of this training. The combination of Shaila's pragmatic style and theoretical knowledge produces a striking invitation for the reader to apply these instructions and master the complete practice for awakening.

I highly recommend *Wisdom Wide and Deep* to any serious meditator who wants to practice what the Buddha discovered and taught.

Pa-Auk Sayadaw

PA-AUK SAYADAW is the abbot of Pa Auk Forest Monastery in Burma. He has spent his life promoting the teachings of the Buddha through study, practice, and realization. He teaches worldwide and is the author of *The Workings of Kamma* and *Knowing and Seeing*.

ACKNOWLEDGMENTS

A DETAILED AND COMPREHENSIVE BOOK of this nature represents the work of many individuals who have each brought their insightful and caring attention to these pages.

I am deeply grateful to the Buddhist tradition, past and present, and the countless unknown individuals who have preserved, translated, and articulated these teachings and trainings. It is remarkable that I can sit in a suburban town thousands of years and thousands of miles removed from the culture of ancient India where the Buddha lived and taught, and find my life deeply touched by his teachings. The rich legacy left by generations of meditators includes detailed records of the Buddha's ministry, instruction manuals, and commentaries that remain remarkably relevant to contemporary explorations of mind.

The approach presented in *Wisdom Wide and Deep* shares the teachings that I was privileged to receive from Venerable Pa-Auk Tawya Sayadaw during a 2008 retreat held at the Insight Meditation Society, in the USA. Venerable Pa-Auk Sayadaw carefully guided me through this training. His mastery of these teachings, his patient and flexible teaching style, his extraordinary devotion to meditation, and the wisdom that he earned during more than seventy years of practice combined to create an astonishing presentation of this profound and systematic approach to direct insight. The Sayadaw's assistant, Venerable U Jāgara, brought a practical clarity that helped to make these traditional methods relevant and accessible for Western practitioners. Anonymous practitioners at Pa-Auk Monastery have devoted countless hours to a careful editing of

Sayadaw's teachings and the preparation of detailed English language course material. The publishing team at Wisdom Publications—including Josh Bartok, Laura Cunningham, Eric Shutt, Gopa&Ted2, Joe Evans, Denise Getz, Tony Lulek, and Megan Anderson—dedicated to a vision that values both contemporary and traditional approaches to Buddhist wisdom, worked diligently to present this book to modern readers. The joy and patience that pervaded each communication, and the respect for the dhamma that I see reflected in their work, has been an inspiration for me at every stage of this project.

I could not have completed this project without the thoughtful assistance of Theresa Farrah, Ann Smith Dillon, Faith Lindsay, and David Collins who poured over early drafts of the manuscript. Their feedback clarified numerous points, streamlined the presentation, and made rarefied practices more accessible to contemporary readers. Glenn Smith captured the essence of this work when he suggested the title *Wisdom Wide and Deep*. Additionally, more than a dozen friends, students, and teachers provided valuable feedback on one or more sections of this work, including Annie Belt, John Kelly, Noa Ronkin, Leslie Knight, Anne Macquarie, Sayalay Anattarā, Sayalay Muditā Vihāri, Susan Larson, Janet Taylor, James Macdonald, Jami Milton, Christopher Titmuss, Lila Kate Wheeler, and anonymous readers at Pa-Auk Monastery.

The tables were composed with material gathered from several sources. I drew on the Pa-Auk course material, worksheets from an Abhidhamma course taught by Andy Olendzki at the Barre Center for Buddhist Studies, and charts of Buddhist lists that twelve members of Insight Meditation South Bay had collaboratively drafted for our web site (www.imsb.org). Several tables were inspired by the elegant clarity of tables included in Bhikkhu Bodhi's translation of *A Comprehensive Manual of Abhidhamma* and Pa-Auk Tawya Sayadaw's *The Workings of Kamma*. My respect and appreciation is especially extended to Maureen O'Brien, whose artful and careful attention to each chart transformed rather mechanical details into a presentation that exposes the refreshing beauty of well-organized, systematic thought.

This project has been silently supported by a continuous influx of encouragement and generosity from my meditation community and

family. Many volunteers at Insight Meditation South Bay, most notably Lois Gerchman, took on additional duties in order to free up my
time for writing. My siblings, Lisa and Philip, provide a continuous
source of strength in my life. My mother, Elizabeth Tromovitch, has
supported every phase of this work with endless love, patience, and
encouragement.

I offer copious thanks to the many named and unnamed people who
generously contributed their time and wisdom to this project. May they
be happy and well.

INTRODUCTION
Approaching Deep Calm and Insight

One who stops trains of thought
As a shower settles a cloud of dust,
With a mind that has quelled thoughts
Attains in this life the state of peace.
—THE ITIVUTTAKA[1]

THIS BOOK, *Wisdom Wide and Deep,* follows my first, *Focused and Fearless: A Meditator's Guide to States of Deep Joy, Calm, and Clarity,* which contains the initial instructions for developing concentration in daily life, overcoming obstacles such as restlessness and distraction, building conditions for tranquility and calmness, and establishing the deep meditative absorptions called *jhāna. Wisdom Wide and Deep* extends the training of concentration and insight by drawing extensively on the wisdom preserved in two traditional sources— *The Visuddhimagga,* a traditional manual for Buddhist practice, and the Abhidhamma, a branch of Buddhist philosophy that emphasizes a systematic and analytical approach to understanding the mind. The structure for these practices and many illustrations are derived directly from the teachings that I received from the meditation master Venerable Pa-Auk Tawya Sayadaw of Burma (Myanmar). *Wisdom Wide and Deep* is not, however, a strict presentation of Venerable Pa-Auk Sayadaw's work. Rather, I have infused each topic with related teachings, personal examples, and wisdom gleaned from other Buddhist sources that have also supported my path of practice as a Western lay practitioner.

Wisdom Wide and Deep is an extended introduction to an in-depth training that emphasizes the application of concentrated attention to profound and liberating insight. With calm, tranquility, and composure established through a practical experience of jhāna, or deep concentration, meditators are able to halt the seemingly endless battle against hindrances, eliminate distraction, and facilitate a penetrative insight into the subtle nature of matter and mind. It was for this reason the Buddha frequently exhorted his students, "Develop concentration; one who is concentrated understands things as they really are."[2]

The reader will learn how to establish jhāna using a host of objects: breath; body; colors; elements; immaterial perceptions of infinite space, consciousness, nothingness, and the stilling of perception; heartfelt social attitudes of loving-kindness, compassion, appreciative joy, and equanimity; as well as recollections of the Buddha, impermanence, and death. Each potential meditation subject has unique qualities that foster a deeper penetration of reality. Each concentration subject can usher the mind into sublime states of blissful absorption and then serve as an effective foundation for the clear perception of reality. This well-structured and time-honored curriculum cultivates a refined and focused attention that is capable of examining subtleties of mind and matter. It is a system of training in concentration and insight that will ultimately lead the meditator to a direct realization of the peace of nibbāna.

Some meditators will find jhāna practice easy; they will quickly experience deep levels of absorption and be able to periodically access jhāna during busy lay life. Other meditators may initially find jhāna practice more difficult and will progress slowly, gradually strengthening the spiritual faculties. They may shift back and forth between concentration and mindfulness practices while endeavoring to overcome distraction, self-interest, and hindrances. The majority of meditators have the capacity to succeed at jhāna practice if they dedicate the time and create the conditions for concentration. The Buddha compared the training of the mind to the taming of a wild horse. Some horses learn quickly, others develop slowly; some horses seem to enjoy the training, other horses resist.

Although everyone might hope for pleasant and rapid progress, our rate of development may not conform to our wishes as we each progress with pleasure or pain, quickly or slowly.[3] The continuum of pleasant and painful practice experience is determined by how strongly our nature is disposed to lust, hatred, and delusion. And the sluggish-to-quick continuum is determined by the strength of the five controlling faculties of faith, energy and effort, mindfulness, concentration, and wisdom. These will be explained and discussed further in chapter 2. But whether your progress is quick or slow, pleasant or painful, is of little importance—a wise practitioner will strive to develop every aspect of the path, both the factors that come easily and those that require arduous effort. You can know for yourself bliss beyond sensory pleasures, directly experience transformative insight, and learn how to sustain deep joy and clarity within the complex dynamic of daily life.

Although it has been widely assumed that jhāna states are difficult to attain, and that even if they are attained in the protected conditions of retreat, they cannot be maintained in daily lay life, please do not allow these misconceptions to thwart your explorations. Even in the Buddha's time, some people denied the existence of the bliss of jhāna concentration, like a person born blind might deny the existence of color, arguing, "I do not know this. I do not see this. Therefore, it does not exist."[4] Yet the Buddha taught jhāna practice to laypeople as well as to renunciates, enabling even busy merchants and political leaders to periodically abide in the bliss of jhāna.[5] Although it will require effort, attaining and maintaining access to jhāna is a real possibility, even when immersed in a busy lay life.

We do not stop with the development of concentration. We apply this profound stability to the meticulous discernment, analysis, and contemplation of reality as it is actually occurring. You will learn how to sustain an in-depth examination of the nuances of mind and matter to unravel deeply conditioned patterns that perpetuate suffering. Based on the sturdy foundation of deep concentration, a pragmatic application of the Buddhist psychology of Abhidhamma, and a careful analysis of causes and effects, this training will culminate in a direct and unmistakable realization of liberation. It is the aim of this book to present a practical guide for applying concentration and insight to the fulfillment of the Buddha's path.

Wisdom Wide and Deep is intended as a practice manual; it is not a scholarly or critical exposition. I have largely ignored the philosophical criticisms commonly levied against Abhidhamma scholasticism and the historical controversies that might keep practitioners from a pragmatic application of this course of training. The trainings contained in these pages illuminate the teachings of the Buddha as preserved in the Discourses of the Buddha, along with elaborations and interpretations offered by the tradition of practitioners who followed after the Buddha. The tradition offers us a remarkably effective training in virtue, meditation, and wisdom, and a direct path for realizing the peace of nibbāna.

There are many ways of applying and interpreting the Buddhist path. The approach described in this book is one that I have found to be profoundly effective. With full confidence in the efficacy of this method, I am inspired to present this training in a format accessible to Western lay practitioners. Readers will discover that most chapters include two parallel approaches. First, I have included refined meditation instructions that were derived from the *Visuddhimagga* and the methods taught by Venerable Pa-Auk Sayadaw. Many of these practices will be difficult to understand if you have not practiced in a retreat context with the guidance of a teacher who is trained in these techniques. Second, these rigorous traditional instructions are complemented by a parallel presentation of contemporary reflections that are set off in graphic boxes. These exercises encourage contemplation of the general concepts and support a broad integration of concentration, mindfulness, and insight into daily lay life. Such reflective exercises will be of benefit to all readers with or without access to retreat conditions, teachers, or jhāna attainments.

A strict adherent of the systematic approach may cringe when coming across casual passages that encourage a comparatively superficial contemplation of general concepts; likewise, the casual reader may skip over the technical instructions that seem like boring literature. This work, straddling two worlds, respects both formal and casual modes of exploration. At times you may sense a tension between the general and specific exercises; at times it is a struggle to maintain both balance and depth in practice. I view this dual approach as an expression of my own dilemma as a Western lay practitioner with a deep love of this traditional training. In straddling these two worlds, I may occasionally offend the more traditional reader or bore the more modern seeker; however, I sincerely aim to provide Western lay practitioners with an accessible and yet challenging gateway to these profound teachings.

I hope *Wisdom Wide and Deep* will inspire you to redouble your efforts in practice. Although people often speak about spiritual endeavors as valuable, important, and rewarding, few talk about the sheer delight and bliss of meditation. Although this path may at times be challenging, it can also be extraordinary fun. Enjoying practice does not imply a trivial pursuit. When supported by the happiness of a concentrated mind, protected by the shelter of virtuous actions, invigorated by direct insight, and fueled by an unwavering commitment to freedom, even difficult practices may not be burdensome.

How to Use This Book

There are many ways of approaching the liberating teachings—some students will respond to pithy brief teachings, other students will benefit by methodically detailed approaches. You might acquire a useful overview by reading the book from beginning to end, exploring the reflective exercises contained in each chapter, and maintaining a daily meditation practice that employs the breath as the meditation subject according to instructions outlined in chapters 1–3.

For the sake of presenting a concise and readable overview for the contemporary lay practitioner, I have not included every detail one would study when training with a master, but I hope this work will inspire readers to seek thorough training[6] and supplement this material with the meticulously referenced and salient writings of the Venerable Pa-Auk Sayadaw[7] and primary sources in the Pali Canon with its commentaries and manuals.[8]

Although the presentation is sequential, some meditators will benefit by undertaking the training with variations of order or emphasis. Some concentration subjects explained in section II, such as meditations on the body and loving-kindness, can be developed prior to attaining jhāna with the breath. The unique and precise procedures for insight meditation *(vipassanā)* presented in chapters 11–18 require a substantial degree of concentration; however, jhāna is not a requirement. Most readers will need the support of a retreat context to develop sufficient concentration for a stable absorption and to develop mastery in the attainment of jhāna. Many of the highly structured and traditional meditation instructions contained in sections III and IV could serve as a manual during intensive meditation periods but might not be applicable for beginners who are practicing at home. As you read *Wisdom Wide and Deep,* you will quickly recognize the sections that support your aim, and may choose to skim through the more detailed instructions that might be more suitable for intensive practice periods.

The Buddhist tradition preserves an elegant, efficient, and effective structure for meditation. The path to liberation is open to us, but we must choose to make the journey. When the Buddha was asked why some people have reached nibbāna and others have not, he alluded to a road that connects two local towns.[9] Although residents might know that the road exists, they will not reach the other town unless they travel the road for themselves. Similarly, although the Buddhist tradition has provided instructions, identified signposts, and showed the way to nibbāna, we must undertake the training of virtue, concentration, and insight. Now the choice is ours. How do we live and practice? Are you aware of this moment's breath? Are you aware of the impermanence of your bodily and mental experience? Do you endeavor to purify your mind of unwholesome states and cultivate wholesome states each and every day?

Just as the radiant flame depends upon the presence of a candle, wax, and a wick, wisdom arises with the support of concentration, discipline, effort, and skillful methodologies. It is the purpose of this book to offer an enduring training guide for meditators that explains, explores, and celebrates this exciting adventure into the depths of reality.

SECTION I

Establishing Concentration through Mindfulness with Breathing

CHAPTER 1

Clearing the Path: Overcoming the Five Hindrances

> *Whatever states there are that are wholesome, partaking*
> *of the wholesome, pertaining to the wholesome, they are all*
> *rooted in careful attention, converge upon careful attention,*
> *and careful attention is declared to be the chief among them.*
> —SAṂYUTTA NIKĀYA[10]

YOU ARE CLEARING A PATH for concentration and wisdom. Like a trail that provides a clear path through the wilderness, your mindful training opens a pathway to an inner goal that is unhindered by habitual tendencies and the obstruction of desire. It may feel at times that a powerful effort is needed to meditate, like the force of a bulldozer that clears away rubble after a hurricane. At other moments the endeavor may consist in just a light inclination of intention, that abandons doubt as gently as flicking away recently settled dust with a feather duster. Whether it seems as though the sea has parted effortlessly before you, or that you are doggedly carving out a jungle trail, the moment that craving ceases, an unobstructed path opens up.

✦ MEDITATION INSTRUCTION 1.1
Mindfulness with Breathing plus Counting

This is the initial instruction. Begin the development of concentration by using the breath as the meditation object. The breath is a simple and versatile object with which to learn to establish concentration. You are breathing now. Direct your attention to feel the breath as it enters and exits the nostrils. Focus your attention at the area between the nostrils and upper lip to find the breath. In this meditation you will give your attention exclusively to the knowing of the breath at this location. You do not need to feel the expansion and contraction of the body breathing or observe movement; your object is the breath itself. Every other experience, such as a sound in the room, the hardness of the seat, a memory of the novel read last night, a plan for a conversation you hope to have tomorrow, an emotion of excitement, sadness, frustration, or delight, the scent of flowers wafting in from an open window—all experiences other than the simple knowing of the breath are ignored. Let every experience fall into the background as the breath takes center stage. A traditional analogy suggests that the meditator observes the breath as it enters and exits the nostrils, without concern for any other phenomena, just the way a gatekeeper posted at the city gate observes all that enters and exits through that gate but does not leave his post to follow visitors into the marketplace or to travel out with caravans to the next village.[11] Give your attention exclusively and completely to the steady awareness of the whole breath just at the nostril area.

This can be a very challenging exercise at first. You may find that the mind wanders into thought. If it does, simply redirect your attention back to the breath, again and again. You can add a mental count to each breath to help maintain the focus. Breathe in knowing the inhalation, breathe out knowing the exhalation, and count "one." Breathe in knowing the inhalation, breath out knowing the exhalation, and count "two." Continue to know the in-breath and the out-breath, counting up to eight or ten. Then reverse the count. Breathe in knowing the inhalation, breathe out knowing the exhalation, and add the number. When you return to the count of one, progress forward to the count of eight or ten and then backward to the count of one for several cycles. Then observe the breath without adding any numbers. Use the counting method to help direct your attention to the breath, and drop the counting when you no longer need it.[12] Practice mindfulness with breathing like this daily for forty minutes, sixty minutes, or longer as desired. This basic practice of focusing on the breath is the first meditation subject that we shall use to establish concentration and explore jhāna. ✦

ONE PRIMARY OBSTACLE

You don't need to struggle to overcome a multitude of diverse hindrances or employ an arsenal of antidotes to tackle each specific problem. To develop concentration you can address one primary obstacle—unwise attention. As the Buddha said, "Whatever an enemy might do to an enemy or a hater to those he hates, a wrongly directed mind can do even greater harm than that."[13] A deliberate and wise application of attention is the root skill that every meditator cultivates.

One of the first lessons dogs must learn in canine obedience class is to pay attention to their owners. There are many distracting sights and smells, as well as other dogs around, and the urge to go sniffing every provocative scent is powerfully ingrained. This first lesson—to pay attention—is paramount. Just as dogs need to inhibit natural impulses in order to be guided by the commands of their owners, you must gain control over your mind and thereby protect yourself, and others, from the tendencies that dwell within. The Buddha said:

> Controlled while walking,
> Controlled while standing,
> Controlled while sitting,
> Controlled while reclining,
> Controlled in bending and stretching his limbs—
> Above, across and below,
> As far as the world extends.
> A bhikkhu observes how things occur,
> The arising and passing of the aggregates.
> Living thus ardently,
> Of calm and quiet conduct,

Ever mindful, he trains in the course
Of calm tranquility of mind.
Such a bhikkhu is said to be
One who is ever resolute.[14]

Nearly every obstruction to concentration can be traced to a root error in how you are applying your attention. So consider, what is your attention occupied by during daily activities and during a meditation session? If your attention is applied carefully it will augment skillful states, and if it strays unwisely it may breed unprofitable ones.

THE CAUSE OF OUR PROBLEMS

Five classic obstacles confront meditators: (1) desire for sense pleasure; (2) aversion and ill will; (3) sloth, torpor, dullness, and boredom; (4) restlessness and worry; and (5) doubt or obstinate skepticism. These are the places where most people get stuck. As you develop meditative skills, you learn how the hindrances function; you investigate them as habitual forces without adopting them as your personal story. Just as a bird protects chicks in her nest by watching for dangers, you guard your mind with proper attention and do not become prey to these hindering forces.

When mindfulness is weak, it is easy to be swept away with desire, aversion, or speculation. Regarding such hindrances, the Buddha taught that we must know five things:[15] (1) the presence of the hindrance, (2) the absence of the hindrance, (3) the cause for its arising, (4) the way of its abandoning, and (5) the way for the nonarising of it in the future. The cause for the arising of a hindrance is unwise attention, the way of its abandoning is wise attention, and the cultivation of concentration, mindfulness, and insight is the way for the nonarising of that hindrance in the future.

Mindfulness-based meditation practices may emphasize a repeated examination of hindrances, for instance, exploring sleepiness, staying with restlessness, or watching a desire arise and pass away. Such mindful

TABLE 1.1
Five Ways to Investigate Hindrances

Recognize when a hindrance is present.

Recognize when a hindrance is absent.

Understand the conditions that cause a hindrance to arise.

Understand the conditions that cause a hindrance to cease.

Explore how to prevent the hindrance from arising again in the future.

investigation of hindrances will produce valuable clarity regarding the qualities unique to each hindrance.

During concentration-based practices, however, attention is efficient, precise, and perhaps even curt. When practicing to establish jhāna, it is enough to see a hindrance, let it go quickly, and return to the meditation object without delay. In fact, it is essential to do so, because time spent examining hindrances weakens the single-pointed focus of concentration, postponing absorption. Approach the hindrance sufficiently to understand its rudimentary function and supports; study it just enough to untangle the mind from its grip. You don't deny the hindrance in concentration practice, but simply recognize it primarily as the result of unwise attention and quickly remedy the error. Later, when you discern mentality (chapter 13), you will apply the full strength of the unified mind to meticulously analyze nuances of all wholesome and unwholesome states. However, in order to efficiently lay the foundation for jhāna concentration, please bypass most of this investigation and diligently redirect attention to your meditation object as quickly as possible.

The state of jhāna lies beyond the range of hindrances. Therefore, every moment that you spend engaged with the hindrances diverts your attention, postponing unification with your meditation object. You may have planted a garden with tomatoes, daisies, basil, melons, and zucchini; but you may find that among the seedlings you planted, weeds have also sprouted. Although it is important to discern the difference between the weed and the melon and respond appropriately to each, a wise gardener would not spend all his or her time plucking up weeds—energy must also be given to nurturing the plantings. In meditation practice you must abandon the unwholesome states and also give attention to esteemed wholesome states, such as concentration, mindfulness, generosity, patience, and diligence. You learn what to cultivate and what to discard. You learn how to relate wisely to whatever arises in the mind, to consistently and efficiently abandon wrong attention and establish right attention by focusing on the meditation object.

DANGERS THAT ARE JUST ENOUGH

Just as an oyster transforms the irritating presence of a grain of sand into a pearl, meditators convert irritants into wisdom. If you know you are susceptible to certain hindrances, guard your mind; be heedful. Convert challenges into assets that will deepen your practice.

Soon after arriving at a forest monastery in Thailand, I discovered that several vipers lived in the hollow space below the floor of my *kuti*. Each time I descended the three steps that raised the bamboo hut above the jungle floor I had a flashlight in hand—I was alert to the danger. The Buddha listed several "dangers that are just enough"[16]—not causing panic, disability, or paralysis, but just enough to inspire urgency, mindfulness, and wakefulness. His list included snakes and scorpions; stumbling and falling; digestion, bile, and phlegm; criminal gangs; and vicious beasts such as lions, tigers, and spirits. What are the "dangers that are just enough" in your life? What conditions demand that you pay attention, even when you are tired or busy? Vigilance protects us from external dangers, and it effectively protects us from the internal threat posed by the obstructive forces of craving, doubt, and fear.

Continuity of Awareness

For most lay practitioners, formal meditation averages only an hour or so per day—a tiny fraction of our time. Distraction poses a formidable barrier to concentration. Therefore, to build momentum, we must augment the sitting meditation with careful attention during daily activities. To strengthen the focus on the breath, become sensitive to the breath as you are drinking coffee, bathing, cooking, conversing, slipping on shoes, mowing the lawn, photographing your child, balancing your checkbook, delivering a lecture, or eating breakfast. Notice at any time and during any activity how your mind is disposed, where it wanders, how it apprehends sensory objects; then encourage a composed and calm awareness of the breath as you continue to do your work or engage in the activity. During daily activities, it is not possible to exclusively focus on the breath, yet, whether you are walking, working, talking, or eating, you can use your interest in the breath to encourage a balanced state of calm composure.

THE FIVE HINDRANCES

The Buddha compared the presence of the five hindrances to trying to view the reflection of a face in a pot of water. A mind obscured by the hindrances does not produce a mirror-like reflection of reality.[17] Each hindrance clouds the mind in a slightly different manner. While extensive examination of hindrances should not be undertaken during jhāna practice, meditators must learn to recognize and abandon these common obstructions to concentration.

The first hindrance, *sensual desire (kāmacchanda),* obscures consciousness, as colored dyes will diminish the clarity of water, presenting an alluring field of pattern instead of a clear reflection. Desire has the characteristic of projecting onto an object attractiveness that the object itself doesn't intrinsically possess. When you are entranced by beautiful appearances, you see what you want to see, rather than what is actually present. The misperception inherent in craving embellishes objects with the illusion of desirability or hate-ability—the illusion that the object can bring or destroy happiness. But desire and craving never actually result in fulfillment. The sense of satisfaction, of being and having the object of your desires, only lasts until you want something else; it is fragile and destroyed by the next desire that arises.

As you develop concentration and contemplate impermanence, craving will lose its power over you. You won't need to force yourself to let go. Instead, just as children who play with sandcastles will eventually outgrow a fascination with worlds made of sand, we outgrow the compulsive desires that keep us restlessly seeking satisfaction in external perceptions and activities.[18]

Desire arises when there is incorrect attention to pleasant feelings, whether it is a primitive craving for barbecued ribs, a refined attraction for cultural arts, an inclination toward sophisticated intellectual pleasures, or a subtle craving to repeat a perfectly tranquil meditation. Desire removes you from the direct perception of present experience and seduces you into a mental realm of hope and craving.

One *Calvin and Hobbes* comic strip illustrated this nicely: The young boy, Calvin, was looking at the ground and called out: "Look! A Quarter!" He picks up the coin and exclaims "Wow!!! I'm rich beyond my dreams! I can have anything I want! All my prayers have been answered!" In the next frame Calvin stands quietly for a moment. And in the following frame he leaps onto the grass searching: "Maybe there's more."

The lustful mind is blind to the simple presence of things as they are. With the senses continually reaching toward pleasurable encounters, the mind is left unguarded and seduction is a constant threat. To steady the mind, you don't need to change what you see, smell, or feel; you don't need to eliminate pleasant encounters. You need, instead, to control how you relate to sensory experience. The Buddha taught:

A man's sensuality lies in thoughts of passion.
Sensuality does not lie in the world's pretty things;
A man's sensuality lies in thoughts of passion.
While the world's pretty things remain as they are,
The wise remove the desire for them.[19]

Keep your attention focused and be content with the observation of the meditation object. Hold it diligently and stray desires will not have the opportunity to seduce you. Just as when an elephant walks through an Indian market with street-side fruit and vegetable stands, the elephant trainer will have the elephant hold a rod with its trunk to keep it safely occupied, you can curb a mind that tends to wander toward attractions by firmly holding your meditation object. You may still experience sensory pleasures, but you won't get lost in them. As the Buddha describes, "He takes his food experiencing the taste, though not experiencing greed for the taste."[20] With the development of wisdom, you will understand that sensual desire is not pleasure; it is suffering; it is a force that inhibits the deep peace and rest you seek.

The Buddha taught his disciples to divide pleasure into two categories: coarse sensory pleasure, which is to be feared and abandoned, and refined meditative pleasure, which is to be cultivated and welcomed.[21] Just as a connoisseur of fine cuisine will not find pleasure in greasy junk food, the consistent attainment of refined pleasures dissolves the prior fascination with coarser pursuits. The subtle pleasures of deep meditative absorption replace painful preoccupation with temporary sensory pleasures, just as sunlight replaces shadow.[22] This training progressively abandons lesser happiness to attain greater happiness. Through this quest for real peace, the mind eventually releases into a deep and complete awakening.

The second hindrance, *aversion* or *ill will (vyāpāda),* is compared to water that is heated on the fire. It boils up and bubbles over, preventing a clear reflection. Aversion persists when there is incorrect attention to unpleasant feeling. It can take mild forms such as irritation, impatience, and frustration; chronic forms such as pessimism, pity, miserliness, and

Interrupt the Craving

You need not wait until the threshold of jhāna or the direct perception of nibbāna before you abandon cravings. In introductory meditation classes I ask my students to pause every hour during their daily activities—just a brief pause, to interrupt the seduction of familiar activities and bring attention to the body breathing. Periodic pauses of this sort can interrupt the stream of habitual cravings that dominate the busyness of daily life. Pausing provides a moment of quiet ease; an intervention in the obsession with activity, productivity, and identity; an opportunity to make a different choice. When "wanting" arises, we question it: Do I really want this thing? Is this a reliable basis for my happiness? What is the price I pay in money, time, upkeep, relationship conflict, health, self-respect? What is the long-term cost? Do I know that I have the choice to say no? You might discover that you don't even want the things that you crave. If you don't stop to ask yourself a few questions, you might find unused gadgets cluttering your shelves and useless thoughts cluttering your mind. Craving will pick up anything to sustain itself—whatever or whoever passes by.

anxiety; or dramatic forms such as hatred, rage, terror, jealousy, and aggression. Anything can be the trigger for an aversive reaction if there is unwise attention. You might react to theft with rage, to an illness with pity, to traffic with impatience, to a noisy neighbor with hatred, to cold weather with complaints, to a spider with fear. Aversion has the characteristic of projecting onto an object repulsiveness that the object does not inherently contain. Aversion can never end by replacing unpleasant external conditions with comfortable and agreeable conditions, since

Letting Go

Become mindful of the early signs of desire—that initial pull or force that propels your attention toward the desirable object. Distinguish between the force of desire and the object or perception that is attractive to you. Is the force of craving as pleasant as you hope the experience of that object will be? Notice that in the moment of gratification, the desire simultaneously ceases. Distinguish the difference between these two occurrences—the attaining of the object and the ending of desire. Once you see these as two distinctive causes of happiness, then explore your experience to determine if happiness comes from getting what you wanted or from the ending of the desire. Does attaining the coveted object bring happiness, or could the happiness result from the momentary subsiding of that desire?

Observe a desire today. Feel the tug and the yearning associated with wanting something. Make the choice to relinquish that desire. Do not seek to satisfy the yearning. Just observe what happens when you let go of desire. You may or may not still acquire the object, depending upon the conditions already set in motion. Do you feel happy even when you don't actually get what you wanted?

the suffering is not caused by the external conditions. The problem is the quality of attention, not the physical situation that you encounter.

When the mind is obsessed by ill will or aversion, we tend to react aggressively, impatiently, or with avoidance. Feel the separation that aversion perpetuates; recognize the suffering that it creates; become mindful of anger. There are many ways to employ meditation to resolve anger. You may soften the tendency toward ill will by cultivating loving-kindness (chapter 8); you may counter the separation that feeds anger by personally giving a gift to the person who irritates you; you may discern the object of your anger as bare elements such as a mere collection of thirty-two body parts (chapter 5), as a conjunction of material and mental elements (chapters 12–13), or as a process of five aggregates (chapter 14). As explained in the *Visuddhimagga,* "For when he tries the resolution into elements, his anger finds no foothold, like a mustard seed on the point of an awl, or a painting on the air."[23] Through the development of concentration and wisdom, you will understand the danger posed by aversive states. Comprehending the danger it becomes easier to let such states go and peacefully steer your attention back to your meditation object.

The third hindrance, *sloth and torpor (thīnamiddha)* is compared to water that is covered over with slimy moss and water plants, creating a murky mental state in which the object of meditation is obscured. Sloth, sometimes described as dullness, refers to a sluggish and stiff quality of consciousness characterized by a lack of driving power. Torpor refers to a weakness or enfeeblement of mental factors. Torpor is characterized by an unwieldiness of the mind and manifests as laziness, boredom, or drowsiness. Arising together, sloth and torpor create a feeling of inertia, a sense that the mind is thick and drooping, a "paralysis due to lack of urgency and loss of vigor."[24] The hindrance of sloth and torpor is a severe expression of not being awake to what is really happening.

Sleep is not the cure for sloth and torpor. You can distinguish between physical tiredness and the hindrance of sloth and torpor, between the need to rejuvenate and refresh the body and the weariness that wants to just call it a day. The Buddha urged, "To have your mind set on calmness, you must take power over sleepiness, drowsiness, and lethargy. There is no place for laziness and no recourse to pride."[25] Learn what seduces you into the passive withdrawal of sloth and torpor, and conquer the urge to find relaxation through dullness or separation. You will discover that as distractions weaken and concentration develops your vital energy is no longer drained by habitually meandering thoughts. When the hindrances are absent, delight and happiness refresh the mind. Once absorption is stabilized, you will have access to an immense and rejuvenating energy source that intensifies through jhāna practice. Your physical need for sleep will noticeably diminish.

The fourth hindrance, *restlessness and worry (uddhaccakukkucca),* is compared to water that is shaken by wind—it trembles, eddies, and ripples. This agitated state precludes the possibility of clear seeing. Restless and distracting thoughts are the principal obstructions to concentration; therefore I will address this hindrance at length and include several pragmatic methods to overcome the influence of mental restlessness.

It is not easy to stay focused on the breath. Most meditators sit down, apply their attention to the breath, and the mind immediately deviates. The *Visuddhimagga* aptly describes the untamed restless mind like this: "it runs off the track like a chariot harnessed to a wild ox."[26]

Imagine the horror if thoughts took form, had shape, or occupied space; we would all be squeezed right out of the room! Although invisible and silent, thoughts exert tremendous influence over moods, energy, health, emotions, abilities, relationships, and perceptions. Plans and worries scatter attention like a pile of ashes scatters when a rock is thrown into it. Restlessness dissipates your effort to collect attention; it prevents the cohesion of concentration.

When you are restless you are more vulnerable to whims and may act in ways you later regret, fueling worry and remorse. Even if the content of thought is beautiful, excessive thinking tires the mind and obstructs concentration.[27] As the Buddha remarked, "you are eaten by your thoughts."[28]

The primary method for working with thoughts is to learn to let them go. Clear the mind of compulsive clutter. In fact, much of what you will do when you begin meditation is to abandon thoughts. Sweep away fantasies of future events, ruminations about past activities, and commentary about present happenings. Train your mind to be quiet by not allowing your attention to fuel a constant stream of chatter and interpretation. One of my early meditation teachers compared this basic quieting of the mind to watching a football game on television with the sound muted. You don't need the opinions of the commentator. Let go of your internal commentary and watch life's events unfold with a silent mind.

The networking capacity of the mind is both baffling and awe-inspiring. One contact—a sound, a sight, a touch, a thought—may lead the way through a chain of associations, drawn from the archives of memory. A sight of a fruit bowl might trigger the simple thought, "I wonder what I will have for lunch." It could be followed by a yearning for Thai noodles, thoughts of beaches along the coast of Thailand or the latest advances in diving equipment, memories of the friend who taught your children to swim, the recollection that he died of cancer, anxiety about medical insurance, and financial worries. Any thought can remove you from what could otherwise have been a mindful observation of a peach in a bowl.

 Living Mindfully

If the tendency to wander off into thought is a strong pattern, don't wait for your formal daily meditation. Interrupt the habit as you are driving to work, cooking dinner, reaching for the telephone, walking to the toilet, or exercising at the gym. Many times every day, notice what your attention is preoccupied by and repeatedly bring it back to present awareness.

Planning Is a Joke

There is a popular joke: How do you make God laugh? Easy, just tell him your plans! Things never occur as planned, yet the pattern of planning reoccurs. The Buddha said, "What people expect to happen is always different from what actually happens. From this comes great disappointment. This is the way the world works."[29] We can plan almost anything, as grand as our whole lives, as useless as what other people will say about us, as mundane as the shopping list, as subconscious as which foot will reach the stair first, or as exalted as what we will do when we are enlightened.

Planning is a deeply entrenched habit, effective for many professional pursuits, but an enormous obstruction to concentration.

In meditation you must sit with your own mind and notice if there is a tendency to fantasize about the future or dwell in memories of the past. H. W. L. Poonja, one of my teachers, curtly informed disciples who indulged in stories of long past events that they were living in a graveyard, digging up corpses that have been dead for a long time. In meditation you must dispel fascination with the content of your thoughts and stop retreating into a private world of imagination. You wake up to the present moment as it is.

Thoughts may seem elusive because they exist only in your mind. Each meditator must discover how to let go of this habit. I repeatedly remind myself to "make no plans" during meditation. This simple reminder helps cut through the compulsive tendencies of the planning mind. One of my students visualizes holding up a Ping-Pong paddle, imagining thoughts bouncing off with their own momentum, no aversion added. Another student visualizes a soft whisk broom gently sweeping thoughts aside. You may not need to add visualizations to the meditation; it may be enough to diligently return to your meditation object.

Be the Master of Your Mind

If you find that you are often lost, entangled in a quagmire of agitation, plans, and regrets, don't worry. You do not need to remove yourself to Himalayan caves or sequester yourself in a desert retreat. Trekking in a remote corner of the steppes or the wilderness of the Mohave is not the only way to discover spaciousness and quietude, for simply turning the mind away from habitual imaginings clears the space for jhāna to arise. Thoughts such as "what I will do, what I will say, how I will be seen, what did I experience, what will someone think of me" only clutter and weary attention. Through jhāna meditation you develop the ability to abide removed from disruption and entanglement and access an inner dimension that is undistracted, uncluttered, and unperturbed.

The Buddha warned, "Not understanding thoughts, one runs back and forth with wandering mind."[30] Enjoy the opportunity to quiet your mind in meditation; stop racing between stories of past and future. Be at ease where you are and discover the deep rest of concentration.

 What Do You Think?

Take a moment now to sit quietly. Notice if the quality and content of your mind is worthy of respect. Sometimes thoughts run on automatic—out of control—and are scarcely even concerned with topics that you value. Each meditator will discover his or her patterns and tendencies—perhaps self-criticism, blaming, dwelling in past regrets, or anxiety. Identify your vulnerable areas, reflect upon them, and make a firm decision to tackle these obstructions to concentration. On some retreats I create a personal list of the topics I will not permit my mind to think of. If a thought repeats, I add it to my list, effectively excluding the four or five most persistent themes from intruding upon my retreat.

In a conversation recorded between a group of great disciples who discussed their individual approaches to the Dhamma, Venerable Sariputta describes his power over mind thus:

> Here a bhikkhu wields mastery over his mind, he does not let the mind wield mastery over him. In the morning he abides in whatever abiding or attainment he wants to abide in during the morning; at midday he abides in whatever abiding or attainment he wants to at midday; in the evening he abides in whatever abiding or attainment he wants to abide in during the evening. Suppose a king or a king's minister had a chest full of variously colored garments. In the morning he could

put on whatever pair of garments he wanted to put on in the morning; at midday he could put on whatever pair of garments he wanted to put on at midday; in the evening he could put on whatever pair of garments he wanted to put on in the evening. So too, a bhikkhu wields mastery over his mind, he does not let the mind wield mastery over him. In the morning... at midday... in the evening he abides in whatever abiding or attainment he wants to abide in during the evening.[31]

To develop a mind like Sariputta's you will need the impeccable self-discipline that develops with jhāna practice. The Buddha declared, "[A liberated one] will think whatever thought he wishes to think and he will not think any thought that he does not wish to think."[32] Imagine this potential! Try it. If you don't want to think about something, then don't think about it! Focus your attention on something that you wish to dwell upon, such as your meditation object, or a beautiful quality such as loving-kindness. Resolve to not dwell with unskillful thoughts, and if they arise, interrupt the wandering mind and direct your attention to the object of meditation. Train your mind until it comes under your control and responds to your direction. Become skilled like the great monks and nuns who were described as the "masters of their own minds."[33]

The hindrance of doubt *(vicikicchā)*, the final one in this classic list of obstructions to concentration, is likened to water that is stirred up, turbid, muddy, and set in a darkened room. In such a state one cannot see a reflection clearly. Doubt as a hindering force is distinct from intelligent inquiry. The hindrance of doubt describes the exhaustion of mind that comes with excessive conjecture. It might take the form of doubt in your own ability ("I can't do this practice" or "it's too hard for me"); doubt in the teacher ("she's too young to teach" or "he doesn't understand the right way"); or doubt in the teachings ("enlightenment is not possible for contemporary practitioners" or "jhāna can't be maintained by laypeople"). Doubt can manifest as indecisiveness; it can come cloaked as dogmatic opinions; it may perpetuate factional sides in a conflict. Because bewilderment is a painful state, people grasp views to try to gain a feeling of certainty but end up rigid and stubborn.

When mindfulness is not yet strong enough to penetrate the object of attention, then the mind might do what minds do—think. Habitual thinking rarely leads to revelation. Questions will inevitably arise as your practice develops since you cannot fully understand this process until you have genuinely experienced it. Yet it will help to suspend doubt; curb the tendency to intellectualize about phenomena, and stop the thoughts before they digress into conjecture. If agitation, perplexity, indecisiveness, or excessive analysis occupies attention, then exhaustion and doubt will often follow in its wake. You must set aside the tendency to doubt in order to see the true nature of mind—only then will you no longer have doubts about it.

SETTLE ALL DISTRACTIONS

With practice, you will learn to settle all distractions. Never abandon careful attention. If there is only one chair in your house and you are always sitting in it, although unwelcome guests may come to visit, they will not stay long. Maintain your stance of mindful attention and eventually hindrances will stop appearing. The nutriment for all hindrances is careless attention;[34] simply giving consistent and careful attention to your meditation object will starve hindrances of fodder and nourish concentration and insight.

Progress in meditation requires the willingness to abandon the obstacles. Remain vigilant. There will come a time when you look into the mind and see clearly that no hindrances are present. The Buddha commented, "Friends, when a bhikkhu reviews himself thus, if he sees that these evil unwholesome states are not all abandoned in himself, then he should make an effort to abandon them all. But if, when he reviews himself thus, he sees that they are all abandoned in himself, then he can abide happy and glad, training day and night in wholesome states." He offered the analogy of a youth who views her own face in a mirror. If she sees a smudge or blemish, she will make an effort to remove it. And if she finds her face is clean and clear, she will be glad and happy.[35] As your practice deepens and you approach the threshold of jhāna, hindrances are removed. Tremendous relief and joy may flood your awareness when

TABLE 1.2
Five Hindrances (nīvaranas)

Hindrance	Characteristics
Sensual desire	Thoughts in favor; craving, especially sensual pleasure
Aversion or ill-will	Thoughts against; judgment, censure, disliking, malice toward others
Sloth and torpor	Dullness, boredom, lack of energy, sluggishness and weakness of consciousness and mental factors; may manifest as sleepiness
Restlessness and worry	Distracting thoughts that inhibit calmness; remorse, anxiety
Doubt	Absence of trust or confidence, lack of faith, unwise skepticism

these hindrances are set aside. The mind will be radiant, unblemished, and beautiful. You can be happy, and use this opportunity to further develop wholesome states.

Recognizing the mind unthwarted by the hindrances establishes a remarkable confidence and joy that sets the stage for deep concentration. In a sequence of analogies the Buddha compared the gladness of a mind freed from the burden of desire to the happiness of a man whose business prospered and was finally able to repay a large debt.[36] He compared the joy of a mind without aversion to the delight of someone who had recently recovered from a terrible sickness. He compared a mind released from the bonds of sloth and torpor to the joy of a man who had been locked in prison and is finally freed from his confinement. He compared a mind unoccupied by restlessness and worry to the thrill of a slave who is freed from slavery, able to go wherever he liked. And he compared a mind unfettered by doubt to the feeling of a merchant who, fearing for his safety and survival while traveling through a dangerous desert, finally arrives at the edge of a village. These people would surely rejoice.

Until you perceive the disappearance of the hindrances within your own mind, you will suffer as a debtor, sick person, prisoner, slave, and desert traveler. Perceiving the disappearance of those same hindrances, you can celebrate as one released from bonds, dangers, and burdens. "And when he knows that these five hindrances have left him, gladness arises in him, from gladness comes delight, from the delight in his mind his body is tranquilized, with a tranquil body he feels joy, and with joy his mind is concentrated."[37] With the honest recognition that the mind is unhindered, happiness develops, concentration matures, and you gain the prerequisites for entrance into jhāna.

CHAPTER 2

Leading the Way: Enhancing Five Controlling Faculties

So now I will go,
I will go on into the struggle,
This is to my mind delight;
This is where my mind finds bliss.
—SUTTA NIPĀTA[38]

WHILE SIPPING a cup of tea one afternoon, I found an apt quote by Virginia Woolf printed on the tea bag label: "To enjoy freedom, we have to control ourselves." There is an important link between freedom and control. Self-esteem and confidence are necessary to stabilize attention in meditation, and these arise out of self-control. As you stop resisting the fact that some things are pleasurable and other things are painful and cease diverting energy by trying to accumulate pleasant experiences and avoid unpleasant ones, you will discover an untapped potential to make significant change in your life. In other words, when you learn to control your mind, you will discover the freedom to live with ease in the midst of things that are beyond your control. The Buddha taught, "When this concentration is thus developed, thus well-developed by you, then wherever you go, you will go in comfort. Wherever you stand, you will stand in comfort. Wherever you sit, you will sit in comfort. Wherever you lie down, you will lie down in comfort."[39] An effective synthesis of concentration and mindfulness will enable you to live in comfort throughout life—even as the body ages, the economy fluctuates, and life unfolds.

Five particular faculties lead the mind in the development of concentration, mindfulness, and insight. These five are sometimes called controlling factors, spiritual powers, or spiritual faculties—both beginning and experienced meditators rely on them. They are faith, energy, mindfulness, concentration, and wisdom. These factors gauge and control the development of the spiritual life, and when highly refined they are potent attributes providing power for the spiritual path. The Pali term for a controlling function is *indriya,* which refers to "the act of ruling by rulers." Analogous to the way effective governance protects a society from corruption and internal strife through the rule of law, you exercise control or leadership over your own mind through the cultivation of these five mental factors. These faculties balance attention so that the mind is well directed, orderly, and not overpowered by adventitious defilements; they sustain the power that we need to make progress on the path. If you find it difficult to stabilize the deep concentration of jhāna, you might work more directly to reinforce these five controlling faculties. If your jhāna absorptions weaken and crumble before you intend to emerge, you might examine and fortify these indispensable faculties.

A discussion of each of these five controlling factors follows.

FAITH *(SADDHĀ)*

When you open a box of jigsaw puzzle pieces, you trust that everything that is present is necessary, and everything that is necessary is present. You can likewise trust that you possess the basic abilities needed to concentrate the mind. No doubt you will need to bring forth persistent effort and practice diligently. If you live a complex and crowded lay life, some simplification and solitude may be needed. But what is required is already present in this human life. The willingness to place your heart upon your meditation object, and have faith in the unfolding of concentration and insight, launches this journey. Like a spider sailing out on a thin thread, you venture into practice, not demanding a familiar landing place. Boldly engaging in the practice will develop the path until you realize for yourself the great peace of the liberated mind.

Classical Buddhist teachings describe faith *(saddhā)* as bearing the characteristic of trusting; it gives us the confidence to set forth in our practice. Faith manifests as clarity and resolution. The traditional symbol of faith is a magical gem that when dropped into water has the power to cause all impurities to settle to the bottom, producing pure, clear sparkling water to enjoy. Faith can purify the mind, leaving experience clear and sparkling. Faith settles doubt and agitation, leaving the mind ready to apply effective and cohesive effort. In order to attain jhāna, you will need conviction in the practice, clarity regarding the object, and diligence to continue even when the meditation becomes challenging. Faith is indispensable.

Faith, in a Buddhist context, is not a mystical quality. It is a mental factor that is remarkably practical and functions in relationship to the other four spiritual faculties. Faith does not deify Buddha. Faith in the Buddha, rather, inspires us to make the necessary effort to awaken. There is a deep confidence that since he, a human being, awakened to the peace of nibbāna and taught the way, therefore, we can follow the instructions and realize liberation ourselves. Trust the value of the goal, the efficacy of the methods, and the worthiness of your endeavor. Knowing that generations of Buddhist practitioners have succeeded in this practice, confidently place your heart upon your meditation object.

In meditation you may not perceive instant results, but you might see the fruit of the practice gradually. Some people learn fast, others learn more slowly, but speed of attainment is not an important criterion of success. The Buddha compared the progress of disciples to the rates at which camphor, dry wood, or wet wood burn. Just as these substances will all eventually burn, every meditator will eventually develop concentration. There is no need to compare your progress to that of others—this is not a race for jhāna and there is no definitive timeline for completion. Faith in the practice can keep you diligently plodding along, wearing away hindrances, and burning up the defilements, as you gradually develop mindfulness, concentration, and wisdom.

The type of concentration needed for jhāna can develop quickly for some students; for most, though, it is a slow and gradual process. Likened to the lumberjack whose toil slowly wears an imprint of his hand into the handle of his ax, our efforts will, bit by bit, have an effect. The lumberjack cannot say which day the handle became truly worn to his hand, but there is no doubt that his efforts have made it that way. You may not be able to say in which sitting you overcame the alluring seduction of sloth and torpor, or at which moment you secluded the mind from distracting fantasies, and yet your effort has the effect of wearing away the defilements and hindrances.[40] It is a natural law that actions have effects; even if your development is not as rapid you would like, progress occurs through meditation.

If your faith is weak and you are faced with pain or difficulties, doubt can arise. You might wonder if you can really do this practice. You might wonder if you will ever attain jhāna. If conviction slackens, you will need to encourage and inspire yourself. Allowing attention to sink into the meditation object requires a yielding, trusting steadiness. If you don't trust the practice or your direction, you will remain preoccupied with superficial speculation—criticizing, comparing, anticipating, conceptualizing, and analyzing the meditation before it has matured. If the cohesive force of conviction weakens, then endeavor to strengthen your faith.

Although faith is indispensable, it is also vulnerable to error. The Buddhist tradition distinguishes between verified faith, which is confirmed through your own experience, and "bright faith," which is merely aroused from an outside source. Bright faith (sometimes called blind faith) has valuable inspirational properties, but it can be feeble and will not sustain us through obstacles. Verified faith, on the other hand, stands the test of investigation and is not diminished by criticisms. This deeper level of conviction is born out of wise consideration. Because conviction has been confirmed through discernment and personal experience, you can trust it, even when life is hard or pain racks the body. Gradually, by experiencing the benefits of concentration and insight first hand, you will gain confidence that you have the capacity to endure pain with equanimity, that you are able to let go of destructive habits, and that you are worthy of the joy of a deeply tranquil mind. You will test the teachings in your own experience. As you grow and develop, your faith will strengthen. When faith is mature, doubts and questions subside. Energies then focus easily on the task at hand. Eventually, trust grows to a level that merits the designation of a controlling faculty and ushers the mind into deeply settled states.

Enhancing Faith with Recollections

One traditional tool to enhance faith is to contemplate objects that are worthy of trust. Reflect on what is worthy to know, such as the four noble truths, the path of release, the law of causes and effects. Reflect on what is worthy to practice, such as kind and compassionate deeds, honesty, generosity, renunciation, patience, integrity, and perseverance in meditation. Reflect on the people who practice sincerely and successfully.

Reflective meditations can quickly dispel the little agitations that arise in the course of cultivating the mind, thereby soothing unrest, enhancing tranquility, and bringing joy, brightness, and buoyancy to the mind. To develop these contemplations, focus on a subject worthy of respect and continuously dwell with that lovely notion. There are six traditional reflections incorporated into concentration practice; namely, recollections of the Buddha, Dhamma, Saṅgha (community), virtue, generosity, and heavens. Two of these are illustrated below.

⟶ MEDITATION INSTRUCTION 2.1
Recollection of the Buddha

Of the six traditional reflections, recollection of the Buddha incorporates most of the qualities highlighted by the other five. Therefore meditators may favor this recollection, focusing one at a time on admirable qualities that the Buddha possessed. Begin by looking at a Buddha image of which you are fond. Then close your eyes and visualize the image. As you focus your attention upon that mental image of Buddha, reflect on a particularly admirable quality possessed by the Buddha. Choose just one attribute at a time—perhaps his extraordinary wisdom, that he discovered the path to nibbāna, that through countless lifetimes he diligently cultivated wholesome qualities, or that he was a man of integrity who spoke the truth. Allow the contemplation of the perfection of Buddha's conduct, virtue, and knowledge to brighten your mind with delight and happiness. ←

→ **MEDITATION INSTRUCTION 2.2**
Reflection on Virtue and Generosity

You might explore reflective practices with the combined contemplation of virtue and generosity. First, reflect on the spiritual potency of these qualities in general; consider the benefits associated with virtuous and generous acts. Second, think of specific virtuous deeds or generous actions that you have personally performed, and allow attention to dwell on these thoughts. Third, sense that virtue supports your attention, providing a current of joyful wholesome energy that upholds consciousness, making your mind worthy of the happiness of concentration. Sustain the contemplation, repeatedly turning virtuous and generous thoughts over in your mind to massage away underlying feelings of doubt, trepidation, and stinginess. ←

ENERGY AND EFFORT (*VIRIYA*)

The faculty of effort has the function of consolidating and reinforcing the mind. It supports and drives the required mental faculties to accomplish the task of concentrating on your meditation object. Effort, however, isn't just a matter of trying harder, for if you are always striving, you may find yourself fatigued rather than strengthened. Supported by faith, the skillful application of effort brings an energetic engagement with meditation that leads to greater mindfulness. Balanced effort is both fully committed and deeply relaxing.

Although it is possible to strive too forcefully, I more frequently see students procrastinating in their meditation practice, inhibiting the complete engagement that would carry the mind into absorption. Laziness, hesitancy, and partial commitment divert precious energy. There is so much that you actually can do to bring peace into your life. People often underestimate the amount of energy drained by habits, energy that could otherwise be tapped as a resource and strength. As the Buddha exhorted in his final teaching: "All conditioned things are of a nature to decay. Work out your liberation with diligence."[41] Wise and heartfelt persistence nurtures a balance of effort and ease as you give your whole heart and mind to the practice.

 Total Dedication

In what ways do you offer less than 100 percent dedication to awakening?

Learn what drains and diminishes your effort. Notice the effect of daily habits and entertainments on your meditation. Observe the effects that watching TV, engaging in gossip, or surfing the Web might have on your concentration. If you discover that an activity increases distraction or reduces your energy, you can do something different—engage in more supportive pursuits. Confront any obstacles that sap your strength and determination for practice.

Enhancing Effort: A Tiger's Patience, a Spider's Diligence

Tigers are powerful and patient hunters. They are well adapted to pounce on their prey, but only from relatively short distances—they must wait patiently for prey to get close before striking. Naturalists have discovered that tigers succeed in less than one out of every twenty attempts at the hunt; they need forbearance to keep trying without discouragement. You too need patience to keep making the effort, to continue returning to your meditation object, even when it seems redundant and nothing appears to be happening. There may be periods that are calm to the point of dullness and others that are excruciatingly restless. Meditation will not always be exciting or blissful, but a skillful meditator will apply ardent resolve and open ease, diligently continuing to practice.

In the early 1990s, NASA sent a spider into space in an experiment on the effects of zero gravity on web building.[42] Without her body weight as a guide, the spider wove misshapen webs for the first three days. On the fourth day, she spun a near perfect web. Like web-spinning, jhāna does not need perfect conditions, but it does require diligence. You may not enter jhāna in your first attempt, or your first retreat, but like spiders, you will learn if you just keep trying.

Skillful Effort Is "Just Enough"

Effort is not a static quality. You can't rely upon a single decision to be aware and expect that to bring calm or insight. Skill is needed to adjust the quality and quantity of your effort in each meditation session. Like a well-tuned instrument, your effort should be neither too tight nor too loose.[43]

The ability to adjust the quality and quantity of effort is an important meditation skill. For thousands of years teachers have used daily life examples to describe the intuitive adjustments that we make as our attention meets the meditation object. Balanced effort is compared to the way surgery pupils train to use a scalpel by cutting on a lotus leaf that is floating in a dish of water. An arrogant student may cut it in two or submerge it with overconfident, pushy, and forceful energy. A fearful student is too afraid to touch it and will not make the cut. But a student who applies balanced effort makes a precise and careful scalpel stroke on the leaf.

Similarly, a zealous skipper may decide to hoist his sail in a high wind and so send his ship adrift. A hesitant skipper may decide to lower his sail in a light wind and so will not navigate the waters. But "one who hoists full sails in a light wind, takes in half his sails in a high wind, and so arrives safely at his desired destination"[44] demonstrates the correct application of effort. As the *Visuddhimagga* states:

Adjusting the Quality of Effort

Notice in your meditation how much effort it takes to bring attention to meet the breath. If your energy is low, how does the attention respond? If there is too much effort, how do you recognize that force of striving? Experiment by first reducing the effort, then intensifying the meditation with more vigorous effort. What is the result of each adjustment? When is a strong and powerful energy needed, and when is a light touch more appropriate?

To consume a meal, you must apply the right amount of effort for your fork to pierce a potato. If you exert too much force, the fork will smash through the potato. If there is a deficiency of energy, the potato will not be firmly gripped and could slip off the fork and mess up your clothes. Notice how naturally you adjust the application of strength in daily tasks, and consider what amount of effort is required to settle the mind on the breath.

Just as with these similes, so too…one bhikkhu forces his energy, thinking "I shall soon reach absorption." Then his mind lapses into agitation because of his mind's overexerted energy and he is prevented from reaching absorption. Another who sees the defect in overexertion slacks off his energy, thinking, "What is the absorption to me now?" Then his mind lapses into idleness because of his mind's too lax energy and he too is prevented from reaching absorption. Yet another who frees his mind from the idleness even when it is only slightly idle and from agitation when only slightly agitated…with balanced effort, reaches absorption. One should be like this last named.[45]

Four Applications of Energy/Effort

The Buddha described four kinds of effort, each of which has an important function in practice: (1) the effort to avoid or prevent unwholesome states that have not yet arisen; (2) the effort to abandon unwholesome states if they have arisen; (3) the effort to cultivate wholesome states that have not yet arisen; and (4) the effort to maintain wholesome states that have already arisen.

1. *The effort to avoid or prevent unwholesome states that have not yet arisen.* To prevent relapse, an alcoholic may spend the evening at an Alcoholics Anonymous meeting rather than a local bar. To avoid sloth and torpor, a meditator may begin the meditation in an upright posture rather than reclining in bed. Using concentration practice, you prevent the arising of hindrances by occupying your attention with the breath.

   You can also avoid unwholesome states by learning from others' mistakes. The *Visuddhimagga* suggests that when seeing an unprofitable state in someone else, you may strive, thinking, "I shall not behave as he has done in whom this state has now arisen, and this state will not arise in me."[46] Thus you can circumvent many common errors by observing others.

2. *The effort to abandon unwholesome states if they have arisen.* Anytime you notice that aversion, ill will, greed, lust, doubt, restlessness, laziness, or any unwholesome state has arisen, you have a choice—you can entertain that state or abandon it. When you focus your attention in meditation, you have abandoned all other objects to attend to the simple perception of your meditation object. When your attention wanders off the meditation object, you can practice letting go of distraction. In daily activities, notice where your attention dwells and steer it away from patterns that disrupt clarity or happiness.

3. *The effort to cultivate wholesome states that have not yet arisen.* The Buddha encouraged his disciples to examine the mind and cultivate

wholesome states, day and night. This practice develops many wholesome states such as loving-kindness, generosity, compassion, equanimity, wise attention, insight, happiness, tranquility, concentration, and the five factors that are the focus of this chapter—faith, energy, mindfulness, concentration, and wisdom.

 Cultivating Wholesome States

Choose a quality that you would like to develop. Decide how you will remind yourself of that quality and what you will do to strengthen it. Create simple daily projects for yourself. For example, if you wish to cultivate good will, you might remind yourself of loving-kindness by taping a note with a phrase such as *May you be happy and well* on the bathroom mirror and resolve to recite the phrase as you comb your hair each day. If you'd like to strengthen concentration, you might decide to forsake television and movies, and reduce newspaper reading, in order to add a little more time for meditation each day. If you want to refine honesty, you might carry a small notebook and write down every exaggeration, white lie, deception, or inaccurate statement to discover how dishonesty creeps into your speech.

Decide what you'd like to improve, and actually do something about it. Apply your effort.

---

4. *The effort to maintain wholesome states that have already arisen.* Once you have experienced a flicker of calmness, how do you nourish its continuance? When you have done a generous action, do you reflect on it to allow the motivation to mature? After you have cleared your mind of the hindrances, how do you maintain that purity? Once you have experienced jhāna, do you maintain access to deep tranquility

for the next sitting meditation, the next day, and throughout your life? The ability to maintain wholesome states is a subtle and essential mode of effort for jhāna practitioners. Students sometimes experience a brief immersion in jhāna, but then wander about with senses unrestrained, sabotaging the gains they have made. Once jhāna has been established, a gentle yet steady application of interest and energy is required to maintain the concentration. You can develop a continuity of attention, not only in the sitting meditations, but also throughout the day. Just as a young pregnant woman would consider the well-being of her baby while going about her activities—protecting it from harm while she worked, thinking of it while sitting, considering its nourishment while eating—a wise meditator will guard the meditation object in all activities and at all times.[47] For instance, if you are using the breath as your meditation object, also bring awareness to the breath as you walk, eat, bathe, and work. Gently but consistently nurture your contemplation throughout daily life, and then intensify that focus during formal sitting periods.

Wise effort is a simple development toward what is fruitful and away from what brings suffering. A Tibetan proverb says, "With a stout heart a mouse can lift an elephant." At times you will need courage, commitment, and a stout heart as you apply wise effort to prevent or abandon unwholesome states and to cultivate or maintain wholesome states.

Determination to Reach the Goal

You will only succeed if you apply yourself toward your goals: "Whatever wholesome states there are, they are all rooted in diligence, converge upon diligence, and diligence is reckoned the best of them all."[48] The Buddha had great strength of determination. He remarked:

> Two things, O monks, I came to know well: not to be content with good states of mind so far achieved, and to be unremitting in the struggle for the goal. Unremittingly, indeed, did I struggle, and I resolved: "Let only my skin, sinews, and bones remain; let the flesh and blood in my body dry up; yet there

Arousing Energy When You Feel Lax

1. Articulate and reflect upon your intention, purpose, and aim.

2. When you sit for meditation, straighten your spine and maintain an upright posture.

3. Quickly recognize dullness, laziness, or sleepiness as forms of suffering, and dispel them as instinctively as you would withdraw your hand from a flame.

4. Make a clear decision to be awake and energetic. Instruct yourself to stop wandering and pull your energy together, as you energetically lift your mind up to the meditation object.

5. Reflect on death to rouse spiritual urgency. No one has the luxury to procrastinate.

6. Tap the energy of rapture and joy. Delight that you have the opportunity to practice meditation.

7. If dullness threatens to overtake your meditation, open your eyes, roll your eyeballs for a moment, and take a deep breath and hold it before letting it slowly release. If sleepiness frequently overcomes you during meditation, then stretch, walk, or do some other physical activity before you sit in meditation.

shall be no ceasing of energy till I have attained whatever can be won by manly strength, manly energy, manly effort!"... Through diligence have I won enlightenment, through diligence have I won the unsurpassed security from bondage.[49]

Strong determination is needed to turn away from the sensual sphere and enter jhāna. Without this mental energy, concentration would be impossible. Let nothing deter your resolve. Make your focus unwavering, entertain no sidetracks in your pursuit of liberation.

MINDFULNESS (SATI)

Meditation teachers use a variety of terms to describe mindfulness, awareness, attention, and concentration. Some use strongly directive language to describe mindfulness, such as "penetrative attention," "attention that is thrust upon an object," or "awareness that sinks into the object." Other teachers describe mindfulness as a "receptive, relaxed, nonjudgmental observation," and reserve the more forceful language for descriptions of concentration.

Mindfulness is a mental factor that occurs in conjunction with a cluster of associated mental factors. This ensemble of factors creates the state of heightened attention that we generally call "being mindful," in which circumstances, interrelationships, patterns, and objects that are occurring in the mind and body are seen clearly. Whether attention is focused on a fixed object such as the occurrence of the breath, or directed to observe changing sensory phenomena—for example, following the movement of the belly as it rises and falls with each breath, or observing changing emotional responses—mindfulness is the factor that prevents attention from wandering off the chosen object.

Mindfulness does not permit superficiality; it manifests as the direct confrontation with the object of perception. Its function is to prevent confusion and to consistently remember the object of perception, thus enabling attention to sink deeply into a penetrative awareness of the object. You are mindful when you remember to pay attention, and you are unmindful when you are lost in a cloud of associative thinking and forgetfulness. Mindfulness arises in conjunction with all wholesome states; it is not present in unwholesome states such as greed or hatred.

We cannot neatly separate the development of concentration and mindfulness, practicing one on Tuesday and the other on Friday.

Mindfulness is needed for concentration to develop into jhāna, and concentration is needed for mindfulness to sharpen and mature. The development of mindfulness not only precedes jhāna by clearing away hindrances and recollecting the meditation object, but the factor of mindfulness is found in every jhāna state.[50] While absorbed in jhāna, you will not be spaced out in relaxed trancelike states or float off in a cloud of bliss. Quite the contrary, in jhāna mindfulness is pure, continuous, and highly refined.

Mindfulness serves as the guardian of both the mind and the meditation object. The Buddha encouraged meditators to use mindfulness as protection from the dangers of sensual desire, craving, anger, arrogance, and any form of delusion.[51] Guard your mind with mindfulness, and cultivate mindfulness by remembering your meditation object. If you are developing present-moment attention, you can remember to be present with things as they are. If you are struggling to overcome hindrances, you can keep watch for any hint of obstruction. If you are mindful of the breath, you permit nothing to divert your attention. Try to not forget what you are doing. Become sensitive to what you are experiencing. Mindfulness is absolutely essential for the clear observation of things as they are.

Four Foundations of Mindfulness (satipaṭṭhāna)

The Buddha identified four foundations of mindfulness: body, feeling tone, mental states, and objects of mind.

Mindfulness of body includes awareness of posture—whether sitting, standing, reclining, or moving. You can develop mindfulness and clear comprehension not only when you sit still, close your eyes, and focus on a meditation object, but also while engaged in any activity: brushing your teeth, eating, talking, walking, driving, sweeping the floor, dialing the telephone, typing, urinating, folding laundry, solving a puzzle, watching a child play. Maintain a continuity of mindfulness of the body by focusing on the breath in all your activities. The consistent awareness of this basic expression of breath will support the calming and concentrating of attention, and facilitate a rapid development of concentration with the meditation subject of breath.

The second foundation, mindfulness of feeling tone, refers to a bare impression of the pleasantness, unpleasantness, or neutrality of any present experience. This "feeling" is an initial impression, not an elaborate emotional response to that impression of pleasantness, unpleasantness, or neutrality. When you are not mindful of feeling tones, you might grasp what you find pleasant, push away what you experience as unpleasant, or space out for neutral experience. Mindfulness of feeling can free you from the agitation that comes with the push and pull of desire and aversion. An untrained mind reacts for or against the feeling tone, but when mindfulness arises you will remain present and attentive with any feeling without being compelled by attraction, fear, or repulsion. When mindfulness of feeling is developed, your orientation to experience shifts—you will begin to understand feeling as an opportunity to develop a stable equanimous presence, free of the burden of accumulating ever more pleasant sensations and avoiding painful ones.

Mindfulness of mental states, the third foundation, directs attention to the mind as it is colored by emotions such as love, joy, anger, hatred, interest, boredom, tranquility, and fear. Become sensitive and aware of mental phenomena without indulging or wallowing in emotional states. Don't take mental states personally—just notice what is present and what is absent. Any time you notice that your attention is entangled in a story, let go of the thoughts and notice the quality of the mind instead. Sometimes you will find restless agitation and although you try to return to your meditation object, a moment later the attention slides off again. Keep trying. Mindfulness grows with repetitive practice. When mindfulness becomes strong, you will calmly observe the inner workings of the mind. Each jhāna will sport a distinctive degree and quality of happiness, interest, and equanimity. Notice the dominant flavor of each state; remain mindful and understand fully what is occurring.

The fourth foundation is mindfulness of mental objects, which includes an awareness of the functions of mental states. Now you may observe how desire functions as a hindrance, how faith functions as a spiritual ally, how concentration supports insight, and how craving causes suffering. As your application of mindfulness extends beyond the mere ability to return to your meditation object, you may notice the context, connections, interactions, causal relationships, and functions of mental states. This fourth foundation of mindfulness promotes a dynamic understanding of phenomena, how things arise and interact, and how they support or obstruct the development of the mind.

Clear Comprehension (sampajañña)

The development of right mindfulness is often combined with clear comprehension or full understanding. With mindfulness *(sati)* and clear comprehension/full understanding *(sampajañña)* established, the meditator maintains clarity regarding four aspects of every endeavor: (1) clarity regarding the purpose, (2) clarity regarding the suitability, (3) clarity regarding the proper domain, and (4) clarity regarding the undeluded perception of the activity concerned.[52]

To highlight these four modes of clear comprehension, when you perform an action, first consider if the action is aligned with your aim. Ask yourself: *Is this act likely to support a desirable result?* In the case of meditation, consider if your approach has the possibility to increase concentration and insight, and to reduce suffering. We do not meditate to indulge in bliss or accumulate personal powers; the purpose is to realize liberating insight that will transform a fundamental experience of suffering in life. Clear comprehension of the purpose is the basis for making wise choices.

Second, become aware of the broader context that surrounds an action. Ask yourself: *Is the action appropriate to the current conditions?* In the case of meditation, consider the appropriateness of external conditions such as timing and environment, and internal conditions such as your health and mental state. For example, it might not be appropriate to enter jhāna while the fire alarm is warning of danger, when a child needs food, or in an attempt to deny painful emotions such as grief.

Third, you can consider the domain, range, or extent of your activity. The Pali term *(gocara)* is the same word used to describe a pasture or field in which a cow might graze. It implies the field that attention dwells within or the range of perceptions that occupy attention. How large a pasture do you give to your attention, and does that range support your aim? For instance, when developing jhāna using the breath you will intentionally restrict the focus to the breath at the area near the nostrils—whenever the mind wanders off quickly bring the attention back to the breath. Insight practices emphasize the contemplation of changing phenomena—although there are a multitude of objects for vipassanā meditation, we shall focus on a range of formations and contemplate a set of specific characteristics. The scope of your awareness should support your purpose and be appropriate to the conditions that are present.

At one retreat center I volunteered to assist the cooks as part of a team of vegetable choppers; we silently washed, peeled, and chopped piles of vegetables each morning. A new participant at the retreat center joined the team and was given his first task of squeezing six lemons. Dedicated to his mindfulness practice he carefully washed, cut, squeezed, and deseeded the lemons, diligently bringing mindful awareness to each sensation and movement. After twenty minutes he had successfully squeezed only two lemons, after thirty minutes he had only partially completed the third lemon. The cooks looked on aghast and lobbied the managers of the retreat center to reassign him to a different department; the rest of the veggie chopping team put in overtime preparing the mountain of vegetables that were piling up on the counters all around the lemon-squeezing retreatant. Perhaps his concentration and mindfulness were admirable, but clear comprehension of the purpose of the task, the suitability of his pace, and the field of his attention was distorted. Actions must be appropriate to the conditions—sometimes that will require quick movement, and other times you will have the luxury of slowing down.

And fourth, consider if you have an accurate view of your activity. Have you embellished the perception of your meditation subject with fantasy, desire, hope, expectation, or pride? Is the meditation experience a basis for self-grasping, I-formations, or conceit? When your practice finally culminates in insight, you will fully understand phenomena as they are actually occurring; you will experience things free of the delusion that distorts phenomena into objects of attachment. These four aspects of clear comprehension—clarity regarding the purpose, suitability, domain, and undeluded perception—enhance clarity in every activity, including the simple activity of sitting in silence observing the breath.

CONCENTRATION (*SAMĀDHI*)

The mental factor of one-pointedness, with its characteristic of nondistraction, is sometimes used synonymously with the term *concentration*. Mental factors, such as one-pointedness, decision, energy, and mindfulness, work together to drive attention toward the object of meditation, yoke the attention to the chosen object, and consolidate the associated mental factors into a state we commonly recognize as "being concentrated." Concentration, as a controlling faculty, refers to wholesome states in which many factors come together to create a stable unification of attention with the object of perception. It is not restricted to the deep states of jhāna, but it can refer to the mental collectedness that occurs when we investigate changing phenomena.[53]

Although you may emphasize either deep concentration or dynamic investigation at different moments in your practice, the calm, tranquil, and concentrated mode of apprehending an object goes hand in hand with the dynamic, investigative, and insightful mode of engagement. When describing one who correctly practices his teachings, the Buddha stated, "these two things—serenity and insight—occur in him yoked evenly together."[54]

In Buddhist practice, focused attention is far more than a convenient antidote to the painful patterns of anxiety, distraction, and restlessness, and it is more than just a steppingstone for higher attainments. When the Buddha announced, "I shall teach you noble right concentration with its supports and its requisites,"[55] he did not describe specific meditation techniques such as counting breaths or repeating thoughts of kindness. The Buddha described this unification of mind as synonymous with the fulfillment of the noble eightfold path, and as inseparable from right understanding, right intention, right speech, right action, right livelihood, right effort, and right mindfulness. Hence, right concentration is not measured by just the depth of the concentrated state, but by the purpose for which it is attained, and the use to which it is put.[56]

The noble eightfold path lays out a set of integrated factors, each mutually supportive of the others. Clear understanding and intention regarding the purpose of the path provide a wise perspective; careful speech, action, and livelihood create a purity that permits the mind to rest at ease. The triad of effort or energy, concentration, and mindfulness is of particular interest to the meditator endeavoring to attain jhāna. When you focus your attention on a chosen object in meditation, concentration, energy, and mindfulness occur with a cluster of associated mental factors that together aid attention in dwelling consistently with that meditation object.

The mutual dependence and interaction of mindfulness, concentration, and effort are illuminated by the traditional story of three friends who enter a park together for a stroll.

> [The first friend] saw a champack tree in full blossom, but he could not reach the flowers by raising his hand. The second bent down for the first to climb on his back. But although standing on the other's back, he still could not pick them because of his unsteadiness. Then the third offered his shoulder [as support]. So standing on the back of the one and supporting himself on the other's shoulder, he picked as many flowers as he wanted and after adorning himself, he went and enjoyed the festival. And so it is with this. For these last three states beginning with right effort (right effort, right mindfulness, right concentration), which are born together, are like the three friends who enter the park together. The object is like the champack tree in full blossom. Concentration, which cannot of its own nature bring about absorption by unification on the object, is like the man who could not pick the flower by raising his arm. Effort is like the companion who bent down, giving his back to mount upon. Mindfulness is like the friend who stood by, giving his shoulder for support.[57]

Well supported by effort and stabilized by mindfulness, concentration will successfully reach its aim.

Concentration is called a "profitable unification of mind";[58] it sustains a steadfast attention on the object and adds a powerful force to the observing capacity of mindfulness. Concentration is like the lens that magnifies and focuses sunlight to such a degree that it can ignite fire. The focused and continuous mindfulness of your meditation object will bring strength and intensity to your insight.

Concentration and the Four Jhānas

In the Discourses of the Buddha, the sequence of four material jhānas is frequently described as the defining feature of concentration:

> And what, bhikkhus, is the faculty of concentration? Here, bhikkhus, the noble disciple gains concentration, gains one-pointedness of mind, having made release the object. Secluded from sensual pleasures, secluded from unwholesome states, he enters and dwells in the first jhāna, which is accompanied by thought and examination, with rapture and happiness born of seclusion. With the subsiding of thought and examination, he enters and dwells in the second jhāna, which has internal confidence and unification of mind, is without thought and examination, and has rapture and happiness born of concentration. With the fading away as well of rapture, he dwells equanimous and, mindful and clearly comprehending, he experiences happiness with the body; he enters and dwells in the third jhāna of which the noble ones declare: "he is equanimous, mindful, one who dwells happily." With the abandoning of pleasure and pain, and with the previous passing away of joy and displeasure, he enters and dwells in the fourth jhāna, which is neither painful nor pleasant and includes the purification of mindfulness by equanimity. This is called the faculty of concentration.[59]

In this passage, *right concentration* is defined as the experience of jhāna absorptions. Much of this book is devoted to cultivating these refined states of powerful concentration. But perhaps most importantly, the training will apply your hard won concentration to elicit a direct and wise encounter with reality.

WISDOM (PAÑÑĀ)

Wisdom is the ability to clearly discriminate and discern the essence of things—an ability that develops out of sustained mindfulness and concentration. Wisdom illuminates the object of attention, like a lamp illuminates a cave. It transforms an ignorant or deluded way of relating to experience into a wise, clear, and lucid knowledge of reality. Like a skilled guide who, knowing the way through a dark forest, travels the forest paths without bewilderment and leads the way to emerge safely, wisdom is an indispensable faculty on the path of liberation.

At every level of the training, you will make choices based on whatever degree of wisdom you can muster. The Buddha said that thoughts can be divided into two classes, wholesome thoughts and unwholesome thoughts.[60] Unwholesome thoughts lead to an increase in unprofitable states, exacerbating sensual desire, ill will, or cruelty. Wholesome thoughts promote profitable states such as renunciation, loving-kindness, and compassion. The Buddha said, "Whatever a bhikkhu frequently thinks and ponders upon, that will become the inclination of his mind. If he frequently thinks and ponders upon thoughts of sensual desire, he has abandoned the thought of renunciation to cultivate the thought of sensual desire, and then his mind inclines to thoughts of sensual desire."[61] Consider what your thoughts cultivate, and choose, based on reasoned reflection, whether that thought ought to be entertained or abandoned. When you discover that certain thoughts lead to harm, you may wisely choose to let them go.

The Buddha did not merely instruct his disciples to let go of harmful thoughts, but he also taught that there was value in letting go of all preoccupation with thought, even thoughts of kindness, wisdom, or compassion. He examined wholesome thoughts in his mind and considered:

> This does not lead to my own affliction, or to others' affliction, or to the affliction of both; it aids wisdom, does not

cause difficulties, and leads to Nibbāna. If I think and ponder upon this thought even for a night, even for a day, even for a night and a day, I see nothing to fear from it. But, with excessive thinking and pondering I might tire my body, and when the body is tired, the mind becomes disturbed, and when the mind is disturbed, it is far from concentration. So I steadied my mind internally, quieted it, brought it to singleness, and concentrated it. Why is that? So that my mind should not be disturbed.[62]

Although there is nothing wrong with wholesome thoughts, the Buddha chose to develop a calm, quiet, and still mind—a mind absorbed in jhāna. You may not be obsessed by lust, hatred, or cruelty; usually we are

---

 Two Kinds of Thought

Observe your thoughts today and categorize them according to the root intention behind each thought. Make two lists—one for the wholesome and one for the unwholesome. If you notice a thought that is fueling anger, recognize the aversive state at the root, and add it to your unwholesome list. If you notice a thought of compassion, recognize the wholesome root of non-cruelty, and add it to your wholesome list. When you notice impatience, see the underlying force of aversion. When you think about dessert, feel the force of greed. When confused, arrogant, or hypocritical thoughts arise, notice the root of delusion. And when thoughts of impermanence, causes and effects, and the value of honesty intrigue you, notice the wholesome root of wisdom from which they spring. Track your thoughts throughout a day.

just preoccupied by innocuous but incessant stories and personal plans about our own lives. But until you discover your capacity to rest the mind, focused, clear and fully aware, jhāna will be impossible.

After you have calmed the distracted mind, attained jhāna, and emerged from the absorption, you will harness the power of the concentrated mind to discern ultimate mental and material phenomena in order to understand the causes of suffering and realize its ending.

A POWERFUL MIND

The five spiritual faculties discussed in this chapter—faith, energy, mindfulness, concentration, and wisdom—must not only be strongly developed, but also well balanced.[63] Together these five faculties produce a powerful mind. The Buddha said:

> Bhikkhus, so long as noble knowledge [wisdom] has not arisen in the noble disciple, there is as yet no stability of the [other] four faculties, no steadiness of the [other] four faculties. But when noble knowledge [wisdom] has arisen in the noble disciple, then there is stability of the [other] four faculties, then there is steadiness of the [other] four faculties.
>
> It is just as in a house with a peaked roof: so long as the roof peak has not been set in place, there is as yet no stability of the rafters, there is as yet no steadiness of the rafters; but when the roof peak has been set in place, then there is stability of the rafters, then there is steadiness of the rafters... In the case of a noble disciple who possesses wisdom, the faith that follows from it becomes stable; the energy that follows from it becomes stable; the mindfulness that follows from it becomes stable; the concentration that follows from it becomes stable."[64]

When the five faculties are fully developed each factor reinforces and supports each other factor, preparing the mind for success in jhāna and insight practices.

→ MEDITATION INSTRUCTION 2.3
Observing Long and Short Breaths

After you have observed the breath at the nostrils for some time as introduced in meditation instruction 1.1, you'll notice that some breaths are long and others are short. Observe each in-breath and each out-breath as they naturally occur; notice if each half breath is long or short. In order to determine if it is long or short, you must attend to the beginning and ending of each inhalation and each exhalation. You don't need to mentally recite the words *long* or *short,* nor would you precisely measure each breath. Don't alter the length of the breath. Let the breathing occur naturally and quietly; audible breathing usually indicates excessive control. Observe the breath itself—not the sensation on the skin, not the sound of its passing. Simply register the length to foster a continuity of attention from the beginning to the end of each breath.

If the breath seems to disappear, patiently continue directing your attention toward the spot it last appeared. Resist the temptation to make the breath coarser in order to observe it. Gradually, mindfulness will become refined enough to perceive the subtle breath. ←

CHAPTER 3

Eleven Supports for Developing Concentration

One need not rein in the mind from everything
When the mind has come under control.
From whatever it is that evil comes,
From this one should rein in the mind.
—SAṂYUTTA NIKĀYA[65]

THE BUDDHIST TRADITION offers us a handy condensed list of eleven specific ways of supporting concentration.[66] Please reflect on each item, and consider how the practice of each skill might enhance the conditions for focus, calm, and concentration in your life.

1. *Cultivate cleanliness.* Your mind will be less distracted if your physical environment is clean, neat, and organized. When basic bodily hygiene and house cleaning are in order, fewer things will compete for your attention. Simple routines, like brushing your teeth, tidying your room, organizing your desk, filing papers, and generally keeping daily life duties well organized is one basic preparation for concentration. The *Vimuttimagga* recommends arranging that your physical needs are supportive for concentration, such as suitable food, agreeable weather, and comfortable posture.[67]

2. *Avoid extremes.* Develop a balanced attention through cultivating the five controlling faculties of faith, energy, mindfulness, concentration,

and wisdom as discussed in chapter 2. In particular, balance faith with wisdom, so that neither an excessively critical nor an overly gullible stance overshadows awareness. Also balance concentration with energy so that effort and focus grow stable together like a swift chariot drawn by horses of equal strength and endurance.[68] Strive to bring balance to any area of your life that seems to swing between the extremes of deficiency and excess.

3. *Choose a clear subject for meditation, and know your object well.* Develop clarity regarding both the subject and the object. For example, with the meditation subject of the breath, the object of attention might sometimes be the touch sensation, the nimitta, or the recognition of breath. When working with the meditation subject of loving-kindness, the object might be a dear friend, a squirrel, or all living beings. Fully embrace your meditation subject. If you work with the breath as the subject for meditation and someone were to ask you, "how do you experience the breath?" would you be able to describe the perceptions that you experience as the breath? Would you be able to clearly describe the specific object of attention? Be patient. Remain with your chosen meditation subject without succumbing to the temptation to switch to a new one when you feel bored, tired, or challenged. After concentration is well established, you may go on to incorporate a series of additional practices, but in the initial stages it's necessary to remain clearly attentive to a single, distinct meditation subject, allowing the perception of that object to naturally become more and more subtle.

4. *Dispel sluggishness.* If the mind falls into dullness, actively enliven your attention by arousing three enlightenment factors—investigation, energy, and joy. The tradition offers many suggestions for stimulating these factors.[69] You might exert the mind by studying Dhamma, enhance interest by asking questions, gain inspiration by offering alms or performing acts of generosity, generate joy by reflecting on your virtue, inspire urgency by considering the fearful consequences of laziness, energize attention by changing postures or sitting in the

open air, avoid overeating which might cause sluggishness, and set your resolve upon the development of an alert, energetic, and joyful quality of attention.

5. *Calm the mind when it becomes overenthusiastic.* Occasionally you may need to restrain the surging energies that build with concentration. When rapture is intense, excitement and elation can overpower the mind like the swell of a tidal wave. Excessive delight will hinder progress. Learn to calm and channel the energies of pleasure. Don't let the jubilant energy of jhāna seduce you away from a composed presence. If you feel excessive elation or giddiness growing, feel your feet on the ground, take a few slower and deeper breaths, sense the body, and control your thoughts. Intentionally restrain, compose, and calm yourself. Channel your mental energy to develop tranquility, concentration, and equanimity.[70]

6. *Encourage the mind when progress is painful or slow.* Lift the mind up when it becomes discouraged. You may naturally feel disheartened at times, so it is beneficial to know how to uplift your mind when you feel disappointed or frustrated. What might delight your mind without distracting you from your goal? What would inspire your practice and carry you just a little further along the path of awakening, even when you just don't feel like being aware? What actions or reflections have an encouraging effect for you?

You might be inspired by reflecting on Buddha's qualities, cultivating loving-kindness, reading passages from the Discourses of the Buddha or recalling quotes from your teachers, reflecting on your goals, sensing the power of previous acts of generosity, or reciting chants. Any of these activities might infuse a discouraged mind with energy.

Contemplating the Buddha, Dhamma, and Saṅgha can remind us that for thousands of years people have cultivated these practices to free the mind from suffering—you can too! Reflecting on death may stimulate spiritual urgency and dispel procrastination or negligence. Inspire yourself to overcome challenges and strive for your highest potential.

When you are absorbed in jhāna, pain cannot arise, but before and after absorption, pain may sometimes assail you. Chronic or intense pain is exhausting, but you can learn to encourage the listless mind with purposeful urgency and faith. Become sensitive to early signs that the mind is becoming fatigued, overwhelmed, or withered by pain and respond to these clues by easing up or backing off. Respect your vulnerabilities, and face what is difficult a little at a time. Use walking, standing, or reclining meditation to provide some ease for the body while maintaining the continuity of practice. Awareness of pain can, in its own way, bring profound rewards. Facing the fact of pain conveys us toward an experience of peace and compassion that is deeper than what comfort usually affords; when we hurt, we are rarely complacent.

Especially when in a busy lay life, take a moment before you fall to sleep at night to cheer your mind. Reflect on your day, recalling acts of virtue and good things that occurred. If you can't think of anything good, then consider that at least there won't be any more problems to deal with today; perhaps that thought will cheer the mind before you fall to sleep.

7. *Maintain a continuously balanced awareness.* Apply effort that is neither forced nor lax. Sometimes an intensely vigorous resolve is required. Other times you'll refresh attention joyfully with the buoyant energy of enthusiasm. And there will be other times when you look upon your meditation object quietly with equanimity. Adjusting your energetic connection with the meditation object to bring the attention into skillful balance can be a bit like riding a bicycle—when you are on a bike, you are not fixed in a static central position but are continuously returning to balance as you adjust to the variously changing forces of movement, inertia, and gravity. A meditator who is skillful at maintaining a balanced, even, and equanimous attention on the object is likened to a charioteer whose horses progress evenly together.[71]

Your engagement with the meditation subject will invite a dynamic process of continuous adjustment. Self-assessment or judging, however, can interrupt the momentum of concentration. Inhibit any tendency to judge how well the meditation is going, or to measure how close you are to absorption. If rapture begins to arise, don't dissipate it by rushing off to tell someone about it. When concentration begins to intensify, relax any excessive excitement that might otherwise interrupt the tranquility of the meditation. Remain alert; when you feel deeply still and calm, restlessness could re-arise and concoct stories starring your radiantly composed self who performs enlightened activities! When these habits and tendencies arise, balance your awareness, or they will pull you back into distraction.

8–9. Avoid distracted friends, and seek the company of focused friends. You don't need to search out a soul mate or expect that your friends and family will follow a meditative path. Social encounters do, however, leave impressions in memory that can ripple through the mind during later meditations. If your associates frequently engage in unethical activities or harmful speech, it may be wise to find new companions. If your friends don't share your interest in concentration, you might seek out a local meditation group to provide supplemental social support for your practice.

10. Reflect on the peace of absorption. Contemplate the peaceful and admirable qualities associated with the attainment of jhānas and liberation, and let the potential of this deep happiness inspire your practice.

11. Incline the mind to develop concentration. A clear resolve sets the direction for your development. Articulate your intention and recollect it. Recall that intention each and every time you sit to meditate.

→ **MEDITATION INSTRUCTION 3.1**
Observing the Whole Breath

In your daily meditation, focus your attention repeatedly and exclusively on the whole breath. Observe the breath from the very beginning of the inhalation, through the middle, and to the end of each in-breath and each out-breath. Direct your attention to perceive the breath at the spot between the nostrils and upper lip. As your attention dwells with the breath for some time without distraction, certain experiences associated with concentration may arise. When the breath is uninterruptedly known for a long time, the mind becomes light, buoyant, and bright. Perception of the size and shape of the body may change. Feelings of contentment, rapture, and happiness may flood consciousness. It is not a problem to notice these natural changes as subtle shifts in the background of awareness, but do not give your attention directly to these expressions of concentration. Many pleasant mental factors will develop, but if you follow each one, they will distract you from the simplicity of mindfulness with breathing and will stall the deepening of concentration. Consciousness can receive only one object at a time, so if you are observing changing mental factors instead of the breath, you are not sustaining attention on the chosen meditation object. Remain consistently and exclusively attentive to the breath, undeterred by hindrances, and unswayed by the pleasures associated with concentration. ✦

CHAPTER 4

Beyond Distraction: Establishing Jhāna through Mindfulness with Breathing

*Whoever, whether standing or walking, sitting
or lying down, calms his mind and strives for that
inner stillness in which there is no thought, he has the
prerequisite to realize supreme illumination.*
—THE ITIVUTTAKA[72]

MANY MEDITATION CENTERS follow the Asian custom of leaving the shoes at the door before entering the meditation hall. You might also like to leave your busy discursive mind with your shoes before you sit down to meditate. Every person has a unique attentional bias that is reinforced by a lifetime of habit. Your habits may support you in one role but pose formidable barriers in other arenas of life. Sometimes these habits are highly trained skills—doctors are trained to focus on physical symptoms, soldiers are sensitized to signs of threat, parents become responsive to their children's distress. As you train your mind to stay steady, calm, tranquil, and equanimous with the whole breath, you are not merely replacing one habit with another, more spiritual, pattern. Rather, through concentration practice, you enhance the flexibility and durability of attention as you gain control over the attentional bias of your mind. Establishing jhāna is a matter of first steering our attention away from the threat of distractions and hindrances and encouraging the healthy development of wholesome faculties. As concentration increases and the mind stops habitually wandering into old painful patterns, you will discover joy, tolerance, happiness, and peace becoming readily accessible features of a spontaneous response to life. The quality of your consciousness will change; your state of mind will improve.

Prior to entrance to jhāna certain conditions must be present; the presence of these characteristics indicate that you might be approaching the threshold of absorption:

1. It will be very easy to focus on your meditation object without wandering off. Although a few stray thoughts might arise, they will not pull the attention away from the chosen object.

2. There will be a distinct absence of any hindrance. The hindrances of desire, lust, aversion, doubt, sloth, laziness, restlessness, and worry cannot arise to disturb or distract you.

3. Five important intensifying factors, called jhāna factors, will be present and will grow as you maintain a continuous perception of a single meditation object. These factors include (a) the initial application of attention to the meditation object *(vitakka)*, (b) a sustaining of attention on the meditation object *(vicāra)*, (c) delight, pleasure, or rapturous interest in the meditation object *(pīti)*, (d) happiness, joy, and contentment regarding the meditation object *(sukha)*, and (e) a one-pointed unified focus on the meditation object *(ekaggatā)*. These factors, in specific combinations, accompany jhāna absorption, just as a tree is "accompanied by flowers and fruits."[73]

FIVE INTENSIFYING FACTORS

These jhāna factors develop in the natural course of concentration as you apply and sustain your attention on your breath. They may appear somewhat subtly or quite obviously. Each factor overpowers a particular hindrance, and the development of all five prepares the mind for jhāna absorption.[74] A skillful meditator will not permit the changing landscape of these factors to eclipse his or her focus on the breath. As the factors develop internally, the breath becomes an increasingly refined meditation object. While you continue to embrace the breath as the focal point in the foreground of awareness, trust that these jhāna factors are indeed maturing in the background. It can be helpful to have some understanding of these factors at the onset of deep concentration; you will not, however, explicitly investigate the functioning of each jhāna factor until after you have attained a stable absorption in the first jhāna and then emerged from it. Until then, keep the meditation simple and direct—stay attentive to the bare occurrence of the breath.

Factor 1: Vitakka—Directing the Attention to the Breath

Vitakka—the initial application of attention—describes the mind's capacity to aim, direct, and apply attention to any object that it perceives. This is an essential factor for negotiating the world. Inundated with a daily barrage of sensory stimuli, you naturally direct your attention to certain perceptions while screening out other information that is irrelevant to your aim. Without this ability to direct attention, you might become distraught by the demands of daily encounters.

A resolve to return to the breath any time the focus wanders off and fades will strengthen the directed awareness of the breath. Basic counting exercises introduced in earlier chapters support the repeated directing of attention to the meditation object. The *Visuddhimagga* describes this invigorating initial application of the mind as having the function "to strike at and thresh" its object.[75] Such an energized application of attention connects directly with the meditation object and allows no space for the sort of dull withdrawal that feeds sloth and torpor. Vitakka, in this way, counters the hindrance of sloth and torpor.

Factor 2: Vicāra—Sustaining Attention on the Breath

Vicāra is the sustaining function that accompanies the initial application of the mind. It anchors attention in the present moment. Vicāra is the factor that yokes the mind to the object and escorts consciousness into a penetrating experience of what is perceived. According to the *Visuddhimagga*, "[vicāra] has the characteristic of continued pressure on (occupation with) the object. Its function is to keep conascent [mental] states [occupied] with that. It manifests as keeping consciousness anchored [on that object]."[76] The thorough and confident knowledge of the object that is supported by the sustained focus of vicāra dispels the hindrance of doubt.

The meditative exercises introduced thus far are formulated to support a continuity of attention through the full length of the whole breath—without drifting away. The "applying" and "sustaining" functions work together to focus attention on the breath. The Buddhist tradition offers several similes to illustrate this teamwork.[77] The initial arousing of the mind toward its object of perception *(vitakka)* is likened to a bird spreading out its wings when about to soar into the air and forcing its wings downward to cause it to lift into the sky. Continuous attention on the object *(vicāra)* is compared to that bird catching the draft by planing its outspread wings against the currents, quietly but firmly maintaining constant pressure against the wind. Just as the bird must both periodically flap its wings and also maintain firm pressure in order to keep hold of the air and soar, likewise, the meditator must refresh interest to maintain a continuous observation of the object. That initial application of the mind is also compared to the movement of a bee diving directly toward a lotus; while the sustaining function is associated with the bee's hovering above the lotus and investigating the flower. Applied attention *(vitakka)* is further described as "gross and inceptive like the striking of a bell"; whereas the more subtle act of anchoring and maintaining pressure on the object *(vicāra)* resembles the resounding of the bell.[78] Whatever the analogy, directing and sustaining attention on the breath comprise two critical functions that are consciously and intentionally cultivated. Engaging these two forces occupies much of the initial effort to establish jhāna.

Factor 3: Pīti—Joyous Interest in the Breath

Pīti is a quality of distinctly joyous and rapturous interest in your meditation object. It can manifest in several forms: (1) as a feeling of shivers or goose bumps on the skin, (2) as a feeling like lightning streaking through the body, (3) as a surging wavelike sensation, (4) as an uplifting, buoyant experience reminiscent of floating, or (5) as an all-pervading rapture that suffuses consciousness. It is only this fifth degree of pīti, that of pervasive rapture, which is stable enough to support jhāna.[79] The lesser qualities of pīti can flood the entire body and mind with joyous thrills, but these relatively coarse manifestations of rapture are unsuitable for the deeply tranquil states of jhāna. The manifestation of pīti that functions as a jhāna factor and intensifies concentration must arise as a consequence of the exclusive perception of the meditation object. It is a form of nonsensuous delight that arises through the direct knowing of the object of meditation.

Pīti has the characteristic of being pleased with the object of meditation. This intensity of interest in the meditation object serves to overcome the hindrance of aversion. It functions to refresh the body and mind, but it can also intensify to excessive manifestations of elation or excitement. You may be thrilled that something is finally happening, find the energized appearance of rapture pleasant, or consider it quite irritating. Let pīti arise and suffuse the knowing of the breath, but don't allow it to divert your attention from the breath. Observing pīti tends to amplify its more caustic attributes and cause it to manifest as an agitating field of vibration in the body. Whether you like it or hate it, this energized delight must settle in order to perform the function of refreshing consciousness and effectively enabling jhāna. Restrain any direct fascination with pīti itself and do not let it distract you from the continuous observation of the breath. Trust that pīti, along with the other jhāna factors, will all mature in the process; you don't need to fuss over them.

Factor 4: Sukha—Deep Contentment Regarding the Breath as Object
Sukha is a feeling of deep contentment, joy, peace, or ease that occurs as a consequence of the simple observation of the meditation object. It drenches the mind in happiness. Attention to the breath will remain undisturbed and undistracted when the tenor of experience is deep joy. You may feel like you could sit forever and never want to leave this joy-filled state of ease. There will be no wish to hurry toward the next project or experience. The arising of this vast expression of happiness thus

counters the hindrance of restlessness. With the arising of sukha, consciousness will settle even more deeply with the meditation object—the mind is happy to attend to nothing but the breath.

Factor 5: Ekaggatā—One-Pointedness of Attention on the Breath

Ekaggatā is recognized in the classic commentaries as the leader of all wholesome phenomena. It functions to unite and bind the associated mental factors, much like moisture permits the particles of bath powder to form a soap bar, or rennet enables the particles of milk to form a cheese. This one-pointedness of attention that completely unifies the mind with the meditation object transforms the hindrance of desire. A mind infected by sensual desire moves through life by clinging to serial possessions, opinions, pleasures, relationships, and experiences, as a monkey travels through the forest by grasping one branch after another. When perpetually reaching for the next potential source of gratification, the heart lacks inner peace. As an antidote to the compulsive dissatisfaction of desire, one-pointed attention is unified; it is settled on just what is present, and it needs nothing more. When one-pointed attention blossoms as an intensifying factor, there will be no sense of lack. Consciousness will settle exclusively with the meditation object without wandering and without distraction. Like the steady illumination of a lamp's flame when there is no breeze, a strongly unified focus manifests as a peaceful, nonwavering calm. When you can keep your attention focused this way, the scattering tendencies of habit dissipate and your attention unites with the meditation object.

These five jhāna factors—vitakka, vicāra, pīti, sukha, and ekaggatā—will naturally develop into extraordinarily strong assets through the continuous practice of connecting with and sustaining attention on the breath. You don't need to make a special effort to cultivate each factor individually. Resist the temptation to conjure up happiness, enhance rapture, or rev up these novel thrills. It is not necessary to be specifically aware of the strength of these jhāna factors at this stage of the practice. At this point in your meditation, investigation of the individual factors could disperse the unification of mind that you are carefully nurturing. Be satisfied with a consistent knowing of your meditation object, the breath, and trust that all five jhāna factors will develop out of the simple effort to attend to that object.

TABLE 4.1
Five Jhāna Factors

Factor	Definition	Function	Hindrances Overcome
Vitakka	Initial application of the mind	To direct attention to the object	Sloth and torpor
Vicāra	Sustained attention	To sustain attention on the object	Doubt
Pīti	Rapture, delight, pleasure	To refresh and invigorate consciousness	Aversion
Sukha	Happiness, contentment	To gratify and intensify associated states	Restlessness
Ekaggatā	One-pointedness, concentration, collectedness	To unify associated factors with the object; to eliminate distractions	Sensual desire

WHAT IS A NIMITTA?

As you are engaged in the process of directing and sustaining your attention with the breath, at some point a bright light, luminous field, or subtle image associated with the breath might appear. This can be the beginning of a significant transformation in the meditative perception of the breath. With the arising of such a subtle or luminous perception, the coarse perception of breathing is becoming a refined mental sign of the breath. This phenomenon is called "the counterpart sign" or *nimitta*. The Buddhist tradition recognizes that a nimitta can appear in a variety of ways for different people. It may resemble the light touch of soft cotton, silk cloth, or a draft; it may appear as light, color, sparkling gems, geometric forms, blossoming flowers, a mist, a star, or a pearly illumination; it might be an impression of steadiness or stability which traditional commentaries compare to the firmness of a peg made of heartwood.[80] Many meditators first perceive a motley field or smoky gray that gradually brightens into a stable, bright, whitish light, like the hue of cotton or wool. Students may describe it as a sparkling field that gradually becomes vividly luminous, or as a radiant gemstone that at first sparkles and then clarifies, or as a vibrational field that gradually becomes remarkably silky, smooth, and still, or as simply a light that gradually becomes clearer and brighter.

This counterpart sign, the nimitta, is not based on imagination. It is, rather, a subtle meditative perception of the breath, and so it arises in the area where the breath enters and exits the body. The *Visuddhimagga* emphasizes that one must "look for the in-breaths and out-breaths nowhere else than the place normally touched by them."[81] Carefully avoid enchantment with sparkling images, lights, colors, and vibrations that might appear at other locations. Don't be seduced by false nimittas. Your meditation subject remains only the breath, so allow the breath itself to gradually and authentically become transfigured into a mental reflection of breathing. Gently nurture the clarity of this sign by simply continuing to observe the breath with refined attention. Don't wander off the location of the basic point of contact with the breath to search for a conceptual sign. Also, don't get too excited or distracted by the subtle initial appearance of signs. Guard your meditation object with a continuity of attention toward the whole breath until the nimitta naturally becomes consistent and stable. Don't try to fuss with it, demand that it grow brighter, or heave your attention upon it when it appears. If approached with exuberance, arrogance, or force, it will slip away, like a shy friend who is wary of strangers. If the brightness fluctuates with sparkles or appears like distant shimmering gems stones, don't rush out to seize it with attention; simply continue to remain patiently aware of the whole breath. If the nimitta appears with color, shape, or texture, again, there is no need to improve or glorify it; it will naturally purify as concentration develops.

If you try to grasp hold of the nimitta too soon, it can dissolve or proliferate into varying images and impressions. If, on the other hand, you force your attention back to the coarse sensations associated with physical breaths, the nimitta may disappear, like a friend who feels slighted and quietly leaves the party without saying goodbye. Nourish the breath nimitta delicately and diligently, with an attitude of devotion, appreciation, and trust. As the nimitta begins to appear consistently in the meditation and becomes increasingly compelling, it will effortlessly occupy your attention. It may seem as though consciousness is magnetically drawn into the nimitta, that the nimitta engulfs the mind, or that the breath, nimitta, and consciousness all merge as a unified focus on the subtle sign of breath.

The production of the nimitta is a natural consequence of the concentrated mind. It has been likened to the smooth and yet stunning transformation of the night sky as the moon emerges from behind a cloud. Functioning like a biofeedback device, the nimitta provides informative clues regarding the quality of concentration. Although the eye is not involved, the nimitta usually appears as a luminous impression—luminosity is inherent in the attainment, and stronger concentration will create stronger light. Orient to this pure mental expression of the breath and subtle mental "seeing" as you gradually withdraw attention from the coarse material realm.

When you maintain a consistently balanced observation of the breath, mental energies will eventually cohere with the meditation object. As this occurs, the nimitta will automatically become clear, vivid, robust, and stable, and when the mental faculties are mature, the nimitta will magnetically merge with the breath. Just as a good host offers guests whatever they need without disturbing their privacy, a skillful meditator will nourish the development of the nimitta with spacious, equanimous, and continuous ease, and without being intrusive or demanding.

→ **MEDITATION INSTRUCTION 4.1**
Seeing the Nimitta

At the beginning of your sitting meditation resolve to remain
continuously aware of the whole breath as it appears between the
nostrils and upper lip area. Permit nothing to distract you from
this deliberate observation. Allow the rhythm of breathing to flow
unregulated. The physicality of the breath will gradually fall away
as the breath naturally becomes more subtle by focusing upon it.
Although the breath may seem to disappear, keep your attention
focused on the place normally touched by it.[82] If the mind is steady,
but the breath feels coarse, you may draw your attention gently
away from the skin, and center your observation upon the bare
occurrence of the breath just slightly off the body. Try to observe
the breath as the object directly, rather than inferring it through
the mediation of tactile sensations such as temperature, pressure,
or vibration. One of my teachers illustrated this transition from
coarse physical perceptions to the subtle sign *(nimitta)* of the
breath with a story of a carpentry project. Imagine that you wish to
hammer a very small thin nail into a wall. At first you hold the fine
nail between your fingers and strike at that area, using the physical
sensations of your fingertips as a guide. But after the nail is partially
tacked into the wall, you remove your fingers and just hammer at
the nail itself. Similarly, you may at first feel the touch of the breath
held, so to speak, between the nostrils and upper lip, but once
attention consistently meets the breath itself, you won't need to rely
on that sensation of physical touch. Simply continue to direct the
attention to the breath at that area, bringing mindfulness and equanimity to meet the breath in whatever way it now appears there.

As you zero in on the breath at the location just off the body,
between the nostrils and upper lip, the nimitta will grow increasingly compelling. Until the nimitta becomes stable, use your resolve
to stay with the full breath. As you are observing the whole breath,
if there is a hint of light or a glimmer of a field of illumination,
be glad, but don't interfere with it or fuss over it. Let it develop

naturally. Check to be certain that this is an inseparable manifestation of the breath, not a distracting projection based on desire or imagination. It will intensify as you observe the whole breath and diminish when thoughts arise. Only after the nimitta is stable and bright will this mental sign of the breath replace the crude observation of the physical in-breaths and out-breaths. ✦

IS THE NIMITTA NECESSARY?

Some approaches to jhāna do not teach the use of the nimitta; others maintain that jhāna is impossible without it. I reconcile the disagreement among various teachers by considering the inherent faults of perception. Just as multiple eyewitness accounts of an accident will vary, individuals also perceive internal states differently. Just as it is possible to be in contact with the seat of a chair and not feel the texture of the upholstery, or to be wearing sandals and not aware of the sensation of the shoes, or to stare out a window and not notice the trees, I believe that it is possible for a nimitta to arise and a meditator not to identify it as a significant occurrence.

When I first began to explore jhāna practice I received no instruction in the use of the nimitta. The mind was ablaze with light, but I had not attributed any particular significance to this light, nor learned to distinguish the various kinds of brightness, lightness, and spaciousness that arise with deep concentration. Light arose quickly in every meditation and pervaded the awareness of breath; I assumed this was just how meditation with the breath appeared. Blinded by familiarity, I did not isolate it as a significant perception or use it as a tool during those early stages of my jhāna explorations. At one point during a long retreat a visiting teacher offered me a new angle for approaching jhāna—she inquired if I saw a bright white light. Assuming that she must mean some special sort of light, some different light, not what I had gradually but inseparably associated with each in-breath and out-breath, I reported "no" and that ended the conversation. But not long after this meeting my retreat was interrupted with worldly necessities and some weeks passed before I could return to the meditation practice and reestablish jhāna. Upon reentering retreat I recognized the dramatic presentation of the nimitta as a vivid yet familiar expression of concentration and transformation of the breath as a meditation object. Familiarity can make the most obvious things invisible if we do not know their significance. Until I learned to use the nimitta as a tool to facilitate absorption, it was merely a backdrop to the meditation.

Sometime later I studied with Venerable Pa-Auk Sayadaw, whose methodology explicitly employs the nimitta as an essential tool for jhāna. I found these techniques to be astonishingly efficient and effective. The stability of concentration that had previously taken me several weeks to accomplish, now, aided by the visual expression of the concentrated mind, could be easily attained in a matter of days. So if you don't have several extra weeks to devote to leisurely meditation, learn to incorporate the power of the nimitta. Proper tools make any task easier. These techniques have been used successfully for thousands of years and there is no reason they won't also work for you.

A SINGLE OBJECT

Central to the issue of the presence or absence of the nimitta is the question: What is the object of attention? Are you successfully screening out extraneous distractions and exclusively aware of the basic occurrence of breath? If you are thinking about yourself breathing, or imagining yourself developing concentration, such active visualizations will inhibit the formation of the nimitta. Even though the breath is known initially through touch, excessive fascination with ever-changing physical sensations—such as coolness on the skin, flaring of the nostrils, or tingling in the nasal passages—can disrupt the potential for unification with a fixed focus. Know the breath as it occurs, but with minimal embellishment or interpretation. Maintain continuous attention to just the basic occurrence of the breath. The subtle transformation of perception will occur as attention shifts from involvement with physical sensations to a mental sign of the breath.

One common distraction that leads many meditators astray is the perception of impermanence—although usually considered an insightful perception, here it is a potential obstruction to jhāna. If you shift your attention from the directed focus on the breath to observe the arising and passing of calmness, equanimity, rapture, or joy, you have effectively abandoned your meditation object. Consciousness can receive only one object at a time, so it is not possible to be absorbed in jhāna while simultaneously observing changing perceptions. Having a number of different meditation objects will stall the momentum of the single-pointed focus of jhāna practice. Each particular change of object breaks the one-pointed focus that characterizes jhāna, whether it is contact with sound, smell, physical sensations, other thoughts, or fascination with rapture, fluctuating feelings, or various mental factors that interfere. The Buddha taught that "dependent on the mind and mind-objects, mind-consciousness arises; the meeting of the three is contact, with contact as condition there arises a feeling."[83] Repeated contact of three aspects of cognition—in this case, a functioning mind, an object (the breath nimitta), and mind-consciousness (consciousness of the breath nimitta)—create the conditions for absorption. Therefore, in this training we postpone the investigation of mental and material phenomena in order to establish stability and concentration. In later stages of this training, fully invigorated by the clarity of a sharp, steadfast, and concentrated mind, you will emerge from absorption and contemplate impermanent formations.

When You Think Nothing Is Happening

Until the jhāna factors are strongly developed, attention can easily slip away from the nimitta and linger in a dormant state of consciousness—in Pali language this state is called *bhavaṅga*. The Abhidhamma identifies this state as the life-continuum consciousness that arises between every cognitive process. Everyone has uncountable moments of this life-continuum consciousness, although they usually occur below the threshold of awareness. Slower minds will have longer lapses between sensory processes; sharper minds will have relatively brief excursions into the *bhavaṅga* consciousness because attention will readily engage with the next moment of perception and rapidly process cognitive data.

To the meditator, a lapse into the *bhavaṅga* state may seem as though everything has stopped and nothing particular is known. Meditators describe this as being "aware of nothing" and may mistakenly allude to it as an experience of emptiness, yet they will not possess clarity regarding the object of attention. Sometimes it can seem as though time is just lost. The posture may remain upright; hence, it does not have the obvious features usually associated with sleepiness or dullness. It is usually a very pleasant state, and overconfident meditators may presume it is an accomplishment, or perhaps even the attainment of nibbāna. In reality, however, the mental faculties are not yet strong enough to discern the subtle functioning of this state of consciousness that links cognitive processes. If a meditator enjoys the pleasant but unclear state of *bhavaṅga* and repeatedly dwells in it, the meditation will stagnate and soon the mind will dull into complacency.

Extended lapses into *bhavaṅga* are likely to happen prior to jhāna. These commonly occur as the meditator approaches the threshold to jhāna but will not happen while actually absorbed in jhāna. These lapses are compared to a child who is learning to walk—at first the toddler takes just a few steps and then falls down, tries a few more strides, and again collapses. The mind in jhāna, by contrast, is stable and adroit, and the jhāna factors are strong. It is likened to a healthy adult who can walk whenever, wherever, and for however long she desires, without stumbling or hesitation.[84]

Is It Really Jhāna?

Teachers do not all agree where to draw the line between the conditions that precede jhāna and full absorption in the first jhāna. Some teachers require a deep absorption that allows no thought beyond the initial directing of attention toward the meditation object, so that a single stray thought or engagement with sensory perceptions would constitute a breach of jhāna. Other teachers accept quite light states of tranquility as the first jhāna, permitting fleeting thoughts as long as they do not progress into a rambling train of association. And still others may liberally apply the term jhāna to states in which the jhāna factors arise along with bodily impressions, and accept only a basic detachment from corrupting reactions of desire and aversion as the defining feature of the first jhāna.

In this book I use the term *jhāna* for rather deep states of absorption that can be sustained for a significant duration—twenty minutes, thirty minutes, one hour, two hours, or more—without the intrusion of any thought, sound, or sensation, and without the weakening of the supportive jhāna factors. When students report that they have attained jhāna, I expect that the absorption would easily be repeated sitting after sitting, again and again, unless the conditions were dramatically altered, such as by leaving the retreat or experiencing an interpersonal conflict. To support the depth that is possible, I have usually opted for language that describes a rigorous and steady experience of absorption. You may, however, attain genuine but briefer jhāna states.

When practicing in distracting environments, some meditators may choose to lower the standard of duration to fifteen or twenty minutes, or accept tiny intrusions, to help bring the tranquility of concentration into experience. It is certainly possible to experience a deep absorption, momentarily breach, and then moments later easily plunge back into the absorption. This will often occur when practicing in a noisy environment. Even when the hindrances have been set aside and the jhāna factors are growing, if a stranger unexpectedly entered the room, a delivery truck unloaded outside your window, or a radio was suddenly turned on, the mind might naturally break the continuity of absorption with the meditation object in order to register the various sounds, determine if conditions remain safe, and then settle back reassured that the disruption requires nothing from you. You don't need to wait until you have pristine retreat conditions; such disturbances will not thwart your efforts. By quickly returning to your meditation object without entertaining aversive reactions, those environmental sounds will soon fall away from your field of interest, and your concentration will continue to develop. With repeated practice and the support of somewhat conducive conditions, the brief and unstable absorptions that beginners first experience will become durable and refined.

There are some meditators who have a strong disposition toward insight and wisdom and successfully develop strong concentration and attain jhāna, but find that their absorptions cannot last for very long. Hindrances and distractions do not disrupt the absorption, and yet the mind periodically emerges to reflect upon the state, reenters, and emerges again. In this book I emphasize the importance of stability and therefore encourage longer durations to support the cultivation of deep concentration. It should be noted, however, that character type and personal disposition can influence what a reasonable degree of satisfaction and success might be for each individual meditator.

There is no need to quibble over exactly how many minutes you must remain in each jhāna before the concentration is worthy of the label of jhāna. I simply encourage you to establish strong and stable absorptions. Exactly how long you need to remain absorbed without a single intrusive thought before you can call it an authentic experience of jhāna is a question you will answer for yourself. Later, when you have mastery in jhāna practice, you may sustain jhāna for whatever length of time satisfies your purpose. By training the mind carefully and systematically in the beginning of your practice, you will lay a stable foundation that will support a broad range of options for further development.

On the Threshold of Jhāna

When the hindrances are absent and jhāna factors are well developed, concentration grows noticeably stable. The Buddhist tradition has introduced the term *upacāra samādhi*—translated as neighborhood concentration, threshold concentration, access concentration, or access to jhāna—to refer to a nonabsorptive experience of concentration that begins with the arising of the counterpart sign and endures until consciousness enters into full absorption.[85] *Upacāra samādhi* implies concentration that is in the vicinity of jhāna, close to jhāna, or on the threshold of jhāna and describes the experiences that precede absorption, but it does not necessarily lead to jhāna. It may refer to the conditions that precede jhāna; it may refer to experiences that are reminiscent of first jhāna mental factors, but without the seclusion of absorption; and it may describe the mature concentration that accompanies those meditation subjects (such as the discernment of the body parts, and various recollections) that do not have the potential to reach full absorption. The *Vimuttimagga* likens the manifestation of access concentration to a discourse-reciter who had stopped reciting for a long time and so forgets and falters, as compared to a discourse reciter who "keeps himself in training always and does not forget what he recites."[86] Similarly, prior to the genuine absorption into jhāna, a meditator may periodically struggle with distraction, dullness, or hindrances. After jhāna is established, however, the meditation will develop smoothly. Some meditators use the term *upacāra samādhi* so loosely that it merely describes the feeling of being concentrated and a mind that is stable and happy during meditation. For the development of these practices I find it useful to avoid marking this phase as a distinct state, but simply strive to attain the maximum benefit that each meditation subject offers.

ESTABLISHING THE FIRST JHĀNA

> *Secluded from sensual pleasures, secluded from unwholesome states, I entered and dwelt in the first jhāna, which is accompanied by initial and sustained application of the mind, with rapture and happiness born of seclusion.*
> —Bhikkhu Sāriputta[87]

The feelings of pleasure associated with jhāna are deeply healing and positive, and they can be developed systematically. This energized happiness, called "a joy born of seclusion," floods the experience of the first jhāna and highlights the profound relief known when the mind is separated from hindrances. Each of the four jhānas is matched with a traditional description of the saturation of feeling in that state. Illustrating the first jhāna:

> And with this delight and joy born of detachment, he so suffuses, drenches, fills, and irradiates his body that there is no spot in his entire body that is untouched by this delight and joy born of detachment. Just as a skilled bath man or his

assistant, kneading the soap powder which he has sprinkled with water, forms from it, in a metal dish, a soft lump, so that the ball of soap powder becomes one oleaginous mass, bound with oil so that nothing escapes—so this monk suffuses, drenches, fills, and irradiates his body so that no spot remains untouched.[88]

→ **MEDITATION INSTRUCTION 4.2**
Entering the First Jhāna

To establish the first jhāna, continue to observe the breath as it appears in the area just in front of the nostrils. As the nimitta becomes stable and vivid, in a mind free of hindrances, you will reach the threshold of jhāna. Now sit with the repeated and quiet determination to remain attentive to only the nimitta; turn your attention away from competing interests and diligently sustain attention with the mental sign of the breath for a long time. The exact duration will depend upon circumstances, but a meditator on the threshold of jhāna will easily remain attentive to just the nimitta for most of every meditation session throughout the day, and likely be sitting for sessions of one, two, or three hours at a stretch. Patiently permit the nimitta to mature as you resist any temptation to rush into jhāna. Eventually the conditions will ripen as the controlling faculties mature, the jhāna factors grow strong, the nimitta becomes stable and compelling, and all hindrances and distractions fade away. Then lean into this vivid and stable perception of the nimitta with the resolve to enter absorption—release your mindful attention into this single perception. Students have likened this event to diving into a refreshing pool of cool water, submerging in a comforting warm bath, stepping into a safe sanctuary, or entering into the bond of matrimony. As the first jhāna is obtained, energy increases and consciousness coheres in a unified perception of the meditation object. Mindfulness will remain vivid in absorption; the mind will be bright, and the meditation object will be continuously known.

The subtle activity of applying and sustaining attention (vitakka and vicāra) will continue, but these mental factors function so seamlessly that the attention will never fall off the object. Pleasure and happiness (pīti and sukha) will flood the state, but you will not divert your attention from the nimitta to analyze these qualities of rapture and joy. Allow the attention to remain fully and deeply absorbed in the first jhāna for as long as possible. It is best to establish jhāna many times before reflecting upon the characteristics of the mind in absorption. Examining the jhāna factors can weaken concentration.[89] Beginners may enter the first jhāna with a determination to stay for short stretches, such as ten to fifteen minutes, then gradually increase the time with an intention to remain absorbed for twenty minutes, then thirty minutes, forty-five minutes, one hour, two hours, or longer. Practice entering the first jhāna until you can remain undisturbed for at least one hour if you wish. Allow the mind to rest, deeply unified with the object of the breath nimitta. ✦

Are you in a hurry, eager to move on? The Buddha warned that meditators should be neither complacent with achievements and coast passively along nor arrogant and rush superficially through the sequence. Rushing through these states before they mature is a common error.[90] The Buddha compared this to a cow that hopes to find a better pasture and so leaves its field in search of greener terrain. If she does not take the time to know the trail and remember the way, she may get lost. She may neither discover a better patch of grass nor find her way home.[91] If you are overconfident and race ahead from the first jhāna to the second, you may later discover that your path is unclear. Higher attainments may be correspondingly uncertain or unstable, and it may become difficult to reestablish the lower jhānas. Patience, perseverance, and steadfastness are needed in this practice to systematically establish each level of attainment with skill and adeptness. Develop each attainment with care and precision until you gain mastery; permit each attainment to mature until you can repeatedly maintain these practices without any trouble or difficulty.

How long should you remain in the first jhāna? The answer will depend upon your aim. Stabilization of first jhāna is more important for someone who wants to develop the remaining jhānas, whereas deep experience of the first jhāna is less important if the practitioner intends to shift immediately to the insight meditation practices introduced in chapter 12. In the latter case, briefer explorations of the first jhāna, or merely neighborhood concentration, might provide sufficient concentration. Both long, slow immersions as well as quick shifts between jhānas have value. In this practical approach to jhāna practice, I recommend that you first establish facility with longer absorptions and then later, when you are confident with the process, you might choose to move quickly through the lower jhānas to preserve more time to deepen higher attainments.

ESTABLISHING THE SECOND JHĀNA

> *With the subsiding of initial and sustained applications of the mind, I entered and dwelt in the second jhāna, which has internal confidence and unification of mind, is without initial and sustained applications of the mind, and has rapture and happiness born of concentration.*
>
> —Bhikkhu Sāriputta[92]

Although the first jhāna is blissful in comparison to the states in which you did battle with hindrances, the directing (vitakka) and sustaining (vicāra) factors will eventually begin to wear on the mind. At this juncture you begin a remarkable process that is integral to the successful implementation of jhāna as a basis for insight. Not only have you developed wholesome factors, but you will also relinquish those same jhāna factors. You are cultivating useful tools, yet remaining free of attachment. After each factor has served its purpose, you let it go without hesitation.

When attention zooms in with rapt interest, you will no longer require the coarse services of the applying and sustaining functions to maintain riveting focus. The activities of vitakka and vicāra subside, the mind is

bright and confident, energy abounds, the meditation object continues
to be known with intense clarity, and the mind is permeated with a happiness and pleasure born of concentration. The traditional simile that
illustrates the second jhāna describes a natural spring that feeds a lake:
"Just as a lake fed by a spring, with no inflow from east, west, north, or
south, where the rain-god sends moderate showers from time to time,
the water welling up from below, mingling with cool water, would suffuse, fill and irradiate that cool water, so that no part of the pool was
untouched by it—so, with this delight and joy born of concentration he
so suffuses his body that no spot remains untouched."[93]

→ MEDITATION INSTRUCTION 4.3
Emerging, Reflecting, and Progressing

After the first jhāna is stable and can be sustained for at least one
hour, you may explore the next sequence of reflections and prepare
for higher attainments.

1. Emerge from first jhāna and focus on the area of your heart. Just
    as the term *eye door* refers to the immediate mental processes
    that arise dependent upon a visual impact, and *nose door* refers to
    the mental processes associated with the cognition of a smell, the
    mind door (manodvāra) includes the mental processes that arise
    dependent upon the cognition of mental objects. Traditionally,
    the heart base *(hadayavatthu)* is considered to be the material
    support for mental processes, and blood within a chamber of
    your heart is believed to house the specific material elements that
    support consciousness. Whether or not this accords with current
    scientific understandings of anatomy and the role of the brain in
    cognition, I would encourage you to try the following instruc-
    tions. Later (chapters 12–13) we will carefully examine the heart
    base and mind-door processes to analyze their compositions
    and functions. At this stage, however, directing attention to the
    heart base serves as a skillful method for focusing attention on
    the mind, as distinct from the meditation object of the breath.

Simply direct your attention to this area and notice what you perceive at the heart area. You may become conscious of an echo of the nimitta that appears as you direct your attention to the heart. When you perceive this reflection of the nimitta, try to discern the five jhāna factors that arise along with it. This process of discerning and reflecting on the jhāna factors and jhāna states must be performed quickly, clearly, and efficiently, because the factors begin to dissipate after the absorption has ended. To clarify the recognition of each individual factor, first try to notice the occurrence of vitakka; then return attention to the place that you observe the breath just off the body near the nostrils and upper lip. Reenter the first jhāna for a brief absorption, perhaps a couple of minutes; then emerge again, directing attention again to the mind door at the heart base. Try to discern vicāra. Shift attention back to the place where the breath touches, and if you find the nimitta you may immediately reenter the first jhāna. If you don't find the nimitta, observe the breath until the nimitta again becomes strong and compelling. Continue this repetitive sequence by emerging from jhāna, discerning a jhāna factor by the mind door in the heart base, returning attention to the breath nimitta at the nostril area, and reentering the first jhāna, until you have discerned the five jhāna factors of vitakka, vicāra, pīti, sukha, and ekaggatā. Then try to discern the five factors simultaneously. It can be as simple as glancing at your outstretched hand and discerning that you have five fingers. Because repeated checking of jhāna factors can destabilize concentration, it is best to do this exercise carefully, but quickly. You must know when the factors are present and when they are absent; you must be able to recognize each one individually and as a group. Toggle back and forth several times, entering and exiting the absorption and discerning the jhāna factors until you possess intimate and clear knowledge of the factors that characterize the first jhāna. If your concentration begins to weaken, dwell for longer periods of time in the absorption, and check the factors less frequently.

2. Then emerge from the first jhāna, direct attention to the mind door again, and reflect on two disadvantages of the first jhāna:[94]

    (a) The first jhāna is dangerously close to hindrances. Although no hindrances will arise in the first jhāna, if your energy wavered, the mind could easily slip back into the battlefield of distraction and reaction.

    (b) Vitakka and vicāra are gross factors, effortful and unreliable; hence the attention may slip away from the nimitta whenever your effort wanes.

3. Consider the advantages of the second jhāna—pīti, sukha, and ekaggatā are more peaceful factors. The second jhāna is a brighter, steadier, more confident state, marked by the presence of pīti, sukha, and ekaggatā, with the absence of vitakka and vicāra.

4. Inspired to progress, now return your attention to the breath and its sign, with the resolve to attain the second jhāna. For most beginners, the initial attempt to attain the second jhāna will result in a repetition of the first jhāna. This time, however, the coarseness of the first jhāna will be more apparent. Emerge again, draw the attention to the mind door at the heart base, discern the jhāna factors, and reflect on the advantages and dis-advantages. This repeated reflection will dislodge any remaining attachment to the first jhāna. The mind will release its interest in the coarser attainment and unify with the subtler option of the second jhāna when the first jhāna has been well established for a satisfactory period of time.

5. Try again. Return to the nimitta at the nostrils area determined to attain the second jhāna for a specific duration of time, and perhaps it will occur.

6. Develop stability in the second jhāna, and cultivate the five mas-teries as explained in the next meditation instruction. Confirm that you have established stable absorptions and cultivated some

degree of mastery in the first and second jhānas before moving to higher attainments. ⬅

↬ **MEDITATION INSTRUCTION 4.4**
Developing the Five Masteries

To cultivate mastery in each jhāna, you must learn to control your entrance and exit for each absorption and to systematically analyze the factors that characterize each state that you have attained. There are five masteries in jhāna practice:

1. To be able to enter jhāna whenever you wish;

2. To successfully employ specific resolves to remain absorbed in jhāna for a specified duration of time;

3. To emerge at the expected time when your determination is reached;

4. To successfully direct attention to the jhāna factors;

5. To review the jhāna factors that you have observed.

The first mastery is developed when you can consistently enter jhāna at will and attention responds to your intention. The second and third masteries require the ability to decide how long you shall remain absorbed in each jhāna and successfully emerge at the chosen time—not early and not late. When the predetermined duration has expired, the nimitta may fluctuate in brightness, darken, crumble, shake, or vibrate. This dissolving of the nimitta breaks the concentration. If you are mindful enough not to be swept into habitual thoughts, you will easily emerge to discern the jhāna factors reflected in the mind door. The fourth and fifth masteries require a skillful reflection on the jhāna factors that are present in each state. ⬅

ESTABLISHING THE THIRD JHĀNA

With the fading away as well of rapture, I dwelt equanimous and, mindful and clearly comprehending, I experienced happiness with the body; I entered and dwelt in the third jhāna of which the noble ones declare: "He is equanimous, mindful, one who dwells happily."

—Bhikkhu Sāriputta[95]

The essential features of the third jhāna are quiet contentment and singularity of attention—sukha and ekaggatā. The third jhāna affords a deep feeling of happiness without the agitation of rapturous interest (pīti). Your mind will be captivated by a sublime and subtle pleasure, disinterested in anything else, and saturated in happiness. The Buddha said the quality of the third jhāna resembles a lotus: "Just as if, in a pond of blue, red, or white lotuses in which the flowers, born in the water, grown in the water, not growing out of the water, are fed from the water's depths, those blue, red, or white lotuses would be suffused, filled, and irradiated with that cool water—so with this joy devoid of delight the monk suffuses his body so that no spot remains untouched."[96]

The third jhāna is so pleasantly peaceful that it will be easy to sit contented for very long meditations without strain, boredom, or intruding thoughts. Take advantage of this ease and meditate as long as you can.

✣ MEDITATION INSTRUCTION 4.5
Entering the Third Jhāna

Each meditation session will follow a sequential process.

1. Begin every meditation by focusing on the breath as usual. Allow the nimitta to form and stabilize.

2. Resolve to enter the first jhāna and remain for as long as you desire.

3. Emerge from the first jhāna, discern the echo of the nimitta and the jhāna factors in the mind door; reflect on the advantages and

disadvantages of that attainment, and then return to the nimitta
at the place where the breath occurs with the aspiration that
consciousness unify in the second jhāna.

4. Repeat and stabilize the attainment of the second jhāna until
   you are able to remain undisturbed for at least one hour. Let
   yourself be completely saturated with the tenor of second jhāna
   happiness, characterized by the jhāna factors of rapture, contentment, and one-pointedness. Develop mastery with the attainment of the second jhāna. Although the second jhāna will be
   more delightful and focused than the first jhāna, after some time,
   defects may appear. The intensity of rapture (pīti) can appear
   agitating, almost caustic to some meditators; the mind may seek
   a more peaceful and sublime abiding.

5. Emerge from the second jhāna and discern the reflection of
   the nimitta and three jhāna factors echoed in the heart base.
   Consider the disadvantages of the second jhāna: (a) it is uncom-
   fortably close to the gross factors of vitakka and vicāra in the
   first jhāna, and (b) rapt interest (pīti) is coarse. Reflect on the
   advantages of the third jhāna—happiness and one-pointedness
   are more peaceful, subtle, and sublime.

6. Then return attention to the nimitta at the place where the
   breath touches; be determined to attain the third jhāna. Pīti will
   fade through dispassion toward that rapture, and the mind may
   merge into the third absorption. However, the first attempt will
   probably result in a repetition of the second jhāna. Don't worry.
   Simply exit jhāna after a few minutes to check. Discern the jhāna
   factors that are reflected in the mind door, determine which
   absorption actually occurred, reflect once more on the disadvantages and advantages, and then try again. With practice you will
   succeed.

7. Then cultivate the five masteries for the third jhāna as mentioned previously in meditation instruction 4.4. ✦

Establishing the Fourth Jhāna

With the abandoning of pleasure and pain, and with the previous passing away of joy and displeasure, I entered and dwelt in the fourth jhāna, which is neither painful nor pleasant and includes the purification of mindfulness by equanimity.
—Bhikkhu Sāriputta[97]

The shift to the fourth jhāna occurs when happiness fades away and is replaced by a feeling that is neither pleasant nor unpleasant. This is the feeling tone of equanimity *(upekkhā)*. After reflecting on the defects of the third jhāna and the advantages to the fourth jhāna you will willingly trade happiness for equanimity. In the fourth jhāna the mind is totally calmed, equanimous, completely engulfed by peace, and unified with the meditation object. It is profoundly undisturbed and characterized by the salient features of single-pointed attention and the feeling tone of equanimity. The Buddha described the tenor of the fourth jhāna as all encompassing and quiet: "Just as if a man were to sit wrapped from head to foot in a white garment, so that no part of him was untouched by that garment—so his body is suffused by that equanimity so that no spot remains untouched by it."[98]

You will by now be getting the hang of this systematic method. The methodical and repetitive practice creates an easy track or groove of habit; this will facilitate the maintenance of these attainments in the future. Practice so that each level of jhāna is crisply defined. Don't permit your mind to slip and slide between these states. Don't rush. Methodically establish each stage step by step until mastery is attained.

✦ Meditation Instruction 4.6
Entering the Fourth Jhāna

1. Begin as usual with the breath as object and allow the nimitta to arise, stabilize, and mature. Shift to the nimitta as the transfiguration of the breath.

2. With a clear resolve, enter the first jhāna for a specific period of time.

3. Emerge from the first jhāna at the predetermined time; focus on the mind door at the heart base; see the reflection of the nimitta; discern the five jhāna factors; and reflect on the disadvantages and advantages associated with the first jhāna:
   (a) The first jhāna is dangerously close to the hindrances;
   (b) Vitakka and vicāra are coarse;
   (c) The second jhāna will be more peaceful and sublime.

4. Resolve to enter the second jhāna and remain for a specific duration of time.

5. Emerge from the second jhāna and focus on the mind door at the heart base; discern the nimitta; reflect on the three jhāna factors that characterize the second jhāna; contemplate the disadvantages and advantages of those states and factors:
   (a) The second jhāna is threatened by its proximity to the agitation inherent in the first jhāna.
   (b) The factor of pīti is coarse.
   (c) The third jhāna will be more pleasant, peaceful, and sublime.

   After you have developed a satisfactory degree of mastery, you may adopt shorter lengths of time to rest absorbed in the first and second jhānas in order to preserve more time for the higher jhānas, but please do not skip steps.

6. Resolve to enter the third jhāna for a determined period of time and cultivate that attainment.

7. After you have achieved at least one hour of uninterrupted absorption, or are satisfied with the stability of the third jhāna, emerge from the third jhāna and draw your attention to the reflection of the nimitta and mental factors perceivable in the mind door at the heart base. Contemplate the disadvantages and advantages:

(a) The third jhāna is unpleasantly close to the coarser state of the second jhāna.

(b) The factor of sukha is relatively coarse.

(c) The fourth jhāna will be more subtle, peaceful, and sublime.

Contemplating the defects of joy and the advantages of the more peaceful abiding in the fourth jhāna will heighten dispassion and enable consciousness to unify with the fourth jhāna.

8. Then return your attention to the breath nimitta at the area of the nostrils with the desire to release any preference for happiness and to abide in the fourth jhāna, which is characterized by equanimity. The first time, stay in jhāna for just a few minutes and then exit, check the factors, and assess which jhāna actually occurred. Then reflect once again on the disadvantages of the third jhāna and the advantages of the fourth jhāna. It may take beginners several tries before the mind truly releases its attraction to the pervasive bliss of the third jhāna and settles in the quiet sublime stillness of the fourth jhāna.

9. Develop the fourth jhāna, incrementally extending the length of absorption until you can remain undisturbed for more than one hour or as long as you wish.

10. Cultivate this attainment until you have developed the five masteries regarding the fourth jhāna. ⬅

The fourth jhāna is a fabulously useful state that purifies and refines mindfulness through continuous association with equanimity. A mind emerging from the fourth jhāna is balanced and steady—it has attained a workable condition for insight and will serve as a fit vehicle to examine the subtle nature of reality. As the Buddha phrased it, "he...with mind concentrated, purified and cleansed, unblemished, free from impurities, malleable, workable, established, and having gained imperturbability, applies and directs his mind to"[99] the numerous practices for insight meditation.

Most people will need the protected structure of a retreat to learn the way into these deep absorption states. Although some students can enter absorption on retreats as short as one week, many students need a month or more to establish concentration and experience its depth. Yet, jhāna is genuinely attainable and produces fruit worthy of every moment of the endeavor.

TABLE 4.2
Four Jhānas

Jhāna	Factors Abandoned	Factors Acquired or Intensified
First	*Five hindrances:* Sloth and torpor Doubt Ill will/aversion Restlessness Sensual desire	*Five jhāna factors:* Initial application of mind Sustained attention Rapture Happiness One-pointedness
Second	Initial application of mind Sustained attention	Rapture Happiness One-pointedness
Third	Rapture	Subtle happiness One-pointedness
Fourth	Happiness	One-pointedness Equanimity

TABLE 4.3
Progression of Jhāna Factors

FACTORS	JHĀNA			
	First	Second	Third	Fourth
Initial application of the mind (*vitakka*)	▓			
Sustained attention (*vicāra*)	▓			
Rapture (*pīti*)	▓	▓		
Happiness (*sukha*)	▓	▓	▓	
One-pointedness (*ekaggatā*)	▓	▓	▓	▓
Equanimity (*upekkhā*)				▓

 # SECTION II

Concentration Beyond the Breath

INTRODUCTION TO SECTION II:

Concentration Beyond the Breath

His concentrated mind is thus purified, bright,
unblemished, rid of imperfection, malleable, wieldy,
steady, and attained to imperturbability.
—MAJJHIMA NIKĀYA[100]

S OME MEDITATORS want to apply the heightened state of clarity as quickly as possible to the development of insight and may choose to jump immediately into the four elements meditation, which is introduced in chapter 12. Although it is certainly possible to make this leap, I would encourage most meditators to strengthen concentration with the additional jhāna practices that are introduced in section II. These include body parts; colors and elements that form mental impressions called *kasiṇas;* immaterial abidings; immeasurable attitudes of loving-kindness, compassion, appreciative joy, and equanimity; and reflections on death. Facility with at least one kasiṇa will activate intensely focused and expansive features of the concentrated mind. However, you have options; your decisions may be influenced not only by your abilities and aspirations, but also by the pragmatic conditions of access to qualified teachers and time available for retreat.

Although some practitioners may choose to specialize in a particular concentration subject, or may find, for example, that they are satisfied after the development of one kasiṇa rather than all ten kasiṇas, you may enjoy exploring the wealth and range of approaches offered in this comprehensive training system. Few contemporary lay practitioners take the time to comprehend the role each meditation object plays and to experience its unique effect on consciousness, but if you build a sturdy and pliant foundation through a repeated and diverse training in concentration, these rarefied states will remain accessible to you both on retreat and in daily life, and they will not dissipate after just a few glimpses.

The following section includes detailed instructions for deepening and extending the practice by establishing jhāna with additional meditation subjects. Each new meditation subject enhances concentration, brightens attention, expands consciousness, and refines the ability to hold an object with balanced attention while the jhāna factors continue to refresh attention and purify consciousness.

At this juncture, some readers might naturally assume that after establishing the fourth jhāna with the breath as object one would precede in a numerically ascending order to the fifth jhāna and the subsequent immaterial states. It may therefore surprise readers that the next chapter in the training focuses instead on body parts that have the potential to raise the mind only to the first jhāna. Although the sequence might not seem logical at this stage, I encourage you to explore the progression as presented here. Before I had the benefit of systematic training with Venerable Pa-Auk Sayadaw, I had fumbled experimentally through many of these same meditation subjects—I know first-hand the many errors that a haphazard undertaking can produce. The system presented in this book offers a pragmatic and trustworthy approach in which each level of attainment creates a foundation that supports the next, often more subtle, attainment and enables meditators to rapidly develop facility with jhāna. Each concentration practice follows a carefully considered and repetitive progression, building on the methodical procedure laid out in chapter 4. Each meditation subject has unique attributes and offers unique benefits. Each jhāna, each reflection, each determination, and each insight makes an impression on consciousness and molds the mind into a calm, wise, and fit vessel for liberating insight.

The systematic repetition that is a hallmark of this training method can be compared to methods used for fitness training. When I joined a gym, I was assigned a personal trainer who designed my physical training program. My routine began with postural analysis; this was followed by passive muscular release work on firm polystyrene logs; I then progressed through a series of aerobic exercises, and developed strength training with machines and weights, and finally, the session concluded with stretching. Similarly, this systematic approach to the Buddhist path of virtue, meditation, and insight offers a well-crafted program designed to unlock the enormous proficiency and power accessible to a well-trained mind.

Systematic repetition is a necessary part of training, but you can adjust the length of time spent in various jhānas, perhaps sequencing rapidly through the lower jhānas when you wish to preserve more time to dwell in the fourth jhāna or immaterial spheres. In retreat conditions, you may sequence through the entire series as your morning "warm up" meditation, and in succeeding sessions strategically select the particular jhānas that will most effectively intensify concentration, stability, or luminosity. You may benefit from the restorative power of prolonged absorptions and also enhance the flexibility and agility that can develop through quick progressions. As you become proficient in these attainments, you may moderate the amount of time spent in each jhāna and mold the system toward a fruitful exploration of consciousness. The basic rule of thumb is simple: stabilize the lower jhānas before moving to the higher attainments.

Developing concentration through mindfulness with breathing *(ānāpānasati samādhi)* may be the most frequently recommended meditation subject. It is generally considered "foremost among the various meditation subjects."[101] Some students, however, find breath meditation difficult, and may suffer from headaches or find that the focus on breathing highlights preexisting respiratory ailments such as asthma, so that the mind too easily slips into anxiety. These meditators might benefit from emphasizing contemplations of the Buddha, virtue, or loving-kindness as meditation subjects, or developing dispassion through the meditations on the body or death prior to taking the breath as their subject. Other meditators may discover greater tranquility with the expanded concepts of colors and elements through kasiṇa practices.

It is difficult to predict what meditation subject would be most effective for an individual practitioner. Even Venerable Sariputta, the chief disciple of the Buddha, erred by suggesting the repulsive corpse as the meditation subject for one student. Although this young monk exerted himself diligently, he made no progress. Realizing that this young monk had worked with radiantly colored gems during many previous lives as a goldsmith, the Buddha manifested a luminous red lotus as the basis for the red kasiṇa. The monk's attention was captivated by the beautiful red color. His mind easily focused steadily upon this new meditation subject; he soon entered jhāna, and he then developed insight.[102] Therefore, since even Venerable Sariputta could not predict the most appropriate meditation subject, these instructions guide students systematically through the full spectrum of meditation objects, enabling meditators to discover for themselves which objects are most suitable for their goal.

Some meditation subjects require prior attainments and must be learned in sequence, while other subjects can be a starting point for meditators who feel an affinity for those topics. While each new object in the sequence includes a unique set of instructions pertinent to that particular practice, a mind already refined through concentration on the breath will find these techniques can be rapidly and easily integrated. The instructions presented in this section will serve as a manual for meditators who are endeavoring to establish jhāna either in retreat or in diligent practice at home. The same instructions that are so useful and essential to an intensive meditator may, however, appear tedious to the casual reader. Those readers who are reading this book as an overview of Buddhist meditation prior to attaining jhāna may wish to simply continue with the basic breath meditation, contemplate these teachings in a general way, and experiment with the daily reflections that are incorporated throughout section II, but reserve the methodical meditation instructions for a future intensive practice opportunity.

Chapter 10 concludes this section on concentration beyond the breath with a review of the essential skills that develop through the practice of jhāna. The remainder of this book will explore insight and wisdom practices. The teachings in sections III and IV do not depend upon the prior cultivation of jhāna and will have relevance for every reader.

The Buddha recognized that people have different inclinations and desires. Some people prefer the qualities of material jhānas and others seek immaterial states. These sequential attainments invite us to understand both the material and the immaterial aspects of existence, experience the pleasures and peace associated with the full range of absorptions, recognize the limitations of each stage, and thereby cling to none of it. Enjoy the process, exploring this progression of concentration and insight at a rate that supports your path.

CHAPTER 5

Embodying Your World: Contemplating Thirty-Two Parts of the Body

With mindfulness of the body established,
Controlled over contact's sixfold base,
A bhikkhu who is always concentrated
Can know Nibbāna for himself.
—THE UDANA[103]

OW MINDFUL ARE YOU of bodily sensations? Are you aware of your current posture, the touch of this book, the texture of your clothing, the pull of gravity? Are you comfortable in your own skin right now? Do you feel your muscles contract, temperatures fluctuate, and energy ebb and swell as you move? Every movement can serve to enliven your physical sensitivity and mindfulness. Take a sneeze, for example. Observe the sensory experience of a sneeze with careful attention—feel the tingling, sharpness, heat, tension, facial movements, mounting pressure, and explosive release. Though you won't attain jhāna by mindful sneezing you can use any movement, posture, or physical event like a sneeze to strengthen mindfulness of the body. As mindfulness of the body increases, each moment of living becomes more vivid and clear; the mind encounters things with a balanced composure; you are mastering the application of focus and will be able to apply it toward the attainment of jhāna when conditions permit.

Jhāna concentration requires an ability to restrain the sense doors—to

put the brakes on habitual yearning for tasting, touching, feeling, seeing, hearing, and thinking. In order to curb preoccupation with sensory
gratification, it is important to observe and investigate sense contact.
As you move through the day, notice what catches your eye. Do sights
lure you into searching for visual pleasure? What sounds intrigue you?
Do you choose to be engaged with hearing right now? How about the
sensitivity of the tongue? Is it pulled toward tastes and foods that your
body doesn't need? Where does the mind wander? Are you frittering
time away drifting in imagination or dwelling on painful emotions?

It is important to understand that your body, complete with emotions and senses, is not an obstacle to either jhāna or ultimate realization.
We all have bodies. The Buddha had a body. There is no need to fear,
judge, or reject our bodies. Our bodies maintain our lives and serve as
the vehicles that carry us through our spiritual quest.

Knowing the body well and trusting your ability to be mindful of the
body, without judgment or obsession during daily activities, will support
your ability during formal jhāna practice to shift your attention away
from sensory desires. The knowledge accrued through cultivating mindfulness of the body during daily life creates a firm and flexible base for
concentration practice. But for rapid and efficient attainment of jhāna,
minimize attention to body sensations during formal meditations.
When absorbed in jhāna, physical sensations diminish, and emotions
and mental states are surprisingly consistent and predictable. Although
you won't be giving explicit attention to the body during formal jhāna
practice, you also don't need to dull physical perceptions or sustain an
undercurrent of aversion toward the body. Build upon a wise and mindful relationship to your body.

THE THIRTY-TWO PARTS

The next meditation subject in this sequence involves a review of the
parts of the body. Many meditative insight practices encourage mindful
attention to what you actually feel in the body—sensations such as pressure, roughness, softness, cold, and so forth. However, the meditation on
the thirty-two parts invites a different orientation to the body. With this

Full Awareness

How present are you for the life you are living? Remind yourself to be present for daily actions, like brushing your teeth, getting dressed in the morning, turning a key in a lock, sitting in a chair, washing your face. When walking, feel the changing sensations of the foot lifting, moving forward, and lowering to the floor.

Being mindful in daily activities is not difficult in itself, but sometimes it can be difficult to *make the effort* to be mindful, or to *remember* to make the effort. You might place a sticky note or cartoon on something you use each day—such as the bathroom mirror or a door handle—to remind yourself to bring careful attention to activities like brushing your hair or opening the door.

practice, you will still know the experience, characteristics, and expression of the body, but you will give virtually no attention to sensory experiences. In jhāna practice, fascination with the ever-changing sensations of the body is diminished, and instead the detached, focused discernment of the body's elements and parts is emphasized.[104] The thirty-two parts practice is an important meditation subject that offers us additional avenues into jhāna and will structure later insight methods.[105]

This traditional exercise is a form of body scan in which you will discern thirty-two specific parts of the body.[106] The ancient instruction invites meditators to "review the body up from the soles of the feet and down from the top of the hair," discerning the thirty-two parts of the body as clearly as one might sort a bag of grains and recognize which grains are rice, beans, peas, or millet.[107] Similarly, you can move your attention to the various parts of the body, recognizing each distinct part.

Step One

The first step in the practice of discerning the parts of the body is simply to memorize the list of thirty-two parts. The easiest approach is to learn the list in groups of five and six, as follows:

- head hairs, body hairs, nails, teeth, skin,
- flesh, sinews, bones, bone marrow, kidneys,
- heart, liver, diaphragm,[108] spleen, lungs,
- intestines, mesentery, contents of the stomach, feces, brain,[109]
- bile, phlegm, pus, blood, sweat, fat,
- tears, grease, saliva, snot, oil of the joints, and urine.

Step Two

Next, closely examine each part, one by one, starting with head hair. Pluck one. Put it on a sheet of white paper and look at it. What do you notice? What are the colors, shapes, and textures? For example, observe any distinctive blond, gray, red, or black tones; take note of the fineness or thickness of the strand; notice the length of the hair; and observe if it is smooth, dry, soft, or kinky. Reflect on where this body part is located on the body and what it is near. Head hair, for instance, is part of the scalp; it is surrounded by grease and emerges from a follicle that is rooted in the skin. Construct a careful and clear perception of head hair. What can you see and know about that strand of hair?

This practice uses discernment, visualization, and reflection to develop mindfulness of body; it does not use felt sensation. Many of the body parts are internal organs and cannot of course be examined on a piece of white paper. In those cases you visualize and contemplate each part as it appears to you. First, try to envision the color and shape, which is usually easiest to see. Some parts are fixed only in specific locations, while other parts are diffused throughout the body. You might see the part along with the surrounding structures that delimit that part. For example, you might perceive the diaphragm attached to the bones of the spine and surrounded by lungs on one side and intestines on the other. When seeing the brain, you might find it encased in the bones of the skull and infused with veins.

In Buddhist cultures, monastics may observe autopsies in hospitals or decomposing corpses when devout Buddhists have donated their cadavers for such contemplation. I was privileged to engage in these practices as part of my traditional training at a Thai forest monastery. Most meditators in the West will not have this opportunity; anatomy books and medical illustrations can provide clues about each body part and where it is found. Since this is meditative contemplation and not precise medical science, don't feel that it is necessary to get caught up with anatomical intricacies. If your concentration is extremely strong, you will literally perceive the specific body part with the mind. This is a practice of discernment—a noncritical, nonjudgmental contemplation of the body. It involves viewing the body from the perspective of a detached observer, as plainly as one would see a bag of grains and sort through them knowing which were beans, peas, or rice. But, regardless whether you are directly observing the body part or are imagining its appearance, this meditation will develop concentration, clarity, and detachment regarding the body.

→ MEDITATION INSTRUCTION 5.1
Meditating on the Thirty-Two Internal Parts

Begin the meditation by establishing concentration with the breath. This meditation does not require a foundation of jhāna; however, if you have previous expertise with jhāna, proceed up to the fourth jhāna. While abiding in the fourth jhāna, a powerful and bright light will intensify. This light of wisdom *(paññāloka)* is a natural product of deep concentration and can aid the discernment of phenomena.[110] Emerge from the fourth jhāna and, with the support of this light of wisdom, begin to discern the body parts one by one by directing attention to each part inside your own body. Use the light of wisdom to penetrate the body and discern each part by color, shape, location, and the environment that surrounds it.

Start the contemplation with the first pentad (head hairs, body hairs, nails, teeth, skin) in both forward and reverse order, until it becomes easy to contemplate each part clearly. Although skin, hair, and nails are visible on the exterior surface of your body, as constituents of the meditator's body, they will be referred to as "internal parts" and contrasted with "external parts," which belong to another person's body. Then add the next pentad, reciting the parts as you focus on the color, shape, location, and environment that delimits each part. Continue through the list until you can see each part clearly, in the groupings, and as the full list of thirty-two parts in both forward and reverse order. ✦

Contemplating the thirty-two parts of the body can, as a side benefit, neutralize certain aversive reactions. Although I have traveled to places where a host of diverse activities—bathing and grooming, food preparation, and clothes washing—take place at a common water source, I am most accustomed to a typical Western home, where rooms are designed for different activities and most body care occurs in the bathroom. I once lived in an international community of meditators; each person came with different habits, preferences, and customs—some of which I considered rude. One man brought his nail clippers to the dining hall every couple of weeks and stood over the trash bin clipping away, and one woman flossed her teeth at the dining table after eating lunch. Since we were practicing in silence, I could not express my aversion or voice my concern for dining room hygiene or etiquette but instead had to deal with my own reactions. So I practiced reviewing the body parts, emphasizing the contemplation of nails as just nails, teeth and saliva as just teeth and saliva. I literally thought, "nails are just nails" or "this is saliva" as I perceived the color, shape, location, and characteristics of these parts. This simple recitation instantly neutralized my aversive reaction. I would still have preferred that these activities take place in a bathroom, but my reactivity to the whole situation dissipated.

→ **MEDITATION INSTRUCTION 5.2**
Meditating on the Thirty-Two External Parts

To continue the contemplation of the thirty-two parts of the body, begin by establishing concentration with the breath as object and reviewing the thirty-two parts internally as detailed in the previous meditation instruction. For a next step, you may extend the meditation to include the body parts of other people in the room. Close your eyes and concentrate on discerning the parts of another person sitting nearby. Try to visualize each part included in the list in sequence, in both forward and reverse order. Shine the light of wisdom to illuminate each part. If the light fades and the body parts become unclear, you may strengthen concentration by returning to the breath as the meditation object or refresh attention by reestablishing jhāna, before continuing the contemplation of the body. Meditating on our own body parts, whether skin, nails, liver, or phlegm, is considered *internal,* and meditating on the body parts of another person, whether their hair, teeth, spleen, or brain, is referred to as *external.* Alternate contemplating, internally and externally, your own body parts and the body parts of another. Continue until the attention is stable and your concentration remains strong throughout the session. Then contemplate the parts of additional bodies. Having started with people sitting near you, gradually add more and more bodies to your contemplation. Expand your visualization to include bodies that are further and further away. Your vision can ultimately encompass body parts in every direction and throughout the universe. ←

The thirty-two parts meditation practice begins with your own body, then progresses to a nearby human body, and gradually expands outward adding additional human bodies. As the range of the contemplation expands you may incorporate the bodies of land animals, fish, birds, and any other body. Of course, some animals will not have exactly the same parts—just see whatever you see. This exercise is not intended as an anatomical survey; you are probing forms that are often the source of attachment and delusion. When the meditation is strong, you may walk around seeing just parts—parts walking through the door, parts vacuuming the carpet, parts chewing gum, parts clawing at a tree stump, parts flying between trees. After contemplating in this way, wherever you look you will know they are just parts that are grouped together—not woman, not man, not teacher, not brother, but more simply collections of elements that function together to form the concepts of woman, man, teacher, and brother.

Just as you would not pull an onion out of a stew and say, "this is stew," or hold up an airplane seat belt and say, "this is an airplane"— likewise, you would not point to a strand of your hair and say, "this is my body." You cannot find any part of your body about which you can say, "this is myself." All things are constellations of parts—no self is to be found located anywhere. Practice until you can discern every part individually, in sets, and as the whole list, clearly and vividly, internally and externally.

Reflecting on the thirty-two parts can also help reduce sensual, and especially sexual, desire. Some people feel powerless when lustful thoughts arise; they feel weakened and unable to curb the fantasies, restrain the eye, or refrain from indulging their sexual urges. If you find yourself inappropriately lusting after or fantasizing about someone's body—perhaps while you are practicing celibacy on retreat or while spending time with your best friend's spouse—try contemplating the thirty-two parts. Replace thoughts of desire with a perspective on the body that undercuts the lure of craving. As a quick antidote to sexual lust, the first five parts suffice—head hairs, body hairs, nails, teeth, skin. This set of five includes most of what you can see in your daily interactions. Contemplate the body as a cluster of parts; see the color, shape, location, and delimitation, rather than the distorting concept of beauty. It is just head hair, just body hair, just nails, just teeth, just skin, and so on. Let this simple contemplation neutralize sexual enchantment and lust. Historically, this practice has been used by celibate monastics, but it is a valuable tool for laypeople as well. Discerning the body as a body provides a radically different view—what is so attractive about teeth, flesh, nails, lungs, intestines, snot, and urine?

Successful completion of discerning the thirty-two parts will be critical to the scaffolding of further jhāna practice as outlined in the remainder of this book. We will return to the sequence of the thirty-two parts of the body many times throughout the progression of jhāna and insight practice. The thirty-two parts, for instance, are used as the foundation for (1) jhāna based on repulsiveness, (2) the color kasiṇas (presented in chapter 6), (3) the four elements meditations (chapter 12), and (4) as an object for contemplating the changing nature of mental and material experience (chapter 17).[III]

The practice of discerning the thirty-two parts can produce strong concentration and bring the mind into the neighborhood of jhāna, but it cannot draw the mind into full absorption. As discernment progresses, you will notice the jhāna factors strengthening, especially delight. But in order to use the body as an object for a full absorption, a new element must be added: the perception of repulsiveness.

THE REPULSIVE ELEMENT *(ASUBHA)*

We don't often display the repulsive nature of the body. Instead, we preen ourselves with combs and razors, slather ourselves in oils and lotions, mask odors with fragrances and deodorants, disguise sores and pus with bandages, and hide rashes, scars, and blemishes with makeup. We correct disfigurements with reconstructive surgery, ignore the worms and microscopic organisms that breed in our bodies and feed on our flesh, and flush away our excrement and urine with huge quantities of fresh water. When we eat an oatmeal raisin cookie, we rarely contemplate how it will appear in the stomach fifteen minutes later, or what it will smell like as it passes through the intestine, or how it finally leaves our bodies as refuse. Rarely do we look at our own excrement and think about the foods that we ate. Although we live intimately with our own flesh, there is still something disconcerting about materiality.

Some people spend a great deal of time and money grooming head hair with stylish cuts and fancy conditioners and gels, checking how it falls each time we see a mirror. You may admire a thick braid someone wears or a flattering touch of henna, but what is your reaction when you step in the shower at the gym and find the drain covered by a mass of hair? Is there any disgust?

The term *repulsive* has strong connotations. The suggestion to cultivate an attitude of repulsion toward our organic nature may offend readers who prefer to view bodily functions with wonder or scientific interest.

Discovering the Repulsive Element

Please take a cup and spit in it. Now drink that spit. Does the idea instill a sense of revulsion, or are you happy to drink your spit? You swallow your own saliva all day long, yet this little experiment may reveal an underlying response of repulsion to the body.

Repulsiveness, however, is not aversion. The complex biological activities that let us move, digest, reproduce, and perceive are indeed amazing, and during the contemplation of repulsiveness, no anger, hatred, or unwholesome factors arise. Quite the contrary, attention to repulsiveness brings with it a host of wholesome factors that balance the mind and infuse consciousness with lightness, flexibility, uprightness, happiness, mindfulness, joy, balance, and confidence. In your own experience, you may notice the subtle distinction between the wholesome perception of repulsiveness and a moment when the perception is tarnished by the unwholesome state of aversion. A purely repulsive perception does not resist the encounter; therefore, you will be able to remain mindful of the perception, as it appears, and for as long as you wish, without attachment or agitation. In contrast, anger, craving, fear, or resistance express an aversive reaction that obstructs the clear perception of the body; fuels the proliferation of thoughts, opinions, and stories of blame that might condemn the body; and agitates the mind.

With the added element of repulsiveness, the body meditations are powerful objects for jhāna, hurtling the mind into absorptions that are surprisingly stable. Although absorptions through repulsiveness of the body cannot reach beyond the level of the first jhāna, I have found they add remarkable strength to my concentration, supporting detachment and increasing the ease and speed of seclusion. It is a relatively coarse meditation object that I can use even when ill, suffering with a headache, or otherwise struggling to overcome conditions that make working with subtler objects, such as the breath, more challenging.

→ **MEDITATION INSTRUCTION 5.3**
Meditating on Repulsiveness

To explore the perception of repulsiveness as an object for jhāna, establish concentration and then use that light of concentration to discern the sequence of thirty-two parts as you have before—see the color, shape, location, and delimiting environment of the body parts. Next, focus on the concept of repulsiveness as you discern each and every part again. See the color as having a dissatisfactory and repulsive quality. Similarly, see the shape as repulsive, see the location as repulsive, and see the delimiting matter as repulsive. After contemplating the part and its characteristic of color, shape, location, and delimiting matter as repulsive, you may discern the repulsive aspect of smell and taste. Instead of maintaining a neutral, observant attitude toward each part, you will notice a slight shift in attitude as you proceed to intentionally contemplate each part as repulsive. You might recite *repulsive, repulsive* to help focus on the concept of repulsiveness.

If it is difficult to sense the body as repulsive, you might try visualizing each part laid out on a dinner plate, or imagine feeling organs by reaching into a dark bag, or coming upon the body part by chance. Each meditator will find their own way to discover the repulsive aspect of the body. When I visited a morgue in Bangkok, I was shocked to see a bucket of stray body parts, with femurs hanging out like umbrellas left at the door, presumably parts that got separated from their corpses. When I think of that bucket of parts, I easily sense a repulsive quality to flesh, bones, sinews, and such.

The perception of repulsiveness may give way to a bright nimitta—the repulsive sign. It may appear as a bright field of light that is intimately connected with the concept of repulsiveness. Although a description of the nimitta may appear similar to the breath nimitta, a discerning meditator will recognize the distinctive association with the repulsiveness subtly reflected in the perception of this mental sign, and not confuse it with the counterpart sign of the breath. Continue contemplating the body part as repulsive while this nimitta stabilizes. When the nimitta is bright and the mind is preparing to enter the first jhāna, shift your focus to the nimitta, letting go of the specific image of the body part or parts. Establish a resolve for how long you intend to remain in the first jhāna, perhaps starting with ten or fifteen minutes. When you emerge, discern the five factors associated with the first jhāna (as you did in meditation instruction 4.3). In this way, you can contemplate each body part individually for thirty-two separate absorptions. Alternatively, you may enter jhāna based on perceiving groups—as groupings of five or six, or the full sequence of thirty-two. When concentration is weak, it is easier to use just one body part at a time, such as bones. When concentration is firm, the mind can embrace the thirty-two parts at a glance. ❧

The Skeleton

The skeleton is a favorite selection for the contemplation of a single body part; namely, that of bones. Images of skeletons are more available in our society than spleens, sinews, or lungs. Halloween costumes and rock bands sport skeleton designs. Skeletons can be found in medical offices, massage clinics, biology labs, and art classes. Many Buddhist monasteries have skeletons hanging in the meditation hall, sometimes with a plaque and photograph of the person who donated their body, together with a verse to remind us that we are no different than the skeleton we are viewing. When you see a skeleton as a design element in a shop window or as the logo for a commercial product, it may seem cute and cartoonish. When you approach an actual skeleton in a medical or artistic context, your intellectual curiosity or aesthetic sensibility might draw you near to examine it. Such mundane attraction to the form of the body, though, is not going to lead to jhāna, because you will not perceive the repulsive aspect. If you are having trouble seeing the skeleton as repulsive, imagine finding one in an unexpected location—perhaps between your bed sheets or decomposing in your vegetable garden. How would you feel about climbing into bed with a skeleton at night or munching on a fresh radish after unearthing a deteriorating pelvis? If seeing bones as repulsive is still a struggle for you, you can also try a less sanitized perception to support the repulsive element—bits of dried flesh sticking to a few joints, limbs scattered about after being gnawed by animals. Don't elaborate a great deal on this sort of visualization: the point is to discern the repulsiveness of the specific skeleton that you perceive.

→ MEDITATION INSTRUCTION 5.4
The Skeleton

After establishing concentration, focus the light of wisdom on the bones of your own skeleton: see their color, shape, location, delimitation, and if you wish, add the repulsive aspect. You can work with the skeleton either in a mode of neutral discernment or as a repulsive object for jhāna absorption. Discern your own skeleton in various postures, in as much detail as possible. There are 206 bones of various shapes and functions in the human skeleton. It is not necessary to discern each and every bone; a steady perception is more important than anatomical accuracy. This practice is traditionally considered a genuine discernment practice—an actual form of mental seeing, not merely a creative visualization. The powerful light of wisdom can penetrate forms and illuminate what the naked eye cannot apprehend. Whether your discernment is influenced by a visualization or appears to be a genuine penetrative discernment of the unique characteristics of that specific part, continue to concentrate on the skeleton. Then discern the skeleton of one other person. Alternate back and forth between the perception of your own skeleton and other people's bones until your concentration becomes powerful and the discernment is clear.

Now extend the contemplation to include additional people's bones, first those of persons that are nearby, and then gradually include the skeletons of beings further away. Incrementally extend this practice to contemplate skeletons at greater and greater distances. Finally, focus on all the bones in the world and the universe: human, animal, fish, bird, and so on. Shine the light of concentration into the world; see whatever bones appear to you. Continue to contemplate until you perceive the world as filled with a vast multitude of skeletons.[112] In a perception focused on bones, what can you take to be self?

The repulsive concept can elicit first jhāna absorption when the skeleton is our own. The skeleton of another living person brings consciousness only to the threshold of jhāna.[113] ←

The first time I practiced this meditation to the level of jhāna it was near the end of a retreat. Shortly after leaving that retreat, I attended a meeting of colleagues. A particularly slim hand gesturing in conversation, a protruding collarbone, or a shiny tooth—each thing that reminded me of bones illuminated the perception of skeleton. For a brief moment, I sensed myself conversing as a skeleton of bones with a group of other skeletons and as one collection of bones passing the salt to another skeleton munching salad. Not only was this an amusing way to experience an otherwise tedious meeting, but a remarkable evenness pervaded my attitude toward everyone. People who had previously intimidated me, people from whom I had wanted something, and dear old friends, all flashed by as sets of bones—each equal, with no particular significance attributed to gender or social status. There was no place for desire to build and nothing to trigger aversion. There was only the perception of bones and moving skeletons: skeletons sitting, skeletons arguing, skeletons talking.

A momentary glimpse of the world of bones hidden inside these bodies can offer a fresh perspective on ordinary experience. Repulsive meditations enhance dispassion, dislodge enchantment with beauty, weaken lustful tendencies, and produce a joy-filled detachment that ushers consciousness toward jhāna. By reducing entrancement with beauty, and quelling lust and aversion, the repulsive meditations can dissolve deeply conditioned attachment to our bodies. Indeed, each step in this meditative progression, while strengthening and purifying the mind also invites profound insight and new ways of experiencing day-to-day life.

TABLE 5.1
Body Meditations

MEDITATION SUBJECT	BASIS	CONCENTRATION POTENTIAL
Discernment of the features of each part	Any individual part or group of parts included in the thirty-two parts of the body *Internal:* our own body parts *External:* body parts of other beings	Neighborhood concentration
Repulsive quality	Any individual part or group of parts included in the thirty-two parts of the body *Internal:* our own body parts *External:* body parts of other beings	*Internal:* first jhāna *External:* neighborhood concentration
Color kasiṇas based on body parts	Any individual part or group of parts included in the thirty-two parts of the body *Internal:* our own body parts *External:* body parts of other beings	All four jhānas
Discernment of four elements	Any individual part or group of parts included in the thirty-two parts of the body *Internal:* our own body parts *External:* body parts of other beings	Neighborhood or momentary concentration

CHAPTER 6
Expanded Perceptions: Ten Kasiṇa Circles

Mind becomes inwardly steadied, composed,
unified, and concentrated. That concentration is then calm
and refined; it has attained to full tranquility
and achieved mental unification.
—Aṅguttara Nikāya[114]

THE NEXT STAGE of the jhāna progression is to derive color kasiṇas from four of the body parts that you have previously discerned. *Kasiṇa* is a Pali term that literally means *wholeness, complete,* or *all.* The *Vimuttimagga* defines *kasiṇa* as "pervasiveness."[115] It refers to a sequence of ten particular perceptions that are expanded without limit. These ten perceptions are based on the concepts of four colors and six elements.[116] Through concentration, these concepts of colors and elements appear in the form of luminous disks that have a capacity to expand consciousness to unlimited dimensions. There really is no word in English to apply to this class of expansive meditation objects, so *kasiṇa* will have to suffice.

DEVELOPING KASIṆAS BASED ON COLORS

To develop the kasiṇa practices, please begin your sitting with the four jhānas based on the breath. Then review the sequence of thirty-two parts of the body in both forward and reverse order, as introduced in chapter 5, and discern either the internal or external skeleton, perhaps dwelling in the first jhāna with the repulsiveness of the skeleton as the object of your meditation. After this review, emerge from jhāna and focus your attention completely on the color of the skeleton: white. You can emphasize a circular-shaped part of the skeleton such as the skull, or choose a bone that appears the brightest, or simply repeatedly apply your attention to the idea of the whiteness of bones.

This work of carefully discerning the white bones of the skeleton will facilitate the arising of a more abstract object: the white kasiṇa. The essential point now is to focus on the concept of whiteness itself, not the particular details of the white object, nor a general notion of the thing that is white. Keep the attention dwelling with the bare concept—in this case, whiteness—and ignore distinctive shapes, particularities of the object, or any changes of hue, tone, or shadow. Ignore any defect, as well. Highlight just the most basic perception of whiteness.

Silently recite the words *white, white* a few times to direct your attention to color as object. When you are able to concentrate on the whiteness of the bones for some time, the details of the skeleton will naturally disappear. You will find the color white reflected in your mind's eye like a luminous white disk or a shimmering china plate. It may at first appear a little off-white, or as a nebulous creamy hue, and it may arise with or without a distinct circumference. As your attention dwells with the whiteness, the imperfections gradually dissolve and the kasiṇa becomes a radiant bright white, like the glory of a freshly gessoed canvas, or the alluring smoothness of a bowl of creamy yogurt, or the purity of snowflakes settling on a frozen pond.

As your concentration grows stronger, this kasiṇa sign will become more stable and more luminous. You can then gradually expand the appearance of this nimitta through the use of specific resolves, such as, "may the white kasiṇa expand two inches," or "may the kasiṇa expand one hand's width." Or by three-dimensional references as the *Vimuttimagga* recommends: May the white kasiṇa increase "to the size of a wheel, a canopy, the shadow of a tree, a cultivated field, a small neighborhood, a village, a walled village, and a city. Thus should he progress gradually until he fills the great Earth."[117] Intentionally expand the kasiṇa to a comfortable degree. Check that the disk-shaped circle of whiteness expanded according to your intention. When it stabilizes in that larger size, make another intention for it to expand, perhaps six inches this time. Observe the diameter increase in all directions and let it stabilize again. Then expand to one foot, or one meter, or three meters, or fill the room. Continue spreading and expanding the nimitta until it occupies the entire universe—above, below, around, and everywhere.

For some meditators, the white kasiṇa expands rapidly, without the need for explicit incremental resolves. Whether it expanded automatically or was prompted by your intention, now observe the infinite dimension of the nimitta. There will be no place untouched by white, no inside or outside. There will be nothing apart from white—now, the expanded concept of white totally pervades consciousness.

Test the stability of the nimitta by focusing on a small spot of white the size of a tile or seashell within this vast field of whiteness. Is the attention steady when resting in this focused perspective? Try expanding your attention to take in a vast expanse of white like the horizon of Antarctica—white as far as you can imagine. Is the attention still steady with this vaster view? Alternate a few times between an expanded perception of whiteness and a focused dot of whiteness that appears within a broader field of white in front of your face. Enjoy this white spot in a white field, without edges, without defining borders. Notice that you can focus on any spot of whiteness that you choose and the attention will remain at that spot unmoved. Sense the all-encompassing expansiveness of the white nimitta and the stability of the mind as it meets this concentration object.

Once the dimensionlessness of the nimitta is apparent and the nimitta is steady, infinite, and bright, you have a suitable object for absorption. At this point resolve to attain the first jhāna and release your attention to unify with the white nimitta. Allow consciousness to dwell with this borderless perception of the concept white. You may sense a vast, unrestricted, and dimensionless quality to perception.

As consciousness unifies with the expanded kasiṇa, the mind will assume correspondingly expanded qualities. Wherever you place your attention in the field of white, it remains there, undisturbed and un-moved. Place your attention on the nimitta and let it settle there, qui-etly and gently, yet thoroughly absorbed in the perception of whiteness, without slipping off or moving around. One of my teachers compared this to hanging your hat on a wall peg and finding that it remains there without requiring further strain to shore it up. It may feel as though you are merely relaxing into the stability of the jhāna, but consistent effort and clarity of intention are needed to support the durability of absorption.

EMERGING AND PROGRESSING THROUGH THE FOUR JHĀNAS

After you can sustain the first jhāna with the white kasiṇa for more than one hour without interruption, or when you feel satisfied, emerge from absorption and direct your attention to the mind door at the heart base. Discern the five factors present in the first jhāna. Reflect on the two disadvantages: (1) the coarseness of vitakka and vicāra, and (2) the dangerous proximity of the first jhāna to hindrances, especially restlessness. Consider the advantage of the second jhāna: the greater quietness of pīti, sukha, and ekaggatā. Resolve to let go of the directing and sustaining activities of attention and aspire for the second jhāna. Return your attention to the white nimitta and settle in a unified per-ception of the second jhāna with the white kasiṇa as the object of your meditation.

When you have remained in the second jhāna for at least one hour or are satisfied with the level of your attainment, emerge and reflect on the two disadvantages of the second jhāna (proximity to first jhāna and the coarseness of pīti) and the advantage of the third jhāna (an absorption with sukha and ekaggatā will be more sublime). Resolve to abide in the third jhāna, and cultivate it until you are satisfied. When you are ready to progress beyond the third jhāna, emerge, reflect on the two disad-vantages (proximity to second jhāna and coarseness of sukha) and the advantage of the fourth jhāna (upekkhā and ekaggatā are more peace-ful). Resolve to dwell in the fourth jhāna; direct your attention to the white nimitta; and then dwell for as long as you wish in the fourth jhāna, inviting the mind to expand to unlimited dimensions and the light of wisdom to grow strong and bright.

As your meditation progresses, you will continue to cultivate stability at each level and review each previous step. It is better not to skip steps, but you may move quickly through the early stages to reserve the bulk of your meditation time for the higher jhānas or more recent attainments. For instance, you might begin to spend only a few minutes in the lower jhānas with breath as the object and rapidly sequence through the thirty-two parts to preserve more time to dwell with the kasiṇas. With each progression to a new object or level of attainment, repeat the previous jhānas and spend at least one hour immersed in your most recent attainment. To transition between jhānas, please don't just slip and slide between states. Each time that you emerge from a jhāna, identify the jhāna factors, and reflect on the disadvantages and advantages of the jhāna factors and states that characterize the first three jhānas. At this stage, you do not need to reflect on disadvantages of the fourth jhāna; this reflection will be performed later, in preparation for the immaterial attainments (chapter 7).

Don't forget to take the time to systematically expand the kasiṇa to vast proportions. Although you may be able to experience brief absorptions using a confined sense of color, the unique attributes and profound stability offered by kasiṇa practice depends upon the limitless dimensions of the object of your meditation. If your absorptions feel fragile, check that the nimitta has maintained its expansive potential. If it appears to have shrunk, then take the time to spread and expand the kasiṇa once again, and confirm that the mind remains stable when focusing on a small spot and also on a vast horizon.

EXPAND YOUR RANGE WITH ADDITIONAL COLORS

If your time in retreat is limited, you may wish to specialize in just one kasiṇa. The white kasiṇa is generally preferred because it presents the most luminous appearance and generates a strong light. Mastery in one kasiṇa is sufficient to progress through the remaining immaterial absorptions and to develop liberating insight. You may wish, however, to develop the remaining kasiṇas to strengthen concentration further. There are three additional colors recommended in the Theravāda tradition: yellow, red, and a darkish hue, called in Pali *nīla*. This dark color is sometimes described as blue, black, green, or brown; essentially, it is a very dark but luminous color.[118] To produce the *nīla* kasiṇa, we use the dark color of bile, black hair, or the pupil of the eye. To form the yellow kasiṇa, we use the yellow color of our urine. For the red kasiṇa, we use the color of our blood. To produce each colored kasiṇa, progress through the same sequence of steps that you used to produce the white kasiṇa.

To develop the *nīla* kasiṇa, for instance, first quickly sequence through the previous attainments: the four jhānas with breath as the object, the thirty-two parts, the repulsive skeleton, and the four jhānas based on the white kasiṇa. Then return your attention to the bile, focusing on the color. As the color of the bile becomes apparent, give your attention to that dark bluish-brownish-black color as a concept. Disregard any imperfections or aberrations found in bile. The kasiṇas use color as the object of concentration, unbound from the texture, shape, and form of the material object that bore the color. Focus on the pure perception of color, devoid of particular details in the colored material substance. Repeatedly bring your attention to this dark color until a luminous disk appears before your mind's eye. Then, just as for the white kasiṇa, incrementally expand the field of this *nīla* kasiṇa until it is stable, strong, and infinite, without boundaries, extending above, below, around, and everywhere. Try focusing sometimes on a small area and sometimes on a large area. Test the stability of the nimitta, and then, when you feel ready, resolve to enter the first jhāna. Systematically establish the four jhānas, stabilizing each one for a full hour before emerging, reflecting on the jhāna factors, the disadvantages and advantages, and the aspiration for a subtler attainment. This way your concentration will grow strong, your mind will become malleable, and you will develop facility with each level of accomplishment.

In the same way, you can use the color of your urine to form the yellow kasiṇa and the color of blood to cultivate the red kasiṇa. In these cases you capitalize on your recent concentration by beginning with the body parts that you have previously discerned. However, color kasiṇas do not necessarily require an anatomical reference. The yellow kasiṇa does not arise through a contemplation of liquid urine per se; the kasiṇa occurs rather by contemplating the basic concept of yellow, which in this instance is derived from the perception of urine. Likewise, the red kasiṇa is not a tangible red object; it is not the contemplation of red blood as in the thirty-two-part meditation. The red kasiṇa is formed by using the essence of the color red derived from the perception of blood.

Once you have established the color kasiṇas based on body parts, try using any external object in your immediate environment the same way. Bones are not the only white objects in our world. Any white object can stimulate the arising of the white kasiṇa—a bed sheet, a pot of steamed basmati rice, a squirt of titanium white acrylic paint, a white tulip, a blank sheet of paper, an egg. Similarly, the *nīla* kasiṇa could be based on the sight of a crow, a freshly polished boot, a cast iron frying pan, a black coral gemstone, or the black exoskeleton of a dung beetle. Use any nearby yellow object to generate the yellow kasiṇa. Flowers are usually recommended; I, however, was personally inspired by a vacuum cleaner encased in a bright cadmium yellow plastic shell. Similarly, any red object may serve as the foundation for the red kasiṇa: a strawberry, the back of a friend's shirt, a bowl of tomato soup, a stop sign, a fire extinguisher. The particularities of the initial tangible object are of no significance. Let the perception remain simple. If you become fascinated with extraneous details of the physical support for color, whether the temperature of blood, the function of a vacuum cleaner, the texture of a stone, the seeds on the skin of the strawberry, or the scent of a flower, the nimitta will not expand to infinite proportions.

The development of the color kasiṇas represents a significant movement from gross to subtler perceptions that usher consciousness into expanded spacious proportions. You progress from the concentrated discernment of internal body objects to the abstraction of color. You abstract a rudimentary concept from an ordinary perception and use that abstraction—a pure concept of color—as the meditation object. Colors and elements are among the most basic concepts one can create; they are stripped down, unembellished notions. Such bare concepts serve as the expandable mental media that make kasiṇa practice possible.

As your meditation progresses you may notice that the mind is growing incredibly bright. The colors may appear so luminous and radiant that the brightness of the mind minimizes the saturation of color; this may be most noticeable in the fourth jhāna. The intensification of the light of wisdom is a valuable feature of kasiṇa practice and will be used later to illuminate subtle realities of mind and matter.

Kasiṇas Derived from Elements

To begin work with the earth kasiṇa, you start by actually looking at some dirt, soil, or ground. You might go to the garden, by the side of the road, an open field, or any place that you find an open swatch of soil, and draw a circle on the ground delimiting an area to contemplate as "earth." The tradition suggests using reddish color soil, like potter's clay, which is commonly found in northern India where the Buddha lived. Don't worry if you live in a place where the earth is more gray or brown; it does not need to be exactly like reddish clay. It should not be so dark, though, that it would be confused with the *nīla* color kasiṇa, nor should it be textured with gravel, sand, twigs, or moss. A simple circle of earth, one to two feet in diameter, will suffice. Smooth it out, clear out as many imperfections as you can, then sit and gaze at it. Establish concentration again with any meditation subject that you have previously mastered such as the breath or a color kasiṇa. When you emerge from concentration and open your eyes, look at your circle of earth. Close your eyes and notice if you can hold the image of the circle of earth in your mind clearly with closed eyes. If not, then alternate gazing at the circle of earth and concentrating the mind in meditation until the image of earth is well established. Then leave your physical earth circle and return to your room or meditation hall to sit recollecting the mental sign, which is now your kasiṇa of earth. Do not entertain interest in the various physical characteristics of earth, such as its hardness, or roughness. Focus only on the bare concept—*earth*—as an abstraction, separated from the attributes of its particular base. The earth kasiṇa is a basic mental representation of the material quality that we call earth. It is, in other words, a concept.

It is necessary to have a clear image to focus upon. If the image fades, walk back to the place where your material-earth kasiṇa is located and look again—let it register in your memory. Once the image is clear in your mind, it will quickly expand in a similar progression as the color kasiṇas did. It will become totally smooth, without blemish or particularization, purified of all imperfections such as spots, sand, ripples, stones, or textures. Thus, when the concept of earth is held in the mind, it may appear as a smooth, luminous, and stable disk, with a hint of an earth tone color in front of your closed eyes.

→ MEDITATION INSTRUCTION 6.1
Developing the Earth Kasiṇa

To develop the element kasiṇas, begin each meditation by quickly reviewing all your previous meditation subjects. For some meditators this could include the four jhānas based on the breath, thirty-two parts, repulsive skeleton, four white kasiṇa jhānas, four bluish-brownish-black *(nīla)* kasiṇa jhānas, four yellow kasiṇa jhānas, and four red kasiṇa jhānas. This review of concentration practices could appear overwhelming when read in a book this way, but meditators who have developed mastery in these subjects will breeze through this sequence as quickly or as leisurely as they like.

As you transition between each jhāna, reflect on the jhāna factors, their disadvantages and advantages. When emerging from the fourth jhāna of the last color kasiṇa, bring to mind the image of your circle of earth. Mentally recite, *earth, earth*. As you focus on the mental sign of earth—the image of the disk-shaped kasiṇa in your mind's eye—you will find the kasiṇa circle becoming clearer and brighter. When it appears steady, you may incrementally expand the circle the same way you did with the colors, until it extends throughout the infinite universe, inside and outside, above and below, around and in all directions. You can focus on a small spot that might seem to be in front of you, or you can rest in a spacious vision of the expansion of the earth kasiṇa. Wherever you rest your attention, the mind will remain unmoved, like setting an item on a shelf and coming back later to find it exactly where you placed it. When you sense this deep stability, you will easily attain the four jhānas based on earth: follow the systematic procedure for attaining the first jhāna; stabilize it for an hour or until satisfied; emerge and reflect on the jhāna factors with their disadvantages and advantages; and then move methodically through the sequence of four jhānas, based on earth kasiṇa. ←

→ Meditation Instruction 6.2
Using Elements as Jhāna Subjects

Develop the remaining kasiṇas by applying the same systematic method. The only differences lie in the presentation of the initial object.

To perceive the *water kasiṇa* find a dark bowl and fill it to the brim with water. Choose a bowl that is without decoration. A dark bowl will reveal the surface of the water more clearly than a white or colored bowl, which might be confused with the white or colored kasiṇas. Alternatively, you can sit on the bank of a natural body of water, such as a still pond or lake. Observe the surface of the water and contemplate the concept of water. Disregard the characteristics of coldness, wetness, bubbles, ripples, surface reflections, fish, algae, or scientific notions about H_2O. Don't think about things that are conventionally related to water; there is no need to plan your next bath, recollect how many glasses of water you drank today, or focus on sensations of thirst. Just gaze at the surface of the water, until the image remains clear when you close your eyes. Then progress as you did with the other objects. It may help to recite the word *water, water* a few times to direct your attention to just water until a shimmering, whitish disk appears as the counterpart sign of water.

A wood fire is an ideal material basis for the *fire kasiṇa,* since wood produces a memorable reddish cast in the flame. A previous sight of such a fire, perhaps at a campfire, bonfire, or in a wood-burning stove, will be sufficient. It is not necessary to build a physical fire; a clear recollection or brief reminder of fire by glancing at a candle or the pilot light on the stove may spark sufficient inspiration to recall it to memory. Focus on the part of the flame that is reddish-orange and relatively steady. Don't look at the ashes, smoke, or blue spots, or analyze the kind of fuel that is burning, such as wood, paper, oil, or wax. Also, don't highlight the feature of color. It may help to recite the word *fire, fire* a few times to direct your attention to the basic concept of fire, until you perceive a reddish-orange disk. Focus exclusively on that fire kasiṇa. Develop and expand the counterpart sign *(nimitta)* of fire in the usual way until it becomes a reliable support for jhāna.

The *wind kasiṇa* cannot be seen directly; it is known, rather, through its effects, such as swaying branches or moving grasses. You can also know the wind by standing outside and feeling its touch on your skin, feeling a draft enter through a crack in a door, or by feeling your hair moved by its flow.[119] When you focus on the concept of wind, the kasiṇa may appears as a soft white disk, like the hue of steam wafting off a pot of boiling milk. Recite, *wind, wind,* or if you prefer, *air, air.* Develop this sign of wind, expanding and stabilizing the kasiṇa, and use it as the basis for the four jhānas.

The *light kasiṇa* begins with a perception of an indirect light, such as sunrays shining through branches, or shafts of light falling on a wall, or floodlights illuminating a parking lot, or stage lights spotlighting a theatrical performance. Do not be concerned with the shape of the light that is cast, the object it illuminates, its degree of brightness, or the contours of shadows; be concerned only with the concept of light. You may notice a beam of light coming through the window at such an angle that it reveals thousands of dust particles. Don't become distracted by the particles; steady your attention with the repeated perception of just light. Focus, in other words, on the idea of light, rather than on the effects of light. Some lights will have a colored cast; others will reflect the colors of nearby objects. As much as possible, ignore all the particular details and attend to the basic notion of light. Recite the word *light, light* to help direct attention to just this one concept, until the nimitta appears as a field of whitish light. Nurture the nimitta until it becomes stable, and then expand the circle and attain jhāna using the same systematic method described previously for the other colors and elements. The light kasiṇa appears as a field of whitish light, but it is the aspect of light itself, not the hue of whiteness, that grips perception.

There can be a tendency to rush this process by skipping some repetitive details, but I urge you to trust the methodical approach—it will deepen your concentration. Patiently develop control at each stage to protect the mind from rushing too quickly through these experiences before the required skills are established.

The *limited-space kasiṇa* begins with a demarcation of space, such as an archway, a window frame, or a hole in a wall. The limited-space kasiṇa is not derived from a perception of the frame, but from the space that is defined by the frame. "Limited space" is a different object from the immaterial jhāna called "infinite space" (chapter 7). To introduce this meditation, Pa-Auk Sayadaw gave me a piece of black cardboard with a circle cut in it about one foot in diameter. He instructed me to hold the cardboard at arm's length before an area of sky that was devoid of clouds, rooftops, or tree branches, and recite the words *space, space* while focusing on the simple concept of limited space, until I could sense and see a circle representing basic space with my eyes closed. The limited-space kasiṇa may appear differently to different meditators. I experienced it as a disk of whitish light—less intensely bright as compared to the white kasiṇa, and not as luminous as the light kasiṇa or as soft as the wind kasiṇa. ❖

DEVELOPING THE KASIṆA TRAINING

Paddling continuously against the currents of laziness, craving, and distraction takes immense effort. Continuous diligence is needed to complete this endeavor and overcome the chronic hindrances of complacency and undisciplined attention that lurk nearby and might thwart progress. There are still several intriguing objects to explore and a great deal of depth to realize before undertaking the mission of insight meditation. Periodically spark your sense of urgency, and recall your aspiration; the effort that you are putting forth will be worth the investment.

The perception of each kasiṇa and nimitta will be slightly different for each meditator. The relative strength and acuity of material and mental sensitivities affects perception. If you follow the progression of this training, you will learn to recognize each kasiṇa for yourself. Once your kasiṇa appears, develop the meditation by following the systematic instructions detailed above.

Some meditators will have very bright and stable breath nimittas, although many meditators find that the kasiṇas, especially the white kasiṇa, appear bigger, brighter, and more powerful than the nimitta associated with the breath. Kasiṇas, with their infinite and expanded qualities, often dwarf the breath nimittas, which in comparison appear constrained and less impressive.

Kasiṇa meditations were common meditative trainings that predated the Buddha. The Discourses of the Buddha mention these six kasiṇas but provide few practical instructions. The *Visuddhimagga* therefore serves as our treasure trove, filled with explicit instructions and procedural details to support the eager meditator. The nuanced and pragmatic structure for developing this path includes remarkably practical advice—such as to wear your sandals when you visit your physical earth circle so that you won't waste time washing your feet upon returning to your hut![120]

In this book I have followed Venerable Pa-Auk Sayadaw's order of instruction for introducing these practices—beginning with mindfulness with breathing and progressing through the thirty-two parts, repulsive skeleton, and kasiṇas of white, *nīla,* yellow, red, earth, water, fire, wind, light, and limited space. With an approach as meticulously detailed and rigorously traditional as the Sayadaw's general mode of instruction, I was surprised that he introduced me to the kasiṇas in an order that differed from what is found in the *Visuddhimagga* and the Discourses of the Buddha, which generally begin with the earth kasiṇa and ends with the white kasiṇa. When I asked Venerable Pa-Auk Sayadaw about this discrepancy, he explained that based upon his experience teaching many meditators, he found that the modified order provides the most efficient progression. Meditators can certainly begin with the earth kasiṇa if they wish; however, his experience indicates that it usually takes a longer time to succeed when starting with the perception of earth. By using the revised order, meditators harness the power of concentration accrued through mindfulness with breathing and the discernment of thirty-two parts, which are often more accessible practices because they use the physical body as reference. It seems that one can learn the full series of concentration objects using the revised order in the same time that it might take to merely establish the earth kasiṇa with the ancient sequence. The order is simply a practical way to facilitate attaining jhāna. Once you have developed mastery in kasiṇa jhānas, you will easily practice them in any sequence.

Practitioners will find their own relationship to the development of these stable concentration states. Some people will prefer one object to others—perhaps the brightness of the white kasiṇa or the soothing quality of black appears attractive, or perhaps a windy day or a log in the fireplace provides immediate inspiration for kasiṇa practice. The subtleness of the wind kasiṇa or the bare simplicity of the limited-space kasiṇa may dovetail well with an individual's temperament. The beauty of the color kasiṇas may appeal to those with artistic temperaments, while the breath may be the favored subject for another meditator.

Mastery in the entire array of kasiṇa objects is a required foundation for yet another level of concentration practice that develops an astounding quality of fluidity and control regarding both the object of perception and the subjective quality of these states.[121] Like a skilled juggler, one can easily shift between the colors, elements, and all the jhānas in various patterns and at incredible speeds. Mastery in these exercises eventually can become the basis for psychic powers and is considered most useful for eradicating the set of unwholesome states called the higher fetters (chapter 18).

You may choose to specialize in a single kasiṇa or cultivate the full spectrum of subjects; develop mastery with either one or all, according to your preferences and personal inclinations. All these meditation subjects will accomplish the aim of developing concentration to support wisdom; therefore you may choose whichever combination seems most interesting and suitable to you.

TABLE 6.1

Ten Kasiṇas as Meditation Subjects

Meditation Subject	Basis	Jhāna Potential
White kasiṇa	*Internal:* any internal white object such as bones, skull, teeth *External:* any external white object such as the bones of another person, yogurt, sheet of paper, dinner plate, snow, lab coat	All four jhānas
Nīla kasiṇa (Dark blue, brown, green, or black color)	*Internal:* any internal blue-brown-blackish dark object such as bile, hair, pupils of the eyes *External:* any external very dark-colored object such black hair, a beetle, lacquer bowl, licorice candy, fur of a black cat	All four jhānas
Yellow kasiṇa	*Internal:* any internal yellow object such as urine *External:* any external yellow object such as another person's urine, a lemon peel, a daffodil, gold	All four jhānas

Table continues on next page

Red kasiṇa	*Internal:* any internal red object such as blood or flesh *External:* any external red object such as the blood or flesh of another being, ketchup, a rose, a stop sign, nail polish	All four jhānas
Earth kasiṇa	Circle drawn on ground	All four jhānas
Water kasiṇa	Any water such as a pool, bowl of water, still lake, bath, ocean	All four jhānas
Fire kasiṇa	Any flame, such as that in a campfire, wood-burning stove, candle, match	All four jhānas
Wind kasiṇa	Movement of grasses or branches, touch of wind on body	All four jhānas
Light kasiṇa	Sunlight shining through branches, beam of light falling on wall, or any perception of light (not light source)	All four jhānas
Limited-space kasiṇa	Framed area of space such as a hole in a wall, archway, window, or a hole cut in a piece of cardboard about one foot in diameter through which the meditator may look toward a clear patch of sky	All four jhānas

CHAPTER 7

Infinite Perceptions: Four Immaterial Jhānas

For some people, contact, that point where sense plus object meet, is enthralling. And so they are washed by the tides of being, drifting along an empty, pointless road. Nowhere is there any sign of broken chains. But others come to understand their sense activity and because they understand it, the stillness fills them with delight. They see just what contact does, and so their craving ends; they realize the total calm.
—SUTTA NIPĀTA[122]

THE FIRST FOUR JHĀNAS were derived from matter. The earth kasiṇa depends upon earth; although it proceeds from a mere concept of earth, it requires the presence of earth. The yellow kasiṇa is far more refined than urine, yet the concept of color manifests in dependence upon a physical material that reflects the color. Even the limited-space kasiṇa produces a material jhāna because the space is known by the boundaries defined by the material frame. The first four jhānas are referred to as fine material jhānas because they depend on the presence of materiality, albeit of a highly refined nature. The immaterial jhānas, however, do not depend upon the *presence* of material forms, but only arise in the *absence* of the perception of matter; hence, these immaterial jhānas surmount matter.

Four specific attainments carry awareness beyond the crutch of material form. Each immaterial attainment is distinguished by the distinct perception that serves as its base: the bases of infinite space (fifth jhāna), infinite consciousness (sixth jhāna), nothingness (seventh jhāna), and neither-perception-nor-nonperception (eighth jhāna). All four immaterial jhānas have the same two intensifying factors as the fourth jhāna— single-pointedness and equanimity. Whereas the first four jhānas develop through a sequential refinement of *mental factors,* the immaterial abidings develop through a refinement of the *object*—coarser perceptions are removed and replaced by progressively subtler perceptions. Every immaterial attainment has a unique object that corresponds to the specific perception characterizing each sphere of consciousness and serves as the nonphysical basis for concentration to focus and cohere. The nimittas for immaterial abidings appear as luminous fields, reflecting the concept of space, the perception of consciousness, the concept of nothingness, or the consciousness that perceives nothingness. It is difficult to precisely describe the impression of these luminous fields; however, with practice you will quickly learn to recognize the unique quality of each nimitta.

When I wrote *Focused and Fearless* several years ago, I introduced the immaterial abidings after the fourth jhāna attained by mindfulness with breathing. Currently, however, I only teach the immaterial abidings after at least one kasiṇa is firmly established up to the fourth jhāna. I now conform to the more traditional sequence of training because greater stability and ease seem to develop when the immaterial abidings are preceded by kasiṇa practice. Breath meditation focuses attention on a specific and narrow location; kasiṇa practice expands consciousness to unlimited proportions and reduces the perception of materiality to a mere concept. This preparation narrows the gap between the fourth and fifth jhānas and softens what might otherwise appear to be a stark contrast between material and immaterial perceptions. If the leap is too large or the contrast too jarring, a meditator could experience distortions of perception similar to the queasiness induced by a high-rise elevator, the peculiar sensation of stepping onto a moving sidewalk in an airport, or the slight disorientation felt when we first step on solid land after a long journey in a small boat. In *Focused and Fearless,* I cautioned certain meditators from attempting these immaterial attainments because such altered perceptions could cause instability. However, I have found no instability when kasiṇa practice precedes the immaterial jhānas and no lingering perceptional distortions after emerging. Hence, I can now wholeheartedly recommend the immaterial jhānas for practitioners who have attained mastery in the kasiṇas.

→ MEDITATION INSTRUCTION 7.1
Disadvantages of Materiality

A series of reflections sets the stage for the immaterial absorptions by instilling a disinterested attitude toward materiality. To begin, strengthen your concentration with a complete review of previous attainments: sequence through the jhānas based on breath, repulsive element, and kasiṇas.

Reflection 1: After abiding in the fourth jhāna with any kasiṇa except the limited-space kasiṇa, emerge from that absorption and reflect upon the disadvantages of materiality—the many kinds of suffering that arise dependent upon materiality. Seriously consider the vulnerablility of material phenomena to pain, cold, hunger, disease, accident, decay, and so on. Patiently reflect on the gross quality of matter as you inhibit the desire to rush toward the pleasure of higher attainments.

Reflection 2: Next, proceed to contemplate the disadvantages of the fourth jhāna as dangerously close to the coarse pleasure characteristic of the third jhāna.

Reflection 3: And last, reflect on the advantages of higher attainments that are more peaceful and sublime. These three reflections—disadvantages of materiality, dangerous proximity of the fourth jhāna to the happiness in the third jhāna, and advantages of the immaterial abidings that are more peaceful and sublime—can gradually release consciousness from attachment to all material things.

Although you won't need to spend much time reflecting, do not skip this step. You will repeat this reflection with every transition between the fourth and the fifth jhānas as you develop this immaterial sequence and establish dispassion toward materiality. For ease of attaining a stable absorption at this time, encourage the mind to rest in the company of equanimity and one-pointed attention by not contemplating disadvantages to upekkhā and ekaggatā; later, you will contemplate the impermanence, unsatisfactoriness, and emptiness of all mental factors. ✦

WHAT IS SPACE?

Spaciousness is an alluring but often misunderstood notion. Confusion commonly arises if we neglect to distinguish the concept of space that functions as an object of consciousness both from spaciousness as a description of a felt quality and from the indescribable realization beyond the material and immaterial planes. Buddhist teachings present the concept of space in several contexts: (1) as a quality of mental and emotional ease, as when we say that the mind feels "spacious, uncluttered, unburdened"; (2) as a framed area defined by borders, much like an ornate strip of wood surrounds a painted landscape or a wall defines the space in the room or curtains create the space for a theatrical performance; when refined, this way of perceiving space elicits the limited-space kasiṇa (chapter 6); (3) as infinite space that occurs in the absence of perceived material and leads to the attainment of the base of infinite space (fifth jhāna); (4) as a property that delimits matter (chapter 12); and (5) as the taintless realization of emptiness, synonymous with nibbāna and enlightenment. With so many meanings for the term *space,* students commonly confuse one usage for another. I have had innumerable conversations with students who have experienced one aspect of space, but without exploring further, presume their attainment is more complete than, in fact, it is. Just as reading a restaurant menu is not the same as sampling the food and testing the spicing of a soup is not as nourishing as consuming a meal, reading about immaterial perceptions or glimpsing a fleeting spacious quality of mind is no substitute for meditative attainment. Meditators explore the rarefied experiences of the immaterial perceptions through meditative training, encountering many subtleties, analyzing their functions, and learning to distinguish the nuances of the many experiences associated with the English words *space, spacious, empty,* or *void.*

BASE OF INFINITE SPACE (FIFTH JHĀNA)

> *With the complete surmounting of perceptions of materiality, with the passing away of perceptions of sensory impingement, with non-attention to perceptions of diversity, perceiving "space is infinite," a bhikkhu enters and dwells in the base of the infinity of space. That former perception of materiality ceases for him. At that time there is a subtle but true perception of the base of the infinity of space, and he becomes one who is percipient of this true but subtle perception of the base of the infinity of space. In this way some perceptions arise through training, and some pass away through training. And this is that training.*
>
> —The Buddha[123]

Jhāna practice invites a deep unraveling of attachment to all things and all standpoints of existence. You do not add an element of space to your meditative survey or collect yet another attainment, leaving an attraction to matter intact. Although experienced as a series of attainments, the immaterial abidings function as the next rung in the ladder of relinquishment.

To dwell in a steady and uninterrupted perception of space, you shall deliberately remove the kasiṇa from awareness. To do this, first reflect on the dissatisfactory quality of materiality as previously described. Then observe a fourth jhāna kasiṇa and with a strong intention to surmount all materiality, withdraw your attention from the perception of the kasiṇa. Notice the space that it previously occupied. Since the kasiṇa was infinite in proportions, the space it occupied will be of correspondingly infinite dimensions. Repeatedly steer your attention to the notion of infinite space by reciting, *space, space,* or *infinite space, infinite space,* or *boundless space, boundless space.* As absorption nears, suspend verbal recitation to permit the mind to steadily dwell absorbed with the subtle luminous nimitta that is a reflection of the concept of infinite space. Quietly rest, aware of the boundless space that is known by virtue of the absence of the materiality of the fourth jhāna kasiṇa.

If you have difficulty removing the fine material kasiṇa, try focusing on a small space within the kasiṇa and incrementally expand that hole until it seems that empty space occupies infinite proportions. Imagine materiality dissolving to reveal pure space—like the gradual dissipation of steam off a kettle of boiling water or the surprising revelation of space when a window curtain is suddenly drawn back in a high-rise hotel overlooking the ocean. You may also use the less elaborate approach of bare relinquishment by abandoning any residual attraction for the four aspects of perception listed in the Buddha's instructions: bodily sensations, resistance, attraction to diverse perceptions, and defining boundaries. Unbound by these habitual ways of orienting toward sensory phenomena, you may relax into a direct perception of this expanse of basic space.

Let the attainment of infinite space mature, abiding in it for at least one hour without interruption. Let the mind rest in this spacious ease. Grow comfortable with a knowing beyond dependence on matter. Develop the five masteries as described in meditation instruction 4.4.

BASE OF INFINITE CONSCIOUSNESS (SIXTH JHĀNA)

> *By completely surmounting the base of the infinity of space, perceiving "consciousness is infinite," he enters and dwells in the base of the infinity of consciousness. That former subtle but true perception of the base of the infinity of space ceases for him. At that time there is a subtle but true perception of the base of the infinity of consciousness, and he becomes one who is percipient of this true but subtle perception of the base of the infinity of consciousness. In this way some perceptions arise through training, and some pass away through training. And this is that training.*
>
> —The Buddha[124]

To surmount the base of infinite space and attain the base of boundless consciousness, emerge from the base of infinite space, and reflect that this base has the disadvantage of being dangerously near to the coarse materiality of the fourth jhāna and that the base of boundless consciousness has the advantage of being even more sublime. Turn your attention around to perceive the consciousness that knows space—welcome this consciousness as your new object. Now, for the first time in the progression of jhāna, you are using a real object or "ultimate reality" rather than an abstract concept as the basis for absorption—that object being the consciousness that cognizes infinite space.

Alternatively you may simply abandon the perception of space and see what remains. This requires only a very small movement, a glance; a modest shift in perception reveals this brilliant expanse of unbroken knowing. Infinite consciousness is not interrupted or defined by any object that is known. It is simply the stable perception of that consciousness that was aware of infinite space. Note it as *boundless consciousness* or just *consciousness, consciousness* until you attain absorption. Develop the five masteries.

BASE OF NOTHINGNESS (SEVENTH JHĀNA)

> *By completely surmounting the base of the infinity of consciousness, perceiving "there is nothing," he enters and dwells in the base of nothingness. That former subtle but true perception of the base of the infinity of consciousness ceases for him. At that time there is a subtle but true perception of the base of nothingness, and he becomes one who is percipient of this true but subtle perception of the base of nothingness. In this way some perceptions arise through training, and some pass away through training. And this is that training.*
>
> —The Buddha[125]

The concept of absence is the object for the next attainment. First reflect on the danger—the base of infinite consciousness is threatened by its proximity to the base of infinite space—and intuit that the perception of nothingness will be even more peaceful and sublime. Careful and unhurried reflection awakens disenchantment for the prior attainment of infinite consciousness. By relinquishing all desire for the base of infinite consciousness, recall that there can be only one object of consciousness at any one time. Therefore, to apprehend the base of infinite consciousness (sixth jhāna), the previous perception of space (fifth jhāna) had to be absent. Turn your attention to the concept of absence. Dwell knowing the absence of the consciousness that had previously taken space as its object. Note this absence as *nothing, nothing,* or *absence,* or *void,* until you attain absorption (seventh jhāna). Then develop the five masteries.

If you find these instructions confusing, try just dropping the perception of consciousness and notice what is left. You'll find nothing, yet you'll be aware of the absence of things. Without something to grasp, the mind rests with profound ease, unwinding eons of tension compounded by grasping possessions, roles, identities, and experiences. Finally you can relax, unburdened by any "thing" to pursue.

To describe the base of nothingness, the *Visuddhimagga* uses the illustration of entering a hall where everyone has left. Upon entering the hall, you perceive that there is nothing there. You do not think about the people who have left. Rather, you experience a clear steady perception of the absence of things.

BASE OF NEITHER-PERCEPTION-NOR-NONPERCEPTION (EIGHTH JHĀNA)

The consciousness that is aware of the base of nothingness serves as the object for absorption in the base of neither-perception-nor-nonperception. After emerging from the base of nothingness, cultivate dispassion toward the attainment of nothingness by reflecting on its proximity to the lesser attainment of infinite consciousness. Incline toward the stillness of the base of neither-perception-nor-nonperception as more peaceful and sublime.

In addition, contemplate the limitations and disadvantages of perception and feeling. Consider that human beings constantly seek sensory impressions without satisfaction; we become exhausted when driven to accumulate pleasures and avoid pain; we often misinterpret causes, exhaust ourselves comparing transient experiences with impressions long past or yet to occur, and perpetuate habits that lead inevitably to greater anguish. Since perception is dependent on memory, it is inevitably faulty and misleading. Contemplating the faults of raw perception and feeling will instill dispassion at a remarkably subtle level. These contemplations unravel a deeply rooted compulsion to seek experiential satisfaction.

With disgust toward perception established, turn the attention to that consciousness that takes nothingness as its object. Try to see the consciousness that is present while perceiving the nimitta of the base of nothingness. If it is not obvious, you can trick it into revealing itself by praising the seventh jhāna consciousness. What is enjoying the quality of nothingness? Think "oh, this base of nothingness is peaceful and sublime" and quickly turn the attention to capture the consciousness that is aware of the peaceful nature of nothingness.

The *Visuddhimagga* illustrates this perspective with the story of a king who observes the fine work of local craftsmen.[126]

> Suppose a king is proceeding along a city street with the great pomp of royalty, splendidly mounted on the back of an elephant, and he sees craftsmen, each wearing one cloth tightly as a loincloth and another tied around his head, working at various crafts such as ivory carving, etc., their limbs covered with ivory dust, etc.; now while he is pleased with their skill, thinking, "How skilled these craft-masters are, and what crafts they practice!" he does not, however, think, "Oh that I might abandon royalty and become a craftsman like that!" Why not? Because of the great benefits in the majesty of kings; he leaves the craftsmen behind and proceeds on his way.

In such a way, you can praise the exquisite qualities of the base of nothingness without the slightest wish to abide there, because you are heading to the more comfortable dwelling place of the sphere of neither-perception-nor-nonperception.

The consciousness that perceives nothingness is your new object. Note it as *peaceful, peaceful,* cultivating steady awareness of the "non-existence of nothingness" until absorption arises. Then develop the five masteries.

This state of neither-perception-nor-nonperception is difficult to describe, and yet it can have a striking impact on the mind. In this state where no sounds, sensations, thoughts, emotions, or intentions impinge on the mind, and there is nothing to perceive except a subtle past consciousness, the mind finds total relaxation. For many meditators this is a fragile state and the slightest activation of intention will abruptly end the absorption. Only a residue of mental factors colors the base of neither-perception-nor-nonperception, and these are in a subdued state.

The *Visuddhimagga* uses two traditional images to describe the extreme subtlety of this state. The first image is of a bowl with a residue of oil in it:[127] An attendant wants to serve his master some rice gruel. He tells the master, "I have brought rice gruel, but your bowl has oil in it." The master replies, "Go get that other bowl and pour the oil into it, so this bowl can be used to serve the gruel." The attendant responds, "There is no oil to pour out." This is the analogy for the base of neither-perception-nor-nonperception. Just as there is neither oil nor nonoil, but a residue of oil remains, so it is with the base of neither-perception-nor-nonperception: perception is not engaged by taking up objects, and yet perception is not absent. There is a residue of the functions of feeling, perception, mental formations, and consciousness; however, all are extraordinarily subtle.

The *Visuddhimagga*'s second example uses water as the metaphor:[128] A novice and an elder monk who is nearly blind are traveling between villages. The novice sees water on the road ahead and says to the elder, "There is water ahead sir, get out your sandals." The elder responds, "Good, let us take a bath. Where is the towel?" The novice responds, "There is no water for bathing."

The illustration of the presence of water that is not usable attempts to describe the residue of subtle formations. The sphere of neither-perception-nor-nonperception is referred to as not perception because you can't recognize anything about it. And it is referred to as not nonperception, because you can still recognize it. Hence, a state that is a perfection of simplicity has gained a rather long and awkward name.

To attain the base of neither-perception-nor-nonperception, you do not dull or suspend perception, but clearly become aware of the consciousness that is aware of nothing. It is an ultrasubtle and luminous attainment that will diminish residual infatuation with all previous perceptions. This absorption highlights the burdensome character of perception, represented by the five aggregates of clinging—matter, feeling, perception, mental formations, and consciousness (chapter 14)—while regarding them with nonattachment. It thereby instills dispassion for any state of abiding.

A CRITIQUE OF DESIRE

Embedded in jhāna training is a critique of desire. Each attainment illuminates the unsatisfactory quality of the previous jhāna and requires the relinquishing of attachment to the coarser phenomena. Saturated by subtle pleasures in jhāna, you will soon realize that these pleasures are limited and naive infatuation with them gradually ends. Like children who outgrow certain toys and seek more sophisticated pursuits as they age, you will leave many attractions behind through the development of jhāna. With each new stage you may question attachment, asking, "Is desire a reliable basis for my happiness?" Incrementally and experientially, you establish genuine disenchantment with phenomenal existence. Whether or not you believe in past and future lives, you may see how desire propels us into new modes of being, moment by moment. Infatuation controls an untrained mind by compelling a lingering glance toward an attractive person, an unmindful walk to the refrigerator, or an unexamined yearning that might impel you to reappear lifetime after lifetime to revel in sensory stimulation. Unable to resist craving, you may be addicted to sensory stimulation and habitually grasp what you seek. Do you relish the sublimely refined experiences of jhāna, or do you genuinely seek the ending of all attachments? Contemplate the potential of liberation from all constraints, freedom from even the most sublime experiences of mind and matter, the ending of all distress, the cessation of attachment, the realization of nibbāna. Jhāna provides a profound system for training the mind to let go. The training should not harbor refined desires or subtle attachments; the Buddha encouraged his disciples to not even cling to the highest immaterial jhāna or the equanimity associated with the attainment. Although it might be considered the best object of clinging, one "should not delight in that...or remain holding to it."[129] So don't rush the progression just to collect more experiences. Like traveling across a series of steppingstones that span a flowing stream, experience each step in the progression, free of lingering attachment to any stage of the path.

TABLE 7.1
Immaterial Jhānas

MEDITATION SUBJECT	BASIS	JHĀNA POTENTIAL
Infinite space	The removal of any fully expanded kasiṇa (except the limited-space kasiṇa); perception of the space previously occupied by the expanded kasiṇa	Base of infinite space
Infinite consciousness	Removal of the sign of the base of infinite space; perception of the consciousness that cognized infinite space	Base of infinite consciousness
Nothingness	Removal of the sign of the base of infinite consciousness; perception of absence of the consciousness that cognized infinite space	Base of nothingness
Neither-perception-nor-nonperception	Removal of the base of nothingness; perception of the consciousness that cognized nothingness	Base of neither-perception-nor-nonperception

CHAPTER 8

Boundless Heart: Loving-Kindness, Compassion, Appreciative Joy, and Equanimity

May all beings be happy and secure!
May their hearts be wholesome!
Whatever living beings there may be:
Weak or strong, tall or middling,
Short or large, without exception;
Seen or unseen, dwelling far or near,
Already born or yet to be born,
May all beings be happy!
One should cultivate an unlimited loving mind
Without obstruction, anger, or opposition
To the whole world
Above, below, and across.
—SUTTA NIPĀTA[130]

A FAVORITE BUDDHIST STORY recalls a group of monks who were meditating in a forest inhabited by mischievous spirits. Frightened by eerie noises, the monks tried in vain to concentrate, but their efforts to establish jhāna repeatedly collapsed. Terrified by the creepy disruptions and discouraged by lack of progress, the monks sought the Buddha's guidance and received instructions in loving-kindness *(mettā)* meditation.[131] You may not be as concerned with ghosts or spirits, but you may have other fears—fears of being hurt, of loss, of loneliness, or being wrong—that might prevent you from doing things you know are good and useful.

The divine abodes *(brahmavihāras)* of loving-kindness, compassion, appreciative joy, and equanimity represent four modes of relating with openness, friendliness, responsiveness, and steadiness toward all beings. The Buddha taught them as ways of engaging with life that lead to "immeasurable liberations of mind."[132] The series begins with the development of loving-kindness, and it extends to compassion, appreciative joy, and equanimity. When a concentrated mind, imbued with mettā, contemplates beings who are suffering, compassion arises. Contemplating the successes of others elicits appreciative joy. Reflecting on the impact of causes and effects on beings brings equanimity to the fore.

This chapter includes daily life reflective exercises that will enhance these altruistic attitudes for meditators and nonmeditators alike. This chapter also includes explicit instructions for developing loving-kindness, compassion, appreciative joy, and equanimity as meditation subjects that can lead to jhāna. These are versatile subjects that can be used for deep jhāna meditation, for supporting other meditation practices, as a basis for insight,[133] or for simply developing and enhancing a pervasively loving response to life. Although presented in this course of training primarily as a means for cultivating concentration, these beautiful qualities should not be reduced to such a utilitarian purpose. They express the clear, wise, and caring engagement of a free mind with all life.

THE KIND HEART

Loving-kindness *(mettā)* is the universal wish for the welfare and happiness of all living beings. Loving-kindness meditation is a powerful practice that dissolves fear and opens the heart to a genuine connection with life. Mettā, and the happiness associated with it, may arise naturally, it may be cultivated during daily social encounters, or it may be embraced in a formal meditation practice. It is a clear intention that weakens ill will, fear, and blame; it is an attitude of noncontention, a quality of heart that embraces life without conflict. The Pali term, *mettā,* is derived from a word for friendship, and therefore can be understood as a deep friendship with life. This should not imply that mettā is necessarily easy. Deep friendship implies being present, connected, and caring even through difficult times.

Loving-kindness practice generates strong concentration and will produce a quick, buoyant, light, and joyful mind. It brings forth pragmatic skills and wholesome states that steer the meditator clear of pitfalls on the path to liberation. Mettā is both an ideal attitude toward living beings and a versatile meditation subject with numerous benefits. It has the power to dispel anger and fear, protect the mind from ill will, generate happiness, encourage simplicity and upright conduct, support peaceful community relationships, and establish jhāna concentration. You may choose to use it as a daily contemplation to purify your intentions, to soften angry or irritable tendencies, or to enhance a disposition toward happiness and ease. Even a brief experience of mettā is something the Buddha praised: "Monks, if for just the time of a finger-snap, a monk produces a thought of loving-kindness, develops it, gives attention to it, such a one is rightly called a monk. Not in vain does he meditate."[134]

Mettā creates a field of reprieve in which the heart can heal old wounds and the meditator can strengthen restraint, commit to wholesome endeavors, and create resolve for peace, happiness, and insight. It also supports the cultivation of concentration, and so is traditionally compared to kindling that nurtures a fire—meditators may "warm-up" their concentration with loving-kindness practice at the beginning of each meditation session or at the beginning of a retreat.

About Mettā

Loving-kindness is not a passionate response of feeling, but rather a mental factor or attitude that can be cultivated. Feelings change with the vicissitudes of pleasure and pain; you will discover mettā, however, not in your feelings, but in your intentions.

Mettā is a strong receptive quality that bears pain as well as pleasure. You can wish well while remaining open to the complexities of suffering that plague our world. One day I was hiking on the grass-covered hills near my home and saw a hawk swoop down and snatch something from a field; I found only a twitching lizard tail left behind in the grass. With mettā, it was natural to wish the lizard be free of pain, rejoice in the good fortune of the hawk, and contemplate with equanimity the struggles of existence and death. Conflict is part of our existence and mettā practice opens the heart to connect with the truth of life, enabling us to face pain with love.

Mettā's opposite—its "far enemy"—is ill will. Stephen Levine, known for his work with hospice programs, was once asked how he became so loving. He replied, "by noticing all the times my heart was closed." The practice can bring to light any latent tendencies toward ill will, which will weaken through being recognized and create opportunities to replace thoughts that close the heart in judgment and anger with thoughts that promote connection, kindness, and love.

→ **MEDITATION INSTRUCTION 8.1**
A Good Start Each Day

Notice the first thoughts that arise in the morning. If you discover that you wake to irritated, anxious, worried, fearful, grumpy, or demanding mental patterns, exchange them for the happy ease of mettā. If you find that you jump in the shower in the morning already rehearsing how you might respond to confrontations that have not yet occurred, lamenting minor social blunders made in previous days, or armoring yourself against dangers that are not present, your mind has set the stage for a miserable day.

To start each day with the intention of good will, before you crawl out from under your blanket, contemplate mettā by reciting and deeply considering the four traditional phrases:

> May I be safe from harm.
> May I be happy, and free from mental distress.
> May I be healthy, and free from illness and pain.
> May I live with ease in the world.

Align your attitude with the powerful intention of kindness,
and direct these intentions toward the people you might meet that
day. Think of a person and wish:

> May you be safe from harm.
> May you be happy, and free from mental distress.
> May you be healthy, and free from illness and pain.
> May you live with ease in the world.

As you practice mettā at home, the purification of unwholesome tendencies will be accomplished gradually in daily life;
then, when you take mettā as a subject in retreat, it will be easy to
develop concentration. ⤺

Mettā cultivates a deep friendship with life. When mettā is strong,
you can trust your intentions. This confidence supports concentration.
As you trust yourself, faith in the practice grows.

In this practice, "hate has to be abandoned and patience attained";[135]
therefore, the initial instruction is to "review the danger in hate and the
advantage in patience."[136] After all, "one cannot abandon unseen dangers and attain unknown advantages."[137] A person who harbors hatred is
compared to a fool who in anger reaches for a pile of dog poop to throw
at an enemy—she soils herself first.[138] In this practice you train your
mind away from hostility and consistently incline your heart toward
good will for all beings—those whom you like, as well as those you do
not like; those who have helped you, as well as those who have hurt you.
Although you cannot control the words others speak to you, you can
increase your capacity to bear them with peace, free of hatred. As the
ancient illustration describes, when you add a teaspoon of salt to a glass
of water, the taste of salt is strong, but if you add a teaspoon of salt to
a lake, there will be very little impact. Just so, you can develop a mind
so filled with love that it remains unaffected by irritating encounters or
verbal abuse.[139]

Little Moments with a Wide Community

Loving-kindness is cultivated through the little moments of kindness and sensitivity toward yourself, others, and the world. Mettā practice offers an opportunity to shift habitual relationships, even small ones, by widening the circle of your community. Take notice of the little creatures that you share a day with—grasshoppers, butterflies, ants, frogs, cats, raccoons, spiders. You are not alone in this world.

I spent a number of years practicing meditation in monasteries in the forests of Thailand, where I would sit cross-legged on the ground to eat lunch. Large black ants also lived in these jungles. This variety of ant did not travel along orderly highways; each ant, with antennae wiggling, seemed to be on an individual quest for my rice and curry. Whenever an ant had zeroed in on my bowl, it would crawl up my foot or leg, make its way to the bowl, reach in, take one grain of rice, and abscond with its bounty. At first I struggled to keep my bowl bug-free, but this only caused me agitation—I was after all sitting on the ground in a jungle; there was no "bug-free" place. Finally, I began to offer each ant one grain as it approached my leg. The ant would gently accept the rice grain from my finger-tip and scurry away. There was no more struggle or annoyance. It was a simple shift that removed the conflict and cost me only six to ten grains of rice each meal.

Human relations are often more complicated, though, and the people we love the most are often the ones who trigger our anger, because we expect more from them than others. When an untrained mind does not get what it wants, it lashes out. Mettā provides a radically different response.

I once lived in a community that was riddled with conflict; thoughts of my fellow community members did not stimulate immediate and bountiful happiness, so first I generated mettā for the dog who was always willing to walk with me. Mettā is such a powerful attitude that even wishing happiness for a dog prevented ill will from dwelling in my heart and perhaps helped halt the escalation of conflict. Don't wait until you feel loving before you start mettā practice. Loving-kindness develops through practice. Informed by a depth of mettā, we will sense the

Transforming the Little Things

Consider transforming some of your habitual reactions. Notice people that you see on a regular basis but generally disregard; for instance, clerks in stores, at the post office, or cafés. Walking your dog you may pass the mail carrier or someone watering plants. Instead of ignoring these people, try adding a few moments of interest and care by generating thoughts of mettā.

Many of my students enjoy reciting mettā phrases while driving—a welcome alternative to becoming angry at the driver who cut you off in traffic. Wish for his safety and well-being. See how a few thoughts of loving-kindness sprinkled throughout the day can transform your mood.

connection and friendship with life growing within and around us. The contraction around me, and what I want, the stories of who did what to me and why it was not fair, the grasping after what I feel I deserve, and the armor that we weave around our hearts, all melt in the field of mettā.

COMPASSION

Compassion *(karuṇā)* is the wish that all beings be free from suffering and pain. When you recognize suffering, you will want to alleviate it; as such, compassion is expressed in action. People habitually withdraw, avoid, or turn away from pain and suffering. So the challenge karuṇā practice presents is the opportunity to connect and respond. When you see suffering in the news or hear stories of other people's pain, do you sense their pain but ignore or avoid recognizing it? When you meet someone who is suffering, ill, limping, grieving, confused, cold, or hungry, how do you feel and what action do you take?

One time I traveled to Colorado to lead a retreat. I boarded the small nineteen-seat plane and soon realized that another passenger, a young woman traveling with her boyfriend, was in tears. As the plane readied for takeoff her distress increased—she was terrified of flying. Discerning the situation, another passenger moved near and engaged her in friendly conversation, holding her attention with eye contact and simple questions. As the plane prepared for takeoff, the compassionate stranger, who was a trained pilot, proceeded to anticipate the sounds, explain the bumps, and narrate the flight. His reassuring presence convinced her that everything was reasonable and expected. She calmed and their conversation segued into a lively discussion of literature and creative writing punctuated by laughter and delight, interspersed with periodic explanations of bumps or rumbles. The pilot's off-duty intervention helped this young woman transform the grip of terror into joyful interaction and illustrated for me the essence of compassion. Compassion is not reserved for Nobel Prize nominees—notice your response to pain and let it elicit compassion.

The first step in compassion practice is to be willing to perceive suffering without aversion—neither reacting in blame and anger nor withdrawing in fear and denial. Then wisdom can inform action. When your heart is softened by mettā, is moved with compassion, and is strengthened by equanimity, you will be able to consider what a skillful response might be.

My grandfather lived in one city for nearly sixty years, active in church clubs and bingo, with several sisters, brothers, nieces, and nephews living nearby. As his condition deteriorated with age, he was forced to move into a nursing home a couple of miles from his home. Once he was ensconced in the facility, his siblings rarely visited. During the two years that he resided in the institution, his sister, who had lived across the street for six decades, never appeared. When I visited and offered to drive her, she told me, "I can't go in there, it just breaks my heart to see him like that." Through the cultivation of compassion meditation, you become willing to see suffering and respond by opening your heart to the suffering that you witness; you are cultivating the capacity to respond kindly and clearly to the inevitable pain in life.

Compassion may appear as a full, heartfelt feeling; a quivering of the

Don't Turn Away from Suffering

When you wake up in the morning, make the commitment: Today I will not turn away from another person's suffering. As you go about your daily activities, notice what is happening around you. Take note of your response to suffering and don't permit yourself to turn away. You may offer only eye contact, recognition, or a smile; you may do something that could help; you may recognize that the danger is great or your skill level insufficient and choose to wisely withdraw. Learn to meet suffering without resistance or fuss, then ask, "How can I help?" and stay present to consider the response.

heart; a softness in the chest. Like mettā, compassion is a mental factor, an intention or attitude that you bring to experience; it is not a feeling. A condescending attitude of pity is considered the near enemy of compassion. It is a quality that is commonly confused with compassion, but is corrupted by the judgmental stance of self-interest. The far enemy of compassion, its opposite, is cruelty.

APPRECIATIVE JOY

Appreciative joy *(muditā)* is also called sympathetic, empathetic, or altruistic joy. It is the wish that the happiness of others continue and increase. Muditā manifests when mettā meets the success and good fortune of another being. You may experience this quality of happiness when you rejoice with a friend's good news, witness a colleague succeed, or delight in the performance of an athlete. Appreciative joy is the pinnacle of good sportsmanship, permitting us to deeply appreciate our rival's superior performance and our friend's good luck.

The term *muditā* means to be pleased, to have a sense of gladness,

and to be nondemeaning. It develops with the recognition that our happiness does not diminish as the happiness of others increases. Recall a
time in your life when you accomplished something challenging. How
did you feel when someone expressed happiness for you, and how did
you feel when someone reacted with envy? Rejoicing with success and
happiness honors the achievement, delights in the good fortune, and
simultaneously brings joy to your life, almost as if the gains of others are
your own.

 Rejoice!

This week, before you retire to bed each night, write a list of
three to six achievements, fortunate events, or successes that you
personally experienced today. Recognize both trivial and important events; write down anything that comes to mind without
judging it. Perhaps you discovered the perfect setting for the
toaster, successfully balanced your checkbook, or finished a difficult project. Notice the good things in your life; recognize the
frequent little accomplishments that fill your days.

Then, in a second column, write another list of three to six
achievements, fortunate events, or successes that you witnessed
in other beings. Perhaps you saw a squirrel find a stash of acorns,
a student earn a perfect test score, a former lover get married,
or a colleague receive an award. Let the recognition of other
people's good luck and success bring joy to your heart.

There are many little lucky moments every day. When you focus on
good fortune, causes for happiness become apparent everywhere. If a
friend wins at a card game, are you delighted for her or do you sulk at
your own defeat? When neighbors build an addition to their house or

cultivate a terrific rose garden, are you pleased or do you compare their accomplishments with your own and feel poor in comparison? If you go out to lunch with two friends, one of whom can eat anything she wants without gaining weight and the other just lost twenty pounds and looks terrific, how do you respond? Are you genuinely happy for the driver in front of you who got the perfect parking spot? Practice responding with wholehearted joy, uncontaminated by comparison, and without interjecting competitive justifications that imply, "I am happy for you, but I deserve it more." Muditā entertains no sense of entitlement, and no thoughts such as, "but what about me?" It is a simple affirmation of happiness, accomplishment, and good fortune.

In contrast to its far enemies that habitually dampen joy—namely, jealousy, envy, comparison, blame, and chronic judging—muditā produces a very sweet quality of happiness that encourages sharing. It is balanced, not excessive like its near enemies exhilaration and giddiness. When you trust that happiness is not a scarce commodity, you find that rejoicing with the good fortune of anyone and everyone becomes an effective antidote to discontent.

EQUANIMITY

Equanimity *(upekkhā)* refers to the capacity to see all beings without prejudice or partiality, and requires that hatred toward enemies and infatuation toward friends be relinquished. This profound impartiality clears the agitation of preference and personal wishes and brings a cool, refreshing balance to consciousness. As a divine abode, this manifestation of equanimity is directed toward how you relate to beings. It stabilizes mettā, karuṇā, and muditā, and it prevents these joyful factors from becoming imbalanced or excessive.

Equanimity is a state free of attachment, aversion, and reactivity; it is not indifference. Developed through a contemplation of causes and effects, equanimity practice highlights the understanding that everything occurs due to causes and that everyone will inherit the fruits of their own actions. Equanimity does not reject people or conditions. It enhances a profoundly balanced attention, permitting wisdom to guide actions without the corrupting influences of fear, anger, and greed. It cultivates the ability to remain equally close to all things—both the painful and the pleasant. Imagine the peace that will be possible when you relate to all beings without the agitation of like or dislike, preference or prejudice. This deep peace of equanimity takes the struggle out of existence.

 An Impact on Life

In your daily life, notice your reactions and preferences regarding the people you encounter. Observe how kindness is expressed in your behavior and when a balanced countenance pervades your relationships. Who do you like or dislike, admire or judge, tend to avoid or seek out? Are you sad when you see a friend struggling with problems that you know you cannot fix? Are you angry to see crimes and violence as reported in the news? Do you feel excessive responsibility to care for younger siblings even after they have grown to adulthood? Do you overreact to the dilemmas and difficulties of friends? Can you refrain from meddling in the married life of a daughter? It is beautiful to care about people and want to help them, but there are many occasions when all you can do is to cultivate patience, tolerance, and equanimity. Appreciate the people who test the mettle of your equanimity, for they are the ones who challenge you to bring these immeasurable qualities into the down-to-earth reality of everyday encounters. Equanimity practice encourages a balanced mind toward all living beings. Let the effects of this meditation practice spill over into your daily life.

A COMPREHENSIVE TRAINING

Skillful meditators who choose the divine abodes as their primary meditation subjects will discover a rich training in virtue, concentration, and wisdom that leads ultimately to liberation. This practice involves the initial cultivation of mettā, and then extends the good will through the cultivation of compassion, appreciative joy, and equanimity.

When the Buddha taught mettā to the monks who were disturbed by fear in their forest retreat, he contextualized loving-kindness in the path of awakening.[140] The cultivation of mettā incorporates upright conduct, is imbued with mindfulness, concentrates the mind, penetrates the illusion of self, and leads to the deathless liberation. It cannot be separated from intention, mindfulness, and the goal of awakening.

Loving-Kindness as an Immeasurable Deliverance of Mind

Loving-kindness represents a social attitude that is outwardly directed and can radiate boundlessly throughout the universe, encompassing all living beings. When the mind is filled with mettā, you care for all beings as the right hand cares for the left: without selfishness, without greed, and without hate. Those of you who have previously established jhāna based on a kasiṇa have already had an intimate experience with the expansive potential of consciousness. Those who have attained the immaterial absorptions will already know the infinite qualities of mind. Cultivating mettā, compassion, appreciative joy, and equanimity provides another vehicle for expanding consciousness.

Mettā is described in the Buddhist canon as an immeasurable deliverance of mind that is exalted, without hostility, without ill will. It is characterized as immeasurable, because kindness expands consciousness infinitely and because the beings that mettā embraces are countless. A mind absorbed by mettā offers a powerful glimpse of the immeasurable quality of consciousness and an exquisite, though temporary, experience of mind free from the corruptions of desire, hate, and self-preoccupation.

A Labyrinth of Phrases and Categories

Meditators who are just beginning to establish loving-kindness may dedicate considerable time to nurturing mettā, by repeating the mettā phrases and carefully addressing the sequence of specific categories. You may use the traditional four phrases introduced earlier in this chapter, or condense the recitation to just one phrase, such as, "May you be happy and well," or "May I be happy, peaceful, and free of suffering." Feel free to compose your own mettā phrases, but they should be simple and reflect the basic wish that all beings share—to be happy and not suffer. Personally, I use longer reflective phrases when inserting mettā into busy daily life, and short pithy phrases when using mettā as a jhāna practice. I generally recommend that students begin by reciting the four traditional phrases until the quality of mettā arises and the image of the person for whom you are wishing happiness becomes clear. Then focus on just one phrase. You will quickly find phrasing that resonates well for you.

Begin this practice by cultivating good will toward yourself. Start with a few minutes of contemplating your own genuine wish to be happy and not suffer. Although jhāna cannot be attained with self as the object, you can use yourself as the example, and since you know your own wish to be happy, you can extend that same authentic wish toward others.[141]

Next, cultivate mettā toward a person whom you respect, admire, or feel gratitude toward, such as a teacher or benefactor. It is best not to use a relative or a close friend who might trigger either worry or attachment. For all the categories, use living people for whom there is no sexual attraction. Contemplate people when they are happy, doing something worthwhile, and are at their best. Conjure the image of this person's happy smiling face, and repeat the phrases while seeing a vivid image of the person. The confluence of the meaning of the phrases, such as "may you be well and happy," with a clear visualization of the person in a happy moment, develops a palpable quality you will learn to recognize as mettā. Once mettā arises toward one benefactor, add a second respected person, then a third, and continue until you have cultivated loving-kindness toward five to ten individuals in this category and then in each of the following categories.

The third category, that of dear friends, may include close friends, family members, and associates—people that you generally like. This category poses the challenge of wishing well to people you care for and with whom you are intimate, without triggering attachment, personal affection, or worry.

The fourth class of people includes anyone who occupies a neutral place in your life—people whom you neither like nor dislike. Often students remember a store clerk, a neighbor, or someone they have recently met but are indifferent toward.

The fifth class of beings includes anyone for whom you harbor hostility and anger. There is no need to conjure up hated ones if you can't recall someone who infuriates you. If there is no one that you hate, then you may choose someone who merely annoys you, or simply skip the category.

The individuals in your classifications are fluid and will change; the placement merely reflects current attitudes toward certain people. This exercise should not stereotype or pigeonhole individuals. One meditator's respected person may be another person's neutral or hostile person;

 ### Standard Mettā Sequence

The following progression, from easy to difficult, structures a sequential training in mettā that gradually extends good will toward all kinds of beings, those that are respectable and familiar, as well as those who are unknown or untrustworthy:

- self
- respectable person or benefactor
- dear friend
- neutral person
- enemy or hostile person
- all beings by way of twelve classes and ten directions.

---

a dear friend may slide into the enemy category at some point in time. These classifications provide a simple way to create an order of beings, beginning with those toward whom it is easy to develop mettā and then progressing to those toward whom it is more difficult.

Mettā as the Subject of Jhāna Concentration

With mettā as a jhāna practice, attention will be entirely focused on mettā directed toward each person, unseduced by thoughts about personality, activities, history, or personal details. Notice the development of mettā. The mind will become glad and content, rapture and happiness will automatically fill consciousness, there will be no distractions, and your mind will easily absorb into jhāna. Develop mettā without wavering or interruption. This contemplation of mettā generates intense rapturous happiness and makes the mind extraordinarily conducive to concentration. Notice the difference between mettā and the other pleasant feelings that arise simultaneously with concentration.

To deepen concentration, try to stay very steady with the pure and boundless quality of mettā that is available, without bias, for each and every being. Systematically working through the categories stimulates boundless love. Once you have established mettā with five to ten individuals in each category, you may discover that the categories seem equal. Love extends effortlessly to everyone; your energy remains balanced while you are wishing happiness toward dear friends and toward hated ones. Mettā arises just as rapidly toward respected persons as toward neutral persons. Eventually a profound evenness will permeate your boundless pure intention of good will.

✦ MEDITATION INSTRUCTION 8.2
Cultivating Mettā as a Jhāna Practice

1. Begin the meditation by establishing concentration with the breath, a kasiṇa, or the meditation subject of your choice.

2. Contemplate your own wish to be happy and not suffer. Then consider, "Just as I want to be happy and not suffer, so other

beings share the same wish." Using yourself as the example, begin to generate mettā by reciting the phrases and saturating yourself with kind intentions. You may start by reciting the set of four phrases, and then focus on just one phrase. After some minutes of directing mettā toward yourself, begin the systematic progression, individual by individual, category by category, phrase by phrase.

3. Recite the set of four phrases (introduced in meditation instructions 8.1) while holding the image of a respected person in mind. Take the time to clarify the image of the person. Then focus on just one phrase and one respected individual. Concentrate on the meaning of this wish, and select an image of the person that fits with the phrase. It could be the smiling face of the person, or an expression appropriate to the wish of safety or freedom from distress that might dovetail well with the specific phrase. Let both the meaning of the phrases and the image of the person become very clear and steady. Work with the phrases, image, and individual until undistracted concentration is established, the hindrances are absent, the jhāna factors are strong, and you reach the threshold of absorption.

4. When mettā is strong, resolve: "May my mind be absorbed in mettā," and intensify your focus on the individual being with a pure attitude of good will. The being toward whom you are developing kindness is classically considered the object for this meditation.[142] In jhāna a radiant field may be more apparent than the particularities of the face; the experience of mettā might eclipse the distinctness of the image of the person. You will, however, still retain the sense of the person to whom you are directing mettā: the concept of that person is an integral aspect of this meditation practice. The persons or beings that you are seeing are the causes for the arising of mettā; they are the spark for mettā's glory. As explained in the *Visuddhimagga,* the "object is a single living being or many living beings, as a mental object consisting in a concept."[143] Mettā practice is not an abstract, self-indulgent, or narcissistic feeling; it is not generated based on

generalized ideals of kindness. As a wise attitude toward beings and the wish for their welfare, mettā develops in response to the thought of an actual being.

5. As concentration strengthens, attention will be steady without the repetition of verbal phrases—you will tune in to the frequency of mettā and remain riveted to this field of kindness. The phrases will cease in absorption, and the image of the face of the being who is your object may, or may not, remain vivid—either is fine. As the force of mettā builds through the intensity of this one-pointed attention imbued with mettā, the first jhāna may arise. Allow consciousness to unify with mettā and its object, and dwell in the first jhāna. It will be characterized by the five jhāna factors of applied and sustained attention, rapture, joy, and one-pointedness, and include the manifestation of vivid loving-kindness.

6. After abiding in the first jhāna with mettā for a respected person as object for as long as you wish, emerge from absorption. Direct attention to the heart base—you may see the face of the being to whom you were directing mettā reflected in the mind door. Discern the jhāna factors, and reflect on the disadvantages and advantages of the first jhāna in the same manner performed previously (see meditation instruction 4.3).

7. Apply the same approach to attain the second jhāna with the same respected person and the same phrase, and then the third jhāna with the same respected person and the same phrase. Mettā has the capability to raise the mind to the third jhāna, but not higher. The happiness that is intrinsic to mettā prevents the intensification of equanimity, which characterizes the fourth jhāna and immaterial states.[144]

8. After successfully attaining the first, second, and third jhānas with a respected person, repeat the process with additional benefactors. After attaining all three jhānas with five to ten benefactors and one phrase, choose a second phrase and cultivate mettā

through the three jhānas with this next phrase toward five to ten respected beings. And then do so with a third phrase, and then the fourth phrase. In this way mettā and concentration will grow vibrant and clear.

9. To accomplish so many steps, you will need to shift between jhānas very quickly—perhaps remaining in each jhāna for only a couple of minutes. Some meditators stereotype meditation as a slow and grueling process; however, when concentration is strong it becomes easy to shift quickly between objects. Try to work with ten beings in the respected category, ten beings in the dear friends category, ten beings in the neutral category, and ten in the hated ones group. Attain the three jhānas with each of the four phrases. Work with all the categories—you can do this if you are willing to try it fast! Enjoy this light and playful connection with the categories of beings. This approach is likened to a circus horse that darts quickly around and through all the areas of the circus ring; likewise, the meditator quickly moves through all the delimited categories of beings.[145] ←

Breaking Down the Boundaries

For those who have already suppressed the hindrances and established jhāna with other objects, mettā will arise quickly. Therefore, instead of sustaining long absorptions, in this jhāna sequence you will dissolve the separations between types of beings and emphasize an equality of good will toward beings in all the categories.

→ **MEDITATION INSTRUCTION 8.3**
Breaking Down the Boundaries

To break down the boundaries between classes of beings, repeat the mettā sequence rapidly, with one person per category for self, respected, dear, neutral, and hated beings in quick succession. Abandon the desire to sustain long absorptions; cultivate undistracted attention with limitless kindness. Emphasize a rhythmic progression that equalizes attention toward each and every being you contemplate. Include the category of self to equalize all beings. You will not attain jhāna with self as the object; however, you will be able to attain the first three jhānas with the other categories of beings. Eventually the demarcations between categories will appear superfluous; no one will be excluded from the field of your good will. Mettā will flow unobstructed to any being you contemplate. When it is equally easy to drop into jhāna based on the benefactor, the neutral being, and the hated one, and the quality of mettā appears even and stable as you shift between categories, you will have broken down the boundaries and accessed a universal quality of loving-kindness that can be extended to all beings without exception. ⬸

Universal Friendliness to All

I may not know specifically what would delight an earwig, a porcupine, or my neighbor's nephew, but I have no doubt that just as I wish to be happy and free from suffering, so do they. On a fundamental level there is little difference between a squirrel's effort to store nuggets in holes and a homeowner's struggle to pay mortgage bills—they both want to be well and live with ease.

The traditional development of the class called "all beings" structures the concept of "all" into specified and unspecified variations of totality. Each category includes the same countless beings. The groupings include five inclusive and unspecified terms for all beings and seven parallel sets of categories that specify a broad type of being, such as female or male. Together, they produce twelve ways of contemplating the happiness of all beings. The unspecified categories for all beings are:

- all beings
- all living beings
- all breathing beings
- all individuals or creatures
- all in existence, all personalities, or all who exist with matter and mind.

The specified categories for all beings are:

- all females
- all males
- all enlightened beings
- all unenlightened beings
- all celestial beings (gods, deities, devas)
- all humans
- all in lower realms (ghosts, hell realms, animals, insects).

As your concentration and the quality of mettā grow stronger, you will perceive the abundance of beings in this world and beyond, with a pervasive equality of friendliness.

✦ MEDITATION INSTRUCTION 8.4
Radiating Kindness for All Beings

1. Begin the meditation by establishing concentration with the meditation object of your choice. Generate mettā toward individuals in each of the five preliminary categories—self, benefactor, dear friend, neutral, and hostile persons. If mettā rises quickly, you may need only one person per category, but if it takes some time for mettā to stabilize, you might follow the previous instructions and work with five to ten individuals per category until mettā is strong and the boundaries between classes of beings have dissolved.

2. To extend mettā to all beings in the unspecified categories, select a limited area near you, such as the room, building, or neighborhood. Try to see all the beings that are present as you radiate mettā throughout that area.[146] Hold a clear image of the beings that populate that area and develop loving-kindness toward them by using the five unspecified ways of considering all beings. While focusing on an area, work with one phrase at a time, such as "May all beings be free from danger." As usual, between each jhāna direct attention to the mind door at the heart base where you may see a reflection of the beings and recognize the presence

of mettā. Check the factors reflected there. Confirm which jhāna you experienced. Reflect on the disadvantages and advantages of the attainment and jhāna factors; then shift attention back to the beings in the defined area and aspire for the next jhāna. Follow the systematic process to attain the first, second, and third jhānas.

3. Develop mettā toward the same area, with the same phrase, but expand your consciousness to take all living beings as the object. Proceed through the same sequence until you have accomplished the five unspecified categories, with one phrase and three jhānas.

4. Now, extend the area wider, seeing beings that are in a town, village, or region, and continue with the same progression of three jhānas and the one phrase. Try to actually see the beings that exist in each area. Of course you will not see every being, but when concentration is strong, the mind may apprehend a vast multitude of beings.

5. Develop each unspecified category up to the third jhāna before moving on to the next. When you are ready, incrementally expand the range of mettā, incorporating beings in the country, the continent, the world, the solar system, the universe, the unlimited expanse, and so on. Let there be no boundaries, no limitation, nothing that could stop the flow of mettā. Explore the potential of mind to abide in the deep calm of absorption that is saturated with boundless good will.

6. When you have completed the five unspecified classes with one phrase, extending to the vast reaches of the universe, repeat the sequence with the next phrase. Gradually expand the breadth of mettā by discerning all beings everywhere by way of these comprehensive classes and contemplating the phrases that focus loving-kindness toward beings until mettā fills the immeasurable universe.

7. When you are satisfied with the five unspecified classes, proceed in a similar manner with the seven specified categories as listed above. Contemplate the mettā phrase while you see all the designated beings in a delimited area. Extend the light of concentration to try to really see the beings for whom you wish well. For instance, if you are contemplating all males in the building, use the light of the concentrated mind to discern the males that are present in that building; if you are radiating loving-kindness toward all unenlightened beings on the continent, try to see all those beings as you wish them well. The light of concentration will keep the images fresh, vivid, and pertinent.

8. When these seven ways of radiating mettā toward all beings are clear and easy, generate mettā by way of all twelve groupings for all beings again, progressing from near to far. To accomplish this in a reasonable period of time, you will need to make the absorptions very quick. Let the practice be light and fun. Sweep through the categories without preference or differentiation.

9. Next, contemplate these same twelve categories, but now structure the expansion by way of the ten directions. The ten directions traditionally specify the north, northeast, east, southeast, south, southwest, west, northwest, above, and below. You may simplify it to front, behind, right, left, above, and below. Choose a pattern that spirals methodically and direct mettā to all beings in that direction until you have encompassed the entire universe with profound good will.

10. Try the series at various paces. This meditation can be done very quickly. Mettā practice is energizing and can be intensely vivid. Allow loving-kindness to permeate your perception of everyone you encounter. In this approach it is the singularity of focus, rather than the duration of absorption, that enhances concentration. ✦

→ **MEDITATION INSTRUCTION 8.5**
Cultivating Compassion as a Jhāna Practice

   1. Begin the meditation by establishing concentration with breath,
   kasiṇa, or a meditation object of your choice.

   2. Establish mettā up to the third jhāna by reviewing the loving-
   kindness practices using one being per category and one general phrase such as "may you be happy and well." Practice until
   mettā is clear, strong, and the boundaries that limit its radiance
   dissolve.

   Extend mettā to a few people who you know are suffering.
   Choose beings whose suffering is easily recognized and toward
   whom it is easy to feel compassion—a friend struggling with
   cancer, a child whose parent recently died, a colleague who was
   injured and disabled. Newspapers provide an apparently endless
   pool of suffering beings—a starving child in Somalia, refugees of
   civil war in Sri Lanka, a homeless woman who suffered frostbite
   on the streets of Boston. Although you have selected suffering
   beings, focus on a time when those people were happy; focus on
   their smiling faces. Zero in on one suffering person and recite the
   mettā phrases. Establish concentration with mettā and enter brief
   absorptions into the first, second, and third jhānas with mettā
   toward the suffering person as the object. Similarly generate mettā
   toward several beings whose suffering you can easily discern.

   3. Next, select one phrase that highlights a compassionate wish for
   a specific being to be free from pain and suffering. Continue to
   focus on the happy face of the person as you contemplate one of
   the following phrases:

   May you be free from pain and suffering.
   May you be free of pain.
   May you be free of suffering.

Boundless Heart 171

4. When the factor of karuṇā is strong and absorption seems accessible, resolve to enter the first jhāna. Follow the standard training as you have learned—enter, remain, emerge, discern the factors, contemplate the disadvantages and advantages of the jhāna, and aspire for higher attainments with each level of absorption. Like mettā, karuṇā has the capacity to raise the mind to the first, second, and third jhānas only. Karuṇā cannot produce a fourth jhāna absorption because happiness is intrinsic to compassion.

5. After exploring the first three jhānas with one suffering person, repeat the process with another suffering person, developing the karuṇā meditation by including several suffering persons. Then, extend the range of compassion to include self, five to ten respected ones, five to ten dear ones, five to ten neutral people, a few hated ones, and a few people who cause suffering through cruelty, greed, or ignorance. In this way you will develop karuṇā toward individual beings and attain the first three jhānas with each being.

6. As you become confident with the karuṇā practice, move rapidly through the sequence, employing one phrase, one being per category, and three jhānas, until you notice that it is equally easy to establish karuṇā jhānas with any being in any category, without preference. This process breaks down the barriers between classes of beings and produces a universal response of compassion.

7. Once the boundaries are dissolved between beings you like and those you do not like, between those who have helped you and those who have harmed you, cultivate compassion by way of the twelve groups that encompass all beings. Use these twelve unspecified and specified categories to continue to establish the first three jhānas toward all beings, in all directions, extending incrementally from those that exist nearby to those that live far away. Continue until compassion extends throughout the infinite universe. ⬸

→ **MEDITATION INSTRUCTION 8.6**
Cultivating Joy as a Jhāna Practice

1. Begin the meditation by warming up your concentration with the breath, a kasiṇa, or a meditation subject of your choice.

2. Establish mettā to the third jhāna by quickly sequencing through the categories using one being per category and one general phrase, such as "May you be well and happy." Then cultivate compassion, up to the third jhāna, using one being per category, with one phrase.

3. Extend mettā to a few people who you consider successful and fortunate. Select people who are virtuous, kind, generous, and frequently offer their resources for the welfare of others. Establish concentration with mettā toward a successful person; enter brief absorptions into the first, second, and third jhānas. Repeat the first three jhānas with mettā toward several additional fortunate persons.

4. Next select one phrase that highlights the altruistic wish for this person's good fortune to continue. Continue to focus on the smiling face of a fortunate person as you contemplate one of the following phrases:

   May your happiness continue and increase.
   May your good fortune and success never end.
   May your achievements not be lost.

5. When muditā is strong and absorption is accessible, resolve to enter the first jhāna. Follow the standard sequence of training to enter, remain, emerge, reflect on the factors, contemplate the disadvantages and advantages of the jhāna, and aspire for higher attainments with each level of absorption. Like mettā and karuṇā, muditā has the capacity to raise the mind to the first, second, and third jhānas only. Because happiness and pleasure come along with the manifestation of joy, muditā cannot produce a fourth jhāna absorption.

6. After exploring the first three jhānas with one fortunate person, repeat the process with another fortunate person, developing the meditation to include several lucky and successful beings. Extend the range of appreciative joy to include yourself, five to ten respected ones, five to ten dear ones, five to ten neutral people, and a few hated ones. Finally, rejoice for a few people toward whom you may have harbored envy, frequently compete against, or consider as your rival. Establish the three jhānas with appreciative joy for each individual being as the object.

7. When you are confident that mudita is strong enough to extend to your rivals, progress through the sequence quickly highlighting just one being per category. As you move rapidly through the meditative absorptions, with one phrase, one being, and three jhānas, it will become equally easy to establish mudita jhānas with any being in any category, without preference. This process will expose an equality in your regard for all beings, break down the barriers, and produce an unlimited and universal response of appreciation.

8. Once the boundaries are dissolved between the individuals, cultivate appreciative joy by way of the twelve groupings of all beings. Use these twelve categories to continue to establish the first three jhānas with mudita toward all beings near and far, and in all directions, extending the radiance of mudita incrementally until it expands without bounds throughout the infinite universe. ←

→ **MEDITATION INSTRUCTION 8.7**
Cultivating Equanimity as a Jhāna Practice

In this traditional sequence, equanimity is always developed dependent upon loving-kindness, compassion, and appreciative joy. The *Visuddhimagga* explains, "for just as the gable rafters cannot be placed in the air without [one] having first set up the scaffolding and built the framework of beams, so it is not possible to develop the fourth [jhāna in the fourth divine abiding] without having already developed the third jhāna in the earlier [three divine abidings]."[147] The establishment of the first three jhānas, based on the first three qualities of loving-kindness, compassion, and joy, serves as the foundation for the establishing of the fourth jhāna based on equanimity toward beings.

1. Begin the meditation by cultivating concentration with the breath, a kasiṇa, or a meditation subject of your choice. Review the loving-kindness, compassion, and appreciative joy practices to the extent that you wish.

2. Establish mettā to the third jhāna with a few people that you feel indifferent toward; cultivate compassion up to the third jhāna with a few neutral persons; cultivate altruistic joy up to the third jhāna with a few neutral persons.

3. Reflect on the disadvantages of loving-kindness, compassion, and appreciative joy, and the advantages of equanimity—namely, that the first three divine abidings are agitated by joy and are close to the dangers of affection, preference, and elation, while equanimity is more peaceful.

4. To attain the fourth jhāna based on equanimity, adopt a phrase that brings forth equanimity toward beings. Traditionally we contemplate causes and effects and the basic functioning of kamma (actions). Reflect: even though you may radiate mettā, karuṇā, and muditā, the condition of each being will depend on his or her own actions. All beings have kamma as their property. Continue to focus on the face of a neutral person as you recite: *All beings are the heirs of their own actions; their happiness or unhappiness depends upon their actions, not upon my wishes for them.*

    The following four phrases[148] highlight a particular aspect of equanimity; however, it is not necessary to practice with all of them.

    (a) All beings are the heirs of their own action; action is the possession of beings *(sabba satta kammassakata).*

(b) All beings spring from their action. Action is their source; they originate from their action *(sabba satta kamma yoni).*

(c) All beings are related to their action *(sabba satta kamma bandhu).*

(d) All beings have action as their refuge *(sabba satta kamma pati sarana).*

For brevity's sake, my teacher suggested that I recite the condensed phrase—*"kamma ssako,"* which roughly translates "to possess one's own action *(kamma)."* As you meditate upon each neutral being, recite one of these recollections or a variation, in the language of your choice, contemplating the unavoidable and impersonal nature of causes and effects.

5. When equanimity is strong and absorption seems accessible, enter the fourth jhāna. Since equanimity is characterized by a neutral feeling, it facilitates absorption into the fourth jhāna.[149] Follow the standard sequence of training, learning to enter, remain, emerge, and reflect on the factors and states.

6. After establishing the fourth jhāna with equanimity toward one neutral person, repeat the process with several additional neutral people. Extend the range of equanimity to establish the fourth jhāna with five to ten respected ones as objects, and then five to ten dear ones. Practice equanimity toward yourself even though the category of self is not stable enough to produce jhāna absorption. Then establish the fourth jhāna by focusing on a few hated ones. You can add some suffering ones, cruel ones, or rivals if you wish to cultivate more objects.

7. As equanimity grows strong, progress through the sequence quickly, using just one being per category to break down the boundaries. That is,

(a) Develop mettā, karunā, mudiutā, and upekkhā toward yourself with the appropriate phrases. The category of self as object does not lead to authentic absorption into jhāna, but it is still important to cultivate these qualities toward yourself.

(b) Develop mettā, karuṇā, and muditā toward respected and/ or dear friends up to the third jhāna and upekkhā toward respected and/or dear ones with the fourth jhāna.

(c) Develop mettā, karuṇā, muditā, and upekkhā toward neutral beings up to their respective jhānas.

(d) Develop mettā, karuṇā, muditā, and upekkhā toward hated ones (if there is still anyone who fits into this category) up to their respective jhānas.

As you move rapidly through the meditations, it will become equally easy to establish upekkhā jhānas with all the categories, without preference; your attitude toward beings in each category will equalize. In this way you will have broken down the barriers and accessed a pervasive quality of impartiality toward all types of beings.

8. Once the boundaries are dissolved between beings, cultivate equanimity by way of the twelve unspecified and specified groupings of all beings. Use the twelve categories to continue to repeatedly establish the first three jhānas with mettā, karuṇā, muditā, and the fourth jhāna with equanimity; incorporating all beings, near and far, in all directions. Extend each variation of all beings incrementally from those that exist nearby to those that live far away. Each time that you select a new area, range, or direction, radiate mettā, karuṇā, and muditā and progress up to the third jhāna before you expand to suffuse that area with upekkhā and enter the fourth jhāna. Continue this cyclical progression until immeasurable equanimity extends throughout the infinite universe and the light of the fourth jhāna is bright, stable, and strong. ✦

Manifesting Boundless Intentions

These beautiful and healing qualities are not suitable meditation subjects for everyone. They offer impressive benefits, but also pose predictable dangers—especially for young, attractive practitioners. In a world where many people crave love, a compelling expression of mettā can easily be

TABLE 8.1
Four Divine Abodes as Meditation Subjects

BRAHMAVIHĀRA	NEAR ENEMY	FAR ENEMY	JHĀNA POTENTIAL
Loving-kindness *(mettā)*	Attachment	Hatred, ill will	First, second, third
Compassion *(karuṇā)*	Pity, grief	Cruelty	First, second, third
Appreciative joy *(muditā)*	Joy tinged with insincerity or personal identification; forms of joy that are excessive, such as elation, exuberance	Envy, jealousy, aversion	First, second, third
Equanimity *(upekkhā)*	Indifference, foolish unknowing	Taking of sides, partiality, resentment, reactivity	Fourth

misinterpreted as seductive, or support deluded fantasies of a special relationship, even when the meditator's intentions are pure. Mettā has sometimes been associated with instances of sexual manipulation and social rivalry, as vulnerable students or friends seeking love vie for a place close to the charismatic leader. Mettā can easily be confused with its near enemy of affection or attachment. When wisdom wanes, mindfulness lapses, or fatigue weakens the purity of mettā, the meditator may become seduced by desire and slide unaware into a state of attachment. Meditators who cultivate the *brahmavihāras* as a primary feature of their meditation practice, especially to the level of jhāna, would be wise to be watchful for potential dangers, welcome criticisms from teachers and friends, and balance their training with mindfulness-based wisdom practices.

Some people will find that these boundless intentions arise naturally; they express pervasive good will and may feel no need to cultivate them through methodical training. Other people will employ these practices as antidotes to soften periodic bouts of agitation. Some meditators will discover an affinity with the qualities and training methods and choose to adopt the *brahmavihāras* as a primary feature of their practice. Eventually, each meditator will select the meditation subjects most suitable for his or her disposition, interest, and needs.

While developing loving-kindness, compassion, appreciative joy, and equanimity you will be inviting images of many people, creatures, and beings into your consciousness. When you have the beneficial conditions of seclusion in retreat, allow concentration to deepen and these qualities to mature as pure meditation subjects. Then in daily life, you can integrate these immeasurable qualities of heart into your work, family, and social engagements with or without the formalities of meditative methods. These limitless attitudes are not bound by technique; they are powerful, natural forces that express the immeasurable liberation of mind.

May all beings be happy and well!

CHAPTER 9

Reflections on Death: Contemplating the Corpse

*Mindfulness of death, if developed and cultivated, brings great fruit and
benefit; it merges in the Deathless, ends in the Deathless. Therefore, you
should develop mindfulness of death.*

—ANGUTTARA NIKĀYA[150]

O NE DAY as the Buddha sat warming his aged back in the late
afternoon sun, Ananda remarked, "The Blessed One's complexion is no longer pure and bright, his limbs are all flaccid
and wrinkled, his body is stooped, and some alteration is seen in his
faculties—in the eye faculty, the ear faculty, the nose faculty, the tongue
faculty, the body faculty." And the Buddha replied, "So it is, Ananda! In
youth one is subject to aging; in health one is subject to illness; while
alive one is subject to death...Death spares none along the way, but
comes crushing everything."[151]

Even though we don't like the idea, we all age, fall ill, and die. But,
if you are currently endowed with favorable conditions such as reasonable health, intelligence, and access to these teachings, you can reflect:
"Before this unwelcome, disagreeable, displeasing thing happens, let me
first make an effort for the attaining of the as-yet-unattained, the reaching of the as-yet-unreached, the realization of the as-yet-unrealized."[152]

People often do not want to hear of death, think of death, or prepare
for death. We don't generally sprinkle small talk at cocktail parties with
reflections on death. Yet vulnerability to death is one thing that we all

share. The Buddha plainly stated, "Both the young and the old, whether they are foolish or wise, are going to be trapped by death. All beings move towards death."[153] It is certain that we will die, only the time and the way is uncertain.

How frequently do you see death? At a monastery in Thailand, I waited to meet the abbot in a waiting room where I sat facing a shriveling corpse in a glass case. I was surrounded by skeletons hanging in corners and glass cases displaying shriveled corpses. Shelves were lined with jars of fetuses and body parts that were preserved in formaldehyde. Photographs and news articles of car accidents covered the walls. All were reminders of death, presented for mindful contemplation.

LIFE IS SO SHORT

To reflect on death is a way to reflect on how you are living. Are you living fully or frittering away your precious life with mindless entertainment and other trivial activities? The life of any human is brief. The Buddha compared a human life span to the ephemeral existence of a dewdrop on a leaf, a bubble on water that disappears soon after forming, a line drawn on water that vanishes without a trace, and to a cow that with each rising hoof steps closer to slaughter: "Short is the life of human beings, limited and brief; it is full of suffering, full of tribulation. This one should wisely understand. One should do good and live a pure life; for none who is born can escape death."[154] By remembering impermanence and death, you will keep your priorities clear, and waste no time. Opportunities for practice are precious, so appreciate your opportunities to grow, even when things are difficult. Every day, whatever you do, you trade a day of your life for it. Did you spend today well? Were you mindful and awake for whatever and whomever you encountered?

The Buddha, known for clear, honest, and straightforward speech, pronounced, "Before long, alas! this body will lie upon the earth, unheeded and lifeless, like a useless log."[155] Surely it is not news to you that you will die. But how deeply do you know that the end of rising is falling, that the end of meeting is parting, and that the end of living is dying? Have you learned this truth so well that you no longer grasp at

Daily Reminders of Death

You see reminders of death each day, but do you use those opportunities to reflect? When a fly perishes on a windowsill, when you drive by a squirrel killed on the road, when you see a favorite object inherited from a grandparent, consider the pervasiveness of death. The next time you pass a mortuary, take a moment to reflect on the inevitability of death. Open your address book or photo album and reflect that people you know and love all die. But also reflect on the fact that it is not just to others that death comes. Contemplate the phrase "I also will die," so that this certain knowledge of death deepens enough to stir you to urgency.

transient things? Is this knowledge so vivid that attention to sickness cannot produce aversion but only ends a sense of entitlement to health; that the signs of aging don't ignite despair but free you from youthful pride; and that the sight of death does not cause fear but fixes your attention on the impermanence of your own life?

Knowledge of death teaches us that happiness cannot be found through impermanent sensory formations that continuously appear and disappear. There is no possession, no relationship, no sensual delight that will support us in death. The Buddha showed us the way to genuine happiness, to a freedom that is unborn and deathless. Mindful of death you can live lightly, without the burden of grasping.

When students begin to contemplate death, many imagine their death occurring in a distant future. People think, "Yes, I know I will die, but not soon." My ninety-four-year-old aunty is active and blessed with good mental and physical health, but she misses her elder sister who died several years earlier at the age of 101. Thinking about her sister she recently remarked, "I just didn't expect her to die so soon." Most

Friends Who Share Suffering

You know that all beings that are born will die. All beings wish for happiness and wish to avoid suffering. Can you live viewing all beings as friends who share birth, old age, sickness, and death? Recite and contemplate this one sentence: "All beings are my friends who share birth, aging, sickness, and death." With every person or animal that you see, with each sound you hear, each sensation you feel, each taste you experience, quietly consider all the beings involved and reflect: "You are my friend who shares birth, old age, sickness, and death." With each contact—be they bugs, neighbors, children, birds, be it the sound of people passing on the road, the smell of cooked meat, the awareness of passengers in airplanes overhead, memories of people, portraits in the newspaper—contemplate that one sentence: "You are my friend who shares birth, old age, sickness, and death."

people are surprised by death; most people don't live informed by the understanding that death can happen anytime. The Buddha corrected disciples who contemplated death as though it could happen as late as tomorrow.[156] He admonished that it is indolent to think that one may live for a day, an hour, or even for the time it takes to complete an inhalation and exhalation. He urged them to practice mindfulness of death more diligently, to reflect that one might die before a single in- or out-breath is completed or within the time it takes to swallow a mouthful of food that has already been chewed.[157]

Embracing the inevitability of death is not a depressing or morbid meditative exercise. Meditative practices that reflect upon death will not isolate you or create the disconnection that feeds depression. Instead, reflecting on death can motivate you to have a heightened presence in

Five Remembrances

The Buddhist tradition recommends five daily remembrances.[158] Recite them each morning and allow the reflection to influence your choices each day.

1. I am of the nature to age. I have not gone beyond aging.

2. I am of the nature to sicken. I have not gone beyond sickness.

3. I am of the nature to die. I have not gone beyond death.

4. All that is mine, beloved and pleasing, will become otherwise, will become separated from me.

5. I am the owner of my action *(kamma),* heir to my action, born of my action, related to my action, abide supported by my action. Whatever action I shall do, for good or for ill, of that I will be the heir.

your own life. Traditional death reflections are structured to inspire vigor and urgency. When you are mindful of death, you won't squander the precious resources that you are temporarily blessed with: a little time and opportunity. Reflections on death protect you from laziness and complacency. The Buddha urged, "The days and nights are relentlessly passing; how well am I spending my time? This should be reflected upon again and again, by one who has gone forth."[159]

In many Buddhist monasteries, practitioners chant the five recollections every morning and evening—a practice easily incorporated into lay life. You may recite the formal chant, reflect on the inevitability of death, or consider if you are completely satisfied with your spiritual accomplishments. The Buddha taught:

If, on reflection, that monk realizes that evil, unwholesome qualities still remain within him, then he should, with strong resolve, apply all his effort, vigor, and exertion, [together with] mindfulness and clear comprehension, to abandon them…Just as a man whose turban or hair is on fire would resolutely apply all his effort, vigor, and exertion, [together with] mindfulness and clear comprehension, to extinguish the fire; even so should that monk resolutely apply all his effort, vigor, and exertion, [together with] mindfulness and clear comprehension, to abandon those evil, unwholesome qualities.[160]

The Buddha compared meditators to four kinds of horses.[161] One horse is alert and ready to respond to the work of the day as soon as he sees the shadow of the goad. Similarly, urgency arises in some meditators when they hear that someone in a distant village or town is ill or dying. A second horse becomes alert when the goad touches his hair, just as urgency may arise for some meditators when they see someone in their town suffering with illness or dying. A third horse only becomes alert when his skin is pricked with the goad, like those meditators who becomes heedful only after one of their close relatives is stricken with illness or death. And the last horse is stirred only after the goad pierces his flesh to the bone, as some meditators may remain complacent until they are afflicted with pain or diagnosed with a terminal illness. What does it take to stir you?

Inspired by mindfulness of death, you are reminded of the deepest meaning for your life. The Buddha offers us a profound path to peace with these teachings: "Mindfulness of death, if developed and cultivated, brings great fruit and benefit; it merges in the Deathless, ends in the Deathless."[162] Nurture the urgency to travel this path to its end.

PREPARING FOR DEATH

Students sometimes ask, "How can I prepare for death?" The first step is to look upon death as a fact of living—everyone that you know will die.

Spiritual Urgency

> ▸ Are you living carelessly or using this precious life fully?
> ▸ Is there anything that you need to do before you die?
> ▸ What is most important in your life?

Then, armed with this conceptual knowledge, you may stop turning away from the multitude of daily opportunities you have to be close to people who are aging, ill, and dying in your community. Notice death, become familiar with the process, and recognize the natural and inevitable role of death. Often death is hidden from sight. Hospitals sometimes transport bodies to the morgue costumed with surgical cap and an oxygen tube to create the illusion that the patient is being whisked into surgery. Some children's wards use specially designed bi-level gurneys where a corpse is transported in a covered lower compartment making it appear that an orderly is pushing an empty mattress through the halls. Funeral parlors have professional makeup artists who add blush and powder to the faces of corpses so that they look almost alive for their funerals.

Death is happening everywhere, yet surrounded by a cultural obscuration of death, meditators must actively look for death and contemplate it. Mindful that you are dying, you may become inspired to let go along the way and embrace each moment of life with a readiness for death.

To develop a seminar on the Buddha's approach to illness and death, I collected the various instructions that he gave to sick and dying monks. Interestingly, the instructions he gave to dying monastics are the same teachings he offered to all. The Buddha, on visiting the sick ward of a monastic community in Vesali, taught, "A bhikkhu should await his time mindful and clearly comprehending."[163] He instructed the sick monks to practice mindfulness of the body, of feelings, of mind, and of phenomena, and then he proceeded to give the standard instructions for clarity of consciousness while moving, eating, urinating, walking, standing, falling asleep, speaking, and in all other activities. His instruction emphasized equanimity toward all feelings, and no doubt this audience experienced a great deal of physical pain: "If he feels a [pleasant, unpleasant, or neutral] feeling, he understands: 'It is impermanent'; he understands, 'It is not held to'; he understands, 'It is not delighted in.' If he feels a [pleasant, unpleasant, or neutral] feeling, he feels it detached."[164]

This teaching applies to all of us. In the sick ward, the Buddha said further: "Just as, bhikkhus, an oil lamp burns in dependence on the oil and the wick, and with the exhaustion of the oil and the wick it is extinguished through lack of fuel, so too, bhikkhus...with the breakup of the body, following the exhaustion of life, all that is felt, not being delighted in, will become cool right here."[165] The defilements have no fuel to burn, and free of defilements you can abide cooled and at ease. The material elements will take their natural course. The body will eventually perish, yet during the course of this life, and in the process of dying, the mind can rest at peace, undisturbed by fear and dread.

CONTEMPLATION OF THE CORPSE

Buddhist traditions have developed specific death meditations such as the contemplation of the corpse. The instructions are simple—observe a corpse and reflect that your own body, this cherished material process, will end up as a rotting corpse too. The Buddha teaches as follows:

> Again, bhikkhus, as though he were to see a corpse thrown aside in a charnel ground, one, two, or three days dead, bloated, livid, and oozing matter, a bhikkhu compares this same body with it thus: "This body too is of the same nature, it will be like that, it is not exempt from that fate."
>
> Again, as though he were to see a corpse thrown aside in a charnel ground, being devoured by crows, hawks, vultures, dogs, jackals, or various kinds of worms, a bhikkhu compares this same body with it thus: "this body too is of the same nature, it will be like that, it is not exempt from that fate."
>
> Again, as though he were to see a corpse thrown aside in a

charnel ground, a skeleton with flesh and blood, held together with sinews...here a hand bone, there a foot bone, here a shin bone, there a thigh bone, here a hip bone, there a back bone, here a rib bone, there a breast bone, here an arm bone, there a shoulder bone, here a neck bone, there a jaw bone, here a tooth, there the skull—a bhikkhu compares this same body with it thus: This body too is of the same nature, it will be like that, it is not exempt from that fate.[166]

What an invitation to wake up! Death will surely come—even if you have made other plans for that day.

A Vehicle for Jhāna

The decomposing body is a powerful meditation subject that can instill an urgency for awakening and reduce attachment to transitory sensual pleasures. It can also serve as a vehicle for jhāna. The traditional course of instruction for this practice begins with a fresh corpse and goes on to identify eleven stages of decomposition, each of which can be an object for meditation. The stages are: recently dead, bloated, livid, festering, cut up, gnawed, scattered, hacked and scattered, bleeding, worm infested, and skeleton. For this practice it is useful to visualize a body that you have actually seen. If you have access to a charnel ground, morgue, or funeral parlor, visit it. In India, I spent many hours on the banks of the river Ganges watching bodies brought to cremation, observing as layers of flesh dissolved in the flames. Legs or arms periodically popped off as gasses inside the body expanded. Sometimes bodies that had been disposed of without cremation—bloated, discolored, and partially eaten—would surface in the river. In many cultures, the process of decay and death is exposed for all to view. If, however, you live in a culture that hides death from sight, it can be enough to recall a single corpse that you saw at one time. Supplement the visualizations with photographs or descriptions as you trace the process from the "fresh" phase through the various stages of decomposition. If you have never seen an actual dead human body, you can still reflect upon the inevitability of death.

Traditionally, however, recollecting the sight of an actual corpse is recommended as the initial object for this meditation.

A REPULSIVE CORPSE

The meditation subject of the corpse can progress in two distinct directions: (1) mindfully discerning and reflecting upon a corpse can dispel lust and heighten spiritual urgency, and (2) with the addition of the perception of repulsiveness the corpse can become a suitable object for jhāna.

The repulsive quality of the corpse is not something that is always obvious. Sometimes the fascination of a new contemplation object or the rapid arising of pleasant jhāna factors can obscure the recognition of the repulsive aspect. In your contemplation of the corpse you may look at the corpse in several ways before discovering a way of regarding it as "repulsive." Many cultures consider death dirty and relegate the handling of corpses to low castes or social outcasts. Even in the less-stratified societies of the West, undertakers are the brunt of stereotypes and jokes. In my own case I sensed the repulsive aspect through a personal encounter. A few days before a friend of mine died, we had a lovely visit; she knew she was dying and would probably not survive the weekend. Yet she still exuded an enormous vitality and expressed a remarkable warmth and inner beauty with her touch. We hugged, held hands, and joyfully shared each other's presence. Just three days later, I was sitting beside her corpse. I sat at the vigil for many hours, but felt no urge to hold her. The repulsive quality does not imply the corpse is ugly; actually my friend's body was arranged in a simple, beautiful, and elegant manner. The repulsive quality manifested as my disinclination to touch.

The death reflections that follow are not intended to be gruesome exercises; rather, they are undertaken to deepen concentration, to cultivate spiritual urgency and wise dispassion, and ultimately to lead toward the deathless liberation. As the Buddha explained, "In one who often contemplates these facts, the path arises. He now regularly pursues, develops, and cultivates that path and while he is doing so the fetters are abandoned and the underlying tendencies eliminated."[167]

→ **MEDITATION INSTRUCTION 9.1**
Decomposition of the Corpse

This systematic meditation progresses by visualizing the stage-by-stage decomposition of a corpse, followed by a reflection on the inevitability of your own death. Begin by establishing concentration with a method of your choice. Next, recall a previously seen corpse. Select a body whose attributes have never sparked you to feel sexual attraction. It may sound hideous or inconceivable that a corpse could stimulate sexual desire, but concentration brings pleasant mental factors of rapture, pleasure, and delight that could, if mindfulness weakens, slide toward lust. Even if you consider this concern unrealistic, choose a body for whom you genuinely feel no attraction. Choosing a corpse of the same gender as yourself may facilitate a seamless transition to the reflection that "I too am subject to death."

Look closely at the corpse if it is actually in front of you; otherwise, take some time to remember one you have previously seen, or examine photos of a corpse. Hold its image firmly in your mind. First, just see the corpse—how the legs and arms are positioned, the color of the skin, the overall shape, and so on. Then, to use the corpse as an object for jhāna, focus on the corpse not as a neutral image, but as a repulsive one. Emphasize the repulsive aspect of the corpse until the sign of repulsiveness arises, similar to the procedure for the repulsive skeleton introduced in chapter 5. Gradually, the nimitta will become bright and stable enough to invite absorption into the first jhāna. The object of the repulsive corpse can only raise consciousness to the first jhāna; it cannot carry the mind into higher attainments. After dwelling in the first jhāna based on the repulsive sign associated with the corpse, emerge and reflect on the five jhāna factors. Then shift your reflection to contemplate, "I will also die some day; I am subject to death; I cannot avoid death."

Now return your attention to the corpse and visualize your own dead body in the place previously occupied by the corpse. See your own death as certain. See your own dead body before you, perhaps laid out on a slab. You are not trying to feel what it might be like to die, or trying to imagine going through a dying process; the practice simply lets the truth that *I too will die, just like that corpse* register very deeply. ✦

✦ MEDITATION INSTRUCTION 9.2
Meditating on More Corpses

After contemplating one repulsive corpse as a jhāna object and awakening urgency by reflecting on the inevitability of your own death, you may wish to develop the corpse meditation subject with further images. Choose another one that you have seen and progressively imagine the eleven stages of decomposition occurring to that single corpse. Each stage of decomposition can elicit the first jhāna; thus, you may attain eleven first jhāna absorptions by following the sequential decomposition of each corpse. After emerging from absorption, you may replace the image of the corpse with a visualization of your own body at each stage of decomposition. In this way you will contemplate the stage-by-stage disintegration of this life's cherished body. Jhāna is accessible by visualizing the corpse of another person, but the contemplation of our own death will not carry us beyond neighborhood concentration.

To loosen the grip of attachment to our friends and family, and to face the inevitable fact that everyone is subject to death, you can follow a similar procedure by envisioning friends and family members as corpses. With these reflections you may contemplate, "I am not the only one who is sure to become old, to fall ill and to die...all are subject to old age, illness, and death."[168] ✦

CHAPTER 10
Eleven Skills for Jhāna Meditation

I must become skilled in knowing the ways of my own mind.
—Aṅguttara Nikāya[169]

THE BUDDHA PROVIDED a practical list of eleven essential skills related to the primary themes and most common errors meditators confront in jhāna practice.[170] You might use this checklist to pinpoint your weak areas and strive to strengthen that meditative skill. This review can be especially helpful to the meditator who has experienced brief absorptions and is trying to stabilize the attainments. By identifying your weaknesses you can strategically focus your effort and effectively apply your mind to the development of concentration and wisdom. These eleven skills for jhāna meditation are:

- attainment
- concentration
- maintenance
- emergence
- pliancy
- object in relation to concentration
- range
- resolution
- thoroughness
- persistence
- suitability.

1. *Skill in attainment (samāpatti kusala).* Have you experienced the genuine attainment of jhāna? The skill in attainment refers to the basic ability to attain jhāna easily where, when, and for as long as one wishes. Most practitioners must rigorously struggle to overcome hindrances and withdraw attention from worldly activities in order to attain authentic absorptions. Some meditators may succeed in entering jhāna but find the absorption to be fragile, with the state soon dissolving; they may not be certain if these fragile absorptions would qualify as an authentic attainment of jhāna. If it is difficult for you to sustain the seclusion necessary for jhāna, you might simplify conditions by relinquishing worldly attachments, enhance wholesome states with acts of giving and kindness, strengthen your determination and resolve, and balance the quality of your effort. Diligently create supportive conditions in your life, patiently focus on your meditation object, and then, when conditions ripen, allow the mind to release into absorption. Continuity of practice, heedful attention that guards the six sense doors between meditation sessions, impeccable virtue, and joyful acts of generosity nurture the trust necessary to experience and then stabilize the attainment of jhāna.

2. *Skill in concentration (samādhi kusala).* Can you easily discern the factors of each jhāna upon emerging? The skill in concentration implies a clear recognition of the subjective experience of the state. Upon emerging from jhāna it is important to become proficient at identifying the presence or absence of jhāna factors, reflect on the disadvantages and advantages of the factors and states, and discern the pertinent distinctions between jhānas. Sometimes practitioners who are facile in attaining jhāna still must struggle to identify the subtle nuances that characterize each state. This systematic training asks that you inhibit the desire to indulge in the bliss, or slide seamlessly into the next absorption; it requires that you develop skill regarding concentration through repeatedly reflecting upon the jhāna factors between absorptions. The skillful observation of jhāna factors not only supports an intelligent engagement with the jhāna practice, but it will enhance your ability to recognize the state of mind that is

knowing an object during insight practices as well. To improve your ability to discern the state of mind, systematically recognize the presence or absence of jhāna factors by directing your attention to the mind door after emerging from each absorption. Although you may consistently find exactly the same factors that you would expect to find, still arouse interest for discerning the specific factors that characterize each state. Refresh your curiosity for directly understanding the nature of the experience.

3. *Skill in stability (ṭhiti kusala)*. The skill of stabilizing jhāna refers to the meditator's ability to remain in a steady absorption, continuously focused on the object, without wavering, for a long time. The ability to maintain jhāna develops with the maturation of the controlling faculties of faith, energy, mindfulness, concentration, and wisdom. Usually the initial encounters with absorption are brief. Gradually extend your ability with incremental resolves—ten minutes, twenty minutes, thirty minutes, one hour, two hours—until you are satisfied that you can remain in jhāna for as long as you desire.

Meditative skills, including mindfulness and concentration, must be stabilized and maintained. Musicians practice to maintain proficiency with their musical instruments; if they stop playing music, their facility will diminish. Similarly, if you do not practice meditation, the subtle mental skills that sustain concentration will diminish. Some people may be athletic, trim, and strong in their youth, but if they eat potato chips in front of the television every evening, they will become fat and weak. Although powerful wholesome states may arise in meditation, if you are negligent and cease to practice, break ethical precepts, or become attached to a stressful lifestyle, you may lose access to such attainments. Skill in maintaining jhāna opposes the tendency to become complacent, lazy, and negligent— to just coast along. So, after succeeding in establishing jhāna, it is important to maintain conducive life conditions or these attainments may not remain readily accessible. It is indeed possible to maintain jhāna in daily lay life, if you are willing to create supportive conditions such as reducing distracting entertainments, dedicating time to daily meditation, and continuing to hone your meditative skills.

4. *Skill in emergence (vuṭṭhāna kusala).* Someone who is skilled in emergence has mastered the ability to exit the absorption state at a predetermined time. To practice this, decide how long you will remain in jhāna prior to entering any jhāna state and then notice when you emerge. Did you come out late? Did you come out early? A meditator who tends to fall out early may find that the hindrances of doubt, impatience, desire, and self-interest are only barely suppressed and sneak back in quickly with a momentary weakening of energy. Continuity of mindful attention between meditation sessions will reduce agitation that can accrue during daily activities. Reflecting on the disadvantages of sensory pursuits and the advantages of concentration may further support the seclusion. On the other hand, the meditator who tends to come out late and overstay the duration of his or her resolves may be seduced by the quiet pleasures of jhāna and overindulge in the tranquil states. Reflection on the highest aim and the enduring peace produced by direct insight, rather than on the pleasures of concentration, can inspire disenchantment with temporary jhāna bliss. Use concentration to fully cultivate the mind, while keeping the practice progressing toward the liberating expression of nonclinging. Also, sometimes just moving through the jhānas quickly can draw out a dynamic, buoyant quality that supports timely emergence.

5. *Skill in pliancy (kallitā kusala).* Jhāna is not an inert state; it is able and ready. The concentrated mind is pliant, flexible, quick, buoyant, and wieldy; it is a state of sound mental health. If you begin to feel stiff or rigid, intentionally enliven and gladden awareness. You may remain longer in the jhānas that you prefer, permitting the happiness of those states to saturate and suffuse awareness. You may try cycling rapidly through the full sequence, challenging the attention to enter and emerge quickly without fault. You might gladden the mind with reflections on virtue, generosity, qualities of the Buddha, Dhamma, or loving-kindness. The strategy that best promotes

pliancy of consciousness will depend on the preferences and abilities of the individual.

6. *Skill in the object (ārammaṇa kusala).* This skill highlights the significance of the object. In the development of jhāna, through the continuity of one-pointed attention, the initial perception transforms into a mental counterpart sign *(nimitta).* When concentration is strong, the brightness, color, and dimensions of the nimitta will be constant and smooth, without fluctuations, fluttering, or dissipation. As you continue to dwell with full attention on your meditation object, the nimitta grows stable and vivid. The stability of the nimitta is a reflection of the stability of the concentrated mind and the maturity of one-pointed attention.

This training becomes most vivid during kasiṇa practice after your repertoire of meditation subjects has expanded and you have learned to move crisply between objects and jhānas without confusion. When working with a series of meditation objects, it is important to maintain clarity regarding the object of attention. For example, a meditator with skill regarding the object will not confuse the various kasiṇas and will be able to quickly produce and distinguish kasiṇas that may at a cursory glance all resemble luminous discs. Similarly, you can clearly distinguish between the meditation object and the mental factors that arise through the knowing of that object, and learn to hold your object with stability and wisdom. This ability to keep the desired object firmly in mind obviously supports the development of concentration, but it will also strengthen insight when you analyze and investigate precise and fleeting mental formations.

7. *Skill in the range (gocara kusala).* This term *gocara* may be translated as domain, resort, or range, and points to the arena of attention. It is closely aligned with the previous item, *the skill in the object.* The skill in the range highlights the capacity to determine the field or domain of attention, whereas the skill in the object highlights the ability to firmly keep the selected object in mind.

This skill in the range invites the recollection of the four aspects of clear comprehension presented in chapter 2: (1) clarity regarding the purpose, (2) clarity regarding the suitability, (3) clarity regarding the proper domain, and (4) clarity regarding the undeluded conception of the activity concerned. Your meditation subject should be suitable for your purpose. Choose a meditation subject that supports clarity regarding these four principles of clear comprehension.

Each meditation subject has a certain range and effect on consciousness. A meditator who is skilled in the range has developed a proficiency to take an array of subjects to their highest level of absorption. All meditation subjects are not equal; the different characteristics of the objects permit distinct levels of concentration. For example, mindfulness with breathing may effectively be used to attain the first, second, third, and fourth jhānas. The thirty-two body parts, skeleton, and repulsive perceptions, on the other hand, cannot surmount the first jhāna, because sustaining the concept of the unattractiveness of the specific object depends upon the directing *(vitakka)* and sustaining *(vicāra)* functions. The kasiṇas are expansive and each one (with the exception of limited space) can effectively attune consciousness to the first four jhānas, and through their removal they provide an entrance into the four immaterial abidings. Consciousness absorbed in loving-kindness is immeasurable, yet it cannot surmount the third jhāna since happiness *(sukha)* is intrinsic to loving-kindness. When emanating equanimity *(upekkhā)* toward all beings as the meditation practice, the mind can only enter the fourth jhāna, since the dominance of equanimity prevents the intensification of rapture *(pīti)* and happiness *(sukha)* that characterize the lower three states.

8. *Skill in resolution (abhinīhāra kusala)*. Our intentions move our minds. Skillful resolution employs clear and conscious decisions to raise the mind from the first jhāna to the second jhāna, from second to third, from third to fourth, and then to remove the realm of material perceptions and abide absorbed by immaterial perceptions. Resolving to remove or enhance mental factors, you develop the skill to make controlled and tidy shifts between various objects and levels

TABLE 10.1
Jhāna Potential of Meditation Subjects

Meditation Subject	Jhāna Potential
Breath	First, second, third, fourth jhānas
Four elements	Neighborhood or momentary concentration
Thirty-two parts of the body	Access to jhāna
Ten kasiṇas White, dark-colored *(nīla),* yellow, red, earth, water, fire, wind, light, limited space	First, second, third, fourth jhānas

Immaterial jhānas:
   Infinite space
   Infinite consciousness
   Nothingness
   Neither-perception-nor-nonperception
	
	Base of infinite space
	Base of infinite consciousness
	Base of nothingness
	Base of neither-perception-nor-nonperception

Brahmaviharas:
   Loving-kindness
   Compassion
   Appreciative joy
   Equanimity
	
	First, second, third jhānas
	First, second, third jhānas
	First, second, third jhānas
	Fourth jhāna

Six reflections	Access to jhāna
Repulsive corpses	First jhāna
Death reflection	Access to jhāna

of jhāna. When you have developed skill in resolve, your intentions manifest quickly, easily, and without fuss. Some meditators must generate strong determination to lift a sluggish or clumsy mind toward subtler states. Other meditators will need determination to slow the pace of their progression to prevent uncontrolled sliding between jhānas, inhibit an instinctive rush through the attainments, and resist the seductive lure of higher attainments. Through resolve you stabilize each attainment, train the mind to move according to the determination, and gain mastery at each level of jhāna before aspiring for more sublime abidings.

9. Skill in thoroughness (sakkaccakāri kusala). How full and thorough is your endeavor? Are you careful and attentive to your concentration throughout the day? Have you created a lifestyle that supports concentration and reduces needless distractions? Are you willing to simplify your life—from time to time reduce worldly activities, minimize writing and reading, avoid trivial chatter and excessive conversation, and practice celibacy? You make many choices in daily life and on retreat—notice how these choices affect your practice. Whatever you must do to fulfill your social duties, care for your health, and meet economic obligations, do them while keeping your meditation practice in the forefront of your concern. At all times, and in all places, know where you are placing your attention and consider the effects of that object on the quality of your mind. If you notice that you dwell in anxious worry when driving to work each day, make a point of focusing on the mirrors, road, steering wheel, sensations of sitting, and present experience of driving. If you notice that you are unmindful in the latrine, take extra care to be attentive and composed. When you are taking time for intensive practice, observe where your mind dwells between the sitting meditations. Notice the effect that perceptions have on your mind and trust you can make wise choices about what to notice and what to think about.

10. Skill in persistence (sātacca kusala). It takes time to learn these methods. Continuity and persistence is needed. If you want to boil water but take the pot off the stove every few minutes, the water will never get hot enough to boil. Similarly, to build a momentum of concentration and mindfulness, you must persist in your practice, tenaciously nurturing your connection with the meditation object. Frequent breaks—to relax in the sun, communicate your great insights to others, or write that novel you've been wanting to start—will not support jhāna. Nor will waking up late, skipping morning meditation, or going to bed at the first sign of boredom and weariness. Continuity of effort and enduring persistence are needed to support a lifetime of practice.

11. Skill in suitability (sappāya kusala). A skilled builder will have many kinds of drill bits designed for making large or small holes in concrete, metal, or wood. A professional chef does not use the same knife to open a pumpkin, slice a strawberry, carve a radish, and debone a chicken. Although all drills make holes and all knives cut, the builder and the chef will choose the most effective tool for the selected task.

Skill in the suitability of objects is the ability to choose the appropriate object, at the right time, for the specific purpose at hand. Starting with the physical reference point of the breath offers a convenient entrance to this system that quickly dispels distraction in a daily meditation. Repulsive meditations can be especially helpful for abandoning lustful fantasies, while the recollection of the Buddha can be used to inspire faith. Loving-kindness might be the ideal meditation subject if ill will, harsh judgments, or irritation torment the mind. The white, fire, and light kasiṇas produce the brightest light to effectively illuminate refined matter. The base of neither-perception-nor-nonperception is too subtle to support every kind of insight contemplation, but might free you from subtle attachments. Sometimes the coarseness of repulsive objects brings quick and strong absorption, sparked by dispassion and sustained by urgency. Yet, at other times, the agitation of the lower jhānas disrupts the process and you may prefer to dwell mostly in the higher states.

Each jhāna can be used as the basis for insight meditation. Each object, however, has unique attributes that produce different degrees of brightness, seclusion, and limberness of mind. As you progress systematically through this system and learn the qualities related to each object and attainment, you will be able to apply the most suitable tool for your purpose.

The Buddha aptly described the well-concentrated mind as "fit for work."[171] With proficiency in these eleven essential skills, your concentration will be strong and stable; your mind will be supple and quick. Concentrated and balanced, you will be capable of directing your attention to penetrate the subtle nature of things.

 **SECTION III**

Discerning Ultimate Realities

CHAPTER 11

Concepts and Reality: Penetrating the Illusion of Compactness

Perceiving what can be expressed through concepts,
Beings take their stand on what is expressed.
Not fully understanding the expressed,
They come under the bondage of Death.
Understanding what is expressed,
The peaceful one delights in the peaceful state.
Standing on Dharma, clearly knowing,
One freely makes use of concepts
But no more enters into the range of concepts.
—THE ITIVUTTAKA[172]

A N ABILITY TO CONCEPTUALIZE experience and to compare a current experience to a past one is a normal capacity of a healthy, dynamic, well-functioning mind. We apply concepts to our perceptions to make sense of the daily barrage of sensory data. We compare a current predicament to previous encounters in order to make decisions. We remember things via concepts and we learn by making comparisons; it is a regular part of how we interact with sensory input. Indeed, it is necessary for our survival as higher organisms on this earth. However, this conceptualizing process can also be reductive; our concepts often suppress insight and distort a truer perception of reality. Meditation examines a subtle proposition—that things exist in a mode radically different than the way we usually conceive them to be. For instance, the body is often considered to be an independent, enduring form, when it is actually a network of ever-changing interrelated processes. As the Buddha succinctly stated, "In whatever way we conceive, the fact is other than that."[173] Concepts are merely mental constructions—they are useful, but limited and inaccurate.

Comparisons are always relative—something is "long" only as conceived in relation to something shorter. Similarly, measurements such as big and small, high and low, and success and failure are relative concepts. Since we cannot compare things of different classes—like the sight of a rabbit with the sound of rain on a roof, or the color green with an aspiration of compassion—we habitually reduce an immediate sensory encounter to a concept and then relate that concept to other concepts. For example, when we see a black color and hear a certain cawing sound, we might identify the visual and auditory encounter as a perception of a crow. Understanding that there is a crow in the field, we might compare the bird to another kind of bird that is twittering in a nearby tree, or relate the presence of the crow to a memory of previous visits of crows to that field. This ability to conceptualize serves as a survival strategy, helping us negotiate the rapidly changing field of sensory impressions that might otherwise degenerate into overwhelming and chaotic encounters with the world. By transforming perceptions into conceptual comparisons, the mind can quickly distinguish a dangerous threat from a welcome refuge. The formation of mental concepts, however, also has the effect of constructing a world of ideas that people tend to wrongly identify as their personal reality.

When beginning meditators experience physical twinges or discomfort during their sittings, they usually squirm because a habitual fear of pain follows on the heels of the sensation. In such a circumstance it can be useful to ask yourself if you are agitated by the present feelings of pressure, tingling, burning, and prickling sensations, or by an imagined future of agony and disability. When you can open to the basic fact of unpleasant sensations in the present moment, you may discover that they are not as dreadful as those imagined scenarios. When concepts proliferate, you forget they are merely mental constructions and take them to be the thing itself. This limits and distorts your perception of reality.

The Comparing Mind

Sit quietly and observe your mind; reflect on the thoughts that arose today. Make a list of all your thoughts that are essentially comparisons; include ranking, judging, and assessing thoughts. Do you compare yourself with others or rate your performance against memories of how you functioned in youth? Do you compare the weather that you hope will occur on the day that you scheduled a picnic with the wind and sun as it is actually appearing? Do you assess your present mood against ideal standards? Note how frequently comparison occurs as a feature of your mental life. Are those assessments verifiable? Do you know them to be true?

If you believe your concepts are real, you will dwell confused. I usually consider myself short, for instance. But recently I was walking with an elderly friend whose head barely approached my shoulders. I experienced an oddly unfamiliar feeling—I had the rare impression of being tall. So, am I tall or am I short? Comparisons, always relative, change with the situation. To the extent that you base an identity on characteristics defined through comparison, you will be disconnected from the truth of things.

TIDES OF CONCEIVING

The Buddha referred to "tides of conceiving"[174] that may wash over us when we don't perceive the reality of things. How might you be swept away by concepts, stories, assumptions, and imaginings moment after moment, hour after hour, day after day? When mindfulness is weak we stay at a surface recognition of things and don't really know the things themselves. Once concept-forming is activated, the conceptual mode of recognition dominates, overshadowing the possibility of a fresh perspective and reinforcing the rut of habit, prejudice, and assumption. You may have a superficial perception of an object—something impinges on the senses and you name it as rock, person, shoe, or glass. If you examined the encounter more closely, however, you would find an infinite number of more fundamental perceptions: opacity, shape, attention, odor, growth, disintegration, one-pointedness, energy, and so on. Similarly, when you treat a relationship as permanent, consider a mental state as an enduring source of personal gratification, or view a material object as possessable, you might hold to the concept and miss the reality. This is unwise attention.

Disciplines such as science and art look beyond presumptive concepts. A physicist will examine patterns in the motion of objects to understand the function of unseen gravitational forces and magnetic fields. An impressionist painter may try to dislodge habitual object-oriented perspectives by illustrating the effects of light rather than the contours of objects. Meditation practice also invites us to look deeper than conventional reality, to see beyond mental constructs, to discern the subtle properties of what you perceive, and to investigate the conceptualizing functions of mind.

BREAKING DOWN COMPACTNESS OF CONCEPTS

The meditative discernment of extremely subtle elements of matter and mind, which will be introduced in the chapters that follow, is designed to deconstruct limiting assumptions. A false sense of solidity or compactness is often attributed to things, concepts, and groups. The careful meditative discernment of the ultimate constituents of matter and mind, as the hallmark of this approach, deconstructs the compactness of concepts in four specific areas: (1) the compactness of continuity *(santatighana)*, (2) the compactness of mass *(samūhaghana)*, (3) the compactness of function *(kiccaghana)*, and (4) the compactness of object *(ārammaṇaghana)*. These misperceptions only arise when you do not see phenomena carefully.[175]

A Profound Presence

Narrative thought has its foundation in the idea of time—past, present, and future. When a memory arises of last night's baseball game, it is only a concept arising in the present—there is no yesterday and no baseball game. You might feel excitement as you remember the home run or disappointment when you remember that your favorite batter struck out. But the past exists only as a concept that occurs in the present. It has no reality beyond a momentary mental impression. Similarly, you can become ensnared in anticipation, planning, fantasy, anxiety, and worry regarding future possibilities. Once you create a concept of past or future, you then respond to the narrative—living within the story and missing your present and immediate life. Notice when you anticipate future results or seek sanctuary in ruminations over past events. When you become aware of the wandering mind, you have an opportunity to disentangle your attention from the web of concept and reconnect with your meditation object or a simple perception in the present moment.

1. *The compactness of continuity (santatighana).* Often, we do not look closely at experience. A cursory glance is frequently enough for us to identify the object, trigger a conceptual comprehension of an experience, bring forth a socially appropriate response from the storehouse of conditioned patterns, and get on with the day. Easily deceived by the rapidity of change, the mind tends to stop at a superficial recognition and cease investigating. When a performer twirls a lit torch, the viewer sees a ring of fire even though there is no substantial ring. The moment that the viewer applies the concept "circle" to the sight of

the whirling torch, that concept can overshadow the momentary and constantly changing positions of the light. In this way, the concept obscures the potential for insight into the impermanent and insubstantial nature of things.

When a film is pulled frame by frame across a path of light, movie viewers see a series of rapidly appearing and disappearing images on the screen that produce the illusion of a motion picture. Viewers interpret the characters as moving, but is this really the case? What is actually moving? A similar process of illusion occurs for us outside the theater when the mind blurs the ending of each incremental bit of sensory data with the beginning of the next bit and, thereby, weaves a coherent experience out of what are actually many momentary parcels of cognitive data. Conceptual interpretations offer efficient means for summarizing a barrage of sensory data, but in meditation you will carry out a more careful inquiry in order to understand the true nature of experience.

Look into your sensory experience. Is there anything that is not changing? Try a little experiment. Stand up and take a few steps. Now ask yourself, what moved? On a conventional level you might say that you moved your body from one past position in the room to a different present position in the room—you were sitting over there before and now you are standing over here. But can you take a step in the past or in the future? Is the material body that was previously sitting the same material body that is now standing and walking? When we do not perceive the distinctly momentary nature of phenomena, we use concepts to construct a sense of continuity through experiences and then we fabricate an enduring self who experiences them. All the tiny parcels of mental and material phenomena blur together when we don't look carefully and so we assume that experiences continue and persist. In the extreme, we might assume that they are permanent.

Insight into impermanence counters the illusion of continuity. Seeing the characteristic of change invites you to look deeply into the assumption of continuity. What is continuity? Is there really duration? Although you know things are continually changing, how often do you pause to consciously notice change? Insight into impermanence is among the most transformative perceptions. Are you ever surprised when looking through old photo albums at how much clothing styles, body shapes, and faces have changed with growth and age? Often, though, people just don't notice change in the little fluctuations that occur day by day.

Certainly you know that you were born and that you will die. The exercises in chapter 12 will refine the perception that there is no continuity to materiality. This body is not always present; it did not exist in the same way a moment earlier and will not exist in the same way a moment later. Only concepts and views create the impression of enduring features. In reality, matter has only momentary expressions, without the slightest endurance across time. Through the careful examination of ultimate materiality, the illusion of continuity regarding matter is removed.

 ### *Watching Emotions Ebb and Flow*

How long does an emotion last? Have you ever felt that you were angry for a couple of hours or sad all day long? Look closely at that angry feeling or that sad feeling. Notice the story: the thoughts of loss that triggered sadness, the threat that triggered anger. Do such thoughts remain static or are they intermittent, or cyclical? Notice sensations in the body: perhaps heaviness in the chest, an ache in the stomach, an indistinct disoriented sensation, heat or cold, a hollow feeling. Are these sensations lasting, stable, or fluctuating? Do they increase or decrease? Notice the intensity of the anger or sadness: does it remain stable, or come as waves that intensify when triggered by certain thoughts, smells, or sights and then diminish when attention is distracted by exercise, meals, and conversation?

Fixed concepts cloud and obscure perception; they are not a refuge to stand upon. The Buddha compared the perception of impermanence to the sun appearing after the monsoon season: "Just as in the autumn, when the sky is clear and cloudless, the sun, ascending in the sky dispels all darkness from space as it shines and beams and radiates, so too, when the perception of impermanence is developed and cultivated, it eliminates all sensual lust, it eliminates all lust for existence, it eliminates all ignorance, it uproots all conceit 'I am.'"[176]

The illusion of duration occurs when you don't look closely enough to see the momentary nature of the cognitive process. When you observe the rapidly occurring sequence of individual mind-moments that form a single moment of cognition, you see only momentary microprocesses connected by causal relationships. By discerning the momentary existence of matter, the unique role each moment of consciousness plays in the cognitive process, and the discontinuity between each individual moment and those before and subsequent to it, you break down the delusion of continuity. Nothing lasts, nothing merges, nothing blends, nothing continues from one state into the next state; hence, the assumption of continuity is radically interrupted.

2. *The compactness of mass (samūhaghana).* This aspect is variously translated as the compactness of group, synthesis, or mass. Through the meditative processes introduced in the following chapters, you will deconstruct mental and material groupings into their component elements. Just as a stew can be sorted into carrots, celery, beef, onions, broth, potatoes, and spices, you can remove the delusion of mass when you discover that each material form and mental process is composed of individual elements. When you discern earth, water, fire, and wind as individual elements that compose a group or discern the thirty-four mental factors that arise with the first jhāna, you will see for yourself that many individual components arise within each grouping. This recognition breaks down the compactness of mass.

Conventionally, we speak as though there is man, stadium, wall, bread, cow, and computer, but these are only concepts. Just as an automobile is a construction of various parts—wheel, engine, carburetor, fuel, transmission, paint, hoses, window glass—so what we take to be "myself" is a conglomeration of mental and material phenomena. We organize the "parts" (hand, lungs, hair, beliefs, personality, past actions, relationships, preferences) into a form we call "I."[177] In reality, however, there is nothing but momentary conditions that arise together and disperse in a rapidly unfolding process. When you look very closely, there is no place to call "I," nothing that is mine, and no one to whom experience occurs.

To intimately experience selflessness, do not try to analyze the question of identity philosophically. Instead, drop into a mindful experience of the present moment and see if you really exist as an independent entity here and now. Is there anything that you can control, stop from changing, or claim as self? When you see, feel, or cognize any object of the senses, fixed concepts can distort the perception, construing it as *I, me,* or *mine.* With the arising of the thought "I am," there is alienation. The position of the doer, the knower, even the meditator, takes birth. But when you explore the meditations that distill clusters and concepts into component parts, you will find only complex conjunctions of momentary causes and conditions—no entity, no self.

On one occasion when Venerables Sariputta and Ananda were discussing jhāna attainments, Sariputta mentioned that he no longer conceives that "I have attained" the jhānas and yet he attains them. Ananda remarks, "It must be because I-making, mine-making, and the underlying tendency to conceit have been thoroughly uprooted in the Venerable Sariputta for a long time that such thoughts did not occur to him."[178] Personalizing experience, even meditative attainments, generates fear of loss, death, and suffering. Notice the moments when the exhausting thought *I am* ceases; rest in the absence of personal stories.

3. *The compactness of function (kiccaghana).* The examination of material realities in chapter 12 will demonstrate that every material element performs a specific function within its unit—the life faculty

Present Awareness

Reach down and feel the rug or the floor. What are you feeling? One answer may be "rug"; but "rug" is a concept. Another response might be "pressure, hardness, roughness, coolness," pointing toward a more direct encounter with sensory phenomena. As you engage in daily activities, rest as often as possible in the simple perception of changing sensory events. Feel the temperature of the room in which you are reading, notice the movement of your ribs on an inhalation, settle into a mindful appreciation of the present configuration of current conditions. Strengthen insight by connecting with the here and now, as it is actually occurring.

maintains the material elements and establishes them in their group; nutritive essence feeds materiality; space delimits matter and displays the boundaries of each material group; the tongue element draws the mind to flavors; and so on. Just as physicists use linear accelerators to smash matter into components so small that they are no longer directly discernible as distinctive units but can be recognized only by their effects on observed phenomena, so too through an ultrasubtle analysis, you can observe the interdependent functioning of material phenomena in your body and dislodge the coarse notion that you are the agent of your actions.

The Buddha described humanity as attached to self-production, to *I am*. One who sees clearly, however, does not claim, "I am the doer," nor does he claim that "another is the doer."[179] The wind blows, but you do not construe a blower. Although you may use conventional language to say, "I reach for the door," you don't need to presume there is a doer that opens the door. Similarly, the world does not exist as we conventionally know it. This practice exposes that not only the concept of self but also the concept of everything is merely an array of mental and material processes, each limited by its specific characteristics and functions, that arise and pass away according to causal conditions.

To dislodge the illusion of compactness regarding function, explore the meditation instructions in the following chapters for analyzing the momentary groupings of material phenomena, mental factors, and consciousness. Specifically, discern the individual functions that each element and factor performs within its group or mind-moment. This meditative endeavor is remarkably precise; the nuances unravel deeply conditioned assumptions. Although the exercises may appear lengthy, or burdened by archaic definitions of the characteristics, functions, and manifestations of individual factors, the clarity and depth of peace that these explorations can provide is well worth the effort.

4. *The compactness of object (ārammaṇaghana).*[180] This fourth category of deconstruction is performed only in relation to mentality and will be practiced during later stages of insight training *(vipassanā)*. Pragmatic instructions are included in meditation instructions 17.11 and 18.3. It is sometimes called "object compactness" or "subject compactness". "Object" is a more literal translation from the Pali, but the English term "subject" illuminates the intended meaning. The insight into this form of compactness occurs by recognizing the impermanence, unsatisfactoriness, and emptiness of the knowing function that arises in conjunction with insight knowledge. For the meditator to be conscious of impermanent phenomena, a cognitive process must occur. Therefore, to thoroughly examine phenomena you will turn attention to that process and recognize the impermanence, unsatisfactoriness, and emptiness of the mental and material processes that are engaging the practice of insight meditation itself.

Contemplating consciousness in a moment of insight breaks down the compactness of the knower or perceiving subject. Contemplating what meditates, you interrupt the reification of yourself as meditator, as doer, as a knowing self, or as the one who discerns ultimate mentality. This understanding untangles a fundamentally dualistic process—the habit of constructing a subject that views an object.

This fourth category does not represent a new form of compactness; it is a reiteration of the first three, now applied to insight knowledge. This endeavor highlights three kinds of compactness in multiple dimensions: the compactness of continuity, mass, and function is dissolved regarding (1) materiality, (2) mentality, and (3) the cognitive process active during insight knowledge.

By carefully examining material and mental phenomena as instructed in chapters 12–14, you will discover and deconstruct false assumptions about the nature of things, loosen the bonds of craving, and identify subtle objects that you will use in further contemplations. The triad of deep concentration, refined mindfulness, and careful examination merge to uproot the illusion of an enduring self-existence and to enhance the liberating potential of awareness.

CHAPTER 12

Explorations of Matter: Four Elements Meditation

With mindfulness of the body established,
Controlled over contact's sixfold base,
A bhikkhu who is always concentrated
Can know Nibbāna for himself.
—THE UDĀNA[181]

THOUSANDS OF YEARS before the invention of the microscope, meditators, alchemists, and ancient physicians developed methods for using the discerning capacity of a concentrated mind to study the fundamental nature of matter. Ancient meditators probed the frontiers of an inner landscape, inquiring: How does matter form? Where does it come from? How does it function? How do organisms grow, convert food into fuel, and reproduce? How is the world perceived by the senses and interpreted by the mind?

Equipped with jhāna and skilled in a time-honored tradition of investigation, seekers explored the fundamental elements of phenomena. Today, Buddhist meditators continue to apply the light of concentration to illuminate refined strata of material and mental processes and reveal the ultimate objects for vipassanā contemplation.

Strong concentration is needed to glimpse these subtle formations of matter, and even stronger concentration is required to discern the function of each element and formation. While jhāna is a valuable asset in the quest of a direct perception of refined phenomena, it is not an absolute requirement. The four elements meditation is a meditative training that is designed to enable you to see these subtle material properties. It is a meditation that may be undertaken with or without the foundation of jhāna.

What a meditator perceives through this meditation may at times correspond to Western scientific concepts and at times not. The intent of the four elements meditation is not to propose a scientific explanation of reality. Rather, the intent of the four elements meditation is to illuminate phenomena beyond our constructed concepts and thereby create an effective vantage point for perceiving the emptiness of all phenomena.[182]

In this chapter I only aim to provide an overview of the four elements meditation as a practical framework for understanding how this analysis of matter bridges concentration and insight practices. These practices are subtle and difficult to describe. They are best undertaken with the assistance of a qualified instructor who has already seen these elements for herself or himself and can confirm the accuracy and extent of your discoveries.

DISCOVERING WHAT IS REAL

The Abhidhamma-piṭaka, a division of the ancient Buddhist scripture, calls for a refined examination of constituents of experience in their most distilled and nonconceptual forms. To facilitate a precise analysis of phenomena, Abhidhamma theory proposes a pragmatic categorization that divides all experiential phenomena into four categories of irreducible realities *(paramattha dhammas)*. These include: (1) materiality *(rūpa)*, (2) consciousness *(citta)*, (3) mental factors that are associated with consciousness *(cetasika)*, and (4) the unconditioned element *(nibbāna)*. The first category—materiality—includes some of the most classical objects for vipassanā. It will be the focus of this chapter.

The *paramattha dhammas* theory has been the focus of historic controversies among Buddhist schools for the last two thousand years. *Paramattha,* a term indicating that something is further, beyond, or supreme, was used in the early Discourses of the Buddha to refer to the transcendent, ultimate goal; namely, the realization of nibbāna. Later

Abhidhamma theory came to use the term *paramattha* to refer to the nonconventional, nonconceptual, intrinsic, irreducible, and therefore "ultimate" building blocks of experience. The exacting analysis undertaken in Abhidhamma-influenced training scrutinizes experiential reality to resolve phenomena into their nonconceptual and irreducible functions.

The term *dhamma* can be translated as *thing, phenomenon, state,* or *reality*. In the early Discourses of the Buddha, *dhamma* primarily referred to the doctrine that the Buddha preached, but in the Abhidhamma literature the term *dhamma* came to refer to the final units of experience that can be discerned and examined through meditation. Meditation techniques were devised to highlight these ultrasubtle momentary psychophysical events. The terms *ultimate (paramattha)* and *reality (dhamma)* do not imply that there is an enduring essence that can be possessed; both conditioned and unconditioned phenomena are devoid of substantial self-existence. Through the power of your own direct insight and with the support of a concentrated and careful examination, you can discern the specific and nonconceptual constituents of experience. By pursuing a rigorous examination of phenomena, you will realize that no thing, no substance, no essence can be found; all designations, terms, labels, and names merely refer to instances of causally related processes.

TABLE 12.1
Four Ultimate Realities

FOUR ULTIMATE REALITIES	PALI TERM	NUMBER OF TYPES
Materiality/matter	*rūpa*	18 concrete types 10 nonconcrete types
Consciousness	*citta*	89
Mental factors	*cetasikā*	52
The unconditioned element	*nibbāna*	1

In contemporary Buddhism, the four elements meditation and the direct perception of ultimate realities have been largely overlooked, appearing to some to be overly complex, academic, and tedious. We are thus in danger of losing these techniques through neglect and disuse. However, by using these practices, we can strip away interpretations, break apart groupings and compounds, and look at bare phenomena below the level of concept to contemplate their impermanence, unsatisfactoriness, and emptiness. Thus, these practices provide a powerful tool for insight, and they are simpler and easier to employ than they first appear.

In this training we analyze our meditation object until we discover highly refined and real phenomena. We dissect groupings, masses, or concepts that are applied to clusters of elemental properties. In nature it is rare to find a pure element such as mercury, iron, oxygen, or sodium. Just as early chemists separated substances into their constituent elements to examine their properties and further scientific knowledge, meditators discern the subtle interactions, functions, and processes of matter and cognition in their quest to understand the mind and body.

The four elements meditation functions as a bridge between attention-sharpening concentration methods and analytical investigative processes. It might be considered the centerpiece of the meditation system explained in this book. At Pa-Auk Monastery in Burma (Myanmar), while jhāna practice is strongly encouraged, it is considered optional. On the other hand, everyone must practice four elements meditation. It is considered indispensable to a precise undertaking of vipassanā. This meditation is the means by which we gather the material that we later examine as vipassanā objects.

PHASE 1: A DETAILED MATTER—THE FOUR ELEMENTS

The materiality aggregate includes internal elements that occur within our own bodies and external elements that occur as organic or inorganic forms outside our bodies. As previously noted, the primary elements of matter are considered to be earth, water, fire, and wind.

The *earth element* has the property of resistance—it resists being displaced from the space that it occupies. We experience the quality

Summary of the Five Phases
to Four Elements Meditation[183]

This system describes all material phenomena as made of the four elements: earth, water, fire, and wind. Each of the four elements has a function and is characterized by certain properties.

- Earth element *(paṭhavīdhātu):* hardness, roughness, heaviness, softness, smoothness, lightness.
- Water element *(āpodhātu):* flowing, cohesion.
- Fire element *(tejodhātu):* heat, cold.
- Wind element *(vāyodhātu):* supporting, pushing.

The existence of any element requires the support of the other elements. Thus, they always occur in groups that include all four primary elements, along with several from a list of twenty-four derived material phenomena (see Table 12.2).[184]

Such a group is called a *rūpa kalāpa. Rūpa* means "matter" and *kalāpa* means "grouping." The constituent elements *(rūpas)* of the group are considered the ultimate realities, and the groupings *(kalāpas)* are concepts that refer to a momentary configuration of these elements that arise and pass as a mutually dependent unit. Although every physical manifestation in the world—whether hair, leaf, blood, strawberry, stone, or steel—contains all four mutually dependent elements, one element may be noticeably dominant. In the four elements meditation, we repeatedly observe the characteristics of the primary elements within the body. We know earth by sensing hardness, roughness, heaviness, softness, smoothness, or lightness; water by properties of flowing or cohesion; fire by the spectrum of temperature from hot to cold; wind by the properties of supporting and pushing.

Box continues on next page

1. To begin the process, we contemplate twelve specific characteristics of material phenomena.

2. After comprehending the characteristics of matter, we look more closely to see that materiality consists of small groups of elements.

3. After seeing the material formations, we deconstruct them into their constituent parts: the four primary elements of earth, water, fire, wind; plus twenty-four additional material properties (See Tables 12.2–12.6). This phase of practice is referred to as the discerning of ultimate materiality.

4. Next we analyze materiality by discerning the causes, functions, and interactions of the material elements; watching as fundamental particles of matter interact with other material elements, reproduce, cause movement, and impinge on the mind.

5. Last, we contemplate all ultimate materiality as just materiality. We discern, analyze, and contemplate the six sense bases and forty-two parts of the body internally and externally (the thirty-two parts that were introduced in chapter 5, plus four fire elements and six wind elements presented in chapter 12), including animate and inanimate material.[185]

These five phases may progress very quickly for a meditator who easily discerns phenomena through brief instruction, or they may progress slowly and methodically for a meditator who benefits from detailed, careful, systematic, and nuanced instructions.

TABLE 12.2
Twenty-Eight Types of Material Phenomena (rūpa)

CONCRETE MATERIALITIES (18)	NONCONCRETE MATERIALITIES (10)
Great Essentials	19. Space element *(ākāsadhātu)*
1. Earth element *(paṭhavīdhātu)*	20. Bodily intimation *(kāyaviññatti)*
2. Water element *(āpodhātu)*	21. Verbal intimation *(vacīviññatti)*
3. Fire element *(tejodhātu)*	22. Lightness *(lahutā)*
4. Wind element *(vāyodhātu)*	23. Malleability *(mudutā)*
	24. Workability *(kammaññatā)*
Sensitive Phenomena	25. Production *(upacaya)*
5. Eye-sensitivity *(cakkhupasāda)*	26. Continuity *(santati)*
6. Ear-sensitivity *(sotapasāda)*	27. Aging *(jaratā)*
7. Nose-sensitivity *(ghānapasāda)*	28. Impermanence *(aniccatā)*
8. Tongue-sensitivity *(jivhāpasāda)*	
9. Body-sensitivity *(kāyapasāda)*	
Objective Phenomena	
10. Color *(vaṇṇa)*	
11. Sound *(sadda)*	
12. Odor *(gandha)*	
13. Flavor *(rasa)*	
Other Phenomena	
14. Femininity *(itthibhāva rūpa)*	
15. Masculinity *(purisabhāva rūpa)*	
16. Heart materiality *(hadayarūpa)*	
17. Life faculty *(jīvitindriya)*	
18. Nutritive essence *(ojā)*	

of earth as hardness, softness; roughness, smoothness; heaviness, lightness. The Abhidhamma describes earth as having the characteristic of
hardness, functioning as a material foundation for other elements that
arise together as a group, manifesting through receiving those material
elements that exist in the same kalāpa, and arising dependent upon the
presence of the other three primary elements (water, fire, and wind) that
exist in its own group. The property of earth occurs in every material
particle of the body, but it will be most obvious in the bones of the skeleton, firm nails, and hard teeth. The traditional reflection on the four
elements begins with the familiar sequence of solid body parts from the
thirty-two parts meditation (see chapter 5):

> What, friends, is the earth element? The earth element may
> be either internal or external. What is the internal earth ele-
> ment? Whatever internally, belonging to oneself, is solid,
> solidified, and clung-to; that is, head hairs, body hairs, nails,
> teeth, skin, flesh, sinews, bones, bone marrow, kidneys, heart,
> liver, diaphragm, spleen, lungs, large intestines, small intes-
> tines, contents of the stomach, feces, or whatever else inter-
> nally, belonging to oneself, is solid, solidified, and clung-to;
> this is called the internal earth element. Now both the inter-
> nal earth element and the external earth element are simply
> the earth element. And that should be seen as it actually is
> with proper wisdom thus: "This is not mine, this I am not,
> this is not myself." When one sees it thus as it actually is with
> proper wisdom, one becomes disenchanted with the earth
> element and makes the mind dispassionate toward the earth
> element.[186]

The *water element* has properties of cohesion, fluidity, and binding.
To bake a cake a cook adjusts the cohesive properties of the batter by
modifying the proportions of liquid and flour. Adding water to flour
causes the wheat particles to cohere into dough; adding lots of water
causes the batter to ooze around in the pan. If the quantity of water
is minimal, the flour particles will not cohere; if there is an excess of

water, the dough might lose cohesiveness. We cannot directly feel the element of water; it is not a tangible experience. The properties of water are known through inference as we observe their effects. For instance, when you place your hand in a bucket of water, you infer the element of water from the combined experience of other characteristics: coldness, softness, and pushing. The Abhidhamma describes the characteristic of water as flowing, trickling, and oozing; its function is to intensify the other elements of its own group; it manifests as the holding together or cohesion of the material phenomena; and it arises dependent upon the other three primary elements (earth, fire, and wind) in its own group. The Buddha described it this way:

> What, friends, is the water element? The water element may be either internal or external. What is the internal water element? Whatever internally, belonging to oneself, is water, watery, and clung-to; that is, bile, phlegm, pus, blood, sweat, fat, tears, grease, spittle, snot, oil of the joints, and urine, or whatever else internally, belonging to oneself, is water, watery, and clung-to: this is called the internal water element. Now both the internal water element and the external water element are simply water element. And that should be seen as it actually is with proper wisdom thus: "This is not mine, this I am not, this is not myself." When one sees it thus as it actually is with proper wisdom, one becomes disenchanted with the water element and makes the mind dispassionate toward the water element.[187]

The *fire element* has the property of maturation or ripening. Fire burns fuel, whether as a candle flame consuming wax, a lamp flame consuming oil, or digestive fire transforming garlic mashed potato into caloric energy units. It is the fire element that causes fruit to ripen, food to digest, skin to age, and bodies to decay. We experience the fire element as the feeling of heat and cold. The Abhidhamma describes the characteristic of the fire element as heat or cold; its function is to mature or ripen the elements in its own group; it manifests as pliancy or softness;

and it arises dependent upon the other three primary elements (earth, water, and wind) in its own group. The Buddha taught:

> What, friends, is the fire element? The fire element may be either internal or external. What is the internal fire element? Whatever internally, belonging to oneself, is fire, fiery, and clung-to; that is, that by which one is warmed, ages, and is consumed, and that by which what is eaten, drunk, consumed, and tasted gets completely digested, or whatever else internally, belonging to oneself, is fire, fiery, and clung-to: this is called the internal fire element.[188]

The *wind element,* alternatively called the *air element,* has the properties of pressure, movement, and vibration. It can be experienced as expansion and contraction in breathing, envisioned through the inflating and deflating of balloons, compared to a breeze that causes a flag to flutter, or recognized in a gust that catches in a sail and propels a boat across a lake. The Abhidhamma describes the characteristic of wind as physically supporting the other elements in its own group; it functions by pushing, which causes motion in the other material phenomena; it manifests as propulsion, to set going, by being the cause for the successive arising in locations nearby which create an illusion of continuous movement, or as conveying to other places; and it arises dependent upon the other three primary elements (earth, water, and fire) in its own group.

In reality no element ever moves or changes its location. When we walk or make a physical gesture, the wind element provokes a successive arising in nearby locations, thereby causing a stream of events that appear as movement. It also provides stabilization and support for matter, thereby preventing total dissolution and collapse. You can discern the kinetic energy experienced as the continuum of supporting and pushing to glimpse the nature of the wind element. The Buddha said:

> What, friends, is the air element? The air element may be either internal or external. What is the internal air element?

Whatever internally, belonging to oneself, is air, airy, and clung-to; that is up-going winds, down-going winds, winds in the belly, winds in the bowels, winds that course through the limbs, in-breath and out-breath, or whatever else internally, belonging to oneself is air.[189]

A complex conjunction of these elemental properties is integral to every physical experience. When you walk to the store, the element of wind manifests as the dynamic pushing and supporting that moves your legs forward and keeps your body erect. When eating toast you might notice the warmth (fire element) of the bread, the roughness (earth element) of the crusts, heat (fire element) in your belly as digestion converts

---

 Four Elements in Your Daily Life

Practice continuously seeing four elements in every activity and every object you see, touch, taste, or smell. You eat, touch, and interact with four elements all day long. Your morning coffee is a cluster of elements. Your knee pain includes elements. The chair that you are sitting on is composed of elements. The book in your hand is just elements. As the meditation progresses you will understand all matter as nothing but elements and interactions of elements.

You may periodically highlight a characteristic. For example, observe the manifestation of hardness for fifteen minutes in everything you touch or encounter, or watch the fluctuations of temperature during a meal. You might examine the experience of painful sensations by teasing out the rigidity, stiffness, softness, heaviness, cohesion, and pushing characteristics as expressions of earth, water, fire, and wind.

the nutrients into fuel, the flowing (water element) of moist saliva as you chew, and the pulsing contractions of swallowing (wind element). Waving your arms in the air demonstrates the characteristic of earth through momentary expressions of heaviness and lightness, the characteristic of wind through the dynamic gestures, the subtle element of water that holds the configuration of elements together to form an arm, and the element of fire that produces temperature changes.

The Twelve Characteristics of Matter

The first phase in the four elements meditation is to contemplate twelve specific characteristics; these are the hallmarks of the four elements. To facilitate a clear recognition of each characteristic, Pa-Auk Sayadaw sometimes introduces beginners to the characteristics in order of how easily they can be sensed: pushing, hardness, roughness, heaviness, supporting, softness, smoothness, lightness, heat, coldness, cohesion, and flowing. After discerning them clearly in this order, the meditator then switches to the traditional order to develop the four elements meditation: hardness, roughness, heaviness, softness, smoothness, lightness, flowing, cohesion, heat, cold, supporting, and pushing.

→ **MEDITATION INSTRUCTION 12.1**
Identifying the Four Elements through Twelve Characteristics

We shall use the easier order to introduce these elemental properties one by one, and then by groupings. Begin every meditation by establishing concentration. If you have skill in jhānas, you can refresh concentration with absorption, ideally establishing the fourth jhāna using the breath or any kasiṇa. Then, apply your concentrated mind to discern material characteristics found in your body. If you do not have skill in jhāna, you may focus on the breath or a meditation subject of your choice until your attention is steady and your mind cleared of distraction. Alternatively, you may begin directly with the four elements meditation and allow concentration to gradually accrue in the course of this exercise. As you discern the characteristics again and again with increasing clarity and speed, distractions fall away, concentration increases, and the mind grows supple, pure, and steady.

Pushing: Try to sense a genuine expression of pushing in your body. You might notice the sensations caused by the breath pushing inside the chest or belly. Once you feel a sensation of pushing in a place that is obvious, such as the rising belly, try to find the characteristic of pushing in every part of your body by scanning outward from the diaphragm to the chest, arms, hands, legs, feet, back, neck, and head. Wherever there is movement, try to discern the characteristic of pushing. Contemplate the characteristic of pushing in whatever way that you experience it in your body. Scan from head to toe, again and again, mindfully observing the body until the characteristic of pushing is vividly clear.

Hardness: To discover an obvious expression of hardness in your body, clench your teeth together or press two finger nails together. Once you sense the characteristic of hardness, begin to scan from head to toe, discerning the characteristic of hardness as it appears throughout your body. Then discern pushing and hardness together as you continue to scan attention through your body. Use the knowledge you have of your body beyond physical sensations. Do this many times until it becomes easy and clear.

Roughness: Stroke an area of rough, calloused skin such as your heel or elbow, or rub your tongue against the rough edge at the tip of a tooth. Once you have a vivid sense of roughness, scan through the body, discerning roughness in subtle and obvious areas. Then look for the three qualities together—pushing, hardness, and roughness. Repeat the body scan many times.

Heaviness: Lean your weight on one leg to amplify heaviness in the lower body, or drop your head forward and feel its heaviness. Repeatedly scan from your head to your toes for the characteristic of heaviness; then continue scanning while discerning pushing, hardness, roughness, and heaviness together. If it is difficult to see them together at a glance, then alternate observing each characteristic individually until concentration builds. Then try again to see them together at a glance.

Supporting: The supporting characteristic is what holds the body upright, stabilizes posture, and resists movement. Whereas pushing causes the body to move, supporting stabilizes the body and enables us to halt and control movement. To identify the supporting quality, mindfully slump forward and then correct your posture to an upright alignment, hold your jaw closed, or feel the dynamic interplay of pushing and supporting as you walk. Once you sense the characteristic of supporting and discern it throughout the entire body, repeat the meditative scan many times and include the previous characteristics, either by sequencing through the series or observing them together within one body scan.

Softness: You might feel softness if you stroke your lips with your tongue or caress a protected fatty area (such as your belly) with your hand. After the characteristic of softness is clear in an obvious location, discern softness throughout the body; then incorporate the previous characteristics. Repeat many times to build concentration and clarity.

Smoothness: Press your tongue against the inside of the lower lip and sense a sensation of smoothness. Discern smoothness throughout the body. Continue mindfully developing the body scan by adding all the previous characteristics—pushing, hardness, roughness, heaviness, supporting, softness, smoothness— either alternately or as a group.

Lightness: Wiggling a little finger or gently fluttering the eyelids may demonstrate lightness. Notice the characteristic of lightness and then observe it throughout the body. First notice it in isolation, then in conjunction with the previous characteristics.

Heat: Hold your hands together and feel the warmth that they generate. Notice warmth in enclosed places such as the space under your arms or inside your mouth; feel the warmth of the exhalation. Use

the mindful body scan to discern the characteristic of heat throughout the body, and then include all the previous characteristics.

Cold: You may feel cold on the skin as sweat evaporates or feel
the coolness of an inhalation in the nostrils. Discern cold in a
specific location and then throughout the whole body. Scan the
body from head to toe many times, discerning these first ten
characteristics—pushing, hardness, roughness, heaviness, supporting, softness, smoothness, lightness, heat, cold—individually
and together.

Cohesion: The water element, known by its characteristics of
flowing and cohesion, is not felt directly; rather it is inferred
through the previous ten tangible qualities. Since cohesion is not
a tangible quality, you must infer the characteristic through the
associated impact of pushing, pressure, supporting, or hardness.
Imagine the sense of cohesion by squeezing your forearm with
your hand. It is the binding characteristic, the function of holding things together, that we distinguish in this contemplation.
Once you have a sense of the characteristic of cohesion, discern
it throughout the body, scanning for cohesion from head to toe.
Then incorporate the previous characteristics.

Flowing: Notice your saliva flowing inside your mouth; sense the
movement of fluids circulating throughout your body—trickling
of blood, oozing of pus, dripping of mucous, expelling of urine.
Although flowing is not a tangible quality, you can infer the
characteristic through the associated impact of pushing, pressure,
or changing temperatures. Discern all aspects of the body where
there is flowing, both subtle and gross.

Discern all twelve characteristics together many times: Pushing,
hardness, roughness, heaviness, supporting, softness, smoothness, lightness, heat, coldness, cohesion, flowing. Rapidly scan
the body until you can complete two or three rounds within one
minute. Then shift to discerning the same twelve characteristics,
but in the traditional order: hardness, roughness, heaviness,

softness, smoothness, lightness, flowing, cohesion, heat, cold, supporting, pushing.

Although the detailed nature of this presentation may appear tedious or create the impression that this is a time-consuming process, do not worry. With a foundation of concentration, you'll find this sequence can be learned quickly, and you'll be well prepared to develop the meditation as an insight practice. The pace of incorporating each characteristic into the meditation varies depending upon the time available and the temperament of the meditator. In a brief approach, a meditator may quickly explore all twelve characteristics in just a few hours. For a more detailed training, a meditator might focus on just one or two characteristics per day, strengthening concentration and examining subtle nuances of matter through steady attention on the featured characteristics over a period of days or weeks of intensive practice.

Contemplate these twelve characteristics of material elements in all postures—while walking, standing, sitting, showering, eating, and defecating—until you perceive them easily and clearly. Perceive the body as just a compendium of elements, or an interaction of functions and characteristics. There is nothing solid, lasting, or personal—no self can be found in the body. ❖

PHASE 2: FOLLOWING THE CLUES— SMOKE, GLASS, ICE, DIAMONDS, AND DOTS

By discerning the characteristics as previously described, meditators prepare to begin the second phase of this practice: seeing the fundamental nature of matter. This phase of the four elements meditation depends upon a willingness to see with the mind, independent of sensation or feeling. Meditators do not literally *see* subatomic properties with the physical eye; the eyes remain closed during meditation, and the eye organ is inactive. However, these subtle material formations might appear in a virtual visual field. "Seeing" is a convenient term that refers to the "eye of wisdom" or the "eye of knowledge."[190] This approach to meditation represents a departure from methods of mindfulness meditation that rely upon the feeling of physical contact or sensory awareness practices, or ones that avoid every type of visualization. Meditators may need some time to adjust to this distinctive approach of discerning phenomena with the eye of wisdom. Although it required a period of transition in my own practice, I found that a skillful use of the mental (apparently visual) field opened great possibilities for deep concentration and for discerning things that simply cannot be felt, including both animate and inanimate material phenomena that lie outside our own bodies.

Some meditators will quickly perceive the pure subtle characteristics of matter. Other meditators may experience a gradual transformation of perception through which matter appears in a variety of forms before finally resolving into a clear perception of the interdependent and fundamental functions characteristic of material phenomena. Perceptions can vary from meditator to meditator, but commonly, after some practice, the body may begin to appear smoky, then it may whiten, brighten, and clarify to produce a translucent block that resembles glass or ice, until it eventually breaks down into small particles that appear to twinkle like stars, sparkle like diamonds, or flicker like tiny blinking dots.

The Buddha used the image of a gemstone to illustrate his instructions on reviewing the four elements of the body: "It is just as if there were a gem...pure, excellent, well cut into eight facets, clear, bright, unflawed, perfect in every respect, strung on a blue, yellow, red, white, or orange cord. A man with good eyesight, taking it in his hand and inspecting it, would describe it as such. In the same way, a monk with mind concentrated, purified, and cleansed...directs his mind toward knowing and seeing. And he knows: 'This, my body, is material, made up of the four great elements.'"[191] Through practice, each meditator will learn to identify and distinguish between ultimate materiality as the characteristics of matter (*rūpas*), and the subtle conceptual mass (*rūpa kalāpas*) that appears as a variety of perceptions, and confirm that perception with their teacher. Whatever you actually see—the smoky body, white body, transparent body, sparkles, diamonds, dots, or a raw intuition of the characteristics of matter themselves—it is a conglomeration of the twelve fundamental characteristics that you practiced observing in the first phase of this practice. This is neither a figment of your imagination nor a perceptual distortion resulting from concentration; it is a glimpse at the subtle workings of matter. Understanding what you are seeing and receiving proper instructions in the four elements meditation will enable you to use this remarkable vantage point to comprehend the nature of all things.

→ MEDITATION INSTRUCTION 12.2
Discerning Eight Nonopposing Characteristics

A meditator cannot perceive contradictory characteristics in any single cluster *(kalāpa)* of elements. You may find:

▶ hardness *or* softness
▶ roughness *or* smoothness
▶ heaviness *or* lightness
▶ flowing
▶ cohesion
▶ heat *or* cold
▶ supporting
▶ pushing.

Discern the eight nonopposing characteristics that appear in the body. Alternate between discerning these characteristics in the whole body and then in a single rūpa kalāpa or cluster of elemental functions. When you can easily discern the twelve characteristics as sets of eight nonopposing characteristics, then divide them into four categories: earth, water, fire, and wind. Recite *earth, water, fire, and wind* while observing gray, white, translucent, reflective, or dotted body material. Let the twelve characteristics become vividly clear before abbreviating the discernment to the categories of four elements. You may continue scanning from head to toe, or develop more stillness by viewing the body from the perspective of an outside observer peering down at your body from over your shoulder. Repeatedly discern all the characteristics—really try to see them. You are not repeating a mantra or chanting a series of words; you are directing your mind to perceive these elements in every material formation. ←

Overcoming Potential Difficulties

For some meditators, this practice is easy—the characteristics of matter are clear, easily discerned, and logically divided into four elements. To these meditators, the small groups of elements *(rūpa kalāpas)* appear quickly and vividly. Even if you have already seen rūpa kalāpas or experienced the body dissolving into discrete functions or bewildering arrays of dots, intensify concentration by repeatedly and rapidly discerning the elemental nature of matter. It is essential to recognize the subtle characteristics of matter and not be impressed by what might appear to be special or altered perceptions.

1. *Refresh your concentration.* Discerning ultimate materiality does not require superpowers, but it does require strong concentration. Any time you feel tired during the four elements meditation, refresh your attention by enhancing your concentration. If you have a foundation in jhāna, you may renew your energy with quick dips into jhāna—even just a few minutes sequencing through the jhānas or resting for five or ten minutes in a single absorption can invigorate the attention, facilitate the task of subtle discernment, and brighten the light of wisdom. Without a foundation in jhāna you may refresh attention by focusing on the breath, mettā, or a calming practice of your choice. Intertwine rejuvenating rests in concentration-oriented practices, with this more active discerning technique until you succeed.

2. *Balance the elements.* It is possible that some meditators may periodically experience an imbalance in the elements, such as a feeling of excessive heat or intense pressure in the body. You can correct imbalances of the elements by giving greater emphasis to discerning the opposite characteristic. If you feel very hot, emphasize coldness, rather than heat, as the characteristic of the fire element. If you feel heavy and inert, focus on the characteristic of lightness of the earth element. You can shift the emphasis of your attention to optimize balance, stability, and clarity.

3. *Ignore changing impressions.* Stay focused on the characteristics of elements. If you notice a field of flickering light, vibrations, or swells, don't let these impressions distract you. Perceptions of change can diminish concentration. Although matter is indeed changing, ignore its fluctuating nature at this time. At this stage it is important to focus exclusively on the salient aspects that characterize each specific element, without giving attention to the impermanence of matter.

4. *Explore the spaces.* If your attention remains with the translucent body for a long time, that ice-like translucent block may not break apart effortlessly. If it lasts for more than forty minutes through successive meditation sessions, then strategically look for small holes or spaces in that translucent appearance of the body.[192] Since matter is naturally discontinuous, as your attention to the material body becomes increasingly refined, you may notice the spaces that surround material units. The perception of space in the body is a traditional entry point for the discernment of the material elements.[193]

If the meditation continues without much progress, you might gradually contemplate the relationship of space and matter by first considering the grosser occurrences such as the space in the mouth, ears, or nose. Second, consider the more subtle spaces between the flesh and bones, and between various organs, until finally you realize that it is the space element that divides the material groupings *(rūpa kalāpas)*. Space delimits matter; any spaces you discover are ultimately the boundaries of rūpa kalāpas. Intentionally penetrate through the spaces to see the rūpa kalāpas that may appear like sparkling diamonds around the holes.

Many meditators will discover that as their concentration increases, the body scan becomes more rapid and smooth, and the discernment of the characteristics becomes clear. The mind naturally becomes pure, lustrous, light, and supple. It is this clarity of the mind, not a conceptualized visualization, that will produce a genuine discernment of ultimate materiality.

5. *Overcome skeptical doubts.* Maybe you have already seen rūpa kalāpas but disregarded their appearance, doubted that they were really elements of matter, or criticized them into oblivion. When I first received the instruction to observe the characteristics of material elements, I thought that it sounded farfetched, if not impossible, to "see" such ephemeral phenomena. When these formations became apparent during the meditations, I did not believe my own perception; I doubted their significance and waited many days before reporting the observations to my teacher. Doubt can manifest in subtle ways: rampant speculation, wistful hopes that avoid actual commitment, expectations of failure, blaming external distractions for our slow progress, rebelling by withdrawing interest, grasping concepts prior to authentic experience, or excessive testing, judging, and probing of the observation. Doubt can lead to endless speculations: What does all this mean? Are these practices the precursors of modern science? Do their findings conform to recent discoveries in the fields of physics, genetics, biology, and medicine? Is this a mere projection of creative imagination or a sneak preview for a new Star Trek movie? Comparing traditional methods with contemporary scientific processes may lead to doubt for people who are concerned with aspects that diverge from modern scientific methods and theories. On the other hand, speculative comparisons could spark excessive excitement, fascination, and blind faith for meditators who correlate recent advances in genetic research, neuroscience, or quantum physics to processes "seen" by ancient meditators.

Do not think you are free and clear of hindrances if you have been able to enter jhāna. At any point in the practice, you may need to unravel subtle traces of hindrances. Meeting after meeting, Sayadaw would urge me: "please try harder, you must try, please try to see." No benefit comes through giving up, and there is no substitute for determination. Through the four elements meditation we vividly discern real matter. This is neither a perceptual distortion nor a creative visualization. The mind's potential is largely untapped, and we do not know the limits of what the mind can know and see. Enjoy the expansion of possibility that meditation offers.

Try to trust what you see, even if it is just an ordinary, uninteresting, indistinguishable dot. Find a way to set aside your doubts and let the practice unfold. The four elements meditation serves an important function within the training of concentration and insight—whether or not the meditator's observations correspond to Western scientific concepts. It produces astounding clarity of mind, it precisely defines the material objects that we contemplate in vipassanā practice, and it untangles clinging at an extraordinarily refined level. By directly perceiving only elements in the body—finding no being, no soul—you will have a powerful insight into the emptiness of beings.[194] Develop the four elements meditation because it has its own purpose and reward.

PHASE 3: TWENTY-EIGHT TYPES OF MATERIAL PHENOMENA

Once you have discerned the four primary elements in rūpa kalāpas, you may proceed through a detailed examination of the constituent components, causes, functions, and interactions of each material grouping. This microscopic contemplation of matter reveals the elements common to all material phenomena and begins an odyssey of meticulous discernment that will reveal twenty-eight types of ultimate materiality (Table 12.2). These twenty-eight types of matter are divided into two primary categories: concrete or real materiality *(nipphannarūpa)* and nonconcrete or unreal materiality *(anipphannarūpa)*. Concrete materialities are produced by kamma, mind, temperature, or nutriment; nonconcrete materialities arise as an attribute of concrete materiality.[195] The eighteen elements classified as real or concrete rūpas are emphasized in this training because they will later serve as objects for vipassanā contemplation: earth, water, fire, and wind; the sensitivity of the eye, ear, nose, tongue, and body; color, sound, odor, and flavor; nutritive essence, life faculty, and heart-base materiality; and sex-determining material elements.[196] The ten nonconcrete materialities—space, bodily intimation, verbal intimation, and the lightness, pliancy, wieldiness, growth, continuity, aging, and impermanence of concrete material—are examined in meditation instruction 12.4. The meditative practice presented in this chapter is designed to initiate a precise and direct perception of ultrasubtle materialities, not speculation or reflection on abstract ideas about matter.

There are three basic types of rūpa kalāpas that form the materiality of our bodies:

▸ Octad kalāpas contain eight types of rūpa.
▸ Nonad kalāpas contain nine types of rūpa.
▸ Decad kalāpas contain ten types of rūpa.

Rūpa kalāpas are traditionally identified according to the quantity and type of rūpas that they contain (see Table 12.3):

▸ *Nutritive-essence octad kalāpas* are inanimate materialities found throughout our bodies. They contain eight types of rūpas and are named after the eighth type of rūpa, nutritive essence.
▸ *Life nonad kalāpas* are animate materialities found throughout our bodies. They contain nine types of rūpas and are named after the ninth type of rūpa, the life faculty.

There are eight types of decad kalāpas:

▸ *Eye decad kalāpa, ear decad kalāpa, nose decad kalāpa,* and *tongue decad kalāpa* are animate materialities that contain ten types of rūpas and are found in their respective sense organs. Each type is named after the tenth rūpa that is responsive to the sensory impact of color, sound, smell, or taste.
▸ *Body decad kalāpas* are animate materialities that are sensitive to the impact of touch, contain ten types of rūpas, and are found dispersed throughout the body.
▸ *Heart decad kalāpas* are found only in the heart base. They are animate, contain ten types of rūpas, and function to support consciousness.
▸ *Sex-determining decad kalāpas* are animate materialities with the sex-determining rūpa as the tenth factor. Women have *female-sex-determining decad kalāpas* and men have *male-sex-determining decad kalāpas* throughout their bodies.

Rūpa kalāpas may also be classified according to their origins:

▸ Kamma-produced materiality

- ► Mind-produced materiality
- ► Temperature-produced materiality
- ► Nutriment-produced materiality.

In the instructions that follow you will be guided through the meditative procedure to see and analyze the subtle materiality in your body. With a powerfully concentrated mind you can examine these subtle material formations to discern nuances in color, smell, and taste. Noticing variations in opacity, sharpness, and softness will assist you to identify the subtle presence of nutritive essence, life faculty, heart-base materiality, and sex-determining material elements. By carefully discerning variations between rūpa kalāpas, you will learn to distinguish and sort the eighteen types of real rūpas by kind. The accuracy of your discernment can be confirmed through repetition, by observing the manifestations and functions of matter in all parts of the body, and by verbally describing your perceptions to a qualified teacher.

✦ MEDITATION INSTRUCTION 12.3
Analyzing Real Materialities[197]

Summary of Method: Begin by establishing concentration. Then shine the light of wisdom onto a location in the body such as a material base that enables sensory encounters with the world: eye base, ear base, nose base, tongue base, and body base; and the material support for consciousness, the heart base. Examine the ultimate materiality that comprises the sense bases, and then examine the thirty-two body parts. You will discover various types of rūpa kalāpas present at each sense base and each body part.

The Procedure: First look at a field of rūpa kalāpas such as what occurs in the eye base. Discern the components of earth, water, fire, and wind in each grouping. Sort the rūpa kalāpas into two categories: those that appear translucent, reflective, or transparent and those that appear opaque or not translucent. Then, notice the color of individual rūpa kalāpas.

In the eye, ear, nose, and tongue bases there are two types of
translucent decad kalāpas. To distinguish between eye-sensitive
elements and body-sensitive elements in the eye base, find a translucent rūpa to analyze. Discern the four elements of earth, water, fire,
and wind in that translucent rūpa kalāpa. Then look at the color of
a different rūpa in the eye door. If the color impacts the translucent
rūpa, it is an eye-sensitive element. To identify the body-sensitive
element, look at the tangible elements of earth, fire, or wind in
a nearby kalāpa of the eye base and notice if the perception of a
tangible object impacts the translucent rūpa. If the perception of a
tangible element impacts the translucent rūpa, it is a body-sensitive
element. Body-sensitive elements are found in all the sense bases,
plus most of the body parts.

Matter also has odor. Try to discern the smell of rūpa kalāpas.
Odors impact the nose-sensitive element and are known by mind-
consciousness. To harness both the material sensitivity and the
mental perception that will facilitate the discernment of odor, find
the nose-sensitive element by looking for a translucent rūpa in the
nose, and then discern the mind door. Try to discern the odor of
a rūpa kalāpa near that translucent rūpa. If the odor impinges on
the translucent rūpa and mind door simultaneously, it is a nose-
sensitive element. If instead the perceptions of earth, fire, or wind
impinge on the translucent rūpa, you will know that it is a body-
sensitive element. After seeing the odor of materiality near the nose,
you will be able to apply this method and use the mind to discern
the odor of other materialities in the body.

Matter has taste. To facilitate the perception of the flavor
of rūpa kalāpas, find a translucent rūpa of the tongue base and
discern the mind door. Observe a rūpa kalāpa in your mouth or
saliva. If flavor simultaneously impacts the translucent element
and the mind door, it is a tongue-sensitive element. If instead the
perceptions of earth, fire, or wind impinge on the translucent
rūpa, you will know that it is a body-sensitive element. After you
are skilled in seeing flavors impact the tongue, you will be able

to use the mind to discern the taste of materialities throughout the body.

Nutritive essence is found in all matter. It supports the reproduction of materiality. Look closely at any rūpa kalāpa and you may see the force of nutritive essence multiplying the materialities like a stream of beads or spray of water drops.

Life faculty is found only in kamma-produced materialities with nine or ten rūpas. It is responsible for maintaining the materialities within each kalāpa. It may be easiest to discern the life faculty first by examining a translucent decad kalāpa. You have already discerned the other nine constituents (earth, water, fire, wind, color, odor, flavor, nutritive essence, and sensitivity); the additional factor is the life faculty.

There are three types of nontranslucent kalāpas that also contain life faculty: heart decad kalāpas, sex decad kalāpas, and the life nonad kalāpas. Heart dacad kalāpas will be found only in the heart base. Look for nontranslucent kalāpas that you can find only in the heart base; they will not appear in the eye base, nose base, liver, bones, or teeth. Discern the ten distinct types of rūpa that make up the heart decad kalāpa. Life nonad kalāpas and sex-determining decad kalāpas are both distributed throughout the body and are present in all the sense bases. Through repeated observation and systematic elimination, you can learn to distinguish the subtle formations that contain the life faculty. Look again and again, in various sense bases and body parts, until you sense the distinctive function of sex-determining materiality and can distinguish the life faculty as it appears in sex-determining decad kalāpas and life nonad kalāpas.

If you have difficulty discerning sex-determining decad kalāpas, you may discern the materiality within yourself and then compare it with other males and females that are sitting nearby. Look for rūpa kalāpas that contain life faculty and are present in all members of the same sex but not present in the opposite sex. With repeated examination you will find a material formation, the sex-determining decad kalāpa, that appears differently in males and females.

Thoroughly examine the materiality of the eye-door, then proceed to examine the ear, nose, tongue, body, and heart bases, followed by the thirty-two parts of the body. See that each rūpa kalāpa is composed of at least four elements (earth, water, fire, wind), plus four ever-present types of matter (color, odor, flavor, nutritive essence), which function together in interdependent units. In each group that is sensitive to the impingement of a specific sensory phenomena such as colors, tangible objects, or odors, an additional two material properties will be found: life faculty and sensitivity to the corresponding sense field (for example, the matter in the eye that is sensitive to the impingement of color, the matter in the tongue that is sensitive to flavors, or the matter in the body that is sensitive to tactile contact). Use Tables 12.3–12.6 to guide your investigation until you easily see all sixty-three types of rūpas in the eye, ear, nose, tongue, and mind bases, the fifty-three types of rūpas in the body, and the varying quantities and types of rūpas in the thirty-two body parts.

I have constructed the tables and the exercises in this book to reveal sixty-three types of rūpas in the eye, ear, nose, tongue, and mind doors, and fifty-three types of rūpas in the body door. You may find references in other traditional Abhidhamma lists and in the *Visuddhimagga* to fifty-four and forty-four types of rūpas.[198] Many traditional sources exclude from the primary lists the nine-factored kalāpa called the life nonad kalāpa (*jīvita navaka kalāpa*) that contains earth, water, fire, wind, color, odor, flavor, nutritive essence, and life faculty. Sometimes this kalāpa is called "digestive fire" and has a dominance of the fire element. It is active in the aging, nourishment, digestion, reproduction, heating up, and breaking down of material formations, and it is found in all the sense doors and throughout most parts of the body. When guided by a teacher, you might be asked to discern this life nonad kalāpa with a dominance of fire element early in the discernment, or only after you can easily distinguish the other fifty-four and forty-four types of rūpas in the sense doors. ✦

TABLE 12.3
Schema of the Material Groups (kalāpas)

Feature		Kalāpas	Eye Decad	Ear Decad	Nose Decad	Tongue Decad	Body Decad	Heart Decad	Sex Decad	Life Nonad	Mind-Produced Octad	Temperature-Produced Octad	Nutriment-Produced Octad
Origin	Kamma		▓	▓	▓	▓	▓	▓	▓	▓			
	Mind										▓		
	Temperature											▓	
	Nutriment												▓
Translucent			▓	▓	▓	▓	▓						
Rūpas	1. Earth		▓	▓	▓	▓	▓	▓	▓	▓	▓	▓	▓
	2. Water		▓	▓	▓	▓	▓	▓	▓	▓	▓	▓	▓
	3. Fire		▓	▓	▓	▓	▓	▓	▓	▓	▓	▓	▓
	4. Wind		▓	▓	▓	▓	▓	▓	▓	▓	▓	▓	▓
	5. Color		▓	▓	▓	▓	▓	▓	▓	▓	▓	▓	▓
	6. Odor		▓	▓	▓	▓	▓	▓	▓	▓	▓	▓	▓
	7. Flavor		▓	▓	▓	▓	▓	▓	▓	▓	▓	▓	▓
	8. Nutriment		▓	▓	▓	▓	▓	▓	▓	▓	▓	▓	▓
	9. Life faculty		▓	▓	▓	▓	▓	▓	▓	▓			
	10. Eye-sensitivity		▓										
	Ear-sensitivity			▓									
	Nose-sensitivity				▓								
	Tongue-sensitivity					▓							
	Body-sensitivity						▓						
	Heart-materiality							▓					
	Sex-determining								▓				
Generations reproduced			4–5	4–5	4–5	4–5	4–5	4–5	4–5	4–5	2–3	10–12	10–12

TABLE 12.4

Sixty-Three Rūpas of the Eye, Ear, Nose, and Tongue Doors

FEATURE		KALĀPAS	Eye Decad* (Cakkhu Dasaka Kalāpas)	Body Decad (Kāya Dasaka Kalāpas)	Sex Decad (Bhāva Dasaka Kalāpas)	Life Nonad (Jīvita Navaka Kalāpas)	Mind-Produced Octad (Cittaja Ojatthamaka Kalāpas)	Temperature-Produced Octad (Utuja Ojatthamaka Kalāpas)	Nutriment-Produced Octad (Ahāraja Ojatthamaka Kalāpas)
Rūpas	1. Earth		■	■	■	■	■	■	■
	2. Water		■	■	■	■	■	■	■
	3. Fire		■	■	■	■	■	■	■
	4. Wind		■	■	■	■	■	■	■
	5. Color		■	■	■	■	■	■	■
	6. Odor		■	■	■	■	■	■	■
	7. Flavor		■	■	■	■	■	■	■
	8. Nutriment		■	■	■	■	■	■	■
	9. Life faculty		■	■	■	■			
	10. Eye-sensitivity*		■						
	Body-sensitivity			■					
	Sex-determining				■				
Origin	Kamma		■	■	■	■			
	Mind						■		
	Temperature							■	
	Nutriment								■
Translucent			■						

*Replace eye with ear, nose, and tongue for the discernments of these sense bases.

TABLE 12.5
Fifty-Three Rūpas of the Body Door (kāya dvāra)

Feature		Kalāpas	Body Decad (Kāya Dasaka Kalāpas)	Sex Decad (Bhāva Dasaka Kalāpas)	Life Nonad (Jīvita Navaka Kalāpas)	Mind-Produced Octad (Cittaja Ojaṭṭhamaka Kalāpas)	Temperature-Produced Octad (Utuja Ojaṭṭhamaka Kalāpas)	Nutriment-Produced Octad (Āhāraja Ojaṭṭhamaka Kalāpas)
Rūpas	1. Earth		■	■	■	■	■	■
	2. Water		■	■	■	■	■	■
	3. Fire		■	■	■	■	■	■
	4. Wind		■	■	■	■	■	■
	5. Color		■	■	■	■	■	■
	6. Odor		■	■	■	■	■	■
	7. Flavor		■	■	■	■	■	■
	8. Nutriment		■	■	■	■	■	■
	9. Life faculty		■	■	■			
	10. Body-sensitivity		■					
	Sex-determining			■				
Origin	Kamma		■	■	■			
	Mind					■		
	Temperature						■	
	Nutriment							■
Translucent			■					

TABLE 12.6
Sixty-Three Rūpas of the Mind Door (mano dvāra)

Feature		Kalāpas	Heart Decad (Hadaya Dasaka Kalāpas)	Body Decad (Kāya Dasaka Kalāpas)	Sex Decad (Bhāva Dasaka Kalāpas)	Life Nonad (Jīvita Navaka Kalāpas)	Mind-Produced Octad (Cittaja Ojatthamaka Kalāpas)	Temperature-Produced Octad (Utuja Ojatthamaka Kalāpas)	Nutriment-Produced Octad (Ahāraja Ojatthamaka Kalāpas)
Rūpas	1. Earth		▓	▓	▓	▓	▓	▓	▓
	2. Water		▓	▓	▓	▓	▓	▓	▓
	3. Fire		▓	▓	▓	▓	▓	▓	▓
	4. Wind		▓	▓	▓	▓	▓	▓	▓
	5. Color		▓	▓	▓	▓	▓	▓	▓
	6. Odor		▓	▓	▓	▓	▓	▓	▓
	7. Flavor		▓	▓	▓	▓	▓	▓	▓
	8. Nutriment		▓	▓	▓	▓	▓	▓	▓
	9. Life faculty		▓	▓	▓	▓			
	10. Heart-base		▓						
	Body-sensitivity			▓					
	Sex-determining				▓				
Origin	Kamma		▓	▓	▓	▓			
	Mind						▓		
	Temperature							▓	
	Nutriment								▓
Translucent				▓					

⤳ MEDITATION INSTRUCTION 12.4
Analyzing Nonreal, Nonconcrete Materialities

Ten additional material properties are classified as nonreal or non-concrete rūpas. These ten nonreal elements of matter are attributes of real matter and include space, bodily intimation, verbal intimation, and the lightness, pliancy, wieldiness, growth, continuity, aging, and impermanence of concrete material.

To discern these elements, first establish concentration. Then, direct your attention to the materiality of the body, beginning with the six sense doors and proceeding to the thirty-two parts of the body (see Table 12.7). Look for each element one by one. If concentration weakens or your attention falters, refresh attention with a brief return to jhāna, concentration on the breath, or contemplation of the characteristics of the four primary elements. If you have done the previous exercises, you will be able to easily intuit the salient aspects of most of these nonconcrete rūpas while examining the ultimate materiality in each sense base and body part.

Bodily intimation refers to the production of intentional physical movement and involves the activation of the wind element in mind-produced materialities. To facilitate the perception of bodily intimation, carefully observe the changes in the rūpa kalāpas in the heart base, arms, and hand during a small intentional movement such as wiggling a finger or making a simple hand gesture. Observe the mode of the wind element in the mind-produced octad kalāpas that arise during an intentional movement. Similarly, to facilitate the perception of verbal intimation—the production of speech—focus your attention on the mind base and the vocal cords while you utter a sound, such as by reciting the alphabet: a, b, c, d, e. Observe the mode of the earth element in mind-produced octad kalāpas; watch as earth elements collide in the vocal cords to produce sound.

Move back and forth between concentration and the discernment process until you have discerned all the concrete (real) and nonconcrete (unreal) rūpas in each sense base and part of the body. ⤆

PHASE 4: DYNAMIC MATTER

After all the twenty-eight real and unreal rūpas have been seen, as clearly as pieces of a jigsaw puzzle spread out on a table, you may begin to analyze how they interact by observing transformations, movements, and reproduction of matter.

✦ MEDITATION INSTRUCTION 12.5
Analyzing the Dynamics of Matter

Explore the behavior of materialities through three easy-to-practice phases.[199]

Phase one—observing mind-produced materiality. The mind generates materiality that is not translucent and distributed throughout the body. To see the generation of mind-produced materiality, called mind-produced nutritive-essence octad kalāpas, focus your attention on the mind door while you make an intentional movement such as wiggling your fingers, reaching, or moving. The mental impulse to act produces a stream of nutritive-essence octad kalāpas that you can see arising in conjunction with the impulse to move. Find these mind-produced nutritive-essence octad kalāpas first in the heart base, then in all the sense bases, and finally examine the body parts to discover where mind-produced nutritive-essence octad kalāpas are found.

Phase two—observing temperature-produced materiality. The fire element is present in every material formation and is a force that multiplies materiality. Each new material formation also contains fire element that has the potential to reproduce more materiality. To observe this process, discern the fire element in the body, for instance in the eye decad kalāpa, and watch as four or five generations of temperature-produced nutritive-essence octad kalāpas are produced from the fire element of the kamma-produced eye decad kalāpa. Discern the production of temperature-produced nutritive-essence octad kalāpas in the sense bases and body parts.

Phase three—observing nutriment-produced materiality. By this point in the training you will have discerned the fire element of many life nonad kalāpas. Sometimes called digestive fire, they are most powerful in the digestive process. You will also have discovered that there are some parts of the body (undigested food, feces, pus, and urine) that are composed of only temperature-produced nutritive-essence octad kalāpas. When the nutritive essence in temperature-produced nutritive-essence octad kalāpas (such as that found in undigested food) meets the fire element in the life nonad kalāpas (digestive fire), the encounter produces many generations of nutriment-produced materiality. As the nutriment-produced materiality spreads throughout the body, the nutriment that it contains continues to support the production of more materiality when activated by the fire element in life nonad kalāpas.

You can observe the production of nutriment-produced materiality while eating. Place a morsel of food, such as a bite of banana, into your mouth. Discern the four elements in the fruit and the eight rūpas that comprise the temperature-produced octad kalāpas that make up a banana. Discern the four elements in your mouth and the various rūpa kalāpas with their constituent elements that comprise your saliva and tongue. Highlight the fire element in life nonad kalāpas in order to watch how it functions as digestive fire. When the nutritive essence of the chewed fruit meets the fire element of the life nonad kalāpas you will see many generations of nutriment-produced nutritive-essence octad kalāpas born. These newly produced materialities will be nontranslucent and contain eight types of materiality. You can watch as generation after generation of rūpa kalāpas rapidly appear. Observe, bite after bite, as the consumption of a banana produces subtle materiality within your body. After the banana is chewed and swallowed, the process of digestion continues. Focus your attention on the digestion in your stomach and then the intestines to observe the dynamic activity that occurs when the forces of nutriment and digestive fire meet.

As nutriment-produced octad kalāpas spread throughout the body and are in proximity to digestive fire, this nourishing team supports the reproduction of kamma-produced, temperature-produced, and mind-produced materialities. Look for the production of new materiality in all the sense bases and body parts. For example, focus on the eye base and discern the materialities present in the eye by specifically seeing the sixty-three types of rūpas present in the eye base (see Tables 12.3 and 12.4). You will find the fire element of life nonad kalāpas present throughout the body, but to a lesser degree than what is available while eating a fruit. You will find nutriment-produced octad kalāpas, along with kamma-, temperature-, and mind-produced materialities, each of which contains its own nutriment. The nutriment within the kamma-, temperature-, and mind-produced materialities will reproduce when supported by the combined presence of nutriment-produced octad kalāpas and digestive fire. The strength of the nutritive essences determines the exact number of generations each is capable of producing (see Table 12.3).

Engage with these processes as you would an interactive video game. Observe their dynamic qualities, behaviors, and functions as you might enjoy a show on a movie screen. ⬸

PHASE 5: THE HEART OF THIS MATTER

After observing the functions and interactions of the most highly refined and subtle material phenomena, recognize that the entire physical world is composed of material elements. Contemplate all these elements within the body and in the world at large as just material elements. Discern the elemental nature of phenomena with an attention that is clear, concentrated, and unobscured by limiting conceptual labels, identities, and names.

TABLE 12.7

Parts of the Body Organized by Element

Dominant Element	Corresponding Element or Part in the Body	
Earth	Pentad 1:	Head hairs, body hairs, nails, teeth, skin
	Pentad 2:	Flesh, sinews, bones, bone marrow, kidneys
	Pentad 3:	Heart, liver, diaphragm, spleen, lungs
	Pentad 4:	Intestines, mesentery, contents of the stomach, feces, brain
Water	Sextet 1:	Bile, phlegm, pus, blood, sweat, fat
	Sextet 2:	Tears, grease, spittle, snot, oil of the joints, urine
Fire		Heat that warms the body Heat that causes maturing and aging Heat of fever Digestive heat
Wind/air		Air that rises up (e.g. belching) Air that goes down (e.g. passing gas) Air in the abdomen outside the intestines Air inside the intestines Air that pervades through the limbs Air that enters and exits the lungs
Space*		Space in the lungs, mouth, nose, ear, and other doors, organs, and body parts Space between different organs and parts such as between skin and bones Space between and inside rūpa kalāpas

*The space element is not a primary element; it is classified as a derived materiality.

→ MEDITATION INSTRUCTION 12.6
A World of Matter

Review each material element found at each sense door and in the parts of the body. So far we have been working with the classic thirty-two parts. At this stage, the list can be expanded to discern forty-two parts by adding four manifestations of heat and six aspect of wind in the body (see Table 12.7).

Contemplate each element within each part of the body individually and then as a group by reflecting: "This is materiality. This is *rūpa, rūpa*, or *matter, matter*." Next, discern the rūpas in someone sitting nearby, contemplating all material elements as "*matter, matter, just rūpa, rūpa*." Alternate contemplating the elements internally (in your own body) and externally (in something or someone outside of yourself). Repeatedly discern and contemplate the materiality of people near and further away until your analysis encompasses the entire universe.

Include inanimate entities by discerning the eight basic types of rūpas found in nonliving material (earth, water, fire, wind, color, odor, flavor, nutritive essence), starting with something near, such as your clothing, and then gradually extending to the floor, the building, and out into the world. After clearly discerning the eight types of rūpas in each nonliving form, contemplate it as just *rūpa, rūpa, matter, matter*. You can continue to contemplate the materiality of the world while walking, reaching, eating, and moving by observing the interaction of all material forms.[200] ←

Observing the material processes at their most fundamental level, we discover only materiality; there is nothing intrinsically beautiful, nothing that offers a suitable support for happiness.[201] When matter is no longer assumed to be solid and enduring, both blind enchantment with pleasant things and habitual repulsion from unpleasant things will fade.

The four elements meditation is primarily concerned with gathering appropriate objects for vipassanā. We have not emphasized the contemplation of impermanence or emptiness, which will be highlighted at a later stage of vipassanā. Even in this early phase, however, the impermanent, ungraspable, unsatisfactory, and empty nature of matter is starkly obvious. By observing the elemental nature of matter, you'll find that attachment to possessions will naturally diminish, the bonds of sense desire will weaken, and the illusion of substantiality and permanence will break down. You may experience inspiring glimpses of freedom from attachment, gain a deeper understanding that nothing material can be a foundation for your happiness, and experience the lightness and ease that comes with this release.

CHAPTER 13
Nature of Mind: Discerning Ultimate Mentality

No other thing do I know, O monks, that changes
so quickly as the mind. It is not easy to give
a simile for how quickly the mind changes.
—AṄGUTTARA NIKĀYA[202]

O NCE YOU HAVE SHARPENED ATTENTION with strong concentration or jhāna, you are ready to apply this hard-won concentration to develop insight. The next step is to gather all the appropriate objects for contemplation. Chapter 12 explored the nature of materiality. Now we shall examine the nature of mentality. This is perhaps the most technical and detailed segment of the training. Please don't let the long lists or technical terms intimidate you; a patient discernment of these factors and processes will reveal subtle nuances of the mind that are worthy of your careful attention.

Worldly objects are neither intrinsically wholesome nor intrinsically unwholesome. A beautiful sunset, a bitter taste, an overheard argument, a peanut butter cookie, a dead moth, a mother singing a lullaby, a $100 bill—all may prompt a mind to enter fruitful states or unfruitful states. The quality of lived experience is affected by the wholesome or unwholesome mental factors that accompany the cognition. An ice cream sundae could trigger painful craving or it could stimulate joy through virtuous sensory restraint. The sight of a corpse may startle an untrained mind into aversive states or inspire a meditator to enter the wholesome states of jhāna. The smell of road kill might spark fear, disgust, or sadness, or it might lead to a fruitful reflection on impermanence. How you apply your attention will determine whether an object functions as an obstacle or as an asset to concentration. Venerable Pa-Auk Sayadaw explains:

> One may go for a walk in the forest, and one may enjoy the flowers, trees, bird singing, and so on, delighting in the "beauty of nature": that is sensual pleasure. Such consciousnesses are associated with pleasant feeling, but they are greed-rooted consciousness: greed-rooted consciousness is not wholesome; it is unwholesome. If however, one enjoys the forest because it is void of people and therefore suitable for meditation, or if one enjoys beautiful flowers with the wholesome intention to use the individual flower as an object to practice the color kasiṇas, or if one enjoys the forest with the wholesome intention to contemplate the ultimate phenomena of the flowers, and trees (analyzing them into the four great essentials and derived materiality), then to contemplate them as impermanent, suffering, and non-self, that enjoyment is not unwholesome. Also, if one enjoys the beautiful flowers as an offering to the Buddha, the pagoda, the Bodhi tree, or one's teacher, that is also wholesome. It depends on one's attention: enjoying flowers for their beauty is pleasant feeling associated with unwise attention; enjoying flowers in the wholesome ways we just explained is pleasant feeling associated with wise attention.[203]

The primary factor that perpetuates unwise attention is delusion—mistaking experiences to be what they are not. When there is contact with a sensory object, consciousness is supported by a cluster of associated mental factors; this consciousness may be affected by wisdom or delusion. When attention is supported by wisdom, the meditator will be able to delve below the superficial conceptual constructs, to know the experience as it actually is—simply impermanent material and mental phenomena that lack individual substance.

The Abhidhamma analysis provides a carefully drafted map of consciousness and the mental factors that arise with every moment of consciousness.[204] This refined model enhances and elaborates on models introduced in the earlier Discourses of the Buddha and defines a precise technical vocabulary used to deconstruct broad conventional concepts into irreducible constituents of experience—factors, functions, components, intervals, causes, and moments. Through meditation we look deeper into the truth of things, rather than settle for superficial, conventional, or broadly sweeping notions. We see the components of existence as raw phenomena. The thrilling precision of this approach is completely devoid of personal drama. Through direct observation you will recognize, with vividness and certainty, that there is no person, me, you, brother, monk, student, or president; no entity; no inherently existing being that possesses experience. Without attachment to our personal narrative, we investigate and map how the mind functions.

THE FIFTY-TWO MENTAL FACTORS

The building blocks of this system include fifty-two primary mental factors, categorized as wholesome, unwholesome, universal, and occasional. When arranged in various combinations, they generate emotions, sensory perceptions, and mental experiences. Each factor represents a piece of the jigsaw puzzle of perception, revealing the complex process of cognition and exposing the conditionality of every conceivable experience.

The fifty-two mental factors always occur in conjunction with consciousness. The relationship between consciousness and the associated mental factors is traditionally compared to a king and his retinue. Although one might say, "the king is coming," a king does not travel alone. He is always accompanied by attendants. Consciousness and the associated mental factors are functionally interdependent; they will always arise and cease together, have the same object, and share the same sensory base.[205]

In this book I have chosen to include both consciousness *(citta)* and the mental factors associated with consciousness *(cetasikas)* together in the numbering scheme when summarizing the mental formations present in any given mind-moment. It is also a valid approach to list consciousness

TABLE 13.1
Fifty-Two Mental Factors

THIRTEEN ETHICALLY VARIABLE FACTORS	TWENTY-FIVE BEAUTIFUL FACTORS
Universals (7):	*Universals (19):*
Contact *(phassa)*	Faith *(saddhā)*
Feeling *(vedanā)*	Mindfulness *(sati)*
Perception *(saññā)*	Shame of wrongdoing *(hiri)*
Volition *(cetanā)*	Fear of wrongdoing *(ottappa)*
One-pointedness *(ekaggatā)*	Nongreed *(alobha)*
Life faculty *(jīvitindriya)*	Nonhatred *(adosa)*
Attention *(manasikāra)*	Evenness of mind *(tatramajjhattatā)*
	Tranquility of mental body *(kāyapassaddhi)*
Occasionals (6):	Tranquility of consciousness *(cittapassaddhi)*
Initial application *(vitakka)*	Lightness of mental body *(kāyalahutā)*
Sustained application *(vicāra)*	Lightness of consciousness *(cittalahutā)*
Decision *(adhimokkha)*	Malleability of mental body *(kāyamudutā)*
Energy *(viriya)*	Malleability of consciousness *(cittamudutā)*
Rapture *(pīti)*	Workability of mental body *(kāyakammaññatā)*
Desire *(chanda)*	Workability of consciousness *(cittakammaññatā)*
	Proficiency of mental body *(kāyapāguññatā)*
FOURTEEN UNWHOLESOME FACTORS	Proficiency of consciousness *(cittapāguññatā)*
Universals (4):	Uprightness of mental body *(kāyujjukatā)*
Delusion *(moha)*	Uprightness of consciousness *(cittujjukatā)*
Shamelessness of wrongdoing *(ahirika)*	
Fearlessness of wrongdoing *(anottappa)*	*Occasionals (6):*
Restlessness *(uddhacca)*	Right speech *(sammāvācā)*
	Right action *(sammākammanta)*
Occasionals (10):	Right livelihood *(sammāājīva)*
Greed *(lobha)*	Compassion *(karuṇā)*
Wrong view *(diṭṭhi)*	Appreciative joy *(muditā)*
Conceit *(māna)*	Wisdom faculty *(paññā)*
Hatred *(dosa)*	
Envy *(issā)*	
Possessiveness *(macchariya)*	
Worry *(kukkucca)*	
Sloth *(thīna)*	
Torpor *(middha)*	
Doubt *(vicikicchā)*	

separately from the associated mental factors. If consciousness had been extracted from the list and counted separately, the tables and exercises would appear to show the mind containing one less mental formation. If you practice carefully, however, not memorizing quantities, but studying the specifics presented in the tables and then actually discerning the constituents of mind, you will know exactly what is present and absent in your mind.

The fifty-two mental factors described below are classified as subtle or ultimate realities because the characteristics and functions of each factor are intrinsic to that factor and cannot be further distilled.

Consciousness plus seven associated universal mental factors compose the *eight universal mental components* of all conscious processes: consciousness (of the object being perceived), contact (of the object being perceived), feeling (of the object being perceived), perception (of the object being perceived), volition (orientated toward the object being perceived), one-pointedness (on the object being perceived), life faculty (that sustains these associated factors as they function to perceive the object), and attention (to the object being perceived). They are universal in the sense that they are required for any cognitive process to occur.

Six occasional mental factors can arise in jhāna or when encountering sensory phenomena: initial application of attention, sustained attention, decision, energy, rapture, and desire. Since they are not present in every mind-moment, they are called occasional factors.

There are *four unwholesome universal mental factors* that always arise together and are universally present in any unwholesome cognitive process: delusion, lack of inner conscience or the shamelessness of wrongdoing, fearlessness of wrongdoing or the lack of social or moral concern, and restlessness.

Ten occasional unwholesome factors, in various combinations, can be found in unwholesome states: greed, wrong view, conceit, hatred, envy, possessiveness, worry, sloth, torpor, and doubt. These factors provide the particular character that we might recognize as a stingy impulse, a greedy desire, a dullness to the mind, or regret about an action. These ten occasional factors combine with other associated mental factors in manifestations of the basic root defilements of greed, hatred, and delusion.

There are *nineteen beautiful universal factors* that arise in all whole-some states. These include faith, mindfulness, shame regarding wrong-doing (a moral conscience that depends on respect for self), fear of wrongdoing (a moral concern that depends on respect for others), non-greed, nonhatred, evenness of mind (equanimity); plus six qualities that are attributed both to the associated mental factors and consciousness: tranquility, lightness, malleability, workability, proficiency, and upright-ness. These factors are included in every wholesome state—a moment of generosity, an expression of loving-kindness, a moment with mindful attention to the breath, a reflection on renunciation, concentration on the nimitta—and they manifest vividly in jhāna and vipassanā practice.

The *three aspects of abstinence or restraint* include right speech, right action, and right livelihood. These factors magnify the mental impulse to not cause harm through our physical and verbal actions. Although they are wholesome factors, they are not universal features of every whole-some state. They arise on occasions when one deliberately refrains from wrongdoing at a time when an opportunity to transgress has arisen. For example, when you have an opportunity to steal, but resist the tempta-tion, the factor of right action has arisen to support restraint. When you have an opportunity to tell a lie, but choose to not deceive your friend, the factor of right speech is supporting restraint. When an unethical business opportunity is present and you choose to pass it by, right liveli-hood is actively supporting restraint. These three occasional factors are not found in jhāna consciousnesses since in jhāna the object is the coun-terpart sign *(nimitta),* not a potential action. These three abstinences also do not arise in the mind of a fully enlightened being *(arahant)* dur-ing mundane activities; because all unwholesome tendencies have been eradicated, there is no need for restraint. They will, however, occur simul-taneously with the supramundane path and fruition attainments at all four stages of enlightenment (chapter 18), eliminating any residual dispo-sition to engage in wrong speech, wrong action, or wrong livelihood.

There are two additional factors called *immeasurable qualities*—compassion *(karuṇā)* and appreciative joy *(muditā)*—which are classi-fied as occasional wholesome factors. These provide the unique flavor to states of compassion and appreciative joy, which you may have experi-enced with the practices introduced in chapter 8. Since loving-kindness

and equanimity are classified as specific modes of the factors of nonhatred (loving-kindness), and neutrality (equanimity), they are not designated separately in this list.

And last, but not least, in the list of fifty-two mental factors is *nondelusion (amoha), knowledge (ñāṇa),* or *wisdom (paññā)*: these terms are used
synonymously in the Abhidhamma. The factor of wisdom penetrates phenomena according to their real nature to reveal things as they actually are.
This is an occasional factor that does not arise in every state, not even every
wholesome state. For example, you might be equanimous and mindful of
a sensation but not have penetrated the real nature of that sensation. You
may become concentrated upon the color of a yellow flower, but without
the support of wisdom you might conceive of the flower as enduring.

→ MEDITATION INSTRUCTION 13.1
Observing Mind-Body Responses

1. Establish concentration and discern real and unreal matter *(rūpa)*
   by reviewing the exercises in chapter 12. Discern the heart base and
   then look for all the various material phenomena (twenty-eight
   material phenomena) found in each sense door and throughout
   the body. As you see the various components of matter, notice
   that there is a mental process that accompanies the knowing of the
   matter. Mind and matter function together to enable cognition.

2. Now, focus your attention on the mind that knows the matter.
   If you see the material objects with the wisdom that recognizes
   matter as impermanent material formations, wholesome mental factors will arise in conjunction with the perception of that
   object. Notice those wholesome factors. If the perception of
   the material phenomena is accompanied by attachment, aversion, lust, or ignorance, unwholesome mental factors will arise.
   Observe those unwholesome factors.

3. Mental states are not dependent upon the object perceived, but
   upon how you perceive them. How do you relate to the things
   that you see, hear, smell, taste, touch, and cognize?

Experiment: Notice a painful sensation of pressure while maintaining the well-grounded perception that it is an imperma-nent experience that has an excess of earth and wind elements; you'll find that the mind remains calm and equanimous, and that only wholesome mental states arise. Notice pain again, but entertain a little angst, fear, irritation, or thoughts of blame; you'll find that unwholesome mental states follow.

It is also possible that an object generally considered beneficial, such as a Buddha image, could trigger wholesome states of faith in a meditator, but anger or fear in a fundamentalist of another religion, or greed in a thief who covets the Buddha image for per-sonal wealth. As the saying goes, "when a thief meets a saint, he only sees his pockets." Our attitude determines what we perceive and how we interpret it. By what features do you distinguish the difference between a wholesome and unwholesome state?

4. Observe some of the mental states that arise in the course of your day. When you must endure an irritating sound, such as a lawn mower, rather than judging the sound or becoming gener-ally aware of the irritation, try to discern the components that make up irritation. For example you might recognize the pres-ence of hatred, restlessness, a feeling tone, and the absence of delight, malleability, and mindfulness. Try to discern the eight-een or twenty mental factors that compose an angry state (see Table 13.7). Recognize the root of anger that is operating in the moment of contact with the sound. Similarly, when you smell freshly baked apricot strudel, notice the mental factors that are present—a greedy response might include greed, restlessness, delusion, and attention, and not include faith, tranquility, or wisdom. Try to discern the nineteen to twenty-two mental fac-tors that are present when there is greed for sensual pleasure. Contrast your experience of unwholesome mental states with the quality of wholesome mental states. For example, notice your experience while helping someone, giving a gift, or studying Dhamma. Try to discern the thirty-four mental formations that

may be present during those wholesome actions. At this initial point in the discerning of mentality, all the details may not yet be clear, but you might already be able to notice the general character of mind during wholesome and unwholesome actions and recognize that each is characterized by a different set of mental factors. The exercises that follow will provide more precise methods for analyzing the subtleties of each state. ←

→ **MEDITATION INSTRUCTION 13.2**
Discerning Mental Formations Characteristic of Jhāna

1. A meditator who has already established jhāna with the breath, a kasiṇa, or the repulsive meditation subjects will find it easiest to begin with the thirty-four mental formations associated with wholesome states (consciousness plus thirty-three associated mental factors). To begin, memorize the list of mental factors associated with jhāna (see Table 13.2). If you had chosen compassion or appreciative joy as your meditation subject, the additional factor of either compassion or appreciative joy would increase the quantity by one additional mental factor in an experience of first jhāna.

2. Establish jhāna meditation using the breath or a kasiṇa of your choice. Upon emerging from absorption direct your attention to the heart base. When the nimitta appears in the heart base, discern the relevant jhāna factors. You will find five jhāna factors in the first jhāna (vitakka, vicāra, pīti, sukha, ekaggatā), three jhāna factors in the second jhāna (pīti, sukha, ekaggatā), two jhāna factors in both the third (sukha, ekaggatā) and the fourth (upekkhā, ekaggatā) jhānas. You might recall that when you first learned to discern the jhāna factors in the mind door (chapter 4), you did so one at a time by repeatedly shifting back and forth between absorption and discerning the jhāna factors at the mind door until you could easily recognize which were present and which were absent.

TABLE 13.2
Mental Formations Associated with Jhāna

ONE CONSCIOUSNESS FORMATION	TWENTY-TWO BEAUTIFUL FACTORS
1. Consciousness *(citta)*	*Universals (19):*
	15.Faith *(saddhā)*
	16.Mindfulness *(sati)*
THIRTEEN ETHICALLY VARIABLE FACTORS	17.Shame of wrongdoing *(hiri)*
	18.Fear of wrongdoing *(ottappa)*
Universals (7):	19.Nongreed *(alobha)*
2. Contact *(phassa)*	20.Nonhatred *(adosa)*
3. Feeling *(vedanā)*	21.Evenness of mind *(tatramajjhattatā)*
4. Perception *(saññā)*	22.Tranquility of mental body *(kāyapassaddhi)*
5. Volition *(cetanā)*	23.Tranquility of consciousness *(cittapassaddhi)*
6. One-pointedness *(ekaggatā)*	24.Lightness of mental body *(kāyalahutā)*
7. Life faculty *(jīvitindriya)*	25.Lightness of consciousness *(cittalahutā)*
8. Attention *(manasikāra)*	26.Malleability of mental body *(kāyamudutā)*
Occasionals (6):	27.Malleability of consciousness *(cittamudutā)*
9. Initial application *(vitakka)*	28.Workability of mental body *(kāyakammaññatā)*
10.Sustained application *(vicāra)*	29.Workability of consciousness *(cittakammaññatā)*
11.Decision *(adhimokkha)*	30.Proficiency of mental body *(kāyapāguññatā)*
12.Energy *(viriya)*	31.Proficiency of consciousness *(cittapāguññatā)*
13.Rapture *(pīti)*	32.Uprightness of mental body *(kāyujjukatā)*
14.Desire *(chanda)*	33.Uprightness of consciousness *(cittujjukatā)*
	Occasionals (3):
	34.Wisdom faculty *(paññā)*
	35.Compassion *(karunā)*
	36.Appreciative joy *(muditā)*

3. Proceed in a similar manner to discern each of the wholesome
    factors associated with jhāna. In this practice you will be alternat-
    ing between moments when the mind is absorbed in jhāna and
    moments of actively discerning mental factors. Contemplate the
    factors in a cumulative but sequential order. First discern con-
    sciousness; include contact, so you are discerning consciousness and
    contact together; include feeling, so you are discerning conscious-
    ness, contact, and feeling together; include perception, so you are
    discerning consciousness, contact, feeling, and perception together.
    Continue until you are observing all the factors at a glance.

4. With the breath or a kasiṇa as object, you will find thirty-one
    mental formations in the third, fourth, and immaterial jhānas;
    thirty-two formations in the second jhāna; and thirty-four for-
    mations in the first jhāna (see Table 13.2). If you are analyzing
    karuṇā or muditā jhānas as the base, the additional factor of
    compassion or appreciative joy will be obvious. To genuinely dis-
    cern these factors you must return to jhāna frequently so that the
    nimitta continues to appear in the mind door at the heart base.
    It may feel as though you are merely touching into jhāna; a few
    seconds in jhāna will be enough. This exercise emphasizes dis-
    cerning mental formations, not sustained absorption; however,
    you must still enter jhāna, if only briefly, to generate the forma-
    tions that you will discern. You might then observe the factors
    in groupings, frequently moving back and forth between the
    modes of absorption and discernment. With practice you will
    learn to perceive all the wholesome jhāna factors at a glance as
    easily as you can see ten fingers when you stretch out your hands.

5. After clearly discerning all the factors that arise with jhāna
    individually and collectively, contemplate them as elements of
    mentality *(nāmas);* they are just mentality. Notice that men-
    tality has the characteristic of bending toward its object. You
    might mentally recite *nāma, nāma, nāma* or *mental phenom-*
    ena, mental phenomena to direct your attention to the simple
    fact that they are nothing more than mental constituents.

6. In this way, discern the mental factors associated with every jhāna subject that you have previously learned. For those of you who have accomplished all the subjects offered in the previous section, it may take several hours to review them all, and the exercise may appear redundant since the mental factors remain virtually the same for each jhāna object. Repeated practice increases agility, proficiency, speed, and clarity of attention and is an effective exercise for training the mind.

This exercise will expand your comprehension of jhāna—there is more to a jhāna state than the basic five jhāna factors that were emphasized in the formative stages of concentration practice. ←

THE COGNITIVE PROCESS

Although multitasking has a certain appeal in our fast-paced contemporary society, it is an illusion. We can only be aware of one thing at a time. Consciousness always arises with a specific object that it cognizes, and only one object can occur in any conscious moment. It appears as though we are seeing the orange color of the carrot in our bowl, tasting the flavor of salt in the vegetable broth, feeling the warmth of the soup, listening to music on the radio, and feeling the ache of tired feet, all at the same time. In reality, however, these sensory impressions are processed in rapid succession.

The subtle interplay of matter and mind can be observed and analyzed. A material element is known through the combined process of seventeen consciousnesses. A rūpa is traditionally thought to exist for a duration of sixteen mind-moments and perishes with the occurrence of the seventeenth mind-moment. If each consciousness is divided into three briefer moments—arising, standing, and perishing—the existence of a rūpa is then calculated at fifty-one mind-moments ($17 \times 3 = 51$), with one brief moment of arising, forty-nine brief mind-moments of standing, and one small mind-moment of perishing. According to ancient Buddhist theory, mental and material phenomena arise together in mutual dependence and yet exist for different durations: "Herein, although materiality is slow to cease and heavy to change and consciousness is quick to cease and swift to change, [nevertheless] the material cannot occur without the immaterial, nor the immaterial without the material." It is likened to a tall man and a dwarf who travel together; a single stride of the tall man is matched by multiple strides of the dwarf as their journeys occur together.[206]

By observing the fifty-two mental factors that combine to form various mental and emotional impressions, you have seen how clusters of components interact to produce experience. This represents a significant departure from the conventional mode of identifying with our personal narratives of continuous experience. The Abhidhamma further enhances this distillation of phenomena into their ultimate constituents by presenting an analytical model that reduces each cognitive process into seventeen discrete momentary events. In this training we will discover a seventeen-part cognitive series for sense-sphere cognitive processes, and a variable number of sequences for mind-door cognitive processes.

Discerning the precise mental formations that arise in each segment of the seventeen mind-moment sequence is a subtle endeavor that requires intense concentration, stillness, and patience. Strong concentration is emphasized in the first half of this book in order to train the mind to properly hold subtle objects for sustained examination. But now, rather than meditating upon objects that enhance the stability of concentration, you are meditating upon these ultimate constituents of mind and matter as they are actually occurring. Just as it is possible to focus on one car in a motor race and watch how it moves through the pack in the midst of potential distractions—other contestants racing past at incredible speeds, flashing colors, dust, smoke, roar of engines, cheers of spectators—you can observe the mental formations that arise and pass in the speedy whirl of cognition.

This meditation practice invites you to end habitual fascination with concepts and enter into an intimate and clear encounter with reality. As mindfulness, concentration, and understanding deepen, the minutely incremental nature of the cognitive process is exposed. Through this examination of the minutia of cognition, you will realize again and again that experience is merely an impersonal series of conditioned events.

OVERVIEW OF THE COGNITIVE SERIES

Mind-door processes take mental formations, materialities, and concepts as objects; these function through a variable series of consciousnesses. Sense-door processes, also called five-door processes, reflect objects that occur via the five sense bases of eye, ear, nose, tongue, and body; these function in accordance with a standard sequence of seventeen consciousnesses.

We shall dissect the cognitive processes to reveal a series of momentary occurrences of consciousnesses; these events may be called "mind-moments." Each momentary unit includes consciousness unified with a set of associated mental factors. These factors represent various combinations of the fifty-two mental factors introduced earlier in this chapter. Each mental factor performs a specific function in its momentary cluster. For example, feeling produces the pleasant, unpleasant, or neutral flavor of the contact; applied thought directs attention to the object; rapture experiences delight in the object; perception recognizes the object; and so on. The mental factors arise together, perform their specialized function within their unit, and pass away together as soon as they have originated, thereby forming an uninterrupted continuum of momentary events. Once you have carefully examined the mental factors contained in each mind-moment, you may progress to examine the role that each moment of consciousness plays within the cognitive series.

Each refined moment of consciousness is designated by a term that describes its function within the cognitive series such as adverting, sense-door sensitivity, receiving, investigating, determining, and so on. There are seventeen parts in the sense-door processes and a variable number of stages in the mind-door and jhāna processes. See Tables 13.3 and 13.4.

TABLE 13.3
Seventeen Consciousnesses in Sense-Sphere Cognitive Process

Life-continuum	Vibration of life-continuum	Arresting of life-continuum	Five-door adverting	Sense-door	Receiving	Investigating	Determining	Seven impulsions	Two registrations*
1	2	3	4	5	6	7	8	9–15	16–17

* Registration consciousnesses do not arise in all sense-door processes. They only occur with vivid sense-sphere objects.

TABLE 13.4
Variable Consciousnesses in Mind-Door Cognitive Process

Life-continuum	Mind-door adverting	Impulsions[1]	Two registrations[2]
1	2	3–9	10–11

1 The number of impulsions vary. There are usually seven impulsions, but jhāna can have more and particularly weak objects can have fewer.

2 Registration consciousnesses do not arise in all mind-door processes. They cannot arise when the object is a concept; they occur only with vivid sense-sphere objects. Thus, they are not a part of jhāna cognitive processes, and they do not accompany states, such as loving-kindness, that depend on the concept of "beings."

The first three steps (life-continuum consciousness, vibrational life-continuum consciousness, and arresting life-continuum consciousness) identify the phases in which the activation of the life-continuum consciousness causes the dormant phase to cease, and enables consciousness to emerge from that resting phase *(bhavaṅga)* between processes. These first few moments in the chain are ultrasubtle and usually occur below the threshold of awareness. Because it is very difficult to discern these formations, we shall initially focus on the more vivid elements of consciousness. After you learn the meditative procedure and become facile with the discernment, you will be able to discern these ultrasubtle consciousness moments as well.

After these initial three moments pass, the mind is capable of orienting toward sensory phenomena (five-door adverting consciousness). Sense-door consciousness occurs and sparks a rapid chain of infinitesimal mind-moments oriented toward that particular sensory input. The sensory object is received, examined, and a determination is made regarding how the mind will relate to it. The determination may bring a wholesome or unwholesome response. A series of consciousnesses called impulsion consciousnesses *(javana)* immediately follow from the determination and produce the more notable and vivid component of experience. With the impulsion consciousnesses, the person is fully experiencing the object through a repeated sequence of momentary consciousness units that are characterized by exactly the same set of mental factors. Because they are identical in character, they may at first appear to the meditator as one long moment; however, as the discernment becomes increasingly refined, you will be able to discern, and even count, the arising and passing of each of the seven distinct impulsion mind-moments. Finally, the last two registration consciousnesses permit the process to quiet down and settle before sliding back into the transitional life-continuum phase of cognition.

A mind-door cognitive process operates through a similar, but abbreviated, sequence. The steps that are needed to orient to a sense door, and engage with sensory information through receiving, investigating, and determining, are not required. Mind-door objects arise directly as mental phenomena and are instantly received by the mind without the need to interpret data from the five sense doors.

The refined resolution of this examination invites repeated observation of the functioning of subtle and causally connected events until each momentary arising is distinctly and certainly seen through the direct knowledge of the meditator. This is a pragmatic endeavor, not an intellectual pursuit. Therefore, it requires strong concentration and a steady mind.

Jhāna consciousness is especially potent and can produce an extended series of impulsion consciousnesses; therefore it is the easiest process for the meditator to discern. If you have already discerned the mental factors that arise within jhāna (meditation instruction 13.2), the basic constituents will be familiar. Now we shall analyze those mental factors according to the cognitive series and discern them in the order in which they perform the function of cognition.

✦ MEDITATION INSTRUCTION 13.3
Discerning the Jhāna Cognitive Process

1. To begin, reestablish the first jhāna with the breath or a kasiṇa of your choice. Direct your attention to the mind door at the heart base and discern the jhāna factors and mental formations as you practiced in meditation instruction 13.2. You may shift between absorption in jhāna and the discerning process until it is clear.

2. After emerging from jhāna and perceiving the appearance of a reflection of the nimitta in the mind door, focus on the jhāna mind-door processes that just occurred. You will find that twelve mental formations arise in the initial mind-moment, followed by a stream of momentary events that contain thirty-four mental factors (consciousnesses plus thirty-three associated mental factors).

3. This discernment procedure is similar to the previous discernment; however, now you will be attentive to the functions of consciousness in a sequential process, noting at a glance the individual mental factors that permit each consciousness to perform

its special role in the jhāna cognitive process. The sequence of mind-moments in the jhāna cognitive process are named according to their functions: mind-door adverting consciousness, preparatory consciousness, access consciousness, conformity consciousness, change of lineage consciousness, and jhāna impulsion consciousness (see Table 13.5).

4. Notice the characteristic that is common to all mental phenomena—they bend toward their object. Recognize this characteristic of mentality in each of the momentary occurrences of consciousness.

5. Proceed to discern and analyze the cognitive processes associated with the second, third, and fourth jhānas. You will find that the second jhāna has the same initial twelve formations (consciousness plus eleven associated mental factors), followed by a brief spike of thirty-four factors (consciousness plus thirty-three associated mental factors) as the mind orients toward the object, and then settles into a stream of thirty-two mental formations (consciousness plus thirty-one associated mental factors) that compose the subsequent impulsion consciousnesses. The third, fourth, and immaterial jhānas will contain the initial twelve formations, followed by thirty-one formations in the impulsion consciousness. The fourth and immaterial jhānas invariably exclude pīti at every stage of the cognitive process.

6. Proceed to review each and every jhāna that you have attained. The pattern will be similar, with the addition of compassion or appreciative joy pertinent to those immeasurable attainments. ✦

TABLE 13.5

Mental Formations Present in Jhāna

JHĀNA	TYPE OF CONSCIOUSNESS	Mind-door adverting	Preparatory	Access	Conformity	Change of lineage	Jhāna impulsion
First	12	34	34	34	34	34
Second	12	34	34	34	34	32^1
Third	12	34	34	34	34	31^2
Fourth	12	33^3	33	33	33	31^4
Immaterial	12	33^3	33	33	33	31^5

1 Initial and sustained applications of mind have been removed.

2 Rapture has been further removed.

3 Rapture does not arise with fourth or immaterial jhānas therefore there are only thirty-three factors that precede the impulsion consciousness.

4 Equanimity replaces happiness as the feeling tone.

5 Factors remain similar to fourth jhāna.

TABLE 13.6
First Jhāna Cognitive Process with Associated Mental Formations

ASSOCIATED MENTAL FACTORS	TYPE OF CONSCIOUSNESS	Mind-door adverting	Preparatory	Access	Conformity	Change of lineage	Jhāna impulsion
1. Consciousness							
2. Contact							
3. Feeling							
4. Perception							
5. Volition							
6. One-pointedness							
7. Life faculty							
8. Attention							
9. Initial application							
10. Sustained application							
11. Decision							
12. Energy							
13. Rapture							
14. Desire							
15. Faith							
16. Mindfulness							
17. Shame of wrongdoing							
18. Fear of wrongdoing							
19. Nongreed							

20. Nonhatred						
21. Evenness of mind						
22. Tranquility of mental formations						
23. Tranquility of consciousness						
24. Lightness of mental formations						
25. Lightness of consciousness						
26. Malleability of mental formations						
27. Malleability of consciousness						
28. Workability of mental formations						
29. Workability of consciousness						
30. Proficiency of mental formations						
31. Proficiency of consciousness						
32. Uprightness of mental formations						
33. Uprightness of consciousness						
34. Wisdom, nondelusion						

Note: For jhānas based on appreciative joy and compassion, you will find the additional factor of joy and compassion.

MIND-DOOR COGNITIVE PROCESSES

Mind-door processes occur every time you are aware of a thought, concept, idea, emotion, material formation, or mental factor; they are not exclusive to jhāna states. When you think about a past event, imagine a variation of that event occurring in the future, rehearse how you might respond to it, and plan what you will say, you are engaging mental processes. If you are inclined to a revenge fantasy or an anxious state, you will be engaged in unwholesome mind-door processes. Not recognizing that these are merely momentary mental processes, you might give credence to the mental constructions and fabricate an illusion of continuity, imagine who you are and how you will be over time: "I am an angry person," or "I am an anxious person." In reality it is only a sequence of conditioned momentary factors.

The mind-door cognitive process (excluding jhāna and supramundane processes) contains three primary phases, each with corresponding mental factors. The three primary phases in a mind-door process are the following:

1. A mind-door adverting consciousness composed of consciousness plus eleven associated mental factors making a total of twelve mental formations.

2. Seven impulsion consciousnesses with variable mental formations:
   (a) If there is unwise attention and the mental state is unwholesome, there can be sixteen, eighteen, nineteen, twenty, twenty-one, or twenty-two mental formations.
   (b) If there is wise attention and the mental state is wholesome, there can be thirty-two, thirty-three, thirty-four, or thirty-five mental formations.

3. Two registration consciousnesses that will contain either thirty-four, thirty-three, thirty-two, twelve, or eleven mental formations. Registration consciousnesses do not occur in all mind-door processes. They require a vivid sense-sphere object. Since registration consciousnesses cannot arise when the object is a concept, they are not a part of jhāna cognitive processes, and they do not accompany states, such as lovingkindness, that depend on the concept of "beings."

Our examination will focus on these three active elements, postponing the formations of the ultrasubtle life-continuum consciousnesses *(bhavaṅga)* for a later stage in the meditative discernment. Meditators can employ this careful analysis of the momentary nature of cognition to break down the delusion that things are solid, enduring, and stable. When we look carefully, we only find fleeting contingent processes that function for a brief moment and vanish. In reality, there is nothing substantial to bind us; clear seeing dispels the only effective fetter—the fetter of ignorance.

TABLE 13.7

Formations that Comprise the Impulsion Consciousness of Unwholesome Mental States

Associated Mental Factors	Type of Mental State	Greed-based view	Greed-based conceit	Hatred/anger	Hate-based envy	Hate-based possessiveness	Hate-based worry	Delusion-based restlessness	Delusion-based doubt
Consciousness									
Ethically variable universals:									
Contact									
Feeling									
Perception									
Volition									
One-pointedness									
Life faculty									
Attention									
Ethically variable occasionals:									
Initial application									
Sustained application									
Decision									
Energy									

Table continues on next page

Associated Mental Factors	Type of Mental State	Greed-based view	Greed-based conceit	Hatred/anger	Hate-based envy	Hate-based possessiveness	Hate-based worry	Delusion-based restlessness	Delusion-based doubt
Rapture		*	*						
Desire		▓	▓	▓	▓	▓	▓		
Unwholesome univerals:									
Delusion		▓	▓	▓	▓	▓	▓	▓	▓
Shamelessness of wrongdoing		▓	▓	▓	▓	▓	▓	▓	▓
Fearlessness of wrongdoing		▓	▓	▓	▓	▓	▓	▓	▓
Restlessness		▓	▓	▓	▓	▓	▓	▓	▓
Unwholesome occasionals:									
Greed		▓	▓						
Wrong view		▓							
Conceit			▓						
Hatred				▓	▓	▓	▓		
Envy					▓				
Possessiveness						▓			
Worry							▓		
Sloth		*	*	*	*	*	*		

Associated Mental Factors	Type of Mental State	Greed-based view	Greed-based conceit	Hatred/anger	Hate-based envy	Hate-based possessiveness	Hate-based worry	Delusion-based restlessness	Delusion-based doubt
Torpor		*	*	*	*	*	*		
Doubt									
Total:		19–22	19–22	18 or 20	19 or 21	19 or 21	19 or 21	16	16

*These factors are variable—they may or may not be present where indicated. Their presence or absence accounts for the variable number of factors for some of the unwholesome mind states. Sloth and torpor always appear together.

→ **MEDITATION INSTRUCTION 13.4**
Discerning the Mind-Door Cognitive Process

1. Establish strong concentration.

2. The discernment of the mind-door cognitive process will focus primarily on three aspects: the mind-door adverting, impulsion, and registration consciousnesses (Table 13.4). Discern the materiality supporting the mind door (sixty-three rūpas of the heart base) and then the eye-sensitive element (the translucent element that you discerned in chapter 12).

3. When the eye-sensitive element appears in consciousness, recognize it with wise attention. Know that this is the eye-sensitive element, this is materiality, or this is impermanent. Wise attention supports the occurrence of a wholesome cognition.

4. Discern the different clusters of mental formation that are
   included in the three primary phases of the mind-door cognitive
   process that is knowing the eye-sensitive element. Do this precisely and carefully.

   (a) Start with the first phase—a mind-door adverting consciousness. Discern the twelve mental formations. You might begin
   with consciousness; when you recognize it clearly, discern
   consciousness and contact; then consciousness, contact, and
   feeling; then consciousness, contact, feeling, and perception; continuing until you have included all twelve factors:
   (1) consciousness, (2) contact, (3) feeling, (4) perception, (5)
   volition, (6) one-pointedness, (7) life faculty, (8) attention,
   (9) initial application, (10) sustained attention, (11) decision,
   and (12) energy.

   (b) Next, examine the impulsion consciousnesses that are experiencing the eye-sensitive element. Although these occur in the
   midst of the sequence, these represent the basic experience of
   the object and will be most clear. Discern the mental factors
   that are present until you determine which specific factors
   flavor the cognition.

   (c) Notice that the impulsion consciousness is not one steady
   formation, but arises as a series of repeated momentary events
   that contain identical factors and respond to the same object
   (in this case, the perception of the eye-sensitive element). Try
   to count the seven impulsion consciousnesses.

   (d) Similarly, if two registration consciousnesses arise, discern
   their associated mental formations. The number of factors
   may vary with the occasional presence or absence of joy and
   wisdom.

   (e) Repeat this discernment until it is clear.

5. Follow the same method using each of the twenty-eight kinds of
   ultimate materiality discerned in chapter 12 to stimulate a mind-
   door cognitive process. ←

SENSE-SPHERE COGNITIVE PROCESS

Since the cognitive process associated with the five sense-spheres (also called the five-door process) is neither inherently wholesome nor unwholesome, meditators must discern the mental factors that contribute to the skillful or unskillful bias of each experience. Exposing these subtle inclinations of perception can transform your relationship to conditioned events, providing a means for purifying habitual patterns, actions, and thoughts.

TABLE 13.8

Mental Formations in Wholesome Five-Door Cognitive Processes

ASSOCIATED MENTAL FORMATIONS	TYPES OF CONSCIOUSNESS	Five-door adverting	Sense-door	Receiving	Investigating	Determining	Impulsion (×7)	Registration (×2)	Life-continuum	Mind-door adverting[1]	Impulsion (×7)[2]	Registration (×2)[3]
1. Consciousness												
Ethically variable universals:												
2. Contact												
3. Feeling												
4. Perception												
5. Volition												
6. One-pointedness												
7. Life faculty												
8. Attention												

Table continues on next page

Associated Mental Formations	Types of Consciousness	Five-door adverting	Sense-door	Receiving	Investigating	Determining	Impulsion (×7)	Registration (×2)	Life-continuum	Mind-door adverting[1]	Impulsion (×7)[2]	Registration (×2)[3]

Ethically variable occasionals:

9. Initial application		▓		▓	▓	▓	▓	▓		▓	▓	
10. Sustained application		▓		▓	▓	▓	▓	▓		▓	▓	
11. Decision		▓		▓	▓	▓	▓	▓		▓	▓	
12. Energy						▓	▓	▓		▓	▓	▓
13. Rapture					*		*	*	*		*	*	*
14. Desire							▓	▓			▓	▓

Beautiful universals:

15. Faith							▓		▓		▓	▓	▓
16. Mindfulness							▓		▓		▓	▓	▓
17. Shame of wrongdoing							▓		▓		▓	▓	▓
18. Fear of wrongdoing							▓		▓		▓	▓	▓
19. Nongreed							▓		▓		▓	▓	▓
20. Nonhatred							▓		▓		▓	▓	▓
21. Evenness of mind							▓		▓		▓	▓	▓

* These factors are variable—they may or may not be present where indicated. Their presence or absence accounts for the variable number of factors for some of the consciousnesses. If a variable factor is present at the start of the series, it will be present for the remainder of the series—if absent at the start of the series, it will continue to be absent.

1 Factors present in the mind-door adverting process must match those in determining consciousness.

2 Factors present in the second series of seven impulsion consciousnesses must match those in the previous series of seven impulsion consciousnesses.

3 Factors present in the second set of two registration consciousnesses must match those in the previous set of two registration consciousnesses.

Associated Mental Formations	Types of Consciousness	Five-door adverting	Sense-door	Receiving	Investigating	Determining	Impulsion (×7)	Registration (×2)	Life-continuum	Mind-door adverting[1]	Impulsion (×7)[2]	Registration (×2)[3]
22. Tranquility of mental body												
23. Tranquility of consciousness												
24. Lightness of mental body												
25. Lightness of consciousness												
26. Malleability of mental body												
27. Malleability of consciousness												
28. Workability of mental body												
29. Workability of consciousness												
30. Proficiency of mental body												
31. Proficiency of consciousness												
32. Uprightness of mental body												
33. Uprightness of consciousness												
Beautiful occasionals:												
34. Wisdom faculty							*	*			*	*
Total		11	8	11	11 or 12	12	32–34	11–12 / 32–34	34	12	32–34	11–12 / 32–34

TABLE 13.9
Mental Formations in Unwholesome Five-Door Cognitive Processes

Associated Mental Factors	Type of Consciousness	Five-door adverting	Sense-door	Receiving	Investigating (greed-based states)	Investigating (nongreed-based states)	Determining	Impulsion (x7)[1]	Registration (x2)	Life-continuum	Mind-door adverting[2]	Impulsion (x7)[3]	Registration (x2)[4]
1. Consciousness													
Ethically variable universals:													
2. Contact								See Table 13.7				See Table 13.7	
3. Feeling													
4. Perception													
5. Volition													
6. One-pointedness													
7. Life faculty													
8. Attention													
Ethically variable occasionals:													
9. Initial application								See Table 13.7				See Table 13.7	
10. Sustained application													
11. Decision													
12. Energy													
13. Rapture					*			*	*			*	*
14. Desire													

1 See Table 13.7.

2 Factors present in the mind-door adverting process must match those in determining consciousness.

3 Factors present in the second series of seven impulsion consciousnesses must match those in the previous series of seven impulsion consciousnesses.

4 Factors present in the second set of two registration consciousnesses must match those in the previous set of two registration consciousnesses.

* These factors are variable—they may or may not be present where indicated. Their presence or absence accounts for the variable number of factors for some of the consciousnesses. If a variable factor is present at the start of the series, it will be present for the remainder of the series—if absent at the start of the series, it will continue to be absent.

Associated Mental Factors	Type of Consciousness	Five-door adverting	Sense-door	Receiving	Investigating (greed-based states)	Investigating (nongreed-based states)	Determining	Impulsion $(x7)^1$	Registration $(x2)$	Life-continuum	Mind-door adverting[2]	Impulsion $(x7)^3$	Registration $(x2)^4$
Beautiful universals:													
15. Faith													
16. Mindfulness													
17. Shame of wrongdoing													
18. Fear of wrongdoing													
19. Nongreed													
20. Nonhatred													
21. Evenness of mind													
22. Tranquility of mental body													
23. Tranquility of consciousness													
24. Lightness of mental body													
25. Lightness of consciousness													
26. Malleability of mental body													
27. Malleability of consciousness													
28. Workability of mental body													
29. Workability of consciousness								See Table 13.7				See Table 13.7	
30. Proficiency of mental body													

Table continues on next page

Associated Mental Factors	Type of Consciousness	Five-door adverting	Sense-door	Receiving	Investigating (greed-based states)	Investigating (nongreed-based states)	Determining	Impulsion (x7)[1]	Registration (x2)	Life-continuum	Mind-door adverting[2]	Impulsion (x7)[3]	Registration (x2)[4]
31. Proficiency of consciousness								See Table 13.7				See Table 13.7	
32. Uprightness of mental body													
33. Uprightness of consciousness													
Beautiful occasionals:													
34. Wisdom faculty									*				*
Total		11	8	11	11 or 12	11	12	11–12	32–34	34	12	11–12	32–34

TABLE 13.10

Mental Formations in Wholesome Mind-Door Cognitive Processes

ASSOCIATED MENTAL FACTORS	Type of Consciousness	Mind-Door Adverting	Impulsion (×7)					Registration (×2)		Life-Continuum
			Right speech	Right action	Right livelihood	Compassion (not jhāna)	Appreciative joy (not jhāna)	Right speech, right action, and right livelihood	Compassion (not jhāna) and appreciative joy (not jhāna)	
1. Consciousness										
Ethically variable universals:										
2. Contact										
3. Feeling										
4. Perception										
5. Volition										
6. One-pointedness								No Registration		
7. Life faculty										
8. Attention										
Ethically variable occasionals:										
9. Initial application										
10. Sustained application										
11. Decision										
12. Energy								No Registration		
13. Rapture			*	*	*	*	*	*	*	
14. Desire										

*These factors are variable—they may or may not be present where indicated. Their presence or absence accounts for the variable number of factors for some of the consciousnesses. If a variable factor is present at the start of the series, it will be present for the remainder of the series—if absent at the start of the series, it will continue to be absent.

Table continues on next page

Associated Mental Factors	Type of Consciousness	Mind-Door Adverting	Impulsion (×7)					Registration (×2)		Life-Continuum
			Right speech	Right action	Right livelihood	Compassion (not jhāna)	Appreciative joy (not jhāna)	Right speech, right action, and right livelihood	Compassion (not jhāna) and appreciative joy (not jhāna)	
Beautiful universals:										
15. Faith										
16. Mindfulness										
17. Shame of wrongdoing										
18. Fear of wrongdoing										
19. Nongreed										
20. Nonhatred										
21. Evenness of mind										
22. Tranquility of mental body										
23. Tranquility of consciousness										
24. Lightness of mental body										
25. Lightness of consciousness										
26. Malleability of mental body										
27. Malleability of consciousness										
28. Workability of mental body										
29. Workability of consciousness										
30. Proficiency of mental body										
31. Proficiency of consciousness										
32. Uprightness of mental body										
33. Uprightness of consciousness										

No Registration

ASSOCIATED MENTAL FACTORS	TYPE OF CONSCIOUSNESS	Mind-Door Adverting	Impulsion (×7)					Registration (×2)		Life-Continuum
			Right speech	Right action	Right livelihood	Compassion (not jhāna)	Appreciative joy (not jhāna)	Right speech, right action, and right livelihood	Compassion (not jhāna) and appreciative joy (not jhāna)	
Beautiful occasionals:										
34. Right speech			▨							
35. Right action				▨						
36. Right livelihood					▨					
37. Compassion						▨				
38. Appreciative joy							▨			
39. Wisdom faculty			*	*	*	*	*		*	▨
Total	12		33–35	33–35	33–35	33–35	33–35	11 or 12	32–34	34

No Registration

⇥ **MEDITATION INSTRUCTION 13.5**
Discerning the Sense-Sphere Cognitive Process

 1. Prepare the mind with concentration or jhāna practice.

 2. To discern the mental formations, you must first cause a sense-sphere process to occur. To do this, discern the eye-sensitive element, the mind door, and then both together. Concentrate on the color of a group of nearby rūpa kalāpas as they appear in both the eye and mind doors. Cognize the color with wise attention by knowing that this is color.

 3. Seeing color will initiate an eye-door cognitive process, followed by many mind-door processes that all take the same color as object. Observe the mental factors found in each stage of the cognitive series. See Table 13.8.

   (a) A five-door adverting consciousness: eleven mental formations that include consciousness, seven universal factors, and three occasional factors *(vitakka, vicāra, adhimokkha)*.

   (b) An eye consciousness: eight mental formations that include consciousness and seven universal factors.

   (c) A receiving consciousness: eleven mental formations that include consciousness, seven universal factors, and three occasional factors *(vitakka, vicāra, adhimokkha)*.

   (d) An investigating consciousness: eleven or twelve mental formations that include consciousness, seven universal factors, and three or four occasional factors *(vitakka, vicāra, adhimokkha,* and sometimes *pīti)*.

   (e) A determining consciousness: twelve mental formations that include consciousness, seven universal factors, and four occasional factors *(vitakka, vicāra, adhimokkha, viriya)*.

   (f) Seven impulsion consciousnesses: if unwholesome, there can be sixteen, eighteen, nineteen, twenty, twenty-one, or twenty-two mental formations; if wholesome, there can be thirty-two, thirty-three, thirty-four, or thirty-five mental formations.

(g) Two registration consciousnesses: eleven, twelve, thirty-two, thirty-three, or thirty-four mental formations.

After these registration consciousnesses pass, a series of life-continuum *(bhavaṅga)* consciousnesses will link the sense-sphere process with a subsequent mind-door process that takes the same color as object and follows the three-part pattern as previously described for mind-door processes. The quantity of mental factors in the mind-door process will parallel the factors found in the preceding determining, impulsion, and registration consciousnesses:

(a) A mind-door adverting consciousness

(b) Seven impulsion consciousnesses

(c) Two registration consciousnesses

4. Repeatedly examine the eye-door process until you are satisfied. Then apply the same discernment to formations with the other four sense doors: ear, nose, tongue, and body.

5. After the wholesome states are clear, discern unwholesome states by following the same procedure with the five sense objects, but pay unwise attention to the objects. For instance, when you perceive color, view it as an object for personal gratification; when you hear a sound, consider it enduring; when you recognize a tangible object, interpret it as a possession. When wrong view enters the field of perception, the resulting mental formations will be unwholesome. Explore this process to discover the precise character of unwholesome states. See Table 13.7.

6. After the meditation session concludes and you are walking around, working, talking, eating, or showering, notice how you encounter experience. Observe the quality of the mind that is calmly playing with a child, gratefully receiving a compliment, awkward at a party, excited before an interview, jealously watching a friend. Mental formations arise in every conscious moment and affect your relationship to experience. Try to apply what you have learned in the refined environment of meditation to bolster the purity of your response during cruder daily encounters. ✦

Once you have thoroughly explored the internal processes that occur when consciousness meets an object, you can extend the discernment to realize the nature of all mentality, both internal and external. In chapter 12, you deconstructed the matter of the world into its subtle constituents beginning with your clothes, then gradually perceiving the chair and floor, and then incrementally extending the discernment to expose the subtle matter that composes the building, the ultimate materialities in the town, region, world, and universe. Now you can follow a similarly thorough investigation of the world of mind. This is not your personal mind, but mentality, anywhere and everywhere in the universe.

⇥ MEDITATION INSTRUCTION 13.6
A Real World

1. Concentrate the mind.

2. Review the discernment of materiality (meditation instruction 12.6).

3. Review the discernment of mentality internally (meditation instruction 13.5).

4. In a similar way, now discern the cognitive processes that are occurring externally, that is, in minds other than your own. Use other beings in general as the base; don't try to penetrate a particular person's consciousness. Just direct your attention to external mentality to perceive an eye-sensitive element and a color. Proceed with the discernment according to the steps in meditation instruction 13.5 without concern as to whose eye-sensitive element you might be apprehending. You will discover a world of mental and material phenomena—impersonal attributes and functions that can be analyzed.

5. Continue this process alternately discerning internal and external phenomena at all the sense doors, incrementally extending the discernment further and further away. For example, you might first direct your external discernment toward beings that

are present in the building where you sit, then extend to beings in the neighborhood, town, region, country, hemisphere, planet, and so on. Thoroughly discern the ultimate mental and material processes that occur in each consciousness moment throughout the infinite universe.

6. Finally, conclude the investigation by meditating upon the totality of mental and material processes as just that: phenomena. See that there is no *I/you, woman/man, sister/brother;* see concepts as mere designations that have no ultimate reality. ✦

The painstaking exercise of identifying, defining, and analyzing the subtle nuances of cognitive processes illuminates refined strata of mental experience. However, you do not need to turn this into an exercise in mathematics, obsessively counting and correlating mental factors with charts. If you are reading this book as an overview, it is enough to understand the basic sequence. Then, when you are training in retreat with the guidance of a teacher, the nuances and specificities of these formations will become both useful and clear.

Yet even a cursory review of this material may reveal interesting insights into the nature of mentality and habitual mental patterns. You might learn to quickly recognize the heaviness and rigidity that is associated with a mind-state devoid of the nineteen beautiful universal factors that include tranquility, lightness, malleability, workability, and so on, and use this sensation as a signal to dispel unwholesome states whenever they arise. You might sense the danger rooted in delusion that accompanies the wandering mind and resolve to interrupt habitual daydreaming. Seeing that greed and hatred never arise in the same mind-moment, that rapture and anger are equally incompatible, and that every unwholesome state includes restlessness and shamelessness of wrongdoing can provide clues to unpack the deeply conditioned roots of action and kamma. By studying the mind, factor by factor, and state by state, you will become attuned to the distinctions between states both during formal meditation sessions and also during dynamic daily encounters. By teasing out the factors that compose mental states, you will see the ways

Untangling Decision-Making Angst

Do you struggle with decision-making, wondering how to decide what is best? Do you sometimes do things that are destructive, even when you know that they are wrong? By teasing out the basic components that compose experience, and examining mental factors associated with a decision to act, you will understand what propels addictive, callous, or disrespectful conduct, and what supports wise action.

Before you make your next decision, whether it is a minor daily selection, a major career move, or an important health issue, examine your mind. If you sense the presence of restlessness and the associated unwholesome factors, wait before you decide what to do. Resolve not to decide or act when unwholesome states dominate. Spend some time cultivating calmness, kindness, and mindful awareness, and then pose the dilemma again for fresh consideration. If you sense that mindfulness and the associated wholesome factors are supporting the decision-making process, trust your intention as you determine your course of action.

in which you might be sustaining or countering the basic root tendencies of greed, nongreed, hatred, nonhatred, delusion, and nondelusion. Empowered with this knowledge of mentality, you will be able to change any patterns that disrupt the peaceful clarity of your mind.

In the chapters that follow, we use these ultimate constituents of matter and mind (defined here and in chapter 12) as the building blocks of a nuanced and profound approach to insight meditation. With the objects and processes carefully defined and analyzed, when you plunge into the contemplations of insight meditation you will discover a thrilling clarity and liberating potential built upon this direct perception of the subtle components of mind and matter.

 Distinguishing Choiceless Awareness from the Wandering Mind

Were you surprised to learn that mindfulness can never arise along with greed, hatred, or delusion, and that restlessness can never arise in a wholesome state? Look into your own mind and see if it is true.

Identify times in the day when your mind tends to wander, such as when walking the dog or eating a snack. Occasionally dissect the habitually wandering mind and see what mental factors it contains. What mental factors sustain a romantic fantasy? You may discover that the pleasure of fantasy is merely the agitation caused by pīti, while the state is devoid of the deeply wholesome factors of mindfulness, tranquility, equanimity, nongreed, nonhate, uprightness, and faith.

Notice the object and quality of attention. When exploring hatred you may see that when mindfulness arises there is wise attention, perhaps taking the mental factors associated with hatred as the object of consciousness; when hatred consumes the mind there will be unwise attention to a hated object. Attention may rapidly flicker between cognitive processes that are characterized by mindfulness or by hatred, but hate and mindfulness cannot arise in exactly the same moment.

At times in daily life, and also in meditation, you may allow the mind to relax with an undirected, choiceless quality of

Box continues on next page

awareness. What is the experience of genuine relaxation? What specific mental factors constitute an experience of relaxation? Notice if choiceless awareness is supporting the development of associated wholesome states, or if the mind slides into unwholesome states of restless imaginings, laziness, fear, or conceit. Let your observations inform the degree to which you direct, restrain, and focus your attention, or creatively respond to the stimuli of living.

CHAPTER 14

A Magic Show: Emptiness of the Five Aggregates

Everything could disappear in an instant.
Materialities are like balls of foam,
Feelings are like bubbles,
Perceptions are like mirages,
Volitions are like banana trees,
Consciousnesses are like magical illusions.
—SAṂYUTTA NIKĀYA[207]

A CHILD MAY ARRANGE her crayons in several different ways, for instance, according to hue, tone, size, age, saturation, or personal associations. However they are arranged, the set includes all her crayons. Individuals devise filing systems for their home computers and may organize documents by date, topic, function, author, category, or idiosyncratic associations. However they are arranged, they encompass the collection of electronic documents. Similarly, any group of material can be organized into different categories using different classification systems, but, when taken together, remain the same collection of material. Our next step is to divide every material element and mental constituent that was discussed in chapters 12 and 13 into pragmatic classification schemes that will serve as the structure for systematic contemplation. Commonly used categories are the (1) the two categories of materiality and mentality; (2) the five aggregates of materiality, feeling, perception, mental formations, and consciousness; (3)

the twelve bases, which include six sense doors and six sense objects; (4) the eighteen elements which include six sense doors, six sense objects, and six sense consciousnesses; and (5) the twelve factors of dependent arising.[208] A skilled teacher may guide you to use one or another model, depending upon temperament, conditions, and the purpose of the exploration.[209] Each model presents a complete approach to insight; each encompasses every conceivable mental and material experience. This chapter highlights the second scheme in the above list, the model of the five aggregates.

THE FIVE AGGREGATES OF EXPERIENCE (KHANDHA)

The scheme of five aggregates organizes the very same constituents of material and mental phenomena that you discerned through the exercises in chapters 12 and 13 into a fivefold model of experience: (1) materiality, (2) feeling, (3) perception, (4) mental formations, and (5) consciousness. When we identify with the functioning of these intrinsically impersonal aggregates or cling to a formation of self-grasping, we suffer from the delusion that these five aggregates are *mine, I,* or *myself.*

Psychophysical processes arise and pass at lightning speed, hence the Buddha compared the five aggregates to ephemeral bubbles, lumps of froth, banana trees, illusory mirages, and magic tricks—such is the insubstantiality of self constructions. In this meditation we examine each aggregate individually and observe how the five function as an inseparable unit.

1. Materiality (rūpa) includes all matter, internal and external—sights, sounds, smells, tastes, touches, and the material support for consciousness. Materiality, an aspect of psychophysical processes, includes the images that the mind constructs when stimulated by objects in the world. Materiality refers not only to a physical tree, bus, pencil, mountain, cat, or sister but also to the impact the physical perception of those things has on the mind. Neuroscientists might define materiality as the mental activity that results when sensory impressions are transmitted to the brain. The four elements meditation introduced in chapter 12 illuminated subtle aspects of the materiality aggregate and defined twenty-eight concrete and nonconcrete material elements.

When we closely examine matter, we discover that it is insubstantial; it is ephemeral. Ancient Buddhist texts compare materiality to balls of foam or lumps of froth on water.[210] Just as balls of foam on ocean waves break apart and disappear, bodies perish, solid objects break apart, and sensory impressions change. Experiences of the body, if not recognized as ephemeral, insubstantial expressions of causal factors, can lead to the fundamental error underlying self-grasping—the belief that "I am the body."

2. *Feeling tone (vedanā)* refers to the characteristic feeling of an object— the experience of the contact as pleasant, unpleasant, or neutral. Feeling tone points to a basic mental factor, not a complex emotion. Every experience of mind or body has a feeling component that is embedded within it and conditioned by causes. Feelings are fleeting; they continuously change throughout our lives. The untrained mind reacts to feelings by grasping for more pleasant feelings, pushing away unpleasant encounters, and ignoring neutral events. These reactions quickly develop into patterns of attachment and identification. When your shoulder hurts, for example, you may not explicitly have the thought that the tingle, pressure, or tightness is really who you are; however, if the sensation is irritating, you might squirm, react, or massage the tense muscle. The pressure of the massage might be soothing, and you could want that pleasant feeling to linger. Habitual reactions that seek pleasure by trying to make pleasant encounters last, and avoid pain by trying to make unpleasant events end, arise as conditioned responses to feeling. These conditioned reactions ignore the simple fact that feelings change without our interference. Reacting to a feeling does not succeed in altering the duration of a feeling—feelings are by nature fleeting. Reactions serve to construct the illusion of an enduring entity that possesses those experiences.

Feelings are like ephemeral bubbles on water; they arise due to momentary conditions, exist for just an instant, and then pop—they vanish and leave nothing behind.[211] "Just as a bubble both arises and ceases in this or that drop of water and has no length of duration, so indeed feeling also arises and ceases and has no length of duration. In the moment of one snapping of the fingers it arises and ceases many times."[212]

3. *Perception (saññā)* has the characteristic of perceiving the qualities of an object; it compares present sensory data with memory to identify the encounter—that a given object is a fork, friend, leaf, or threat. Perception is the mental function that recognizes, conceptualizes, and labels the things that we see, hear, smell, taste, touch, and think. As such, it picks out distinguishing marks of an experience, gives it a name, compares it to previous encounters, and stores it in memory for future reference. It manifests through how we interpret the object. Perception makes sense of the barrage of daily stimuli, filters out superfluous data, and registers the useful information.

Since perception is mediated through our ideas and past experiences, it can be inaccurate. Children may imagine there are ghosts when fear affects their response to the sound of creaking floorboards. After a serious car accident, even a glimpse of the same color, make, and model car can trigger a sense of panic. When expecting a special guest to arrive, anyone approaching from a distance who matches her general height, weight, and complexion might startle you into thinking she has arrived early. Perception is often skewed by the influence of desires, fears, hopes, plans, and memories; it can be affected by stereotypes, habitual patterns, and belief systems. Impressions accrued through past events can distort the perception of current events. Once I introduced two friends at a party; for no apparent reason one distrusted the other. Later, when looking at old photographs, we realized that he bore a striking resemblance to an ex-boyfriend who had deceived her.

Clinging to perceptions of things seen, heard, smelled, tasted, or touched is likened to clinging to mirages, which are unsubstantial, ungraspable, and deceptive.[213] The Buddhist commentary explains, "For one cannot grasp [a mirage] and drink it, or wash in it, or bathe in it, or fill a pot with it...And just as a mirage deceives travelers and makes them say that a full lake has been seen, perception also deceives them and makes them say 'this is blue, beautiful, pleasant, and permanent.'"[214]

The concept of self arises when we try to organize perceptions. We create the past through memory. We create future through projection. We organize each sensory contact through the filter of concepts of *my* past and *my* future. We build a self-referential position in the center of our personalized universe. When we perceive the world from a preconceived vantage point of *me,* this central organizing structure creates an illusion of the person to whom experience occurs. The world is then recognized by how it impacts *me* and *my* personal interests.

4. *Mental formations (saṅkhāra)* include all the formations of mind—wholesome and unwholesome—such as hindrances, intentions, compassion, tranquility, thoughts, images, hopes, fears, plans, mindfulness, effort, anger, determination, memories, opinions, attitudes, joy, envy. This is a vast category of mental phenomena that includes qualities we endeavor to cultivate, qualities we seek to abandon, and all the thoughts that proceed from the basic perception of an object. This category encompasses the fifty-two mental factors defined in chapter 13, but excludes feeling, perception, and consciousness since they appear as specific aggregates in the context of this model.

The scope of this aggregate is vast. Although experiences are composed of many mental factors that function together to form the interdependent state, they are essentially hollow and without a core—like a banana tree.[215] As the traditional commentary explains, "One cannot take anything from a plantain stem and bring it away to make even as much as a rafter...A plantain stem is a combination of many sheaths, so also the formations aggregate is a combination of many states."[216]

5. *Consciousness (viññāṇa, citta, manas)* has the characteristic of cognizing an object. It is a rudimentary quality of knowing. Consciousness refers to the basic functioning of cognition; it is the awareness that something is impacting the senses. Consciousness functions as the forerunner of the many interdependent mental factors that combine

What Moved? What Decides? What Knows?

When you have an intention to shift your posture during meditation, to turn away from a cold draft, scratch an itch, look at
your watch, or to adjust your seat, consider what decided to
move. You might say "I" decided to move. But which aspect of
mind conditioned the desire to move? Was it fear, restlessness,
compassion, desire? Are you that aspect of mind? When you
make the decision that "I will not move," which aspect of mind
conditioned the decision to remain still? Was it confidence,
resolution, determination, embarrassment, pride, commitment,
or desire to achieve?

to form the experience of the object; it manifests as a continuity of processes that leads and links the elements of the cognitive sequence.

Consciousness can only arise with the impact of an object. The
Buddha explained that "consciousness is reckoned by the particular
condition dependent upon which it arises. When consciousness arises
dependent on eye and materiality, it is reckoned as eye-consciousness;
when consciousness arises dependent on ear and sound, it is reckoned as ear-consciousness."[217] There is no preexisting consciousness
just waiting for a perception to impinge. Consciousness contains no
intrinsic qualities; it simply performs the function of cognizing whatever objects impact the senses. Individual disposition and personality
are expressed by the patterns of associated mental formations, not by
an intrinsic feature of consciousness. This rudimentary function of
cognition is like a magical illusion;[218] it is not as it appears, and its
apparent solidity is not real. "Just as an illusion...deceives the many
and makes them grasp anything at all as gold, silver, or pearl, consciousness too deceives the many and makes them take it as though it

Tracking the Experiences of Mind and Body

Bring mindfulness to your daily events; notice how mind and body interact. As your observing powers increase, attention will rest more frequently in present-moment experiences, without the drama of elaborate stories that remove you from the here and now. Observe how you receive information from the senses. Do you make a story out of it—a reaction of liking or not liking, wanting or aversion? Do you judge it? Do you fabricate a self-reference point—the sense of being someone who is having the experience? Try to identify the function of the five aggregates in daily experiences at home, at work, while exercising, while shopping. Do you see how difficult it is to separate the aggregates from one another? That is because they always function together.

were coming and going and standing and sitting with the same consciousness. But there is one consciousness at the moment of coming and another at the moment of going."[219] When we cease attributing solidity to mental and material processes, we recognize the ancient web of attachments to be deceptive.

CONSTRUCTING THE SELF

We experience our lives through the functioning of the five aggregates. You may observe these constituents of experience in everyday activities. For example, when eating a bowl of noodles, you might notice the temperature of the broth and the soft texture of the noodles—heat and softness are characteristics of matter. The pleasure you experience in contact with the salty taste reveals the feeling tone. Recognition that it is a bowl of noodles is accomplished through the function of perception. Your mental orientation to the bowl, attention to the meal, and desire for the next bite are elements of the mental formations aggregate. And the conscious impact of the contact with the noodles is accomplished by the consciousness aggregate. Through the refined practices of discerning the five aggregates in meditation, as well as daily activities, you will confirm with your direct knowledge that experience arises with changing mental and material conditions and does not belong to anyone.

The five aggregates affected by clinging—materiality, feeling, perceptions, mental formations, and consciousness—provide a structure for contemplative inquiry into *how* this psychophysical process works in a world of interdependent experience. To what extent is the interaction of materiality, feeling, perception, mental formations, and consciousness simply the manifestation of a deep and clear presence in life and to what extent are they distorted by formations of *I*-making, *mine*-making, and self-grasping? The concept of self *(I)* coupled with the concept of possessiveness *(mine)* is the primary form of misperception. You might identify with sensory experiences or feelings (*my* pain, *my* frustration, *my* joy). You might identify with views and opinions (*I* believe). You might identify with the knowing of experience (*I* am, *I* know, *I* realize). Yet, when we carefully analyze mind and body, we find no one who does actions, no entity who is the owner of the body, no guarantee that we can control any conditions: we find only causally related events. When we understand *I*-ing and *my*-ing as a process of grasping, we will then fearlessly recognize not-self. Understand that this process itself is not a personal process.

When with meditative awareness we look below the surface of the conditioned patterns to discern the five aggregates, we discover something more profound than preconceived concepts. We search internally and externally, near and far, throughout the infinite universe and, yet, only conditioned elements of materiality and mentality are found. There is nothing in this world of change that will not collapse, decay, and disappear. Knowing the suffering that ensues from trying to hold on to unstable experiences, the Buddha advised, "Whatever is not yours, abandon it; when you have abandoned it, that will lead to your welfare

Notice the Constructions of I *and* Mine

Notice in your daily activities when the activities of *I*-making and *mine*-making form. Watch for the construction of a possessive relationship to experiences. Learn how identification and possessiveness operate. You will find they occur when a sensory contact is met without wise attention. When you enter a room and take your seat, consider if there is a possessive relationship to that place. Do you think of it as "*my* seat"? Who do you choose to sit next to and why? If there is any attachment to that position, you could be constructing a sense of being the one who has a place or exists in relation to another. It can be interesting to observe these formations of *I, me,* and *mine* arising in community dining rooms where no one owns anything; sometimes people form an entrenched routine and feel threatened if that routine is interrupted.

When you spot your favorite tea mug on the shelf, is it an experience of simply seeing, or is the seeing infested with *mine*-making? When you feel a stinging sensation on the arm, is it a simple sensation or are you outraged, complaining that "a mosquito is biting *me*!" When a feeling of grief sweeps over the heart, notice if there is an unadulterated wave of grief or if the mind constructs elaborate stories of beautiful moments shared and lost? How strong is the formation of *I* or *mine* in daily experience? Is your self-image threatened when illness affects the body? Did conceit swell up hoping to be recognized when you first achieved jhāna? Noticing the fabrication of *I* and *mine* can enhance the intimate experience of seeing, hearing, smelling, tasting, touching, or thinking. It strengthens mindfulness of the encounter, free from the distorting intrusion of self concepts.

and happiness for a long time. What is it that is not yours? Material-ity [feelings, perceptions, formations, and consciousness] is not yours. Abandon it. When you have abandoned it, that will lead to your welfare and happiness for a long time."[220] Our job is to unravel the clinging, and the most intimate arena for clinging is the process that fuels identifica-tion and possessiveness. Although people commonly attribute personal significance to their life story and experiences of the five aggregates, fun-damentally these are not ours.

As you recognize habitual grasping for what it really is, you will not be deceived, seduced, or confused by it. You will learn to stop grasping after transient experiences. This nongrasping will not bring even the slightest sense of deprivation or disquiet. On the contrary, you will enjoy the deep ease and freedom that comes with letting go.

MEDITATIVE INVESTIGATION

Buddhist teachings may or may not have convinced you that you are not a fixed entity. But you don't need to grasp intellectual concepts of emptiness or accept not-self on faith. This training invites you to closely examine the processes of mind and body that habitually inject a sense of self into experience. The quality of the meditative inquiry is gentle, peaceful, and nonmanipulative. You will not see into the nature of mind if you hunt out the ego with the attitude of a predator. It would also be arrogant to adopt the stance of a creator who constructs an improved enlightened self. The process is simpler: see clearly how you encounter experience and notice if experiences are embellished with constructs of *I, me,* and *mine*. It is the process of grasping that produces the illusion of self—it matters little what is grasped. You will experience just what you are naturally experiencing, but you will remain informed by clear seeing, and mental and material processes will be known to be void of the distortions of self-grasping. The futility of self-grasping is illustrated by the proverb, "It can seem difficult to catch a black cat in a dark room, especially if it is not there." The insight into not-self may appear chal-lenging, but you will discover through a careful examination of your own experience that there is nothing to get rid of and there is nothing at the core of experience to claim as self.

 Question Identity

Ask yourself, in the midst of a thought, in the middle of an experience, during the course of a conversation, while working out at the gym: *Am I this thought? Am I this feeling? Is this emotion me? Is this sensation what I am?*

My favorite inquiry questions emphasize one word: really. *Really,* am I that? *Really,* is this tension mine? Am I *really* this thought? Is this sensation *really* me? Whenever you notice that you have identified with something, are attached to something desirable, or withdraw from something painful, ask yourself, *"really?"* Dislodge the tight shell of grasping that welds a sense of being onto a momentary occurrence. Experience your daily events free from deceptive self-reference.

Self is a fabricated concept that occurs whenever experience is met with clinging. When we are not grasping self-concepts, sensory experience continues, unimpeded and without a self to whom it is happening. As your vipassanā practice progresses, you will further analyze the aggregates, their causes, and how they function and contemplate their arising and perishing. Through direct observation you will investigate if, and when, experience is affected by clinging.

Emptiness is not a state of blankness; it is just empty of self-grasping. Practice to know your experience, unaffected by clinging. Rest in the present configuration of changing conditions—life being known through the functioning of the five aggregates. Wake up in the morning, get dressed, eat, and work, but live unburdened by the notion that *I* am doing it. Then you will recognize processes as they are occurring, free from the distorting lens of *I*-making or *mine*-making, and unrestricted by the role of agent of the action. This extraordinary clarity regarding mind-body processes can dislodge deeply rooted concepts of *I, me,* and *mine.*

✦ MEDITATION INSTRUCTION 14.1
Discerning Five Aggregates

Divide mental and material phenomena into the categories of the five aggregates. Discern cognitive processes at each sense door according to these five groups following the sequence of instructions given in chapter 13 (meditation instructions 13.3, 13.4, 13.5), only now categorize phenomena according to the five aggregates model. Specifically, you will discern the materiality that composes the basis for consciousness, sense door, and object; the feeling tone that arises on contact; the perception; the mental formations including all additional associated mental factors; and consciousnesses as they arise in each mind-moment of the cognitive series. Discern both wholesome and unwholesome cognitive processes at each sense door with phenomena now divided according to the five aggregates scheme.

This is an excellent opportunity to carefully examine certain features of experience, such as feeling tone (*vedanā*). For example, you might notice that within each sense-door cognitive process the adverting, receiving, and determining consciousnesses always carry a neutral or equanimous feeling tone, however investigating, impulsion, and receiving consciousnesses have pleasant, unpleasant, or neutral feeling tones. You might also discover that the body door is only affected by pleasure or pain, not neutral feelings, whereas the ear, nose, and tongue doors register only neutral feelings. Feeling tone is not continuous; it fluctuates even within the subtle stages of a single cognitive process. Explore what the five aggregates model might reveal about the psychophysical experience. ✦

MODELS FOR EXPLORING SUFFERING

Understanding the mechanisms of suffering is integral to a genuine realization of liberation. As the Buddha stated, "The purpose of the holy life is the full understanding of suffering."[221] After exploring the five aggregates model presented in this chapter, the examination will extend in the following chapter to include causal relationships governing phenomena. The Buddha taught that these two models (the five aggregates and twelve links of dependent arising) work together in the quest for the end of suffering:

> One who sees dependent arising sees the Dhamma. One who sees the Dhamma sees dependent arising. And these five aggregates [matter, feelings, perceptions, formations, and consciousness] affected by clinging are dependently arising. The desire, indulgence, inclination, and holding based on these five aggregates affected by clinging are the origin of suffering. The removal of desire and lust, the abandonment of desire and lust for these five aggregates affected by clinging is the cessation of suffering.[222]

In practice, these two models intertwine to reveal the complex mechanisms through which suffering is formed and ceases. Aided by these models, meditators can analyze causal conditioning from two perspectives that represent a shift in time scale. You may explore the moment-by-moment dynamics of suffering, and also see how the entire round of existence is inextricably bound to suffering, and glimpse your potential to free the mind from the bonds of ignorance.

CHAPTER 15

Causes and Effects: Twelve Links of Dependent Arising

Action makes the world go round,
Action makes the generation turn.
Living beings are bound by action
Like the chariot wheel by the pin.
—MAJJHIMA NIKĀYA[223]

SIMPLE WISDOM WARNS: squeeze the tube slowly, because once the toothpaste is out, it is pretty hard to get it back in. The Pali term *kamma* describes the process by which intentional actions produce effects. It is a system in which causes *(hetu)* and conditions *(paccaya)* are linked to results; actions have consequences. The Buddha said, "Intention *[cetanā]*, I tell you is action *[kamma]*. Intending, one does action by way of body, speech, and mind."[224] Our intentional actions of body, speech, and mind condition how we will experience future events. Buddhist teachings stress that "beings are owners of their actions, heirs of their actions, they originate from their actions, are bound to their actions, have their actions as their refuge. It is action that distinguishes beings as superior or inferior."[225] However, we are not trapped by the past or condemned to repeat patterns; the key to relating to kamma is in how we respond to the present.

When a fire alarm sounded, I saw most people walk straight past well-marked emergency exits, single-mindedly heading for the familiar exit at the front door. We are conditioned by our routines and repeated actions.

Mental states are conditioned by repetition, and we constantly influence ourselves by how we act and react to life. If you frequently become irritated at red traffic signals, you condition the response of impatience. If you frequently cultivate loving-kindness toward your colleagues, you contribute to a caring work community and condition a response of tolerance. Physical states are also conditioned by repetition. If you frequently round your back forward when you work at a computer, you are conditioning the muscular response of collapse. If you frequently establish an upright posture when you meditate, you are creating wakeful and alert conditions for awareness. For better or for worse, we condition our way of being in the world.

Every day intentions arise by the millions—which ones do you enact? Experiences, thoughts, tendencies, feelings, and even our very existence have causes that can be traced to formations of greed, hatred, and delusion or to their counterparts of nongreed, nonhatred, and nondelusion.[226]

Investigating causality brings a vivid and clear comprehension of the

---

 A Wise Pause

To expand the possibility of choice, learn to pause before reacting to daily events. Take a moment to consider your response before you speak, reply to an email, make a decision, or finalize a purchase. Even a split second of calm can create a space in which you become aware of your body, feelings, views, and emotions. A simple willingness to wait a moment can transform a habitual enslavement into a conscious commitment to act in accordance with your core values. Notice how much of your present response to daily events is influenced by personal history, childhood conditioning, or habitual reactions. Consider: what would be a skillful response?

moral foundation of action. How we act, what we do, and how we live is of paramount importance in the development of the liberating path. Our meditative practice works to remove tendencies toward greed, hatred, and delusion and simultaneously to cultivate more healthy attitudes, views, and ways of living in the world.

 Five Practical Steps—The Five R's

Five practical steps can help change unwanted habits.

1. Recognize harmful habits and the desire to change. Use the power of your observational skills to examine habitual actions, words, and thoughts and the impact that they have on your mind.

2. Restrain and inhibit conditioned reactions to familiar stimuli. Make the commitment to pause before speaking, acting, and deciding. Give yourself the time to consider your response without reacting to a habitual trigger.

3. Renounce unskillful habitual patterns. Don't act until the harmful impulse to react diminishes and an appropriate response arises.

4. Redirect the mind toward the preferable alternative.

5. Reflect on what you might learn about the patterns and tendencies that lead to suffering, and on a way of being with things that brings ease and clarity.

For example, if you have a tendency to react with angry criticism every time your friend is late, *recognize* your tendency and

Box continues on next page

decide not to react in that familiar way. The next time he is late, *restrain* your familiar irritation, *renounce* the anger, and resolve to remain calm. You might feel your breath as you mindfully track the unfolding of your emotions, thoughts, and feelings. Learn to remain alert in this nonhabitual response; grow comfortable with the practice of restraint. At first, you might not know how else to respond, but if you inhibit the unskillful habit and wait patiently, eventually you will intuit a more skillful response. You don't need to figure out what you will do, plan how you will feel, or script future interactions. This reflection simply suspends the habitual mode of reaction and creates a moment of calm, mindful awareness in which an alternative response might emerge. When a more skillful alternative emerges, *redirect* your energy to this response. Then observe and *reflect* to learn if this mode might offer you greater benefits than the habitual response.

THE CYCLE OF DEPENDENT ARISING

The cycle of dependent arising *(paṭiccasamuppāda)* is central to the Buddhist understanding of how things come to be the way that they are. Venerable Ananda once enthusiastically remarked that "Dependent arising is very profound, but to me it seems as clear as clear can be." The Buddha corrected, "Not so Ananda, not so! This dependent arising is profound and appears profound; it is truly very difficult to penetrate. Because they have not understood and penetrated this one principle, beings are caught on the wheel of birth and death and cannot find the means to freedom."[227] Listed in Table 15.1 are twelve factors that comprise the wheel of which the Buddha speaks. A step-by-step presentation of dependent arising is briefly sketched in the following standard summary:

When this exists, that comes to be; with the arising of this, that arises. When this does not exist, that does not come to be; with the cessation of this, that ceases. That is, with ignorance as condition, formations come to be; with formations as condition, consciousness; with consciousness as condition, mentality-materiality; with mentality-materiality as condition, the sixfold [sense] base; with the sixfold [sense] base as condition, contact; with contact as condition, feeling; with feeling as condition, craving; with craving as condition, clinging; with clinging as condition, being; with being as condition, birth; with birth as condition, aging and death, sorrow, lamentation, pain, grief, and despair come to be. Such is the origin of this whole mass of suffering.[228]

The cyclic nature of dependent arising was traditionally illustrated by drawing a circle on the ground.[229] Just as it is nonsensical to say that either the hen or the egg came first, regarding the cycle of dependent arising, the "earliest point cannot be found."[230] Not only is the beginning impossible to detect, the image of the circle poses a profound question: where is the end of this configuration? As long as the cycle continues no release will be found, and beings will continue to wander repeatedly through existences affected by ignorance and suffering. So we ponder how kamma sustains the cycle of suffering and how we might escape this beginningless cycle of suffering.

The image of a circle, however, is not entirely satisfactory. It might give students the erroneous impression that death is the immediate cause of ignorance. In addition to the traditional circle design, Buddhist teachers have presented the twelve factors as a chain, a web, and a knotted ball of thread. The image of a chain highlights the conditioned dependency of each link but may place too much emphasis on a linear sequence. A web design invites a multifaceted and nonsequential exploration of the relations between the twelve factors. A knotted ball of string, however, might offer the most satisfactory image: an image of looping, intertwined, nonlinear sequences of causation.[231] A mind conditioned by ignorance is entangled in suffering through complex patterns that may be difficult to untie. As various threads are patiently pulled, loosened, and rearranged, even tight knots eventually become loose. Similarly, even deeply ingrained mental patterns can be released and abandoned through systematic training. Just as a knotted ball of string can unravel and become useful, a mind confused by ignorance can be purified and see the ultimate nature of things. Meditative investigation of the twelve factors of dependent arising explores not only how the mind gets entangled in patterns that perpetuate suffering, but also encourages the removal of ignorance at every stage of the process.

TABLE 15.1
Twelve Links of Dependent Arising

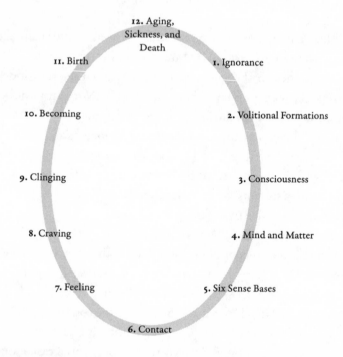

Beginning with Ignorance

The Buddha taught, "Not knowing suffering, not knowing the origin of suffering, not knowing the cessation of suffering, not knowing the way leading to the cessation of suffering. This is called ignorance."[232] An ignorant mind does not comprehend either the subtlety or the magnitude of suffering, and it therefore misses the primary purpose of this path. When we are affected by ignorance, we believe the unreal to be real, disregard the impermanent nature of things, mistake what causes suffering for potential happiness, and misapprehend ephemeral conditions as being self. Ignorance misperceives and distorts perceptions to the point that experience is mistakenly interpreted as stable, a cause of lasting happiness, and a sufficient foundation for self-concepts. According to the Abhidhamma, the characteristic of ignorance is the unknowing of the ultimate constituents of mental and material processes, the function of ignorance is to confuse, and its manifestation is the concealing of the individual essence of things. In daily life ignorance is recognized through its effects: a grasping at fleeting experiences as though they are really mine or myself, resulting in the perpetuation of suffering.

Although we start the description of the twelve links of dependent arising with ignorance, the Buddha cautioned that "a first beginning of ignorance cannot be discerned, of which it can be said, 'before that, there was no ignorance and it came to be after that.'"[233] Although we can never know the origin of ignorance, we can understand that it is activated only when the necessary conditions arise, such as an absence of mindfulness and wise attention.

With Ignorance as Condition, Volitional Formations Come to Be

Volitional formations are clusters of mental formations that enable an experience to come into existence. This element in the chain of causation includes the intention plus the mental formations that arise in association with that intention. Volitional formations can produce kamma. They arise with the volitional activities of body, speech, and mind. The classic definition summarizes volitional formation as having the characteristic of forming, its function is to accumulate kamma, and it manifests through volition. In a multiple lifetime scheme, formations or activities that occur in the previous life instigate the rebirth-linking process that generates the new life. Through observing the causal formations, meditators will recognize how volitional formations that produce renewed existences are invariably linked to ignorance.

With Volitional Formations as Condition, Consciousness Comes to Be

Consciousness has the characteristic of cognizing an object. Consciousness cannot be known separate from materiality, feeling, perceptions, and formations, which arise together as the five aggregates of experience. It occurs in six classes—eye-consciousness, ear-consciousness, nose-consciousness, tongue-consciousness, body-consciousness, and mind-consciousness—as these arise in the various mind-moments that compose the cognitive processes (explored in chapter 13), and in the rebirth-linking process. The volitional formations that accrue during one lifetime ripen through the formation of a new conscious existence. Consciousness also functions as the forerunner of mental factors and manifests as a continuity of processes through bridging cognitive processes during the course of a lifetime of perceptions and supporting the causal relationships that govern the rebirth-linking process.

With Consciousness as Condition, Mentality and Materiality Come to Be

Consciousness and mentality-materiality are interdependent. Mentality does not include materiality, and materiality does not include mentality, yet they occur together in mutual dependence. Traditional teachings illustrate the partnership with a story of two traveling companions—a blind man and a cripple. The cripple (representing mentality) climbs onto the shoulders of the blind man (representing materiality), and by sharing their abilities—one steers and the other provides the momentum—they successfully navigate the road, avoid obstructions, and reach their destination.[234] The aspect of mentality-materiality includes all the elements and factors that are associated with material and mental phenomena. Basically this includes everything that appears to us.

Material factors were addressed in chapter 12 and include the four elements (earth, water, fire, wind) with their derived materialities. The characteristic of materiality is traditionally described as being "molested by change"; its function is to be dispersed or altered; its manifestation is indeterminate, implying that material elements do not possess the nature to produce kamma.

Mental factors were addressed in chapters 13 and 14 and include the fifty-two mental factors, which may alternatively be structured as the four mental aggregates of feeling, perception, formations, and consciousness. Each specific element or factor bears its own characteristics, but in the framework of the twelve links of dependent arising we shall focus on the characteristic of mentality as a whole—how it bends toward its object. Mentality functions to associate with the object of perception; it manifests in this formula through the rebirth-linking between multiple lives.

With Mentality and Materiality as Condition, the Six Sense Bases Come to Be

Sensory experience relies upon mental and material elements. The six sense bases represent the internal material support for eye, ear, nose, tongue, body, and mind. These bases are naturally ready to receive stimulus from the environment. They have the characteristic of enlarging, actuating, or extending the sphere of experience; they function as seeing, hearing, smelling, tasting, touching, and thinking; and they manifest as the state of material base and door. The six sense bases represent the specific dynamic of mental-material phenomena that is responsive to sensory impingement. They are the means through which we make contact with the world.

With the Six Sense Bases as Condition, Contact Comes to Be

Contact describes the meeting of the sense door, consciousness, and sense object. The characteristic of contact is touching; its function is impinging; it manifests as coincidence of material base, object, and consciousness. Likened to a fire that is generated by the rubbing of sticks, contact is produced from impact on the six sense bases.[235] It is in the moment of contact that the accumulation of our conditioning is aroused. If we are under the sway of ignorance as we experience sensory phenomena, then we might react in a mode that will lead to suffering; if we are mindful and attentive to the nature of things, we might respond in a mode that diminishes greed and hate, and lightens the burden of ignorance. Through meditation practice we examine how ignorance conditions moment-to-moment contacts in both refined meditative structures and in the mundane expressions of everyday life.

With Contact as Condition, Feeling Tone Comes to Be

Inherent in contact is a quality of feeling. Feeling tone refers to the pleasantness, unpleasantness, or neutrality experienced in every sensory contact. This is a subjective experience that describes the way that we experience our encounter with the world. Classically, feeling is described as bearing the characteristic of experiencing an object; its function is to exploit the stimulus of the object, and its manifestation is pleasure, pain, bliss, or grief.

The feeling tone is largely conditioned by how we have reacted to past experiences. Wise attention encourages a balanced and equanimous response to feeling, accepting the present-moment occurrence as the natural manifestation of past or present conditions. The Buddha taught a wise response to feeling born of sensory contact: "On seeing a form with the eye, he does not lust after it if it is pleasing; he does not dislike it if it is unpleasant. He abides with mindfulness of the body established, with an immeasurable mind, and he understands as it actually is."[236] If you notice a reaction that causes stress, consider what some contributing factors might be—are there opinions, fears, desires, or prejudices that perpetuate stressful reactions? What might you do to cultivate healthier conditions for the future? We don't try to avoid or suppress feelings; feelings are inevitably produced by contact. A mindful experience of contact will not stop feelings that naturally arise with each sensory encounter, but wisdom and clarity purifies the experience of any ignorance that could generate causes for further suffering.

With Feeling Tone as Condition, Craving Comes to Be

All craving is based on a feeling. Craving cannot exist without the support of a feeling, yet feeling does not invariably lead to craving. Craving is not inherent in external objects; it is generated through an ignorant relationship to the feelings that arise on contact with the sixfold senses. Craving has the characteristic of being a cause of suffering. It functions through delight and manifests as insatiability.

Feel the Feeling

Practice bringing mindful attention to the experience of contact and noticing the associated feeling tone. Scan your body for sensations. Try to discern the present-moment expression of feeling rather than assuming that sensations will carry a predictable feeling quality. Sometimes painful aching muscles also contain moments of pleasant feeling, and sometimes pleasurable activities include painful or irritating moments. If you notice pressure where your buttocks touch the seat, focus on the feeling tone by examining if it is a pleasant or unpleasant quality of pressure. If you notice heat in your palms, recognize if that heat feels pleasant or unpleasant. If you can taste the saliva in your mouth, observe if it is a pleasant or unpleasant experience of taste. If you can hear the sounds from traffic on the street, a barking dog, music from a nearby stereo, the hum of a refrigerator, or the twitter of birds, recognize if the experience of hearing is felt as pleasant or unpleasant. Many times the feeling quality will be neither distinctly pleasant nor unpleasant, but it might fall in a category generally felt as neutral.

Notice craving any time that you seek pleasure or avoid pain. Craving fuels the search for happiness in ways and places where satisfaction can never be found. No matter how many chocolate bars you consume, how much money you have in the bank, how beautiful you look, or how much power you wield, craving creates an unquenchable thirst that cannot be satisfied, like the thirst of a person who drinks salt water.[237] As people struggling to maintain sobriety or overcome addictive behaviors work diligently to bring mindfulness to craving, every meditator who

Drawing Out Desire

When you sit down for your next meal, look at your plate before you eat. Notice the colors. Smell the odors. Observe the mind. Is there craving to take a bite? Have you started salivating yet? Consider if you are presently feeling hungry. What is the feeling quality of hunger? If you do not feel hungry, what is the motivation that causes you to reach for the food? As you take your first bite, chew it, and swallow it mindfully. Taste it fully. Observe the physical sensations, notice the pleasant and unpleasant qualities, and observe your mental response. Notice if and when a desire arises for another bite. If your hand reaches for another forkful even before you have swallowed the quantity that is in your mouth, notice what motivated the movement for more. Enjoy a mindful meal by teasing out the distinctions between the physical sensations that come with the impact of taste, smell, and sight, and the distinctly mental processes of desire, repulsion, fear, and craving.

wishes to free the mind from ignorance must face deeply entrenched patterns of reaching toward gratification that never fully arrives.

With Craving as Condition, Clinging Comes to Be

We often recognize clinging after we have become obsessed or fixated upon a desired object, attainment, belief, or experience. Clinging can manifest as a strong form of craving or as false views. The characteristic of clinging is seizing or grasping. It functions by not releasing its hold. Consciousness becomes narrowed to a compelling quest that pleads, "I need that to be happy." This imperative causes the mind to become obsessed with the object of desire. However, since all things in this world

Investigating Attachments

Identify an obvious attachment in your life and reflect:

▸ What feeling or emotion surrounds the attachment?

▸ Are there emotional cravings, habitual routines, social expectations, material needs, or ideological constructs that sustain the attachment?

▸ Can you feel the force of clinging itself, without the elaboration of story—just the raw, visceral experience of wanting?

▸ What does clinging feel like? Do you feel off balance, disconnected, insecure, stiff, threatened, confused, closed off, angry, impulsive, irrational, desperate, hollow, entitled? Notice the specific quality of this suffering state.

are impermanent, it is not possible to hold on to the things that we desire. Whether or not we temporarily attain the object that we seek, inevitably the quest for pleasure and security remains unfulfilled.

With Clinging as Condition, Becoming Comes to Be

As a cause for rebirth, grasping for existence is likened to a fish that is clinging to the hook through greed for the bait.[238] Becoming, also referred to as *being,* identifies the process of coming into existence. Shaped by grasping, becoming describes the stage where *I am* has formed: I am happy, I am depressed, I am a woman, I am the witness, and so on. This is the point in the cycle when identification manifests. The Abhidhamma defines becoming's function as "to make become" and "to become." Its characteristic is being kamma and kamma-result, that is, the cause or the result of action; and it manifests as having kammically wholesome, unwholesome, or indeterminate qualities.

Observing the Constructions of Self

Observe your speech. Notice when the primary communication is merely your own existence. Sometimes what is said is not very important; what we are really saying is, "notice me, I'm here, I'm special, I am like this—*I am*." Become sensitive to the tendency to seek respect, appreciation, confirmation, praise, or recognition. You don't need to squelch these desires should they arise, but notice how they contribute to the development of self-formations. Are you in a phase in your life when self-formations are valuable, or are you ready to deconstruct these processes?

Also observe your internal dialog, ruminations, and daydreams. Make a note of moments when the thought "I am" forms. How much of your thinking is recreating and reinforcing the story of being you? What would the experience of your life be like without the burden of incessant becoming?

With Becoming as Condition, Birth Comes to Be

Propelled by the forces of ignorance, craving, and clinging, and following upon the impetus of becoming, existence is born. The phase of birth in the cycle is characterized by the first genesis in any sphere of becoming; its function is to consign the formation to a sphere of becoming, and it manifests as the result that emerges out of previous conditions. From the viewpoint of multiple lifetimes, this poignant moment of birth occurs at conception when past causes ripen to give rise to consciousness in any realm of existence; for example, as a human embryo or a celestial being. When this cycle is applied to the moment-to-moment events of our lives, birth describes the uncountable momentary occurrences that arise from the continuously changing dynamic of potentials, conditions, and tendencies.

With Birth a Condition, Aging and Death Come to Be

Everything born will inevitably die. Aging and death refers to the demise of every sentient being, including humans, other animals, celestial beings, insects, fish, and so on. It also refers to the momentary maturing and passing of elemental phenomena, the ending of any particular form of identity, and the cessation of each experiential event. In the traditional language, aging points to the characteristic maturing of the aggregates; its function is to lead on to death, and it manifests as the vanishing of youth. Death is defined as bearing the characteristic of falling, shifting, or passing; it functions to disjoin, and it manifests by a departure from the destiny in which one took birth.

In an untrained mind, resistance toward the process of aging and death may be expressed by sorrow, lamentation, pain, grief, and despair. When ignorance affects the dependently arising chain of phenomenal

 The Scope of Suffering

Notice the frequency of unsatisfactoriness in your day-to-day activities. Begin from the very first moment of waking and tune in to any experience, subtle or gross, that is unsatisfactory, disagreeable, or unwanted during your day. Take note of the little things—the unpleasant taste in the mouth upon waking; hunger and thirst; distress while rushing to an appointment; disappointment with the result of a project; impatience when the email you have been hoping for does not arrive; an aching hip; irritation with traffic; the harsh sensation of winter wind; a concern about being judged; the fear of loss; and so on. Notice the pervasive scope of suffering. How willingly do you observe the unsatisfactory nature of life?

events, we suffer. But suffering is optional. When we are mindful in contact with sensory phenomena, and unaffected by ignorance, suffering is not produced.

DISCERNING PAST CAUSES

The discernments that we practice in conjunction with the examination of dependent arising will tease out causal relationships that arise within the cognitive process when we see, hear, smell, taste, touch, and think. They also illuminate the determining forces that condition a succession of rebirths. The instructions that follow describe specific methods to contemplate our own existence as configurations of the five aggregates and to discern the various causes that condition this existence.

It is important to be honest regarding your own aspiration. What are you willing to give up to be free? You are engaged in a process, an evolution of sorts, and you may not be ready to relinquish all attachments right now. This practice invites an actual examination of reality. It is not about just adopting beliefs about kamma and rebirth. The essence of this practice is to honestly investigate the deep roots of ignorance and craving in the present moment, in the past, and in the future. Learn how suffering forms in attachment.[239] See for yourself how causes produce effects. Consider what would be truly satisfying in a conditioned world, and how strongly you desire further experiences in this life and in future existences. Do you really want more and more sensual experiences? Do you want to be reborn again? If so, what experience are you seeking? What do you really want?

The discernment of the causes from previous lifetimes that produced this existence may require strong concentration, but not psychic powers. While knowing very specific past and future life cycles of oneself and other people may require certain specialized powers, the ability to discern the various formations of mental and material aggregates internally and externally is a natural outcome of concentration and insight and it is within the scope of what a contemporary meditator can attain. Speculation about the specifics of kamma could, however, become a distraction, and inferential and intellectual knowledge is insufficient. The

Buddha said that the complete details of kamma were incomprehensible and warned that excessive conjecture could bring vexation or even madness.[240] This study will not predict how a particular past or present event will affect a particular future result; rather, our approach examines the forces that sustain the psychophysical process, stopping short of interpreting a future that will arise from specific causes.

This system, in other words, does not dictate that a specific cause x must produce the specific effect y, but rather it reveals that because there is an effect y, there invariably must have been a cause x to support it.[241] This logical relationship is illustrated with the example of fruit trees. If there is an apple, we can deduce that there must be an apple tree. Although an apple cannot come into existence without an apple tree, it is possible to have a tree without a fruit. An apple seed, however, can only produce future apples. It can never produce mangos, grapefruit, or peaches. Its potential is limited to the production of apples.[242]

In the remainder of this chapter, I will explain the procedures for discerning your own past kamma and your future potentials. The instructions may appear dubious to some readers; they may not fit neatly into your worldview. When I first received these meditation instructions I was skeptical. I left the interview shaking my head, assailed by doubting thoughts, "Does my teacher seriously expect me to see into past lives? This is too weird! This is impossible..." Fortunately, by this point in the training, I had enough confidence in my teacher and the training that I could set aside the doubt-filled thoughts before they disabled me. I tried to retain an open mind and just see what there might be to discover.

Proficiency in discerning ultimate mental and material components (as in chapters 12 and 13) is a prerequisite to practicing these meditation instructions. By discerning the ultimate material and mental phenomena as discussed in the previous chapters, you have metaphorically laid out all the pieces of the jigsaw puzzle on the table. Now, with the discernment of causal relationships, you are, so to speak, putting the pieces together and seeing how each piece fits together with the other units and functions to give rise to conscious experience and life. If the constituents of mind and matter are clear, you will be able to analyze their interactions and recognize the past, present, and future forces exerted by ignorance, craving, clinging, and kamma potency *(kammasatti)* that sustain the cycle of existence. This meditation also invites you to contemplate the ignorance, craving, clinging, and kamma potency that are accruing through your intentional actions during this present lifetime and consider how they will impact future existence.

The process is analogous to a tracking dog that follows the trace of scent left by a person who has passed by. A meditator can follow her line of mental and material factors back through time by tracing the causal connections through successive lifetimes. As you trace the stream of mentality and materiality back through past lives and into future lives, be wary of the seductive potential of personal stories. This process is not concerned with personal identities, social status, previous careers, or family ties, which are the field of psychic powers. Remain focused on the ultimate and impersonal realities of material and mental phenomena and their causal relationships.

Through a sequence of meditative discernments you can see the subtle processes that function within your own stream of conditioning and gain the direct knowledge that because of the cause of suffering in the past, suffering in the present continues; that as long as there is a cause for suffering in the present, suffering will continue in the future. Although you will not fathom all the subtle workings of kamma, this is a fascinating exploration of causality that may confront you with stark questions. What do you really want? What is the cost of that desire? Are your desires leading to a noble aspiration? What aspects of experience are the results of previous actions, and what aspects of your experience are creating the causes for future effects? Can we choose to change our tendencies? How much of your perception is determined by past causes and how much is affected by present events?

MULTIPLICITY OF CAUSES

The model of the twelve links provides a methodology for examining the causal relationships of mind and matter to describe how experience comes to be. But just as many conditions must come together for a ceramic tea cup to be found on my desk—the presence of clay and water, the previous pressure of the potter's skilled hands, the heat of the kiln, the nutrition that provided strength to the potter, the truck driver who transported the cup to the store, and so on—there are always innumerable complementary aspects that support every existence. There is an ancient Indian story of a king who hears beautiful lute music and demands that his minister bring him the sound. When the minister returns and presents the lute to the king, the king is enraged—he wanted the sound, not a wooden instrument. The minister explains that the sound cannot exist apart from the wood, strings, bow, and musician. Music is the effect produced by a combination of conditions.

The Abhidhamma expands the considerations of conditionality to analyze twenty-four causal relationships that govern the interaction of material and mental phenomena through three primary modes: (1) conditioning states that produce, support, or maintain other states, (2) conditioned states that arise and are maintained by conditions, and (3) conditioning forces that are the particular ways that conditioning states function as conditions for the conditioned states.[243]

Many causal relationships can be discerned. There are some ways in which matter supports mental factors; for example, the material ear organ supports the mental formations related to a sound. There are situations in which mental factors affect and sustain materiality, such as when the craving, ignorance, and kamma in a previous lifetime serve as a cause for conception. There are innumerable situations in which mental and material factors intertwine to create mutually dependent conditions enabling conscious experience to arise. From one viewpoint, an immediately preceding state may be a causal factor, such as when the sight of a limping child serves as the proximate cause for the arising of compassion or when your tongue comes into contact with a salty biscuit and triggers an experience of pleasant taste. From another perspective, associated factors may be contributory causes; for example, the five aggregates must arise together, not individually, and the four elements never arise independently but always as a material group. States occurring in the distant past might produce a result in the future, as when a crime committed at one time may ripen into incarceration later. Sometimes the absence of preceding states is a supporting cause, such as when the ending of one consciousness creates the opportunity for a new moment of consciousness to arise. In reality, a multiplicity of intertwined and mutually dependant conditions come together to produce the birth of any phenomenal event; nothing arises due to a single cause. There are always multiple causes and multiple fruits.

Five Distinct Methods

The traditional training incorporates five distinct methods for exploring dependent arising drawn from teachings in the Pali Canon.[244] Just as someone may uproot a creeper vine by starting at its end, or by pulling it from the root, or by taking hold of its center and tugging one way or the other, a meditator may examine the interdependent and causal relationships from various perspectives.

1. The first method starts at ignorance and progresses to the twelfth link, death. The meditator notices that because of ignorance, volitional formations come to be; because of the arising of volitional formations, consciousness arises; because of consciousness, the sixfold sense base comes to be; and so on.

2. The second method investigates the process starting from the central link of feeling and then observes the links that conditioned feeling and will lead to craving, clinging, becoming, and a new birth.

3. The third method starts at the stage of death and traces the sequence in reverse order from death back through to ignorance (aging and death arise dependent upon birth, birth arises dependent upon becoming, becoming arises dependent on clinging, and so on).

4. The fourth method highlights the role that wrong view plays at each stage in the process from craving back through to ignorance (craving arises because of ignorance, feeling arises supported by ignorance... formations arise due to ignorance).

5. The fifth method emphasizes a discernment that reveals that:
    (a) because of five past causes, five present effects arise
    (b) because of five present causes, five future effects arise.

The meditation sequences that follow conform to the training approach that Venerable Pa-Auk Sayadaw instructed me to develop, beginning with the fifth method and followed by the first method. These exercises provide a structure for contemplating a multiplicity of causes for each event, sufficient for revealing the dynamic, interdependent, and empty nature of experience. Each of the five traditional approaches, however, describes a valid way to discern causal relations.

To understand these processes and root out ignorance, you will trace the causal relationships back through time. You will discern conditionality from many angles and across many lifetimes, observe how unwise and wise attention affects experience, recognize the unmistakably dependent nature of existence, and identify the causal forces that propagate rebirth. Your current life has neither transmigrated from a previous realm of existence, nor has it arisen randomly; rather, your life is a result of causes.[245] By observing the subtle intertwining of past conditioning with present-moment choices, you'll see for yourself that your life is not determined exclusively by past actions, and yet is not totally under your control. Equipped with this direct knowledge of how causes and effects operate in your own kammic stream, you'll learn to respond wisely to whatever conditions arise in your life.

Successful completion of the meditative contemplations will bring the realization that there are only causes and effects in the past, in the present, and in the future. There is no separate self that exists outside constantly changing dependently arising conditions. Nothing exists independently. There is no being who is created and no creator who exists apart from causes and effects. Mental and material processes arise moment-by-moment through contingent relationships. Just as curd is formed from milk, could not arise without milk, but is not milk, our existence arises due to causally related conditions.

The unusual meditation exercises that follow may be challenging or appear repetitive for the casual reader. The ability to discern ultimate realities as demonstrated through the successful completion of the lessons in chapters 12–14 is a prerequisite for accomplishing the detailed exercises described below. In addition, most people will need a qualified teacher to avoid conceptual pitfalls and to steer the discernments toward a liberating knowledge when practicing these techniques. You may choose to skip the meditation instructions that follow and simply continue reading the insight meditation teachings in the next chapters. You can return to these meditation instructions when there is an occasion to practice them in retreat with the guidance of teachers skilled in this method.

MEDITATION INSTRUCTIONS FOR EXPLORING THE RELATION BETWEEN PAST, PRESENT, AND FUTURE CAUSES AND EFFECTS

The following systematic meditation instructions are designed to provide experiential knowledge that expands the teachings on past and future formations. The first five meditation instructions in this section apply to the fifth method for discerning causes and effects. Many of the instructions may appear repetitious; however, each slight change in the sequential contemplation highlights a causal relationship that becomes the focus of that discernment. Each causal relationship in the sequence should be repeatedly contemplated while seeing the functioning of mental and material processes. This careful examination constitutes a direct perception of the dependent arising of phenomena.

✣ MEDITATION INSTRUCTION 15.1
Discerning the Causes for This Human Birth

1. Establish your concentration to the highest level that you have attained, and discern materiality and mentality both internally and externally by reviewing the exercises in chapters 12 and 13.

2. Next, make an aspiration for a desirable rebirth. For example: "by the fruit of this jhāna concentration, may I be reborn in a

heavenly realm," or "may the kammic fruit of this meditation be a contributing cause for opportunities to practice the Dhamma in my next lifetime," or "may the merit of this practice produce a healthy and wealthy human life."

3. Then reestablish your concentration and discern the materiality and mentality associated with your aspiration for a rebirth. Discern materiality and mentality that are occurring externally as well.

4. Try to distinguish the five essential causal components: ignorance, craving, clinging, the mental formations associated with the meritorious action, and the kamma potency created by those formations (see Table 13.7 to review mental factors present in unwholesome states). For example:

(a) Ignorance is the wrong view that conceives of a being, whether that being is a human or a deity. A consciousness affected by wrong view will probably have twenty mental formations. If it is accompanied by equanimity and devoid of rapture, it will have only nineteen, but if it is dulled by sloth and torpor, it could contain twenty-one or twenty-two. Discern the unwholesome formations associated with ignorance. See Table 13.7 for mental formations associated with unwholesome states.

(b) Wanting the experience of a heavenly realm or the comfort of health and wealth as a human being is craving. A consciousness affected by craving will have nineteen to twenty-two mental formations. Discern the unwholesome formations associated with craving.

(c) Clinging to the experiences that are craved is the pertinent grasping. A consciousness affected by clinging will have nineteen to twenty-two mental formations. Discern the unwholesome formations associated with clinging.

(d) The volitional formations that occur with the meritorious action will probably have thirty-one to thirty-five mental factors. Discern those wholesome mental formations.

(e) A kamma potency will be produced by the mental formations
associated with that meritorious deed. Try to sense the force
of the kamma potency embedded in the intentional action.
Specifically, discern the mental formations that arise in the
seventh impulsion consciousness, and see how the powerful
seventh impulsion consciousness, supported by the preceding
mind-moments, produces kamma potency.

These five aspects (ignorance, craving, clinging, volitional formations, and kamma potency) highlight the wholesome kammic
formations and the surrounding unwholesome formations that
produce a future life.

5. Once again, make the aspiration for your next life, and recognize
the unwholesome force of ignorance, craving, and clinging, and
the wholesome mental formations and kamma potency associated with that aspiration.

6. To trace these forces back in time, discern the sixty-three rūpas
in your heart base and a present mind-door cognitive process.
Discern the mentality and materiality (either as mentality and
materiality, or by employing the five aggregates structure). Then
examine the processes that occurred when you made the aspiration
a moment earlier. Next discern the mental and material process
that occurred a few minutes before that when you were developing
concentration, such as occurred when you were perceiving your
meditation object. Use your clear and powerfully concentrated
mind to direct your attention backward in time. Then pick up
sense-door or mind-door processes that occurred earlier—ten
minutes ago, one hour ago, two hours ago, several hours ago,
yesterday, several days ago, several weeks ago, several months ago,
a year ago, two years ago, three years ago, and so on. Examine
sense-door processes such as the smell of oatmeal during yesterday's breakfast or the coolness that you felt when you washed your
hands last week. Examine mind-door processes such as the irritation that you felt while waiting for an appointment last month, the
delight that arose when you entered the retreat, or the experience

of concentration in a previous meditation session. Examine each past experience as just mental and material formations; don't embellish the formations with complex concepts or personal stories. Continue in this way, tracing your life back to the fetal and embryo stages, by discerning mental and material processes.

Have no concern for concepts. If you happen to see images (things, people, a snapshot of yourself at a younger age), break down the compactness of the images, beings, and concepts to discern their constituent mental factors and material elements.

7. When you reach the stage of conception there will be only three kinds of materiality present in that first moment of life: the heart base kalāpas, body kalāpas, and sex-determining kalāpas; each consists of ten kinds of rūpas. Discern those thirty kinds of rūpas. For a human birth the initial mental formations will be wholesome. Discern the mental formations associated with this first moment of life.

8. As you glimpse the threshold between lifetimes, you may notice an ultrasubtle stage of death. Just a little further beyond you will find mental and material formations connected to your kammic stream but belonging to a previous existence.

Discern the sixty-three rūpas in that past being's heart base and discern the cognitive process that is occurring there. Sensitivity to external sensory stimuli will have faded in the dying process, so the final mental process will be a mind-door process active only in the heart base through the functioning of body faculty, mind faculty, and life faculty.[246]

9. What is the object of the last moment of consciousness in the previous life? Do you see an image, shape, symbol, object, color, impression, sign, or nimitta? You will find that the same object will be present in five mind-moments:

(a) a near-death moment that occurred just prior to the death of the first past life,

(b) the first moment of consciousness at conception for this present life,

(c) a series of life-continuum consciousnesses that follow immediately after conception,

(d) the life-continuum consciousnesses that arise throughout the
course of this present lifetime and link cognitive processes,

(e) the eventual death moment when this present life span ends
(you will see this after you discern your death through a
forthcoming exercise).

Look back and forth across the transition between your present life and your past life until you can discern the consistent
object of this subtle consciousness. Many different images may
appear around the time of death, so you should check again
and again to be sure that the action that you discerned actually
produced the effect of the subsequent lifetime. The image that
appears in the last mental process may represent the ripening of
an action done much earlier in the lifetime. Examine the material and mental stream until you find the actual time during the
lifetime that the significant action was performed, and then
identify the ignorance, craving, clinging, and mental formations
that are associated with that action.

10. Contemplate the five past causes as the primary causal forces active
in the production of materiality at conception. For example, reflect:

Five past causes:

(a) Because of the arising of ignorance (you will find nineteen to
twenty-two mental formations), the materiality at conception arises (you will find thirty kinds of materiality). Ignorance is the cause, materiality is the effect.

(b) Because of the arising of craving (you will find nineteen to
twenty-two mental formations), the materiality at conception arises (you will find thirty kinds of materiality). Craving
is the cause, materiality is the effect.

(c) Because of the arising of clinging (you will find nineteen to
twenty-two mental formations), the materiality at conception arises (you will find thirty kinds of materiality). Clinging is the cause, materiality is the effect.

(d) Because of the arising of volitional formations (you will likely find thirty-two to thirty-five mental formations), the materiality at conception arises (you will find thirty kinds of materiality). Volitional formations are the cause, materiality is the effect.

(e) Because of the arising of kamma potency (you will likely find thirty-two to thirty-five mental formations), the materiality at conception arises (you will find thirty kinds of materiality). Kamma potency is the cause, materiality is the effect.

11. To discern the causes that produce mentality in conception, consider:

Five past causes:

(a) Because of the arising of ignorance (you will find nineteen to twenty-two mental formations), feeling, perception, formations, and consciousness at conception arise. Ignorance is the cause; feeling, perception, formations, and consciousness are the effects.

(b) Because of the arising of craving (you will find nineteen to twenty-two mental formations), feeling, perception, formations, and consciousness at conception arise. Craving is the cause; feeling, perception, formations, and consciousness are the effects.

(c) Because of the arising of clinging (you will find nineteen to twenty-two mental formations), feeling, perception, formations, and consciousness at conception arise. Clinging is the cause; feeling, perception, formations, and consciousness are the effects.

(d) Because of the arising of volitional formations (you will probably find thirty-two to thirty-five mental formations), feeling, perception, formations, and consciousness at conception arise. Volitional formations are the cause; feeling, perception, formations, and consciousness are the effects.

(e) Because of the arising of kamma potency (you will probably find thirty-two to thirty-five mental formations), feeling,

perception, formations, and consciousness at conception
arise. Kamma potency is the cause; feeling, perception, formations, and consciousness are the effects.

Three present causes:

(a) Because of the arising of heart-base materiality (discern thirty
types of rūpas arising at conception), feeling, perception, formations, and consciousness at conception arise. The material
base is the cause; feeling, perception, formations, and consciousness are the effects.

(b) Because object arises, feeling, perception, formations, and
consciousness at conception arise. Object is the cause; feeling, perception, formations, and consciousness are the effects.

(c) Because of the arising of contact (with associated mental
formations), feeling, perception, formations, and consciousness at conception arise. Contact (with associated mental
formations) is the cause; feeling, perception, formations, and
consciousness are the effects.

As you meditate upon the workings of kamma, you will recognize two significant relationships: (1) because of past causes
(ignorance, craving, clinging, volitional formations, and kamma
potency), five present effects arise; and, (2) because of the five
present causes, the five future effects will arise.

The effects describe the constituents of a resulting experience
and may be organized according to the five aggregates model
(materiality, feeling, perception, formations, and consciousness)
or the model of dependent arising (consciousness, mentality/
materiality, sixfold sense base, contact, and feeling). ✦

→ **MEDITATION INSTRUCTION 15.2**
Causal Relationships in Sense-Sphere Cognitive Processes

1. Establish your concentration and review the discernment of
mentality and materiality, both internally and externally.

TABLE 15.2
Past and Present Causes

Causes	Formation for Analysis	Material bases	Life-continuum consciousness	Adverting consciousness	Sense-door consciousness (eye, ear, nose, tongue, body)	Receiving consciousness	Investigating consciousness	Determining consciousness	Impulsion consciousness	Registration consciousness
Past:										
Ignorance	▓	▓			▓	▓	▓			▓
Craving	▓	▓			▓	▓	▓			▓
Clinging	▓	▓			▓	▓	▓			▓
Volitional formations	▓	▓			▓	▓	▓			▓
Kamma potency	▓	▓			▓	▓	▓			▓
Total Past Causes:	5	5			5	5	5			5
Present:										
Mind		▓								
Temperature		▓								
Nutriment		▓								
Heart base			▓	▓		▓	▓	▓	▓	▓
Material base (eye, ear, nose, tongue, or body base)					▓					
Object			▓	▓	▓	▓	▓	▓	▓	▓
Contact and associated mental formations			▓	▓	▓	▓	▓	▓	▓	▓
Attention					▓					
Wise or unwise attention									▓	
Pertinent element: light (eye); space (ear); wind (nose); water (tongue); earth (body)					▓					
Total Present Causes:		3	3	3	5	3	3	3	4	3

2. To contemplate the causal relationships as they affect each moment of lived experience, such as in a presently occurring sense-sphere cognitive process (for example, the visual impact of a color), begin by discerning five past causes and three present causes for the occurrence of the material heart base and the material eye base. The detailed instructions require that the material base be discerned in every mind-moment. Specifically, recognize the following:

Five past causes:
   (a) Because of the arising of ignorance (you will find nineteen to twenty-two mental formations), materiality arises (you will find sixty-three kinds of materiality in the eye door [see Table 12.4] and sixty-three kinds of materiality in the heart base [see Table 12.6]). Ignorance is the cause, materiality is the effect.
   (b) Because of the arising of craving (you will find nineteen to twenty-two mental formations), materiality arises. Craving is the cause, materiality is the effect.
   (c) Because of the arising of clinging (you will find nineteen to twenty-two mental formations), materiality arises. Clinging is the cause, materiality is the effect.
   (d) Because of the arising of volitional formations (you will probably find thirty-two to thirty-five mental formations), materiality arises. Volitional formations are the cause, materiality is the effect.
   (e) Because of the arising of kamma potency (you will probably find thirty-two to thirty-five mental formations), materiality arises. Kamma potency is the cause, materiality is the effect.

Three present causes:
   (a) Because of the arising of temperature, materiality arises. Temperature is the cause, materiality is the effect.
   (b) Because of the arising of mind, materiality arises. Mind is the cause, materiality is the effect.
   (c) Because of the arising of nutriment, materiality arises. Nutriment is the cause, materiality is the effect.

Through this discernment you will see that the arising of matter can have five primary past causes (ignorance, craving, clinging, volitional formations, and kamma potency) and three primary present causes: mind, temperature, and nutriment. These forces nourish the production of the material base and object. In other words you will know through your meditative insight that:

(a) The causes of kamma-produced rūpa are ignorance, craving, clinging, volitional formations, kamma potency.

(b) The cause of mind-produced materiality is mind, which depends upon the heart base.

(c) The cause of temperature-produced materiality is the fire element.

(d) The cause of nutriment-produced materiality is nutriment.

3. To identify the causes for mentality, discern an eye-door cognitive process and contemplate the causes and effects links for each of the consciousnesses that compose that series as outlined in Table 15.2. The following examples provide clues to the systematic approach.

Five-door adverting consciousness has three present causes.

(a) Because of the arising of heart-base materiality (discern sixty-three types of rūpas in the heart-base), feeling, perception, formations, and consciousness arise. Material base is the cause; feeling, perception, formations, and consciousness are the effects.

(b) Because object arises, feeling, perception, formations, and consciousness arise. Object is the cause; feeling, perception, formations, and consciousness are the effects.

(c) Because of the arising of contact (including associated mental formations), feeling, perception, formations, and consciousness arise. Contact (including associated mental formations) is the cause; feeling, perception, formations, and consciousness are the effects.[247]

Sensory consciousnesses have five past causes and five present causes.

Five past causes:

    (a) Because of the arising of ignorance (you will find nineteen to twenty-two mental formations), feeling, perception of color, formations (discern the associated mental factors), and eye-consciousness arise. Ignorance is the cause; feeling, perception, formations, and consciousness are the effects.

    (b) Because of the arising of craving (you will find nineteen to twenty-two mental formations), feeling, perception of color, formations, and eye-consciousness arise. Craving is the cause; feeling, perception, formations, and consciousness are the effects.

    (c) Because of the arising of clinging (you will find nineteen to twenty-two mental formations), feeling, perception of color, formations, and eye-consciousness arise. Clinging is the cause; feeling, perception, formations, and consciousness are the effects.

    (d) Because of the arising of volitional formations (you will probably find thirty-two to thirty-five mental formations), feeling, perception of color, formations, and eye-consciousness arise. Volitional formations are the cause; feeling, perception, formations, and consciousness are the effects.

    (e) Because of the arising of kamma potency (you will probably find thirty-two to thirty-five mental formations), feeling, perception of color, formations, and eye-consciousness arise. Kamma potency is the cause; feeling, perception, formations, and consciousness are the effects.

Five present causes:

    (a) Because of the arising of eye-base materiality (discern sixty-three types of rūpas in the eye-base), feeling, perception of color, formations, and eye-consciousness arise. Material base is the cause; feeling, perception, formations, and consciousness are the effects.

    (b) Because object arises, feeling, perception of color, formations, and eye-consciousness arise. Object is the cause; feeling, perception, formations, and consciousness are the effects.

(c) Because of the arising of contact (discern eight mental formations arising with sense-door consciousness), feeling, perception of color, formations, and eye-consciousness arise. Contact (including associated mental formations) is the cause; feeling, perception, formations, and consciousness are the effects.

(d) Because attention arises (discern eleven mental factors associated with the preceding five-door adverting consciousness), feeling, perception of color, formations, and eye-consciousness arise. Attention is the cause; feeling, perception, formations, and consciousness are the effects.

(e) Because light arises, feeling, perception of color, formations, and eye-consciousness arise. Light is the cause; feeling, perception, formations, and consciousness are the effects.

Receiving consciousness and investigating consciousness include five past causes and three present causes.

Five present causes:

(a) Because of the arising of ignorance (you will find nineteen to twenty-two mental formations), feeling, perception of color, formations (discern the associated mental factors), and consciousness arise. Ignorance is the cause; feeling, perception, formations, and consciousness are the effects.

(b) Because of the arising of craving (you will find nineteen to twenty-two mental formations), feeling, perception of color, formations, and consciousness arise. Craving is the cause; feeling, perception, formations, and consciousness are the effects.

(c) Because of the arising of clinging (you will find nineteen to twenty-two mental formations), feeling, perception of color, formations, and consciousness arise. Clinging is the cause; feeling, perception, formations, and consciousness are the effects.

(d) Because of the arising of volitional formations (you will probably find thirty-two to thirty-five mental formations), feeling, perception of color, formations, and consciousness arise. Volitional formations are the cause; feeling, perception, formations, and consciousness are the effects.

(e) Because of the arising of kamma potency (you will probably find thirty-two to thirty-five mental formations), feeling, perception of color, formations, and consciousness arise. Kamma potency is the cause; feeling, perception, formations, and consciousness are the effects.

Three present causes:

(a) Because of the arising of heart-base materiality (discern sixty-three types of rūpas in the heart-base), feeling, perception of color, formations, and consciousness arise. Material base is the cause; feeling, perception, formations, and consciousness are the effects.

(b) Because object arises, feeling, perception of color, formation, and consciousness arise. Object is the cause; feeling, perception, formations, and consciousness are the effects.

(c) Because of the arising of contact (including associated mental formations), feeling, perception of color, formation, and consciousness arise. Contact (including associated mental formations) is the cause; feeling, perception, formations, and consciousness are the effects.[248]

Impulsion consciousnesses have four present causes:

(a) Because of the arising of heart-base materiality (discern sixty-three types of rūpas in the heart-base), feeling, perception of color, formations, and eye-consciousness arise. Material base is the cause; feeling, perception, formations, and consciousness are the effects.

(b) Because object arises, feeling, perception of color, formations, and eye-consciousness arise. Object is the cause; feeling, perception, formations, and consciousness are the effects.

(c) Because of the arising of contact (including associated mental formations), feeling, perception of color, formations, and eye-consciousness arise. Contact (including associated mental formations) is the cause; feeling, perception, formations, and consciousness are the effects.[249]

(d) Because wise or unwise attention arises (discern the twelve mental formations composing the preceding determining consciousness), feeling, perception of color, formations, and eye-consciousness arise. Wise or unwise attention is the cause; feeling, perception, formations, and consciousness are the effects.

Discern and link causes from the past and present life to the production of the five aggregates as they arise in wholesome and unwholesome eye-door cognitive processes (see Table 15.2). Thoroughly examine causes and effects related to every stage of the cognitive series including materiality, and the five-door adverting, sense-door, receiving, investigating, determining, impulsion, registration, and life-continuum mind-moments. Include subsequent mind-door adverting, impulsion, and registration consciousnesses that arise dependent upon the sense objects.[250]

4. When the causal forces producing an eye-door cognitive process are clear, discern the causal relationships occurring with other sense doors: ear door, nose door, tongue door, and body door.

5. Perform the meditative discernments first by applying wise attention and discerning the appropriate quantity of associated mental factors for each wholesome cognitive process. You might apply wise attention by perceiving the object as impermanent, unsatisfactory, not-self, repulsive, or as simple mental-material processes. Then perform the meditative discernment with unwise attention by applying the various unwholesome attitudes listed in Table 13.7 to the perception of the sensory phenomena. Discern the appropriate quantity of associated mental factors for each unwholesome cognitive process. ←

→ MEDITATION INSTRUCTION 15.3
Causal Relationships in Mind-Door Cognitive Processes

1. Establish your concentration and review mentality and materiality, both internally and externally.

2. To contemplate the causal relationships of the five aggregates occurring in each mind-moment of the mind-door cognitive process, focus your attention on the mind door at the heart base. Then, stimulate a mind-door cognitive series by discerning one of the twenty-eight kinds of ultimate materiality presented in chapter 12.

Mind-door adverting consciousness has three present causes:

(a) Because of the arising of heart-base materiality (discern sixty-three types of rūpas in the heart-base), feeling, perception of rūpa, formations, and mind-consciousness arise. Material base is the cause; feeling, perception, formations, and consciousness are the effects.

(b) Because object arises, feeling, perception of rūpa, formations, and mind-consciousness arise. Object is the cause; feeling, perception, formations, and consciousness are the effects.

(c) Because of the arising of contact (including associated mental formations), feeling, perception of rūpa, formations, and mind-consciousness arise. Contact (including associated mental formations) is the cause; feeling, perception, formations, and consciousness are the effects.[251]

Impulsion consciousness has four present causes:

(a) Because of the arising of heart-base materiality (discern sixty-three types of rūpas in the heart-base), feeling, perception of rūpa, formations, and mind-consciousness arise. Material base is the cause; feeling, perception, formations, and consciousness are the effects.

(b) Because object arises, feeling, perception of rūpa, formations, and mind-consciousness arise. Object is the cause; feeling, perception, formations, and consciousness are the effects.

(c) Because of the arising of contact (including associated mental formations), feeling, perception of rūpa, formations, and mind-consciousness arise. Contact (including associated mental formations) is the cause; feeling, perception, formations, and consciousness are the effects.[252]

(d) Because of the arising of attention (discern twelve associated mental formations in the preceding mind-adverting moment), feeling, perception of rūpa, formations, and mind-consciousness arise. Attention is the cause; feeling, perception, formations, and consciousness are the effects.

Stimulate mind-door processes by perceiving each of the twenty-eight kinds of ultimate materiality with wise attention. Recognize the appropriate quantity of mental factors that are associated with wholesome states. Thoroughly examine causes and effects related to every aspect of the cognitive series including materiality, and the life-continuum, mind-door adverting, impulsion, and registration consciousnesses.

3. Then, perceive the twenty-eight kinds of materiality with unwise attention according to the unwholesome states listed in Table 13.7, and recognize the appropriate quantity of mental factors that are associated with each unwholesome state. Also discern causes and effects related to wholesome practices such as recollection of Buddha's qualities or death; the cultivation of loving-kindness, compassion, appreciative joy, and equanimity; virtuous action such as generosity, truthful speaking, right livelihood; and any mediation practice.

4. Next, discern the causes and effects for materiality, and the life-continuum, mind-door adverting, impulsions, and registration consciousnesses that arise with wholesome (nonjhāna) states. This would include practices such as recollection of the Buddha, recollection of death, compassion, appreciative joy, right speech, right action, and right livelihood.

5. If you have attained jhāna, also discern the causal relationships of the five aggregates that occur in each jhāna cognitive series. This exercise expands the discernment of meditation instruction

13.3 beyond the analysis of the components of the cognitive process that occurs in jhāna and examines the causal relationships of those components and processes. The basic procedure will be similar to the above discernments, but the quantity of associated mental factors and the number of impulsion consciousnesses will reflect the relevant level and strength of jhāna. ←

→ **MEDITATION INSTRUCTION 15.4**
Further Back in Time

Once you have successfully discerned the past causes (ignorance, craving, clinging, volitional formations, and kamma potency) that brought forth this lifetime, continue the examination of causes and effects as they occurred further into the past.

1. Discern the mental and material formations that arose shortly before the death of your previous life; then, discern the formations that occurred one hour before death, two hours before death, one day before death, one week before death, one month before death, one year before death, and so on. Gradually work your way back throughout the course of the life span observing wholesome and unwholesome states, feelings, contacts, and mental factors in those moments. Empasize wholesome states, such as generousity, restraint, concentration, and insight.

You may see images related to the life, concerns, or activities of that being; you may gain an impression of lifestyle, values, character, attachments, and social role; you might perceive aspirations, actions, or events. Be careful not to become entranced with concepts. Continue to discern the mental and material realities that occurred at various ages. By discerning the sex-determining kalāpa you will know the gender. By discerning mental formations you will know the frequency of wholesome or unwholesome states.

2. Gradually continue back to the moment of conception of this nearest past life. Discern the materiality in that being's heart base (human beings will have sixty-three rūpas) and discern the cognitive process that is occurring in that being's mind door. Repeat the same methodical procedure practiced in meditation instruction 15.1 to determine the precise unwholesome formations of ignorance, craving, and clinging, and the wholesome volitional formations associated with the meritorious action and kamma potency that were performed in your second past life and were responsible for the production of the first past life. Try to discern the object of consciousness at the near-death moment of the second past life or in the first moment of conception of the first past life. Check that the near-death moment, conception, and the life-continuum process share the same subtle object. Check and link the cause-and-effect relationships across the threshold from the second past life to the conception of your nearest past life.

3. Discern cognitive processes as they appear at periodic intervals by moving backward and forward throughout the course of this first past life. You may discern any sense-door or mind-door cognitive processes but give emphasis to the seeds of virtue, meditation, and wisdom by searching specifically for experiences such as generosity, restraint, concentration, and insight. Carefully link causes and effects between your second and first past lives to see how past causes from the second past life, combined with present causes in the first past life, produced mentality and materiality in each mind-moment of cognitive processes during that first past life.

4. You may apply this procedure to discern causes and effects of the five aggregates of additional past lives, linking the third past life to the second, and linking the fourth past life with the third, and so on. A series of four past lives may be a convenient quantity for a beginner to discern. This can provide a sampling of lifetimes to incorporate into the vipassanā meditations introduced in the next chapter. Additionally, it offers a glimpse of the seeds of meritorious conduct and wisdom, and the roots of the aspiration for awakening, in your kammic stream. Experts in this practice may discern the unbroken stream of conditioning back as far as they like. ✦

→ **MEDITATION INSTRUCTION 15.5**
Discerning Future Existences

1. Establish your concentration and review the discernment of mentality and materiality in the present moment. Review meditation instructions 15.2 and 15.3.

2. Then project your attention into the future and discern the mental and material processes that may occur one minute in the future. Follow the stream of mental and material processes forward a few minutes, and again discern the ultimate realities that you find. Follow the stream of arising and perishing phenomena forward one hour, and discern mentality and materiality again. Discern the future occurrence of the five aggregates at periodic intervals until you reach your near-death moment.

3. Discern your inclination toward the next life. Tease out the ignorance, craving, and clinging that surrounds the inclination.

4. See the near-death sign or nimitta—the object that arises in the last moment of consciousness and the mental formations and kamma potency associated with this sign.

5. Crossover into the next existence and discern the formation of that mentality and materiality. Note that thirty-one to thirty-five mental factors are needed to generate a human or celestial life, and the quantity of factors depends upon the kamma that produced that consciousness. In a human existence the heart base kalāpas, body kalāpas, and sex-determining kalāpas will arise first, but life in various celestial realms may have different material compositions.

6. Observe carefully, until you are confident that there is a causal relationship between the kamma potency that you discerned and the initial production of the materiality at conception. Check that the object of the consciousness at conception is the same object held by the final mental process in the previous life.

Discern back and forth across the threshold between lifetimes, checking and linking causes with effects.

7. You may discern the corpse composed of only temperature-produced matter, or perceive an ultrasubtle state of death where the object of consciousness is that which was known at conception and in the life-continuum moments of the existence that is perishing. This is the final subtle appearance of that object.

8. At intervals throughout the duration of this future lifetime, discern the past and present causes that produce the five aggregates as you find them. When you arrive at the near-death moment of this first future existence, carefully discern the causes that produce an effect of a second future existence. Know the ignorance, craving, clinging, volitional formations, kamma potency, and the sign or object. Link the causes from one life to the effects in the next life. Be sure that the same object is shared by the four states of existence:

   (a) the near-death consciousness in the first future life,
   (b) conception in the second future life,
   (c) life-continuum consciousnesses throughout the course of the second future lifetime,
   (d) the death moment when this second future life ends.

9. Discern the mental and material formations of all future existences until you reach the end of your kammic stream. ✦

✧ MEDITATION INSTRUCTION 15.6
Exploring Causal Relationships between the Twelve Links[253]

The following exercise introduces practical contemplation for the first method of discerning causes and effects that was mentioned in this chapter. This first method describes a way to contemplate each link in the chain of dependent arising in forward order from ignorance to death. This is accomplished by observing the rebirth-linking process through successive past and future lives, and wholesome and unwholesome cognitive processes that occur during the course of each life span (see meditation instructions 15.1–15.5). Since the contemplation focuses on causal relationships, it emphasizes the mind-moments that are the result of past kamma: (1) conception, (2) life continuum, (3) death, (4) eye door, (5) ear door, (6) nose door, (7) tongue door, (8) body door, (9) receiving, (10) investigating, and (11) registration.

Through the previous exercises you will have already seen how ignorance, craving, clinging, volitional formations, and kamma potency that arose at the end of your previous life instigated this present existence. Now link the causal factors in forward order as follows:

1. *Because of the arising of ignorance, volitional formations arise.* Ignorance is the cause; volitional formations are the effects. Be sure that you discern the associated mental factors for each part of the mind-door cognitive series associated with both ignorance and volitional formations. Twelve mental factors compose the mind-door adverting consciousnesses; the unwholesome impulsion consciousness of ignorance will have approximately twenty mental factors; the wholesome impulsion consciousness of volitional formations will have approximately thirty-four mental factors.

2. *Because of the arising of volitional formations, consciousness arises.* To reveal the causal relationships between volitional formations and consciousness, observe sense-sphere cognitive processes while contemplating: because of the arising of volitional formations, consciousness arises; volitional formations are the cause, consciousness is the effect. Discern each specific type of consciousness that arises as a result of kamma: eye door, ear door, nose door, tongue door, body door, receiving, investigating, and registration. Recognize the mental factors associated with each mind-moment. Then discern the rebirth-linking process while continuing to contemplate: because of the arising of volitional formations, consciousness arises; volitional formations are the cause; consciousness is the effect. Focus on the consciousnesses that are the result of past kamma: conception, life-continuum, and death.

3. *Because of the arising of consciousness, mentality-materiality arises.*
The causal connection between consciousness and the mentality-materiality link emphasizes the discernment that our present formation of mentality and materiality is dependent upon the consciousness associated with the wholesome kamma from the previous life.

(a) Discern the mental and material formations associated with the meritorious action in the past life and link them to matter and mind that arise with conception, life-continuum, and death moments as you consider: because of the arising of past consciousness, mentality-materiality arises; consciousness is the cause; mentality-materiality is the effect.

(b) Discern a sensory process, and observe the mental formations that arise in each resultant phase of that cognitive process. Contemplate the support provided by the past consciousness that enables the current process to occur. For example, contemplate: because of the arising of past consciousness, mentality-materiality associated eye, ear, nose, tongue, body, and mind arise; consciousness is the cause, mentality-materiality is the effect. Similarly, contemplate the causal force that is exerted on the resultant phases of receiving, investigating, and registration mind-moments by linking past consciousness with the formation of mentality and materiality.

(c) To consider the concomitant support of consciousness and mentality-materiality, observe each resultant formation and contemplate the causal relationships that intertwine mental and material formations with their associated consciousnesses. Observe the kammically formed consciousnesses that arise with conception, life-continuum, death, eye, ear, nose, tongue, body, mind, receiving, investigating, and registration mind-moments. For example, contemplate: because of the arising of eye-consciousness, mentality-materiality associated with the eye door arises; consciousness is the cause, mentality-

materiality is the effect. Or contemplate: because of the arising of receiving consciousness, mentality-materiality associated with receiving consciousness arises; consciousness is the
cause, mentality-materiality is the effect. Or contemplate:
because of the arising of conception consciousness, mentality-
materiality associated with conception arises; consciousness is
the cause, mentality-materiality is the effect.

4. *Because of the arising of mentality-materiality, six sense bases arise.*
To unravel interconnections between mentality-materiality and
the six sense bases, five distinct causal relationships are highlighted.

(a) Mentality is seen as the cause for the arising of mentality.
Specifically, the cause is the mentality that includes the
mental factors associated with consciousness in any given
mind-moment, and the effect is the mentality that includes
the consciousness arising with those mental factors. While
discerning wholesome and unwholesome cognitive processes
occurring at each sense door, or reviewing the transition
between death and rebirth, contemplate the causal relationship of mentality and materiality occurring in each mind-
moment. Emphasize the mind-moments that are the result of
past kamma.

(b) Mentality is seen as the cause for the arising of materiality.
Specifically, mentality is defined as the mental factors that
arise dependent upon a material sense base that supports
them. Interestingly, the cause arises subsequent to the effect,
and yet their mutual dependence is classified as a causal
relationship.

(c) Materiality is seen as the cause for the arising of materiality.
Specifically, the materiality defined as the four elements of
earth, water, fire, wind, and their derived materialities are the
cause for the arising of the six sense bases. This analysis looks
into each type of kalāpa at the six sense bases to highlight the
fact that the material group *(kalāpa)* depends upon its constituent elements *(rūpas).*

(d) Materiality is seen as the cause for the arising of mentality. Specifically, the material sense base provides the support for consciousness and its associated mental factors.

(e) Mentality-materiality is seen as the cause for the arising of mentality. In this step the mental factors and material sense bases are seen together and function as the cause for the arising of the associated consciousness.

5. *Because of the arising of six sense bases, contact arises.* To contemplate the causal connections between the sense bases and contact, consider the six sense bases to include not only the internal material support for eye, ear, nose, tongue, body, and mind, but also the external object: color, sound, odor, flavor, tactile object, and mental object. Contact includes the momentary arising of the associated mental factors in each phase of the cognitive series. As you discern a cognitive process, observe four conditions as the cause for the arising of contact at each mind-moment: the material base, the object, consciousness, and the associated mental factors. Contact is the term that designates the concurrence of these four mutually dependent conditions.

6. *Because of the arising of contact, feeling arises.* Feeling arises with contact at the eye, ear, nose, tongue, body, or mind doors. As you observe a cognitive process, recognize that feeling is associated with contact. The feeling that arises is directly linked to the type of contact that occurred. For example, the feeling of an ear-door cognitive process depends upon the feeling associated with sound-contact. The feeling that is present during a body-door cognitive process depends upon the feeling associated with touch.

7. *Because of the arising of feeling, craving arises.* Craving may follow immediately after a feeling is experienced, or it may be separated by many moments or cognitive processes. Craving is not an inevitable result of every feeling; every experience of

craving, however, depends upon a feeling. Observe the transition between lifetimes and discern the occurrence of the kamma in the previous life. Focus on the feeling, and contemplate how that feeling is the cause for the craving for renewed existence.

8. *Because of the arising of craving, clinging arises.* To contemplate the link between craving and clinging, focus your attention on the craving for future existence (discerned in meditation instruction 15.5), and see the clinging to new existence that follows from that craving. Also, observe when sensory experiences of craving intensify into clinging during daily life encounters.

9. *Because of the arising of clinging, becoming arises.* Becoming is embedded in the force produced by ignorance, craving, and, clinging. Observe the force produced by any group of ignorance, craving, and clinging that is being accumulated for a future life. Link the cause of clinging to the force for becoming, and see how it might support a new existence.

10. *Because of the arising of becoming, birth arises.* By observing the transitions between lifetimes, observe that this kamma potency of becoming is a cause for the next birth.

11. *Because birth arises, aging, sickness, and death arise.* The causal link between birth and death can be understood by contemplating the life span from birth to death, or by regarding the impermanence of momentary mental and material events. Although aging and death must inevitably follow from birth, the experience of sorrow, lamentation, pain, grief, and despair will depend upon various factors, most notably, the presence of ignorance, craving, and clinging. Notice if and when these amplified manifestations of suffering occur, and trace their roots through the cycle of dependent arising. ❦

CHAPTER 16

A Thorough Examination: Recognizing the Characteristic, Function, Manifestation, and Proximate Cause

When a person has assessed the world from top to bottom;
when there is nothing in the world that raises a flicker
of agitation, then he has become a person free...
He has become calm. He has gone beyond getting old;
he has gone beyond being born.
—SUTTA NIPĀTA[254]

YOU HAVE ALREADY gained a basic overview of mental and material phenomena; however, a detailed training will also include the careful contemplation of each factor according to its characteristic, function, manifestation, and proximate cause. The *characteristic (lakkhaṇa)* highlights the most salient and irreducible quality of the phenomena. The *function (rasa)* identifies the dynamic action of the factor, how it performs a task, or achieves a goal. The *manifestation (paccupaṭṭhāna)* describes how it presents itself in lived experience. The *proximate cause (padaṭṭhāna)* points out immediately preceding conditions that permit the factor to occur.

Readers familiar with the theory of meditation presented in the Abhidhamma may have recognized the fourfold definitions of characteristic, function, manifestation, and proximate cause embedded in the previous chapters and discerned phenomena accordingly. Other students might

have discerned the subtle realities of mind, matter, and dependent arising in a brief or intuitive way, and now they may enhance their understanding by applying this formal structure. In keeping with a traditional
approach to training, at this juncture Pa-Auk Sayadaw asked me to study
the fourfold definitions for each of the twenty-eight kinds of material
elements, fifty-two mental factors, various types of consciousness that
arise in the cognitive process, and twelve links in the chain of dependent
arising. This detailed recapitulation of the ultimate realities marks the
final stage of discernment in which you are gathering and examining
objects that you will use for insight meditation.

The basic exercise is rather simple. First, memorize the traditional
fourfold description for each element and factor as defined in Tables
16.1–16.5. Succinct definitions of the factors can be found in *A Comprehensive Manual of Abhidhamma,*[255] the *Visuddhimagga,* and many
other traditional Buddhist sources. Second, discern each element and
factor explained in chapters 12–15 again, now highlighting the fourfold
defining features. Although you might be eager to move on and want
to skip over what could appear to be a tedious review, there is benefit
in this meticulous and careful identification of each object according to
its traditional fourfold description. Once the specificity of phenomena
is thoroughly clarified, you will be well prepared for the forthcoming
and liberating contemplation of the *general characteristics* of those same
objects—as impermanent, suffering, and not-self. A comprehensive
understanding of phenomena includes the comprehension of both the
specific and general characteristics.

✧ MEDITATION INSTRUCTION 16.1
*Defining Phenomena by Characteristic, Function, Manifestation,
and Proximate Cause*

1. For ease of memorization, you might tackle this exercise in
   sections. Start with the material elements, later progress to consciousness and the associated mental factors, and finish with the
   cycle of dependent arising. Memorize the characteristic, function, manifestation, and proximate causes for each element.

2. Discern and analyze a kalāpa, which you shall define. For example, you may begin with an eye-decad kalāpa that you discern in your eye door. You will find earth, water, fire, and wind elements, along with color, odor, flavor, and nutritive essence, plus an array of nonconcrete materialities such as space, growth, decay, lightness, and so on, composing the eye-decad kalāpa. While discerning the earth element in the eye door, define it according to characteristic, function, manifestation, and proximate cause. Then discern the water element, and contemplate water according to its fourfold definition. Similarly, examine every type of constituent found at each sense door and forty-two parts of the body (see chapters 5 and 12), and define each phenomenon one by one according to its characteristic, function, manifestation, and proximate cause.

3. After you have contemplated the twenty-eight types of material elements, examine the fourfold defining features of consciousness, feeling, perception, and mental factors. Memorize the characteristic, function, manifestation, and proximate causes for each mental component.

4. To define mentality, stimulate a cognitive event—for example, hearing a sound. While focusing on the cognitive process that experiences a sound, discern and define the specific mentality associated with the mind-door adverting consciousness according to characteristic, function, manifestation, and proximate cause. Then discern and define mentality associated with ear-consciousness according to these fourfold definitions. In the same way discern and define the mental constituents associated with receiving, investigating, determining, impulsion, and registration consciousnesses. Carefully examine the cognitive series by applying this fourfold defining structure to your recognition of each type of mentality associated with each mind-moment.

5. Follow the same procedure of discerning and defining each type of mental factor that occurs in eye, ear, nose, tongue, body, and mind-door cognitive processes.

6. Finally, memorize the characteristic, function, manifestation, and proximate causes for each link in the cycle of dependent arising. As you discern a development from your past life to the present life, consider each link in the chain of dependent arising in terms of its characteristic, function, manifestation, and proximate causes.

In this way you will thoroughly understand the subtle components of mind and body. The tables below structure the material, mental, and causal constituents for easy memorization. ⬥

TABLE 16.1
Characteristic, Function, Manifestation, and
Proximate Causes of Twenty-Eight Kinds of Materiality

Key:
C = characteristic
F = function
M = manifestation
P = proximate cause

EIGHTEEN REAL OR CONCRETE MATERIALITIES

1. Earth element—*paṭhavīdhātu*

C:	hardness, roughness, heaviness, softness, smoothness, lightness
F:	to act as a foundation for the other coexisting primary elements and derived materialities in the same kalāpa
M:	as receiving coexisting materialities in the same kalāpa
P:	the other three primary elements in the same kalāpa (water, fire, and wind)

2. Water element—*āpodhātu*

C:	flowing, trickling, or oozing
F:	to intensify the coexisting materialities in the same kalāpa
M:	as the holding together or cohesion of material phenomena in the same kalāpa
P:	the other three primary elements in the same kalāpa (earth, fire, and wind)

3. Fire element—*tejodhātu*

C:	heat (a deficiency of heat is referred to as cold)
F:	to mature, maintain, or ripen other material phenomena in the same kalāpa
M:	as a continuous supply of softness, pliancy
P:	the other three primary elements in the same kalāpa (earth, water, and wind)

4. Wind element—*vāyodhātu*

C:	supporting the coexisting material phenomena in the same kalāpa
F:	movement in the other material phenomena (pushing)
M:	propulsion; the cause for the successive arising of other rūpa kalāpas in locations nearby, thereby creating the appearance of movement or change
P:	the other three primary elements in the same kalāpa (earth, water, and fire)

5. Eye-sensitive element—*cakkhupasāda*

C:	the sensitivity of primary elements in the same kalāpa that is ready for the impact of visible data brought through the impingement of an object; or the sensitivity of primary elements in the same kalāpa produced by kamma and springing from craving to see
F:	to pull the mind to a visible object
M:	as the base for eye-consciousness and mental factors associated with it
P:	the primary elements in the same kalāpa produced by kamma, springing from craving to see

6. Ear-sensitive element—*sotapasāda*

C:	the sensitivity of primary elements in the same kalāpa that is ready for the impact of sounds; or the sensitivity of primary elements in the same kalāpa produced by kamma and springing from craving to hear
F:	to pull the mind to sounds
M:	as the base of ear-consciousness and mental factors associated with it
P:	the primary elements in the same kalāpa produced by kamma and springing from craving to hear

7. Nose-sensitive element—*ghānapasāda*

C:	the sensitivity of primary elements in the same kalāpa that is ready for the impact of odors; or the sensitivity of primary elements in the same kalāpa produced by kamma and springing from craving to smell

Table continues on next page

F:	to pull the mind to the odors
M:	as the base of nose-consciousness and mental factors associated with it
P:	primary elements in the same kalāpa produced by kamma and springing from craving to smell

8. Tongue-sensitive element—*jivhāpasāda*

C:	the sensitivity of primary elements in the same kalāpa that is ready for the impact of flavors; or the sensitivity of primary elements in the same kalāpa produced by kamma and springing from craving to taste
F:	to pull the mind to the flavors
M:	as the base of tongue-consciousness and mental factors associated with it
P:	primary elements in the same kalāpa produced by kamma and springing from craving to taste

9. Body-sensitive element—*kāyapasāda*

C:	the sensitivity of primary elements in the same kalāpa that is ready for the impact of tangible data; or the sensitivity of primary elements in the same kalāpa produced by kamma and springing from craving to touch
F:	to pull the mind to the tangible object
M:	as the base of body-consciousness and mental factors associated with it
P:	primary elements in the same kalāpa produced by kamma and springing from craving to touch

10. Color, visible data, visible object—*vaṇṇa*

C:	impinging on the eye-sensitive element
F:	to be the object of eye-consciousness and mental factors associated with it
M:	as the resort of eye-consciousness and mental factors associated with it
P:	the four primary elements in the same kalāpa

11. Sound—*sadda*

C:	impinging on the ear-sensitive element
F:	to be the object of ear-consciousness and mental factors associated with it
M:	as the resort of ear-consciousness
P:	the four primary elements in the same kalāpa

12. Odor—*gandha*

C:	impinging on the nose-sensitive element
F:	to be the object of nose-consciousness and mental factors associated with it
M:	as the resort of nose-consciousness
P:	the four primary elements in the same kalāpa

13. Flavor—*rasa*

C:	impinging on the tongue-sensitive element
F:	to be the object of tongue-consciousness and mental factors associated with it
M:	as the resort of tongue-consciousness
P:	the four primary elements in the same kalāpa

14. Femininity faculty—*itthibhāva indriya*

C:	the female sex
F:	to show that "this is female"
M:	as the marks, signs, features, and ways of the female
P:	the four primary elements in the same kalāpa

15. Masculinity faculty—*purisabhāva indriya*

C:	the male sex
F:	to show that "this is a male"
M:	as the marks, signs, features, and ways of the male
P:	the four primary elements in the same kalāpa

16. Life faculty—*jīvitindriya*

C:	maintaining the material phenomena in the same kalāpa at the moment of their presence
F:	to make the associated materialities occur from arising until passing away
M:	establishing of their presence
P:	the four primary elements that are maintained in the same kalāpa

17. Heart materiality—*hadayarūpa*

C:	being the material support for mind-consciousness

Table continues on next page

F:	to be the base for mind-consciousness
M:	carrying the elements associated with the heart decad kalāpa
P:	the four primary elements in the same kalāpa

18. Nutriment materiality—*ojārūpa*

C:	nutritive essence; the nutritional substance contained in gross edible food
F:	to sustain the physical body and nourish matter
M:	as the fortifying of the body
P:	gross edible food

TEN UNREAL OR NONCONCRETE MATERIALITIES

19. Space element—*ākāsadhātu*

C:	delimiting matter
F:	to display the boundaries of material kalāpas
M:	as the border of material kalāpas; or as gaps and apertures
P:	the material kalāpas delimited

20. Bodily intimation—*kāyaviññatti*

C:	the mode and alteration in the mind-produced wind element of the four primary elements that causes the occurrence of moving forward, moving backward, reaching, bending, wiggling, etc.; bodily intimation (as a mode of the wind element) is a condition for the stiffening, upholding, and moving of the material body
F:	to display intention
M:	as the cause of bodily excitement or movement
P:	the mind-produced wind element
Note:	For example, walking forward displays the intention of traveling in a forward direction, pointing of a finger displays a directional intention, nodding of the head displays an affirmative response.

21. Verbal intimation—*vacāviññatti*

C:	the mode and alteration in the mind-produced earth element that causes speech utterances; the knocking together of matter in the vocal apparatus
F:	to display intention

M:	as the cause of vocalization and verbal expression
P:	the mind-produced earth element

22. Lightness—*lahutā*

C:	nonsluggishness of real materiality that is produced by mind, temperature, or nutritive essence
F:	to dispel heaviness of those three types of materiality
M:	as lightness and transformability
P:	those three types of light materiality

23. Malleability—*mudutā*

C:	nonrigidity of real materiality produced by mind, temperature, or nutritive essence; pliancy
F:	to dispel stiffness or rigidity of those three types of materiality
M:	as nonresistance to action
P:	those three types of malleable materiality

24. Workability—*kammaññatā*

C:	wieldiness of real materiality produced by mind, temperature, and nutritive essence; conducive to bodily action
F:	to dispel unwieldiness
M:	as nonweakness of materiality
P:	those three types of wieldy materiality

25. Production of real materiality—*rūpassa upacaya*

C:	setting up, emerging, or growth of matter such as in the first stage of fetal formation until the physical faculties are developed
F:	to make matter emerge in the first instance or for the first time
M:	as launching; or as the completed state of the real materiality
P:	produced materiality

26. Continuity of real materiality—*rūpassa santati*

C:	occurrence beginning from the developed state of the faculties
F:	to anchor

Table continues on next page

M:	as noninterruption
P:	materiality that is to be anchored

27. Aging of real materiality—*rūpassa jaratā*

C:	the maturing, aging, or ripening of material phenomena
F:	to lead matter toward its termination
M:	as destruction and fall; as loss of newness without loss of being
P:	materiality that is maturing, decaying, or ripening

28. Impermanence of real materiality—*rūpassa aniccatā*

C:	complete breaking up of material phenomena
F:	to make materialities subside
M:	as destruction and falling away
P:	materiality that is completely breaking up

TABLE 16.2
Characteristic, Function, Manifestation, and Proximate Causes of the Consciousness Aggregate[256]

Key:
C = characteristic
F = function
M = manifestation
P = proximate cause

1. Consciousness—*viññāṇacitta*

C:	the knowing or cognizing of an object
F:	to be the "forerunner" of the mental factors because it presides over them and is always accompanied by them
M:	as a continuity of processes
P:	associated materiality and mental factors which are the object for consciousness

2. Rebirth-linking consciousness—*paṭisandhicitta*

C:	cognizing the object which might be kamma, kamma sign, or rebirth sign
F:	to link the processes of two lives or existences
M:	as a continuity of two existences
P:	associated materiality and mental factors which are the object for consciousness

3. Life-continuum consciousness—*bhavaṅgacitta*

C:	cognizing its object which might be kamma, kamma sign, or rebirth sign
F:	noninterruption of flow of consciousness
M:	as a continuity in the flow of consciousness
P:	associated materiality and mental factors which are the object for consciousness

4. Five-door adverting consciousness—*pañcadvārāvajjana*

C:	being the forerunner of eye-, ear-, nose-, tongue-, and body-consciousness; cognizing the occurrence of sensory data such as color, sound, odor, flavor, tactile impressions, and mental phenomena
F:	to advert
M:	as confrontation of sensory data
P:	the interruption of life-continuum consciousness

Table continues on next page

5. Eye-consciousness—*cakkhuviññāṇa*

C:	being supported by the eye and cognizing visible data
F:	to have only visible data as its object
M:	as occupation with visible data
P:	the cessation of adverting consciousness that has visible data as its object

6. Ear-consciousness—*sotaviññāṇa*

C:	being supported by the ear and cognizing sound
F:	to have only sound as its object
M:	as occupation with sounds
P:	the cessation of adverting consciousness that has sound as its object

7. Nose-consciousness—*ghānaviññāṇa*

C:	being supported by the nose and cognizing odor
F:	to have only odor as its object
M:	as occupation with odors
P:	the cessation of adverting consciousness that has odor as its object

8. Tongue-consciousness—*jivhāviññāṇa*

C:	being supported by the tongue and cognizing taste
F:	to have only flavor as its object
M:	as occupation with flavors
P:	the cessation of adverting consciousness that has flavor as its object

9. Body-consciousness—*kāyaviññāṇa*

C:	being supported by the body and cognizing touch
F:	to have only sensations as its objects
M:	as occupation with bodily sensations
P:	the cessation of adverting consciousness that has tangibles as its object

10. Receiving consciousness—*sampaṭicchanacitta*

C:	cognizing visible data, sound, smell, taste, and touch immediately following the respective sense consciousness

F:	to receive sensory data
M:	as the state of receiving the sensory data
P:	the cessation of the previous moment of eye-, ear-, nose-, tongue-, or body-consciousnesses

11. Investigating consciousness—*santīraṇācitta*

C:	the cognizing of the six sense objects
F:	to investigate the six sense objects
M:	as the state of investigation
P:	the heart base

12. Determining consciousness—*voṭṭhabbanacitta*

C:	cognizing of sense data
F:	to determine or define the object that has been cognized by sense consciousness
M:	as the state of determining or discriminating sense data
P:	the cessation of the preceding investigation consciousness

13. Wholesome or unwholesome impulsion consciousness—*kusala* or *akusala javanacitta*

C:	the presence or absence of fault
F:	as the property of purity or impurity in the experience of sense data
M:	as wholesome or unwholesome, profitable or unprofitable; productive of desirable or undesirable effects
P:	wise or unwise attention

14. Registration consciousness—*tadārammaṇacitta*

C:	cognizing of the six sense objects
F:	to take as object what has been apprehended by the preceding impulsion consciousness
M:	as the state of registration of that sense data
P:	cessation of impulsion consciousness

Table continues on next page

15. Mind-door adverting consciousness—*manodvārāvajjana*

C:	cognizing sensory data
F:	to advert attention at the mind door
M:	as the state of adverting
P:	cessation of the preceding life-continuum consciousness

16. Death consciousness—*cuticitta*

C:	cognizing its object which may be kamma, kamma sign, or rebirth sign
F:	shifting
M:	as the state corresponding to the shift
P:	the cessation of the previous consciousness, which may be an impulsion, registration, or life-continuum consciousness

TABLE 16.3

Characteristic, Function, Manifestation, and Proximate Causes of the Feeling Aggregate

Key:
C = characteristic
F = function
M = manifestation
P = proximate cause

1. Pleasure associated with body-consciousness—*sukha*

C:	experiencing desirable sensory data; pleasure being felt
F:	to intensify or relish the associated mental states
M:	as bodily enjoyment
P:	the body faculty

2. Pain associated with body-consciousness—*dukkha*

C:	experiencing undesirable sensory data; pain being felt
F:	to wither the associated mental states
M:	as bodily affliction
P:	the body faculty

3. Joy, bliss, or pleasure associated with mental objects—*somanassa* or *sukha*

C:	experiencing a desirable object
F:	to exploit the desirable aspect or intensify the associated mental states
M:	as mental enjoyment
P:	tranquility

4. Grief—*domanassa*

C:	experiencing an undesirable object
F:	to exploit the undesirable aspect
M:	as mental affliction
P:	the heart base

Table continues on next page

5. Equanimity as neutral feeling—*upekkhā*

C:	being felt as neutral
F:	to neither intensify nor wither the associated mental states
M:	peacefulness
P:	consciousness without rapture

6. Equanimity in the fourth jhāna—*upekkhā*

C:	enjoying an object midway between the desirable and the undesirable
F:	supporting evenness and balance of the associated mental states
M:	as not being apparent
P:	the cessation of pleasure and bliss

TABLE 16.4

Characteristic, Function, Manifestation, and Proximate Causes of Mental Formations

Key:
C = characteristic
F = function
M = manifestation
P = proximate cause

ETHICALLY VARIABLE UNIVERSALS

1. Contact—*phassa*

C:	touching
F:	impingement; to cause the object and consciousness to impinge
M:	as the concurrence of consciousness, sense faculty (door), and object
P:	an object that has come into focus

2. Feeling—*vedanā*

	see Table 16.3

3. Perception—*saññā*

C:	perceiving the qualities of the object
F:	recognizing what has been previously perceived; or to make a sign as a condition for perceiving again "this is the same"
M:	as interpretation by comparing features that had been previously apprehended
P:	an object in whatever way that it appears

4. Volition—*cetanā*

C:	the state of willing
F:	to accumulate kamma
M:	as coordination or directing of action; the organizing of the associated mental factors to act upon an object
P:	the associated mental formations

Table continues on next page

5. One-pointedness—*ekaggatā*

C:	the unification of mind with its object; nonwandering, nondistraction
F:	to conglomerate or unite the associated mental factors; fixing the mind on its object
M:	as peace; or as wisdom in the mode of effect as the Buddha described: "One who is concentrated understands things as they actually are"[257]
P:	usually happiness

6. Life faculty—*jīvitindriya*

C:	maintaining the associated mental formations in the same consciousness moment
F:	to make them occur
M:	as the establishing of their presence
P:	the mental formations to be maintained

7. Attention—*manasikāra*

C:	conducting the associated mental formations toward the object
F:	to yoke the associated mental formations to the object
M:	as confrontation with an object
P:	the object
Note:	Attention is likened to the rudder of a ship, which directs it to its destination, or a charioteer who drives well-trained horses toward their destination. Similarly, attention directs the associated mental factors toward the object. *Manasikāra* is a necessary factor of cognition, and therefore it should be distinguished from *vitakka*, which is an occasional factor. *Manasikāra* is responsible for turning the mind toward the object, whereas *vitakka* applies the mind to the object.

ETHICALLY VARIABLE OCCASIONALS

1. Initial application—*vitakka*

C:	the directing or mounting of the mind onto the object
F:	to strike at and thresh the object
M:	as the leading of the mind onto an object
P:	the object; or material base plus object plus contact and associated mental formations

2. Sustained application—*vicāra*

C:	continued pressure and occupation with the object; the continued stroking of the object by examining it
F:	sustained application of the associated mental formations to the object
M:	as the anchoring of those phenomena on the object
P:	the object; or material base plus object plus contact and associated mental formations

3. Decision—*adhimokkha*

C:	conviction
F:	not to flounder with uncertainty like a blind man groping in the dark
M:	as decisiveness
P:	the object to be convinced about

4. Energy—*viriya*

C:	supporting, exertion, striving, marshalling, or driving of the mental factors to fulfill their function
F:	to consolidate or support associated mental phenomena
M:	as noncollapse
P:	a sense of spiritual urgency or anything that stirs one to vigorous action
Note:	*Viriya* is compared to strong military reinforcements that enable a king's army to defeat its enemy; similarly, energy supports the associated mental factors enabling them to fulfill their function.

5. Rapture—*pīti*

C:	endearing, pleasure, happiness, or satisfaction
F:	to refresh the body and the mind; or to pervade and thrill with rapture
M:	as elation
P:	the object; material base plus object plus contact and associated mental formations

6. Desire—*chanda*

C:	desire to act toward wholesome or unwholesome deeds
F:	searching for an object

Table continues on next page

M:	as need for an object
P:	that same object
Note:	It should be regarded as the stretching forth of the mind toward the object.

BEAUTIFUL UNIVERSALS

1. Faith—*saddhā*

C:	placing confidence in, having faith, trusting
F:	to clarify; to set forth or enter into, as one might set forth to cross a flood
M:	as nonfogginess, resolution, or the removal of the mind's impurities
P:	something worthy to place faith such as hearing the liberating teachings, good friends, wise attention, diligent practice, etc.

2. Mindfulness—*sati*

C:	not wobbling, not floating away from the object
F:	absence of confusion or nonforgetfulness of the object
M:	as guardianship of mind and object; or as confrontation with an objective field
P:	firm perception; or the four foundations of mindfulness

3. Shame of wrongdoing—*hiri*

C:	disgust at bodily, verbal, or mental misconduct
F:	inhibition of evil actions due to the influence of modesty or internal restraints
M:	as the shrinking away from evil due to internal restraints
P:	respect for oneself

4. Fear of wrongdoing—*ottappa*

C:	dread of bodily, verbal, or mental misconduct
F:	inhibition of evil actions due to concern for the opinions of others, punishment, social consequences, or external restraints
M:	as the shrinking away from evil due to external restraints
P:	respect for others

5. Nongreed—*alobha*

C:	nonattachment toward sensual or worldly objects; or nonadherence to the object like a drop of water on a lotus leaf

F:	to not grasp; likened to a liberated bhikkhu
M:	as detachment, not grasping things as mine
P:	wise attention to the object

6. Nonhatred—*adosa*

C:	lack of ferocity, savagery, aggression, aversion; or noncontention, like a gentle friend
F:	to remove annoyance and aversive states
M:	as agreeableness
P:	wise attention to the object

Loving-kindness—*mettā*

C:	promoting the welfare of living beings
F:	to prefer their welfare
M:	as the removal of ill will and annoyance
P:	seeing beings as lovable
Note:	Loving-kindness succeeds when it makes ill will subside; it fails when it produces selfish affection.

7. Evenness of mind—*tatramajjhattatā*

C:	conveying the associated mental factors and consciousness evenly
F:	to prevent deficiency and excess; to inhibit partiality and attachment
M:	as the state of looking on with equanimity, neutrality, and mental balance; ever-evenness
P:	wise attention; or the material base plus object plus associated mental formations

Equanimity—*upekkhā*

C:	promoting the aspect of neutrality toward beings
F:	to see equality in beings
M:	as the quieting of resentment and approval; impartiality
P:	seeing ownership of kamma thus: "Beings are owners of their kamma"
Note:	*Upekkhā* succeeds when it makes resentment and approval subside; it fails when it produces worldly-minded indifference, unknowing, or ignorance regarding experiences.

Table continues on next page

Equanimity in the third jhāna—*jhānupekkhā*

C:	complete evenness of attention toward the object or *nimitta*
F:	to prevent attraction to mundane sensual forms of happiness
M:	as the state of balance which does not grasp even sublime bliss; ever-evenness
P:	the fading away of rapture

8. Tranquility of associated mental factors—*kāyapassaddhi*

C:	the quieting down of disturbance in the associated mental factors
F:	to crush disturbance of the associated mental factors
M:	as inactivity, peacefulness, and coolness of the associated mental factors
P:	the associated mental factors
Note:	Counters the defilements of restlessness and worry, which create distress.

9. Tranquility of consciousness—*cittapassaddhi*

C:	the quieting down of disturbance in consciousness
F:	to crush disturbance of consciousness
M:	as inactivity, peacefulness, and coolness of consciousness
P:	the associated consciousness
Note:	Counters the defilements of restlessness and worry, which create distress.

10. Lightness of associated mental factors—*kāyalahutā*

C:	the subsiding of heaviness in the associated mental factors
F:	to crush heaviness in the associated mental factors
M:	as nonsluggishness of the associated mental factors, swiftness
P:	the associated mental factors
Note:	Counters the defilements of sloth and torpor, which can create heaviness.

11. Lightness of consciousness—*cittalahutā*

C:	the subsiding of heaviness in consciousness
F:	to crush heaviness in consciousness
M:	as nonsluggishness of consciousness, swiftness
P:	the associated consciousness
Note:	Counters the defilements of sloth and torpor, which can create heaviness.

12. Malleability of associated mental factors—*kāyamudutā*

C:	the subsiding of rigidity in the associated mental factors; pliancy of associated mental factors
F:	to crush rigidity in the associated mental factors
M:	as nonresistance to the object
P:	the associated mental factors
Note:	Counters the defilements of wrong view and conceit, which can create rigidity.

13. Malleability of consciousness—*cittamudutā*

C:	the subsiding of rigidity in consciousness; pliancy of consciousness
F:	to crush rigidity in consciousness
M:	as nonresistance to the object
P:	the associated consciousness
Note:	Counters the defilements of wrong view and conceit, which can create rigidity.

14. Workability of associated mental factors—*kāyakammaññatā*

C:	the subsiding of unwieldiness in the associated mental factors
F:	to crush unwieldiness in the associated mental factors
M:	as success in making something an object of the associated mental factors
P:	the associated mental factors
Note:	Counters the remaining hindrances, which create unwieldiness of the associated mental factors. It is likened to the process of refining gold to produce a workable metal. A workable mind enhances trust in the things that should be trusted, and inclines toward beneficial actions.

15. Workability of consciousness—*cittakammaññatā*

C:	the subsiding of unwieldiness in consciousness
F:	to crush unwieldiness in consciousness
M:	as success in making something an object of consciousness
P:	the associated consciousness
Note:	Counters the remaining hindrances, which create unwieldiness of consciousness. It is likened to the process of refining gold to produce a workable metal. A workable mind enhances trust in the things that should be trusted and inclines toward beneficial actions.

Table continues on next page

16. Proficiency of associated mental factors—*kāyapāguññatā*

C:	healthiness and effectiveness of the associated mental factors
F:	to crush incompetence of the associated mental factors
M:	as absence of disability of the associated mental factors
P:	the associated mental factors
Note:	Counters deficiencies of faith, energy, mindfulness, concentration, and wisdom, which disable the associated mental factors.

17. Proficiency of consciousness—*cittapāguññatā*

C:	healthiness and effectiveness of consciousness
F:	to crush incompetence of consciousness
M:	as absence of disability of consciousness
P:	the associated consciousness
Note:	Counters deficiencies of faith, energy, mindfulness, concentration, and wisdom, which disable consciousness.

18. Uprightness of associated mental factors—*kāyujjukatā*

C:	rectitude or straightness of the associated mental factors
F:	to crush tortuousness of the associated mental factors
M:	as honesty, straightforwardness, noncrookedness, and nondeceptiveness of associated mental factors
P:	the associated mental factors
Note:	Counters hypocrisy, deception, and fraudulence, which create crookedness in the associated mental factors.

19. Uprightness of consciousness—*cittujjukatā*

C:	rectitude or straightness of consciousness
F:	to crush tortuousness of consciousness
M:	as honesty, straightforwardness, noncrookedness, and nondeceptiveness of consciousness
P:	the associated consciousness
Note:	Counters hypocrisy, deception, and fraudulence, which create crookedness in consciousness.

BEAUTIFUL OCCASIONALS

1. Right speech—*sammāvācā*

C:	nontransgression in the field of speech
F:	to refrain from verbal misconduct
M:	abstinence from harmful speech
P:	the special qualities of faith, shame of wrongdoing, fear of wrongdoing, fewness of wishes, etc.
Note:	Should be regarded as the mind's disinclination to do evil.

2. Right action—*sammākammanta*

C:	nontransgression in the field of bodily action
F:	to refrain from bodily misconduct
M:	abstinence from harmful bodily action
P:	the special qualities of faith, shame of wrongdoing, fear of wrongdoing, fewness of wishes, etc.
Note:	Should be regarded as the mind's disinclination to do evil.

3. Right livelihood—*sammāājīva*

C:	nontransgression in the field of livelihood
F:	to refrain from misconduct in livelihood
M:	abstinence from engaging in wrong livelihood
P:	the special qualities of faith, shame of wrongdoing, fear of wrongdoing, fewness of wishes, etc.
Note:	Should be regarded as the mind's disinclination to do evil.

4. Compassion—*karuṇā*

C:	to promote the alleviation of suffering
F:	being unwilling to disregard the suffering of beings
M:	as noncruelty
P:	seeing vulnerability in those overwhelmed by suffering
Note:	It succeeds when it makes cruelty subside, and it fails when it produces sorrow.

Table continues on next page

5. Appreciative joy—*muditā*

C:	gladness and rejoicing produced by the recognition of another's success
F:	being not envious
M:	as the elimination of aversion, envy, jealousy, and boredom
P:	seeing the success of others
Note:	*Muditā* succeeds when it makes jealousy and boredom subside, and it fails when it produces merriment, giddiness, exuberance, or exhilaration.

6. Wisdom faculty—*paññā*

C:	penetrating things according to their intrinsic and ultimate nature
F:	to illuminate the object like a lamp makes objects visible; to abolish the darkness of delusion which conceals the individual essence of states
M:	as clarity of perspective, lucid discernment, nonbewilderment, like a good guide in the forest
P:	wise attention; concentration, because the Buddha said: "One who is concentrated understands things as they really are."[258]

UNWHOLESOME UNIVERSALS

1. Delusion—*moha*

C:	unknowing
F:	to conceal the individual essence of an object
M:	as the absence of right understanding
P:	unwise attention

2. Shamelessness of wrongdoing—*ahirika*

C:	absence of disgust at bodily, verbal, and mental misconduct; or immodesty
F:	to do evil out of an absence of modesty or internal restraint
M:	as not shrinking away from the evil
P:	disrespect for oneself

3. Fearlessness of wrongdoing—*anottappa*

C:	absence of anxiety and dread about bodily, verbal, and mental misconduct

F:	doing evil because of an absence of fear and dread of external consequences
M:	as not shrinking away from evil actions
P:	disrespect for others

4. Restlessness—*uddhacca*

C:	agitation, distraction, and disquiet, like water whipped by the wind
F:	unsteadiness, like a flag or banner whipped by the wind
M:	as turmoil, like ashes flung up when pelted with stones
P:	unwise attention to things that stimulate mental disquiet

UNWHOLESOME OCCASIONALS

1. Greed, attachment—*lobha*

C:	grasping an object as *I* or *mine*; craving for the object
F:	sticking or clinging as meat sticks to a hot pan
M:	as not giving up or adhering
P:	seeing enjoyment in things that lead to bondage
Note:	Greed *(lobha)* includes all forms and degrees of attachment, clinging, longing, and selfish desire.

2. Wrong view—*diṭṭhi*

C:	unwise interpretation of things
F:	to presume
M:	as wrong interpretation, as attachment to opinions; holding the belief that the object is permanent, satisfying, or has self-essence
P:	unwillingness to see Noble Ones, hear the true teachings, and so on

3. Conceit—*māna*

C:	haughtiness, pride
F:	to promote arrogance and self-exaltation
M:	as an attitude of vainglory or the desire to promote oneself, narcissism

Table continues on next page

P:	greed dissociated from wrong views
Note:	Conceit *(māna)* is an unwholesome mental state that is rooted in greed or attachment *(lobha)*. Wrong view is excluded as a proximate cause because the presence of wrong view would generate a state categorized as *lobha diṭṭhi* rather than *lobha māna*. An arrogant attachment to one's genuine accomplishments (meditative or professional) could be a proximate cause for conceit to arise if attachment was present and the event was neither misunderstood nor justified by opinions. Note that although wrong views might be absent, delusion *(moha)*, as a universal feature of every unwholesome state, would still be present.

4. Hatred—*dosa*

C:	savageness, ferocity, animosity
F:	to spread like poison; or to burn up and consume one's own support, like a fire consumes a forest
M:	as persecution, like an enemy who finds an opportunity to attack
P:	the grounds for annoyance and ill will
Note:	Hatred *(dosa)* includes all forms and degrees of aversion, ill will, anger, hostility, fear, impatience, aggression, intolerance, etc.

5. Envy—*issā*

C:	being jealous of others' success and good fortune
F:	to be dissatisfied with the accomplishments of others
M:	as aversion toward the accomplishments of others
P:	another's success

6. Possessiveness—*macchariya*

C:	avarice; concealing one's own success so that it will not benefit others
F:	to obstruct sharing with others
M:	as shrinking away to prevent sharing; as meanness or stinginess
P:	one's own success or good fortune

7. Worry—*kukkucca*

C:	subsequent regret
F:	to sorrow about what has and what has not been done

M:	as remorse
P:	wrongs of commission and omission

8. Sloth—*thīna*

C:	lack of driving power, stiffness
F:	to dispel energy
M:	as subsiding, sluggishness, or sinking mind
P:	unwise attention to boredom and drowsiness

9. Torpor—*middha*

C:	unwieldiness, dullness
F:	to smother
M:	as laziness, nodding, and sleep
P:	unwise attention to boredom and drowsiness

10. Doubt—*vicikicchā*

C:	uncertainty
F:	to waver
M:	as indecisiveness; or as taking various sides
P:	unwise attention

TABLE 16.5

Characteristic, Function, Manifestation, and Proximate Causes
of Twelve Factors of Dependent Arising

Key:
C = characteristic
F = function
M = manifestation
P = proximate cause

1. Ignorance—*avijjā*

C:	unknowing the ultimate, nonconventional reality of things
F:	to confuse
M:	as concealing the ultimate reality of things
P:	the four taints *(āsavas)* of sensual desire, desire for existence, ignorance, and wrong view

2. Volitional formations—*saṅkhārā*

C:	forming
F:	to accumulate kamma, or to endeavor
M:	as volition
P:	ignorance

3. Consciousness—*viññāṇa*

C:	cognizing an object
F:	to go before
M:	as rebirth-linking
P:	volitional formations or the physical base and object

4. Mentality and materiality—*nāma rūpa*

Mentality—nāma

C:	bending toward the object
F:	to associate with other mental factors
M:	as the inseparability of the three mental aggregates that compose mentality (feeling, perception, and mental formations)
P:	consciousness

Materiality—rūpa

C:	being molested by change
F:	to be dispersed and subject to decay and change
M:	as indeterminate, that is, neither intrinsically wholesome nor unwholesome
P:	consciousness

5. Six-fold sense base—*saḷāyatana*

C:	actuating, enlarging, extending
F:	to see, hear, smell, taste, touch, and think
M:	as the state of physical base and door
P:	mentality and materiality

6. Contact—*phassa*

C:	touching
F:	impinging, to cause the object and consciousness to impinge
M:	as the coincidence of internal and external base and consciousness
P:	the six sense bases

7. Feeling—*vedanā*

C:	experiencing
F:	to exploit the stimulus of the object
M:	as mental or bodily pleasure and mental or bodily pain
P:	contact

8. Craving—*taṇhā*

C:	being a cause of suffering
F:	to delight
M:	as insatiability
P:	feeling

9. Clinging—*upādāna*

C:	seizing, attachment, or grasping
F:	not to release

Table continues on next page

M:	as a strong form of craving and as false view
P:	craving

10. Becoming—*bhava*

C:	being kamma and kamma-result
F:	by causing to exist; existence
M:	as wholesome, unwholesome, and indeterminate
P:	clinging

11. Birth—*jāti*

C:	the first genesis in any sphere of becoming
F:	to consign to a sphere of becoming
M:	as an emerging in this existence from a past existence
P:	kamma-process becoming *(kamma-bhava)*

12. Aging and death—*jarāmaraṇa*

Aging—jarā

C:	the maturing of the aggregates
F:	leading on to death
M:	as the vanishing and destruction of youth
P:	birth

Death—maraṇa

C:	a fall, shifting, perishing, or passing
F:	to disjoin
M:	as absence from the destiny in which there was birth
P:	birth

SECTION IV

Realizing the Deathless Liberation

CHAPTER 17

Liberating Insight: Contemplating Three Universal Characteristics[259]

All conditioned things are impermanent.
When one sees this with wisdom
one turns away from suffering.
All conditioned things are unsatisfactory.
When one sees this with wisdom
one turns away from suffering.
All things are not-self.
When one sees this with wisdom
one turns away from suffering.
—THE DHAMMAPADA[260]

WHERE DO YOU search for fresh insight? Do you turn to classes, books, teachers, or nature? Meditation invites us to look carefully into our own material and mental experience. The term "insight meditation" is a translation of the Pali word *vipassanā*, which is derived from the root word *passati*, meaning to see. *Vipassanā* can literally be translated as "clear seeing"—the seeing of things as they are actually occurring, not as you might believe they should be or desire them to be. Vipassanā is more than a practice of watching the breath, being with sensations, or letting go of thoughts. Vipassanā is the insight knowledge that comes when you see things as they are. To this end, vipassanā practices emphasize the contemplation of three particular characteristics: impermanence, unsatisfactoriness, and selflessness.

Many "ah ha" moments and personal revelations will accompany your development, providing general insight into the patterns that dominate daily experiences. However, insights that are based on concepts such as *my body* (with all its anatomy, notions of beauty, associations with health, and aches and pains) or *my feelings and emotions* (such as sadness, happiness, joy, or fear) may not reach the depth necessary to unravel the underlying patterns that perpetuate suffering.

THE OBJECT FOR VIPASSANĀ

It is important to contemplate the correct objects during vipassanā meditation. Only subtle realities and their causes can be held steadily enough to endure the rigorous and exacting contemplation that this method entails. Concepts and groupings cannot endure close scrutiny and will fade away when observed. Even the tiny particulate masses called rūpa kalāpas are not sufficiently refined. If they are taken as the object of vipassanā practice, they may soon vanish, leaving the meditator without a clear object, or the mind may slip into a calm but blank state in which there is no perceived object (*bhavaṅga*, discussed in chapters 4 and 13). Sometimes meditators misinterpret this disappearance of consciousness, or object, or both, to be an advanced stage of insight in which the perception of materiality or consciousness ceases. To avoid this error, meditate only upon the subtle realities of mind and matter.

In this process you will be contemplating the impermanence, suffering, and selfless quality of each moment of consciousness, interaction, causal relationship, component of the cognitive process, mental and material factor, and aggregate of experience, as you directly observe them arising and perishing. You must examine each parcel of material and mental experience, because it is in relationship to sense contact that attention is often ensnared by misperception, grasping, and attachment. Contemplate matter and mind, internally and externally, as impermanent, unsatisfactory, and not-self. Just as a dermatological surgeon systematically roots out a skin cancer by examining many tissue biopsies to trace the extent of the incursion, you can carefully and thoroughly examine every possible type of subtle reality.

Most of the exercises contained in this book rely upon a gentle but clear application of mindfulness that nurtures a profound perception of the object. You may observe the breath as it transforms into a stable nimitta suitable for absorption. You may hold a basic concept such as a color or element until it expands into a kasiṇa. You may hold a tiny material mass *(rūpa kalāpa)* to examine its components or discern the functioning of subtle mental factors in a cognitive series. Throughout the course of this training you are learning how to apply wise attention to objects of perception.

As a doctor will examine multiple x-rays taken from different angles to diagnose a broken wrist, you will look carefully, again and again, from different angles and perspectives, to diagnose the conditions of reality. A single perspective might not adequately diagnose the condition, but if you examine phenomena from different perspectives, you will understand their supporting causes, composition, and function. Try to see as thoroughly as possible that every single object of perception, encompassing the totality of lived experience, is affected by the same three characteristics; that they are all impermanent, unsatisfactory, and without a fixed entity of self. Nothing is excluded from this scrutiny—internal, external; near, far; subtle, gross; past, present, and future. The entire universe of experiential phenomena is examined: sensory encounters, mental states, jhāna factors, and insight knowledge. With a concentrated mind and right effort, this level of detailed contemplation can proceed with relative ease.

Characteristic of Impermanence *(anicca)*

What happened to last summer's vacation, yesterday's meeting, and your first love? Where are all the plans you have made? Why are people repeatedly seduced by fantasies of lasting satisfaction when every event that ever occurs soon ends? The Buddha taught, "What is impermanent is not worth delighting in, not worth welcoming, not worth holding to."[261] Although you were probably convinced even before you picked up this book that things are impermanent, you may still find yourself attached to ephemeral things and suffer when they change. You know that the body, with its sensory organs, is subject to illness, decay, and death. You experience change everywhere you look. Even the way that you see the world changes as the eyes deteriorate with age. Extrapolating from this knowledge, how could any feeling or any state associated with eye-contact last?[262] Ignoring the basic and pervasive fact of change keeps people seeking happiness where it can never be found. This is a great tragedy. The Buddha proclaimed that it would be better to live one day deeply, seeing the truth of impermanence, than to live one hundred years lacking effort and not seeing it.[263] He praised the transformative value of perceiving impermanence, even if this insight lasted merely for the brief duration of a finger-snap.[264] It is by actually engaging in the meditative process and wearing away the underlying tendencies toward misperception that this knowledge becomes potent enough to transform the mind and realize what lies beyond all concepts.

Impermanence refers to a radical change in the nature of a thing, from its present state into what is not its present state. There are three stages in the formation of all material phenomena: the arising stage, the standing stage, and the perishing stage.[265] The standing stage is neither static nor continuous, but refers to an inherent inclination that propels matter from the arising stage to the perishing stage. Matter does not exist the moment prior to its arising, and it does not exist the moment after its perishing. Things are born and die, begin and end, arise and pass. At the ultimate level, no constancy can be found in any material or mental experience. All mental phenomena are impermanent as well.

Mental factors are fleeting. In your daily life, you know the inconstant feature of thoughts and mental states—fluctuating moods, transitory thoughts, dynamic feelings, and uncountable changes in perception. How many different mental states did you experience during this last hour? Were there moments of interest, boredom, irritation, calmness, equanimity? Because you know that the mind changes, you meditate, learn, grow, and cultivate wholesome states. If you had an entrenched belief that things could not change, you would not bother to read this book. Observing the ephemeral nature of mind and matter empowers a deep insight into impermanence. It is a potent practice that removes deeply entrenched obstacles, exhausts the tendency to reach for transient sensual experiences, and reduces attachment, ignorance, and self-pride.[266] The practice leads to the vivid realization that "this is not I." As the Buddha stated so clearly, "Impermanent are all formations, their

 Impermanence in Daily Life

Watch the flow of changing experience as you go about your daily activities. Notice how you feel when you wake up in the morning; contemplate impermanence by recognizing that your moods are likely to be different at breakfast, in the afternoon, in the evening. Notice that your thoughts arise and pass as momentary mental phenomena; contemplate the impermanence in those mental states by recognizing their fleeting and fickle qualities. Notice how sensations change as you sit at the table, as you walk to work, as you chew a piece of toast; contemplate the impermanence in those sensations by tracking changing sensations through the course of an activity. Notice how the breath transitions from an inhalation to an exhalation; contemplate the impermanence of the breath. Notice the temperature of the morning air and pause periodically during the day to notice how it changes; contemplate impermanence of temperature and weather. Notice your emotional states. When you feel irritated, excited, tranquil, angry, or frightened, do you expect to be feeling the very same emotion ten minutes later? Check to notice how emotions change. Highlight how the pervasive characteristic of impermanence affects every single moment of your life.

nature is to arise and vanish. Having arisen, they cease; their appeasement is blissful."[267]

THE CHARACTERISTIC OF SUFFERING (DUKKHA)

Certainly you have experienced painful mental and material experiences such as injury, illness, depression, melancholy, distress, grief, or agitation. But suffering is also experienced in more subtle ways. One of the most pervasive is a basic unpleasant feeling of dissatisfaction. The traditional description of *dukkha* refers to matter as "molested by change" and to mentality as "unstable and without rest." Insight into suffering is intimately linked to the recognition of impermanence.

Insight into the characteristic of *dukkha* is gained by realizing that everything that is impermanent will inevitably bring dissatisfaction or distress. In essence, anything that is pleasant is vulnerable to loss; anything born will die; anything unstable is an unreliable support for happiness. Simply because mental and material phenomena are impermanent, they are the basis for suffering, not happiness.

There simply is no place to rest in the cycle of birth, struggle for survival, aging, and death. The countless activities of living create a relentless impingement on the senses; we move from one activity to the next without ever finding a reliable place of comfort. As such, *dukkha* highlights the burden inherent in mind-body processes. When you directly see that conditioned phenomena are completely unsatisfactory, you will release your attachment to things and open to the insight that "this is not mine."

THE CHARACTERISTIC OF NOT-SELF (ANATTĀ)

The concept of self is one of the most primary mental constructs. The insight into not-self, selflessness, or emptiness reveals that there is no fixed entity behind your experience and no stable definition of who you are. Basically there is no static, fixed essence, no self to whom your life happens. The Buddha taught the insight into not-self by way of impermanence, or suffering, or both impermanence and suffering.[268] Buddhist commentaries explain that when a plate or saucer falls and breaks, impermanence is obvious; and when a person is pierced by a splinter or thorn, suffering is obvious; "but, the characteristic of no-self is unobvious, dark, unclear, difficult to penetrate, difficult to illustrate, difficult to make known."[269]

To tease out the perception of not-self through a refined practice of vipassanā meditation, you observe mental and material phenomena arise and perish; this is the insight into impermanence. You recognize that due to this constant change, there is nothing to hold on to for happiness; this is the insight into suffering. You realize that since all the psychophysical events occur due to causes and conditions and are outside your control, you don't need to take life personally; this is the insight into *anattā*. You cannot decide, "body, do not get sick or grow old!" You cannot decide, "mind, do not become feeble, do not feel pain!" Fundamentally, mind and matter are just impersonal processes that are causally related. You

---

 Three Characteristics of Existence

Apply the standard sequence of three inquiry questions extracted from the Buddha's discourses to examine any experience. When seeing a sight, hearing a sound, feeling a touch, or experiencing an emotion, ask yourself:

► Is this permanent or impermanent?
► Can something that is impermanent bring lasting satisfaction?
► Can something that is impermanent and invariably brings suffering really be taken to be myself?

These questions can be interjected into any moment and nurture a quiet contemplation of whatever the attention is observing—breath, pain, sounds, thoughts, intentions, desires, and so on.

may look very closely, but you will find nothing that transfers intact from the past, to the present, or into the future. Yet there are causal relations that usher the next moment into being. There is no creator of our future, and yet nothing arises without a cause. Meticulously examine experience and discover for yourself that everything you discern, the tiniest of particles and the briefest of mind-moments, is not-self. This understanding elicits the insight regarding mind and matter that "this is not myself." Not-self is not something that you must either create or fear; it is simply the fact of things.

SPOTLIGHT ON EXPERIENCE

Insight is not intended to foster cleverness, speculation, or intellectual knowledge. Insight refers to an immediate knowing that will move you beyond the fragmentation of the conceptual mind. Problems arise only through how you conceive of things. You make experience problematic by conceiving of the impermanent as permanent, by interpreting that which is unreliable as satisfactory, and by viewing what is impermanent and unreliable as self.[270] Vipassanā meditation techniques are designed to counter these misperceptions. With insight, for a brief moment you may step outside conditioned patterns and see beyond familiar frames of reference. This knowledge is not bound by the intellect; it is not limited to ideas and concepts; and it is difficult to adequately describe with language. Yet insight has the power of releasing the tension of grasping, ending the strain of clinging. When you see clearly, you will feel open, at ease, content, unconflicted, unconfused, unagitated, and profoundly peaceful.

Insight transforms the fundamental way people experience life. It is like a spotlight that puts experience into clear view. When we perceive *anicca,* we do not cling. When we perceive *dukkha,* we do not cling. When we perceive *anattā,* we do not cling. These three insights are specifically cultivated in vipassanā practice because they prevent clinging and erode delusion. The direct perception of these characteristics implies a twofold understanding of the cause of suffering and the cessation of suffering. As the Buddha described, "One insight is that grasping is the basis of all suffering. The other insight is that by the complete cooling and cessation of all this grasping there is no more arising of suffering."[271]

We train the attention to perceive these characteristics of impermanence, unreliability, and not-self, but the goal is not to walk around pointing out everything that is impermanent, or to annoy friends by continually discerning the suffering aspect of existence, or to amplify the empty characteristic of every activity. Vipassanā practice is not fixated on the sustained perception of these three characteristics which characterize conditioned existence; rather, the condition of the former infatuation with sensory experience is replaced by an attention that is markedly disenchanted. As the Buddha instructed his son Rāhula: "Seeing thus, Rāhula, a well-taught noble disciple becomes disenchanted with the eye, disenchanted with colors, disenchanted with eye-consciousness, disenchanted with eye-contact, and disenchanted with anything comprised within the feeling, perceptions, formations, and consciousness that arise with eye-contact as condition."[272] Insight leads to a profound disenchantment with mental and material phenomena, while deep joy accompanies this profound release of attachment.

Meditative training invites you to carefully examine phenomena and see, as the Buddha taught, that "both the internal element and the external element are simply [elements]. And that should be seen as it actually is with proper wisdom thus: 'This is not mine, this I am not, this is not myself.' When one sees it thus as it actually is with proper wisdom, one becomes disenchanted with [the element] and makes the mind dispassionate towards [the element]."[273] We see beyond conventional views of phenomena to gain liberating knowledge. The Buddha explained that clearly seeing the impermanence of feeling naturally propels the mind toward dispassion: "Seeing thus, a well-taught noble disciple becomes disenchanted with pleasant feeling, disenchanted with painful feeling, disenchanted with neither-painful-nor-pleasant feeling. Being disenchanted, he becomes dispassionate. Through dispassion [the mind] is liberated."[274] There is an almost automatic transformation that occurs as a consequence of seeing things as they are; it is a natural progression from clear seeing, through disenchantment, dispassion, and detachment, and toward liberation from attachment to the five aggregates.

DIFFICULT "D" WORDS

For some contemporary readers, the terms dispassion, disenchantment, and detachment can, unfortunately, trigger images of an aversive withdrawal from life. Yet if you brave association with these terms, you might come to appreciate how each negates a particular problem and does not suggest a disconnection with life.

Disenchantment describes the absence of the seductive force of titillated desire. It is not an aversive rejection but a simple suspension of the fascination that habitually seeks sensory gratification. A mind that is disenchanted sheds the entanglements that shackle it to this psychophysical process. Ajahn Chah, a master in the Thai Forest Tradition, likened disenchantment in the mind to unscrewing a bolt.[275] The mind is unwound and untangled from entrenched distortions of attention.

Detachment describes the ease of a mind not adhering, not fixated, and not identified with the fleeting stream of lived events. There is a definite quality of release: what was confined and caught becomes unbolted or unhooked.

Dispassion implies the ending of suffering or the absence of passion. The term passion is derived from the Latin root which means suffering. Just as compassion, composed of *com* (with), and *passion* (suffering), describes the heart's capacity to stay open in the presence of suffering, *dispassion* describes the heart's capacity to stay open without suffering. Dispassion refers to a mind that stays steady and unperturbed by truth.

When clear seeing is established, you will find that much of what you had clung to regarding personality, social role, and personal preferences simply no longer feels attractive. You will be meditating on the three characteristics of the first three ultimate realities—matter *(rūpa)*, mental factors *(cetasika)*, and consciousness *(citta)*—in order to realize the fourth ultimate reality, nibbāna. Clearly seeing the impermanent, unsatisfactory, and empty nature of the five aggregates, we realize the fruit of awakening.[276] The clarity of seeing the conditioned is the means to glimpse beyond conditioning. The relationship between the conditioned and the unconditioned is similar to the relationship between any number, big or small, to infinity. Infinity cannot be reached by adding more numbers. Similarly, the goal of the Buddha's path is not attained by adding one more contemplation or practice. At some point, a certain clarity will arise that dislodges attachment and liberates the mind from misperception and ignorance.

BEYOND THE DESCRIBABLE

In a flash of insight, when clinging ceases, you may experience something beyond the describable and analyzable factors of mind and matter. It is as though the mind peels away or recoils from the incessant barrage of conditioned mental and material contacts and is naturally inclined toward what is of deepest importance in the spiritual life—the deathless liberation.[277] At this point, a meditator's "mind shrinks away from [the mental and material], turns back from it, rolls away from it, and is not drawn toward it, and either equanimity or revulsion toward it is established in him. Just as a cock's feather or a strip of sinew, thrown into a fire, shrinks away from it, turns back from it, rolls away from it, and is not drawn toward it."[278] The mind turns toward a vast expression of peace, and rests with the unconditioned, the ultimate, the inexpressible, nibbāna as object. The Buddha said, "Whatever the phenomenon through which [beings] think of seeking their self identity, it turns out to be transitory. It becomes false, for what lasts for a moment is deceptive. The state that is not deceptive is nibbāna: that is what the men of worth know as being real. With this insight into reality their hunger ends: cessation, total calm."[279]

Essentially, the mind finally lets go and experiences release; then later, consciousness again picks up the mundane processes of mind and matter, but something has changed. And when you return to your ordinary life, you will find that a deep shift occurred. Life may seem utterly fresh, while the mind is infused with profound equanimity. The conditioned processes of mind and body will no longer feel like a strong bond, merely an old tiring habit. The chains of craving and attachment have loosened. Ceasing to grasp after transient things for your happiness, security, and identity, you may discover a balance and joy through not-grasping, knowing happiness through letting go. The

way of relating to phenomena has changed from an interaction based
on clinging to an infinitely spacious clarity regarding all things. Allow
clear seeing to inform your life.

STRUCTURED VIPASSANĀ MEDITATION INSTRUCTIONS

Each of the following meditation instructions presents traditional and
refined methods for contemplating the characteristics of matter and
mind. The casual reader may choose to skip or skim these exercises and
continue reading with the next chapter. If you wish to genuinely experience these practices you will need to set some time aside, probably under
retreat conditions. Prepare the mind for each exercise with the concentration practice of your choice and a review of the subtle realities previously discerned, which will include twenty-eight types of materiality
(chapter 12), wholesome and unwholesome mental states (chapter 13),
and causal conditions (chapter 15). Once your objects are clearly discerned, proceed to contemplate them according to each set of instructions. A well-concentrated mind will be quick, flexible, alert, and eager
to apprehend the dynamic nature of conditioned phenomena. Meditators who have prepared their minds according to the instructions given
throughout this book will find these contemplations to be astoundingly
effective vehicles that unravel deeply conditioned patterns and lead to
liberating insight.

→ MEDITATION INSTRUCTION 17.1
Contemplating the Characteristics of Materiality

1. Discern the types of ultimate materiality (rūpa) that exist in one
   sense door (see Tables 12.4–12.6). Be sure to discern ultimate
   material phenomena as individual characteristics, not general
   concepts, masses, or clusters. For this phase of vipassanā meditation, we only contemplate concrete materialities,[280] not the
   nonconcrete materialities.[281] Notice their nature to arise and pass
   away. Contemplate their impermanent nature as you observe
   each concrete rūpa actually arising and perishing. Do the same

for all types of ultimate matter found at each of the six sense doors.

2. Now, consider the characteristic of suffering *(dukkha)*, noticing that each material element is oppressed by constant arising and perishing. Contemplate all types of ultimate materiality at each sense door as suffering.

3. Then, meditate on the characteristic of not-self *(anattā)* by noticing the absence of any indestructible, lasting, or controlling entity in this morass of ephemeral events as you observe material phenomena arising and passing away at each sense door.

4. Similarly, analyze, discern, and contemplate the impermanence, unsatisfactoriness, and selflessness of all materiality by dividing the body into the thirty-two parts scheme presented in chapter 5. For a more thorough contemplation, expand the list by incorporating four manifestations of heat and six aspects of wind to produce a forty-two part scheme (see Table 12.7). ✦

→ **MEDITATION INSTRUCTION 17.2**
Contemplating Phenomena One by One

1. Contemplate each individual component of ultimate material and mental phenomena and each causal relationship that you previously discerned. You will be seeing the same subtle elements and factors, only now you will emphasize the causal matrix within which they arise and pass. To do this, discern them one by one, and contemplate each as impermanent. You must actually discern the phenomena as you contemplate, so that you are perceiving the arising and perishing of subtle phenomena, not merely considering the concept of impermanence.

2. Repeat the sequential discernment of material and mental phenomena, contemplating them as suffering.

3. Repeat the sequence again, discerning all phenomena while contemplating them as not-self.

4. Then, sometimes meditate on their impermanence, sometimes their unsatisfactoriness, and sometimes the characteristic of emptiness. Repeatedly contemplate phenomena that are internal and external, near and far. ←

→ MEDITATION INSTRUCTION 17.3
Contemplating Material and Mental Phenomena as Impermanent, Unsatisfactory, and Not-Self

1. Divide phenomena into two categories: material and mental. Discern a cognitive process occurring at the eye door. Analyze the components of that cognitive process to discern their essential factors and elements.

2. Contemplate each individual component of ultimate material and mental phenomena and each casual relationship that you discern at the eye door as impermanent.

3. Repeat this thorough examination with phenomena occurring at each sense door (ear, nose, tongue, body, and mind).

4. Repeat the sequence of discerning, analyzing, and contemplating material and mental phenomena and their causal relationships, contemplating them as suffering and then again as not-self.

5. Sometimes meditate on mentality and materiality and their causal relationships as impermanent, sometimes as unsatisfactory, and sometimes as not-self. Contemplate phenomena that are internal and external, near and far—all while actually discerning the arising and perishing of each phenomenon. Alternately meditate on the three characteristics of material phenomena. Alternately meditate on the three characteristics of mental phenomena. Then, alternately meditate on the three characteristics of material and mental phenomena paired together.

6. Contemplate materiality and mentality at periodic intervals throughout the span of lifetimes, from the earliest lifetime that

you have discerned through to the present moment, and then through to the end of your future existences.

7. Contemplate the causal relationships that occur throughout the lifetimes you have discerned, from the earliest lifetime through the present, and to the end of your future existences. Contemplate each link and each causal relationship in the chain of dependent arising, past, present, and future as impermanent, suffering, and not-self. ⬅

→ **MEDITATION INSTRUCTION 17.4**
Contemplating the Five Aggregates as Impermanent, Unsatisfactory, and Not-Self

1. Divide phenomena into the categories of the five aggregates (matter, feeling, perception, mental formations, and consciousness) as described in chapter 14. Discern a cognitive process occurring at the eye door as practiced in chapter 13, and contemplate each aggregate as impermanent. You must actually discern the phenomena as you contemplate so that you are perceiving the arising and perishing of ultimate mentalities or materialities, and not merely thinking about the concepts of aggregates or impermanence.

2. Repeat the discernment, analysis, and contemplation of the impermanence of the psychophysical process as broken down into five aggregates through cognitive processes that occur at each remaining sense door (ear, nose, tongue, body, and mind).

3. Contemplate the five aggregates as suffering through cognitive processes occurring at all the six sense doors.

4. Repeat the sequence, contemplating the five aggregates as not-self in conjunction with cognitive processes occurring at all the six sense doors.

5. Sometimes meditate on their impermanence, sometimes on their unsatisfactoriness, and sometimes on their emptiness.

Repeatedly contemplate phenomena that are internal and external; near and far; past, present, and future, while actually discerning the arising and perishing of that phenomenon.

Sometimes you will be meditating on materiality, sometimes on feeling, sometimes on perception, sometimes on formations, sometimes on consciousness, sometimes on impermanence, sometimes on suffering, sometimes on selflessness, sometimes on present phenomena, sometimes on past or future phenomena, sometimes on causal relationships. You can do this many times in many combinations to thoroughly contemplate all phenomena. ←

→ **MEDITATION INSTRUCTION 17.5**
Contemplating Jhāna Factors as Impermanent, Unsatisfactory, and Not-Self

After emerging from jhāna, discern the mental formations in the jhāna cognitive sequence as described in chapter 13. Review the jhāna factors associated with the jhāna cognitive process: the mind-door adverting consciousness will have twelve mental formations (consciousness plus eleven associated factors), and generally the first jhāna impulsion consciousness will have thirty-four mental formations (consciousness plus thirty-three associated factors), the second jhāna will have thirty-two mental formations (consciousness plus thirty-one associated factors), and the third and fourth jhānas will have thirty-one mental formations (consciousness plus thirty associated factors) See Tables 13.5 and 13.6. You may organize them as mentality and materiality, consider each phenomena individually, or you may structure the discernment according to the model of five aggregates.

As you discern the arising and passing of the moments of consciousness and their associated mental factors, contemplate each factor or aggregate as impermanent, unsatisfactory, and not-self. Do this internally, that is, with regard to your own jhāna consciousness, and externally, that is, with regard to any jhāna consciousness occurring for other beings. It is not necessary to specifically discern a particular person's mental state. It is enough to look externally— somewhere someone is practicing jhāna. ◆

◇ **MEDITATION INSTRUCTION 17.6**
Contemplating the Bases and Elements as Impermanent, Unsatisfactory, and Not-Self

As an alternative to the traditional aggregate model, you may do the same exercises suggested in this chapter with regard to the traditional five aggregates, but organize phenomena according to the following five categories:[282]

1. materiality, including all the rūpas in the sense doors—for example the sixty-three rūpas of the eye door;

2. objects—for example, color;

3. consciousness—for example, eye-consciousness;

4. contact—for example, eye-contact;

5. feeling and formations—for example, feeling, perception, and all formations that arise with eye-contact as condition.

In order to include all the types of present mental and material factors you will discern a cognitive series stimulated by contact, for example the impact of color at the eye door. In every mind-moment of the cognitive series that knows color (such as five-door adverting consciousness, eye-consciousness, receiving consciousness, investigating consciousness, and so on), there will be materiality and the mental formations of consciousness, contact, feeling, perception, and associated mental formations. See Tables 13.7 and 13.8.

1. Establish concentration and then discern phenomena according to the five categories listed above.

2. If you have established jhāna, you may contemplate the material and mental factors occurring in the jhāna cognitive process as

instructed in meditation instruction 13.3, but this time organize phenomena as basis, object, consciousness, contact, feeling, and the associated mental factors. If you have not established jhāna, simply continue with step three.

3. To contemplate the sense-sphere processes according to the elements, begin by discerning a cognitive process occurring at the eye door as practiced in chapter 13, and contemplate each element as impermanent: contemplate the eye-door materiality as impermanent, the color as impermanent, eye-consciousness as impermanent, eye-contact as impermanent, feeling born of eye-contact plus all the mental factors in the cognitive process as impermanent. This last contemplation would include, for example, contemplating the impermanence of each of the eleven mental formations associated with the five-door adverting consciousness, each of the eight mental formations associated with eye-door consciousness, each of the eleven mental formations associated with receiving consciousness, and so on (see Tables 13.7 and 13.8). You must actually discern the phenomena as you contemplate so that you perceive the arising and perishing of ultimate mental or material phenomena and not merely conceive ideas about impermanent phenomena. Discern, analyze, and contemplate the constituents of both wholesome and unwholesome eye-door processes as impermanent by way of the five categories listed above.

4. Then contemplate each sense door in the same manner. Repeat the discernment, analysis, and contemplation of the impermanence of the psychophysical process as broken down into these five categories while observing cognitive processes that occur at each remaining sense door (ear, nose, tongue, body, and mind).

5. Repeat the sequence of discerning, analyzing, and contemplating both wholesome and unwholesome processes as divided into these five categories, but replace the contemplation of impermanence with a contemplation of suffering and then not-self through all the sense doors.

6. Sometimes meditate on their impermanence, sometimes on their unsatisfactoriness, and sometimes on their emptiness. Repeatedly contemplate phenomena that are internal and external; near and far; past, present, and future, while actually discerning the arising and perishing of that phenomenon.

Sometimes you will be meditating on materiality at the sense-base, sometimes on the materiality of the object, sometimes on consciousness, sometimes on contact, sometimes on feeling and formations, sometimes on impermanence, sometimes on suffering, sometimes on selflessness, sometimes on present phenomena, sometimes on past or future phenomena. You can do this many times in many combinations to thoroughly contemplate all phenomena.

This was the method that the Buddha taught to his son, Rāhula, which effectively conveyed his mind through a series of insights and culminated in complete liberation. ✦

DEEPENING INSIGHT

Sometimes, after applying effort through repetitive exercises, some meditators feel as though they have stalled. The mind might back off from a direct perception of the incessantly changing phenomena by building a conceptual understanding of impermanence, unsatisfactoriness, and not-self. In other words, one might find the mind contemplating the concept of impermanence rather than directly perceiving the impermanence of phenomena—the concept might trump the direct perception. Concepts, however, do not have the power to dislodge subtle clinging. Vipassanā relies on clear seeing—the direct perception of things as they are actually occurring.

A more precise focus on the characteristics may be needed to exhaust the fuel for defilement and free the mind from the underlying tendencies of greed, hatred, and delusion. If the mind does not naturally unravel its attachment to things through the previous exercises, then contemplate each characteristic from multiple angles. You might need to force the mind to face the fact that no happiness can be found in conditioned phenomena. The Buddhist tradition has complied forty ways to view the three basic characteristics of phenomena.[283] Using the forty-part system illuminates greater subtleties and can dramatically enhance dispassion toward phenomena.

⇥ MEDITATION INSTRUCTION 17.7
Forty Ways of Viewing Phenomena with the Three Characteristics

To refine the contemplation of all mental and material phenomena as bound and oppressed by the characteristics of impermanence, suffering, and selflessness, the meditator can review any of the previous vipassanā exercises by highlighting an individual facet of the characteristic. Contemplate phenomena according to the forty ways as listed in Table 17.1, "Forty Ways of Viewing Phenomena with the Three Characteristics."[284] Consider the meaning of each of the forty ways. Use the specificity of this detailed contemplation to understand these characteristics in finer resolution and enhance dispassion toward conditioned phenomena. ⇤

REPELLED TOWARD INSIGHT

Another avenue that can instill dispassion and draw the mind toward liberating insight is the perception of repulsiveness *(asubha)*. In chapter 5 on contemplating thirty-two parts of the body, and chapter 9 on contemplating the corpse, we used the perception of repulsiveness in a mode of concentration to elevate the mind to the first jhāna. Now, the perception of repulsiveness can augment the vipassanā practice. In the mode of insight, the perception of repulsiveness appears as a facet of dukkha. By focusing on the repulsiveness of subtle realities you can intensify your awareness of the incessantly unsatisfactory nature of mental and material phenomena. All the previous vipassanā exercises can be converted to incorporate the repulsive element. Rather than contemplating the primary three characteristics of impermanence, unsatisfactoriness, and not-self, perform the same exercise, but add a fourth characteristic—that of repulsiveness. Consider the repulsive quality of each and every material element, mental factor, and causal relation. Or experiment with the following exercises that highlight the material phenomena of the body.

TABLE 17.1
Forty Ways of Viewing Phenomena with the Three Characteristics

I.   As Impermanent *(anicca)*

1. Impermanent— *aniccato*	They did not exist before they arose; they do not wait to appear. They do not exist after perishing; there is no storehouse, pile, or eternal resting place of material and mental properties.
2. Disintegrating— *palokato*	Their nature is perishing; they crumble with sickness, age, death.
3. Fickle—*calato*	They are unstable; quiver due to sickness, aging, and death; are agitated by gain and loss, love and hate; fluctuating worldly states.
4. Perishable— *paghanguto*	They are affected by effort, and they will perish or disperse in disarray.
5. Unenduring— *addhuvato*	They have no firmness or stability; like fruit that may drop from the tree at any time, material and mental phenomena do not endure.
6. Of changing nature— *viparināma dhammato*	They are subject to change; their arising has an inherent inclination toward perishing; birth leads to death.
7. Coreless—*asārakato*	They are without a stable core; feeble; they will easily perish like sapwood; they have no firm essence.
8. Extinguishable— *vibhavato*	They are subject to annihilation; they perish immediately, without expansion, growth, or increment.
9. Of a mortal nature— *maranadhammato*	They are subject to death.
10. Formed—*sankhatato*	They are produced by causes, formed and restored by repeated supporting conditions.

II.   As Suffering, unsatisfactory *(dukkha)*

1. Suffering—*dukkhato*	They are of an unsatisfactory nature.
2. A disease—*rogato*	They are the base for all bodily and mental diseases.
3. A misery—*aghato*	They are the base for loss to occur.

Table continues on next page

4. A tumor—*gaṇḍato*	It oozes with defilement; they are swollen in the arising phase and erupt in the perishing phase; therefore, they are likened to a boil or tumor.
5. A dart—*sallato*	The ceaseless arising and perishing is oppressive; they are difficult to extract like a piercing spike, thorn, or dart.
6. Affliction—*ābādhato*	They are likened to a severely sick person who is dependent upon the help of a nurse and cannot move without assistance from others, so, material and mental phenomena depend upon causes.
7. Disaster—*upaddavato*	They are the basis for all kinds of adversities such as old age, sickness, punishment, and death.
8. A fearsome thing—*bhayato*	They are seen as a frightful danger here and now, and lead to dangers in future existence.
9. A plague—*itito*	They are seen as a terrifying danger that brings ruin.
10. A menace—*upasaggato*	They always result in loss, such as loss of relatives, friends, health; they are bound up with faults.
11. No protection—*atanato*	They have no protection from inevitable perishing after arising.
12. No shelter—*aleṇato*	They are not a worthy shelter from suffering; they are not a place one can hide from suffering.
13. No refuge—*asaranato*	They are not a refuge from suffering, birth, old age, sickness, and death; they fail to disperse fear.
14. Murderous—*vadhakato*	They are likened to the enemy that poses as a friend and then kills the one whom he has become intimate with; deceived by not seeing clearly, attachment and suffering follow.
15. Root of calamity—*aghamūlato*	They are the cause of unwholesome states, rooted in loss and suffering.
16. A danger—*ādīnavato*	They are a dangerous condition, subject to change, with nothing to rely upon that could avoid perishing.
17. Tainted—*sāsavato*	They are the basis for the arising of the taints of sensual desire, becoming, wrong view, and ignorance.
18. Mara's bait—*mārāmisato*	They are the fuel that sustains Mara (defilement and death).

19. Of a born nature— *jātidhammato*	They are subject to the suffering of birth (arising phase), which is the cause for the inevitable suffering of aging (standing phase) and death (perishing phase).
20. Of an aging nature— *jarādhammato*	They are subject to the suffering of aging and causally related to birth and death.
21. Of an ailing nature— *byādhidhammato*	They are subject to the suffering of sickness and causally related to birth and death.
22. Of a sorrowful nature— *sokadhammato*	They are the basis for sorrow.
23. Of a lamentable nature— *paridevadhammato*	They are the basis for lamentation.
24. Of a despairing nature— *upāyāsadhammato*	They are the basis for despair.
25. Of a defiled nature— *saṁkilesikadhammato*	They are the basis for the defilements, craving, wrong views, and all unwholesome states.

III. As Not-self *(anatta)*

1. Not-self—*anattato*	There is no self to be found, only the functioning of five impermanent aggregates. They are not (1) a self that could own mental and material experience; (2) a self that exists intact throughout successive lifetimes; (3) a self that performs actions; (4) a self that feels objects; (5) a self that decides.
2. Void—*suññato*	They are void of a self that could own mental and material experience; void of a self that exists intact throughout successive lifetimes; void of a self that performs actions; void of a self that feels objects; and void of a self that decides.
3. Alien—*parato*	The five aggregates do not abide by our wishes; they are not under our control; we cannot demand that they not age, sicken, or perish.
4. Empty—*rittato*	They are empty of permanence, happiness, self-existence, and beauty.
5. In vain, worthless— *tucchato*	They exist for only a brief time in the transition from arising to perishing states. They are a worthless support that provides nothing to take a stand upon; trivial.

→ **MEDITATION INSTRUCTION 17.8**
Contemplating the Repulsiveness of Inanimate Material Phenomena

1. Establish concentration, and then review the meditations on the corpse as described in chapter 9. Focus on a corpse, image of a corpse, or recollection of a corpse that you have previously seen, and perceive the faults of the body by recognizing vulnerability to decay, vulgar oozing matter, disgusting smells, and so on. See the body as food for worms, rats, and vultures; it is the breeding ground for flies and bacteria. Emphasize the perception of repulsiveness as you view the corpse.

2. Contemplate your own body as equally repulsive; it bears the same faults as the external corpse. It too will die and decompose like that corpse.

3. Contemplate the faults of an external and internal corpse by moving your attention quickly between the vision of a corpse that you have actually seen and the vision of your own body when it will be dead. For example, you might contemplate the shriveled discolored skin of a corpse that you have seen and then imagine your own skin shriveling and discoloring—seeing both internal and external corpses as repulsive. You might contemplate the stench of decay that surrounds a corpse, and reflect that your own body will smell just as horrible—seeing both internal and external corpses as repulsive. You might contemplate the body festering with worms and larvae, and gnawed on by animals, and know that your own body might fare the same—seeing both internal and external corpses as repulsive. Contemplate quickly back and forth between the internal and external repulsive corpses. Know that those same faults will inevitably befall your own body when it becomes a corpse.

4. You may gradually add additional corpses to the contemplation, giving emphasis to the people who are most dear and beloved to you. Perceive their bodies also as repulsive corpses, recognizing this pervasive repulsive characteristic of matter. As you continue to contemplate corpses and expand the arena of your attention, the perception of repulsiveness will grow strong and you may gradually perceive the entire world as populated only by repulsive corpses.

5. Next, discern the material elements of the corpse. You will find only temperature-produced kalāpas. The only sensitive matter or life faculty might be of an occasional worm or larva. Focus specifically on the ultimate materiality of the corpse. Discern the eight types of rūpas (earth, water, fire, wind, color, odor, flavor, and nutritive essence) that compose those temperature-produced kalāpas in both the external and internal corpse. Contemplate each of the eight types of rūpas as impermanent, unsatisfactory, not-self, and repulsive. You may sense the repulsive quality of even material elements—they are small; their color, smell, and taste are associated with the repulsive corpse; they are subject to birth (arising stage), decay (standing stage), and death (perishing stage) just like the repulsive corpse. Perceive the impermanent, unsatisfactory, not-self, and repulsive characteristics of all the types of rūpas by rapidly alternating between contemplating dead bodies that you have seen and your own body when it becomes a corpse. Notice that in this meditation you are contemplating the repulsive quality at the level of conventional reality (characteristics of corpses), and also at the level of ultimate reality (characteristics of rūpas). ❖

➔ MEDITATION INSTRUCTION 17.9
Contemplating the Repulsiveness of Animate Material Phenomena

1. Establish concentration, and then review the meditations on the thirty-two parts of the body as described in chapter 5. Practice alternately discerning the parts of your own body and the parts of other bodies until gradually you have expanded your perception of body parts, and in every direction throughout the whole world you perceive only body parts. Alternate quickly between discerning internal parts and discerning external parts.

Emphasize the repulsive nature of both internal and external body parts as you practice these meditations.

2. When you are satisfied with the repulsive component of this meditation, next discern the material elements of each part, internally and externally as you did in chapter 12 with the four elements meditation. For many meditators, the ultimate reality of materiality will appear automatically when the repulsive meditation matures. By continuing to alternate quickly between internal and external perceptions, soon all the bodies throughout the whole world will appear as only rūpas or rūpa kalāpas. Discern and analyze all the materiality that you find internally and externally. Contemplate the rūpas as impermanent, unsatisfactory, not-self, and repulsive. You will sense the repulsive quality of even material elements—they are small; their color, smell, and taste is associated with the repulsive body; they are subject to birth (arising stage), decay (standing stage), and death (perishing stage) just like the repulsive body. Perceive the impermanent, unsatisfactory, not-self, and repulsive characteristics of all animate material phenomena.

3. Notice that both your own body and the bodies of all other people are the homes of worms and bacteria that live, breed, feed, excrete their waste, and die within our bodies. Contemplate that the living body, internal and external, is the home of many repulsive things and the repository of filth—highlight the repulsive quality. Then discern, analyze, and contemplate the rūpas that compose the worms and the bacteria as just composed of the four elements and derived materiality. Contemplate the ultimate realities (rūpas) that make up the worms and bacteria as impermanent, unsatisfactory, not-self, and repulsive. Notice that in this meditation you are contemplating the repulsive quality at the level of conventional reality (characteristics of worms and bacteria), and also at the level of ultimate reality (characteristics of rūpas).

4. Then see mental phenomena as repulsive. Observe a cognitive process occurring at the eye door and contemplate each of the five aggregates arising in each mind-moment as repulsive.

Contemplate both the unwholesome and wholesome mental processes as repulsive. The ugly and disquieting qualities of greed, hate, conceit, possessiveness, delusion, and all unwholesome mental processes may be obviously repulsive. Wholesome mental factors as well can be seen as repulsive—they are subject to arising and perishing; they are responsible for producing the five aggregates of clinging in the future. Perhaps the only *dhammas* that are not repulsive are those that arise in conjunction with the perception of nibbāna.

5. In a similar manner, contemplate the mental factors that function in cognitive processes at the remaining sense doors (ear, nose, tongue, body, mind) as repulsive. See all phenomena, internal and external, near and far, mental and material as repulsive.

Highlighting the repulsive quality can elicit powerful dispassion toward material and mental experiences, suspend habitual attachment to mind-body experiences, and support an awakening to the peace that is untouched by any trace of filthy or repugnant qualities. ⤆

CONTEMPLATING PHENOMENA IN INCREMENTAL TIME PERIODS

If you have practiced all the previous exercises but have not yet realized your goal, the following traditional vipassanā method may enhance insight, inspire dispassion, and consume attachment. It is an exhaustive survey of phenomena that emphasizes the limitations and fluctuations of mentality and materiality throughout the course of your lifetime. When I first read the instructions, it appeared so laborious and daunting that I doubted anyone would attempt such a practice. However, with the foundation of strong concentration along with the discernment of ultimate mental and material processes, your mind will be malleable, quick, agile, and balanced, and capable of gaining insight into the nature of phenomena. You may expand and refine this sequence into finer and finer increments, as you wish, apply the contemplation to daily activities, or let the framework inspire a wise and mindful presence by living with the flow of changing phenomena.

The next exercises take the inconstancy of all matter as the primary object, and structure the lesson by sorting materiality in seven ways and then sorting mentality in seven ways. In this approach you will divide your life span into small increments and then contemplate the impermanent, unsatisfactory, and not-self (if you like, you may add repulsive) characteristics of the internal and external phenomena found in each designated period.[285] You already know that materiality is impermanent—so the insight may not bring a radically new discovery regarding the quality of matter. By repeatedly examining the obvious characteristics of matter, internally and externally, near and far, past, present, and future, you wear away any subtle tendency to assume there is anything solid, substantial, or enduring in this life or any other life. It is insufficient to discern just present phenomena, just the matter within your own body, or just a single characteristic. This approach demands a comprehensive review of phenomena to prevent even subtle formations of views, conceit, or attachment from forming through association with mental or material processes.

✧ MEDITATION INSTRUCTION 17.10
Contemplating Phenomena in Incremental Time Periods

Preparation: Establish concentration and conceive of your lifetime, from birth until death, as occurring in a series of time periods. For mathematical simplicity, we will assume a life span of one hundred years. Then, focus on materiality through the seven exercises that follow.

Exercise 1. *Highlighting that Materiality Is Born and Dies*
Casting your meditative discernment into the past, and into the future as practiced in chapter 15, scan your hundred-year life span, from the moment of conception to the moment of your death, observing the continuous arising and perishing of material phenomena in the body. Contemplate the impermanent, unsatisfactory, and not-self characteristics of the internal and external phenomena that you find arising and perishing throughout the course of that hundred-year period. You will have found only

constantly changing materiality. Each element of ultimate materiality will have a rising stage, a standing stage, and a perishing stage. At no time, at no phase of life, not for your body or for the body of another, have you found a single particle of matter that endures. Let this recognition alleviate the insult of aging and end resistance to loss, decay, and death.

Exercise 2. *Highlighting that Materiality Disappears Stage by Stage*

Divide that hundred-year life span into three periods of approximately thirty-three years, which roughly correspond to youth, adulthood, and old age. Next you will divide the hundred-year life span into ten equal parts: ten decades. Throughout this exercise you will continue to divide the life span into incrementally smaller and smaller parts, such as five-year blocks, one-year blocks, one-month blocks, one-week blocks, one-day blocks, until eventually you divide each day into two segments: night and day. Then, finally, divide each day into three segments roughly corresponding to morning, midday, and late afternoon, and divide each night into three segments roughly corresponding to the evening, the middle of the night, and predawn.

Cast your meditative attention into the past as you accomplished in chapter 15. Discern and analyze the rūpa kalāpas that you see arising and perishing, starting at birth and gradually proceeding, stage by stage, until death. Start by dividing the lifetime into thirds. Contemplate all the material phenomena that you can discern in each third as impermanent, unsatisfactory, and not-self, alternating between discerning the materiality that composes your own body at the various times (internal) and the matter that composes other bodies at those times (external). Recognize that the materiality that arises in that phase of life perishes there without ever reaching the subsequent phase of life.

Then divide the life span into smaller increments such as ten decades or twenty five-year blocks and again discern, analyze, and contemplate the impermanent, unsatisfactory, and not-self characteristics of the material phenomena arising in those periods from birth until death, specifically recognizing that materiality arises in one stage, without enduring into the next stage.

Systematically divide your life span into increasingly fine periods: 100 one-year periods, 1,200 one-month periods, 36,500 one-day periods, and so on. Discern, analyze, and contemplate the impermanent, unsatisfactory, and not-self characteristics of the material phenomena arising in those periods from birth until death, internally and externally. In each case see that the materiality does not last or reach the next stage.

Next, consider the various postures that you might take throughout a day, week, month, year, decade, or lifetime.[286] Sitting, standing, walking, and reclining, plus activities such as reaching, bending, stretching, moving forward or backward, looking away or toward, can all be incorporated into this category. You may break down each posture into smaller and smaller increments to discern, analyze, and contemplate the materiality that occurs in each section of movement. For example, you might divide walking into several stages: lifting of the heel, lifting of the foot, moving the foot forward, lowering it, touching the ground, shifting the weight. Reflect that the material phenomenon that arises in one stage of posture, gesture, or activity perishes without reaching the next stage. For example, the matter that manifests while you are sitting does not endure until standing. The wind element that propels your leg forward during walking perishes before the next step. The materiality that reaches for a cashew is not the same materiality that draws the nut toward your mouth. In each phase of the movement, observe and contemplate the material phenomena as impermanent, unsatisfactory, and not-self. Vividly experience the dynamic nature of the body throughout your life span. Every nuance of gesture and every subtle shift of the body is carried by a swirl of microscopic change. Look carefully. Among these currents of changing processes, is there anything that you can claim to be self?

Contemplate the subtle realities by systematically reflecting on the impermanence of materiality, stage by stage, decade by decade, year by year, day by day, hour by hour, activity by activity, gesture by gesture, experience by experience. Carefully discern the impermanence of rūpas during formal meditation by discerning their arising, standing, and perishing phases, and then, as you move about your daily activities, continue to observe the dynamic and ephemeral manifestation of posture and gesture. Mindfully observe an activity, such as putting on your socks or getting out of bed; see the subtle and gross expressions of impermanent phenomena that are born and die posture after posture. Let the insight register: this body is continuously changing, oppressed by change, unstable, and without anything that can be identified as myself.

Exercise 3. *Highlighting Matter Arising from Nutriment*[287]
Sometimes you feel hungry, and at other times you feel no hunger; nutriment is impermanent. The feeling you experience prior to partaking of a buffet is different than the feeling you experience after feasting at the buffet. The popcorn that you ate at the movies last month is not the same matter than will fuel a walk to the store next month. The materiality that is born out of the fuel from a carrot does not remain fixed and stable in any place in the body. Reflect on the impermanence of nutriment.

This exercise highlights matter that arises from nourishment day by day, meal by meal, throughout your life span, by focusing on incremental periods designated by hunger and the satisfaction of hunger. Discern, analyze, and contemplate the impermanent, unsatisfactory, and not-self characteristics of matter arising from nutriment and food consumption. For example, focus on one day and observe the changing material formations that arise and perish during the six periods of the day: before and after breakfast, before and after lunch, and before and after dinner. If your meal schedule differs, modify the instructions accordingly. Observe all material formations, including kamma-produced, temperature-produced, mind-produced, and nutriment-produced materialities, although in this exercise nutriment-produced materialities will be most vivid as you witness the rapid multiplication of nutriment-produced materialities after each meal. Start as a baby, and then examine the next day, and then the next, and then the next until you have examined 36,500 days of food consumption in a hundred-year life span, internally and externally. Notice that at the level of ultimate materiality the quantity of nutriment-produced rūpa kalāpas is minimal when you are hungry, but increases dramatically after eating. No meal has ever lasted, no satisfaction has ever endured; nothing that you gobbled, nibbled, or slurped has formed a solid experience of self. As you approach your next meal, observe your response to hunger, food, and nutriment in light of these contemplations.

Exercise 4. *Highlighting Matter Arising from Temperature*[288]
Notice that cold and heat are continually fluctuating. The temperature at dawn changes before midday. The crisp cold sensation that you perceive as you bite into a chilled slice of melon is replaced by soft warmth as you chew the fruit. The warmth of mother's milk is not the same heat that a middle-aged person feels when mowing the lawn. A simple activity such as taking a shower or washing the dishes can reveal uncountable fluctuations of temperature. Each perception of temperature occurs and then instantly perishes. Temperature does not linger; it is not the same temperature event that arises in the next period of time. Similarly, materiality that is born from temperature arises and perishes instantly, without lingering.

Meditatively review your life span, day by day, from birth until death, highlighting material formations that arise and perish in conjunction with shifts and changes of temperature. Discern materiality (include all ultimate materialities including kamma-produced, mind-produced, nutriment-produced, and temperature-produced materialities), internally and externally, and contemplate those rūpas as impermanent, unsatisfactory, and insubstantial temperature-related phenomena.

You might integrate this perception of temperature into daily activities by periodically tracking the inconstant nature of temperature. Recognize the suffering that stems from incessantly reacting to fluctuations of temperature—preference of season, layers of clothing, adjusting heaters and air-conditioners. Learn to view temperature as simply a dynamic and impersonal material element.

Exercise 5. *Highlighting Materiality that Arises from Kamma*
To expose materiality that is kamma produced, this exercise highlights materiality at each sense door. Discern the sixty-three rūpas in the eye, ear, nose, tongue, and mind doors, and the fifty-three rūpas in the body door as you did in chapter 12 (see Table 12.7). Progress day by day, from birth until death, contemplating the materiality in each sense door, internally and externally, as impermanent, unsatisfactory, and not-self. Although you may accumulate countless sensory experiences in a hundred-year life span, nowhere will you find a single particle that remains stable throughout those encounters.

Exercise 6. *Highlighting Materiality that Is Associated with Happiness*[289]
This traditional approach uses the fluctuations of joy and grief to highlight materiality that arises with consciousness. Reflect on the vicissitudes of joy and grief, happiness and unhappiness. Your mood is fickle. The happiness that you felt when you received a perfect test score on your algebra exam arose and perished then; it is not the same happiness that you experienced when you married. The sadness that you felt when your goldfish died is not the same sadness that you feel reading the obituaries. The happiness that you feel in the moment that you emerge from jhāna is not the same happiness that you feel ten minutes later when you reflect upon it.

Understanding that joy and grief come and go, divide each day in your life into periods designated as being marked by happiness or unhappiness, and then observe materiality that arises in those periods. This exercise highlights the profusion of mind-produced materialities that occur with emotional states, but please discern all materialities, including those that are kamma-produced, nutriment-produced, temperature-produced, and mind-produced. Contemplate the impermanence, unsatisfactoriness, and not-self characteristics of all the material phenomena that arise in association with joy and grief. Discern, analyze, and contemplate rūpas occurring in each period internally and externally.

Then you may notice your mood as you experience daily life. Although nonmeditators may say, "I have been angry all day long," or "I have been grieving continuously since my mother died last year," when you look closely at the mind you will discover that every mood, feeling, emotion, and mental state arises and perishes as a sequence of subtle momentary events. Even the materiality that is associated with joy and grief changes constantly through arising, standing, and perishing phases. It is impossible for sadness to endure or anger to last. One event arises and perishes, and it is followed by another event that arises and perishes, and then another, and so on. Although nonmeditators might take their moods personally, by contemplating moods in the refined structure of formal meditation, and applying that understanding to the intricate dynamics of daily encounters, you will find nothing but fleeting events that are dependent upon ephemeral material formations; nothing is there to build a personal identity upon.

Exercise 7. *Highlighting Natural Materiality*[290]

This exercise highlights inanimate materiality that is not bound up with sense faculties. Consider that all materiality everywhere is impermanent, unsatisfactory, and not-self. Every possession that you cherish, the walls of your home, the wheels of your car, the copper in a penny, the laces that secure your shoes, the flowers in the field, and the rocks that form mountains are all impermanent. Your childhood scooter has long ago decomposed in a landfill. The daffodil bulb that you planted has grown, reproduced, blossomed, and transformed—the matter that is in the current bulb is not the same matter that you planted. The temperature-produced materiality that composes these objects arises and perishes moment by moment. Although a mountain may appear enduring or the wall of a city might seem sturdy, when you discern the rūpas that compose these objects you will find that earth, water, fire, wind, color, odor, flavor, and nutritive essence are continually arising and perishing.

Discern the materiality that surrounds you during each day in your hundred-year life span; emphasize the possessions that you cherish most dearly. Contemplate the impermanent, unsatisfactory, and not-self nature of the material objects. See all things as entirely ephemeral, vulnerable, unpossessable, and insubstantial. ❦

EXPANDING THESE PRACTICES

Each of these exercises demands a comprehensive and systematic examination of ultimate materiality, past, present, and future. Whereas the first six exercises are performed on internal and external phenomena, the seventh exercise includes only external phenomena. By patiently examining matter, dispassion toward material phenomena can grow steady and strong. Again and again, past, present, and future, internally and externally, stage by stage, you will have looked and looked again, and never found anything that can be a stable and enduring expression of matter. This exhaustive survey will wear away attachment to the body and assumptions about a continuity to material forms.

These vipassanā exercises can be expanded as much as you like. You may refine the time increments into smaller and smaller segments until you are viewing material events in each day, each hour, each quarter hour, each minute, each half minute, the time it takes to complete an inhalation or an exhalation—each mind-moment. You might expand the range to incorporate past or future lifetimes, or substitute the forty facets of *anicca, dukkha,* and *anattā* as presented in meditation instruction 17.7 for the three characteristics. As you become more adept with these meditative processes you will find that your inquiry into the nature of phenomena may become playful as well as incisive. Seek to understand the true nature of things and instill dispassion; trust that your practice will wear away any residue of ignorance or tendency toward attachment that might be obstructing your realization of the great peace of release.

Reflection on the Ephemeral Nature of All Phenomena

The traditional instructions for this method emphasize the contemplation of materiality for the preceding seven exercizes. You may, however, notice and reflect that not only is materiality arising and perishing, but feelings, perceptions, mental formations, emotions, moods, and thoughts arise in one period of time and pass instantly; they do not continue into the next time period. For example, the feelings that you felt as a baby crawling on the floor are not the same feelings that you experienced as a teenager learning to drive a car, or as a senior playing a game of cards. The perceptions that you experienced as a child learning to read are not the same perceptions that you experience now as you study this book.

Alternatively, you may combine the mental and material contemplations by discerning phenomena in terms of five aggregates (materiality, feeling, perception, mental formations, and consciousness). Observe cognitive events that occur during each time increment and contemplate internal and external material and mental aggregates as impermanent, unsatisfactory, and not-self. Allow the insight to register deeply, that every single event (including the interdependence of materiality and mentality) that has ever occurred or will ever occur in your life is utterly fleeting, unretainable, and not possessable. Know that feelings, perceptions, mental formations, and consciousness that arise dependent upon materiality also do not last; there are no mental formations that can be owned, controlled, stored, or claimed as *mine*.

→ **MEDITATION INSTRUCTION 17.11**
Focus on Mentality through Seven Exercises[291]

To contemplate the impermanent, unsatisfactory, and not-self characteristics of mental phenomena, the traditional instruction recommends seven exercises that emphasize seeing the impermanence of the meditating phenomena.

Exercise 1. *Highlighting the Meditating Mentality as a Whole Group*

Group together the phenomena discerned through the previous seven methods and then contemplate that the mental process (include mind-door adverting, impulsion, and registration consciousnesses plus all associated mental factors in the cognitive series) that comprehended materiality as impermanent, unsatisfactory, and not-self is also impermanent, unsatisfactory, and not-self. Now you are contemplating the three characteristics of the meditating mind that is aware of the insight into the same three characteristics of materiality. You will, for example, find the standard twelve mental formations in the mind-door adverting consciousness moment of the mind-door process, followed usually by thirty-four mental formations in the impulsion consciousnesses of that meditating mind. With the occasional absence of rapture, however, there may be times when only thirty-three formations are discerned. As you discern the ultimate mentality that composes the meditating mind, contemplate every mental formation in the cognitive series as impermanent, unsatisfactory, and not-self.

Exercise 2. *Highlighting the Meditating Mentality that Occurs in Each of the Seven Separate Methods*
Repeat the previous seven methods that highlight the impermanence, unsatisfactoriness, and emptiness of materiality; then, with regard to each segment, contemplate the mental process that is aware of the three characteristics as also impermanent; then contemplate that mental process as suffering; and then as not-self. For example, you would meditate on rūpas that you find in each stage of life, in the lifting of the foot, in a period of hunger, or in a variation of temperature, and immediately perceive that not only is that matter changing, but the consciousnesses and associated mental factors in the cognitive process that knows the changing matter are also changing. Not only is the matter in that stage of life suffering, but the mental formations involved in knowing it as suffering are also suffering. Not only is the matter throughout your life span not-self, but the mental formations that compose the meditating mind that is knowing the not-self characteristic of matter is also not-self. Thoroughly contemplate every formation in the cognitive process of the mind that is having insight into the three characteristics of materiality throughout the various incremental stages of life.

Exercise 3. *Highlighting a Series of Four Meditating Minds*
This third method is similar; it also focuses on the meditating
mind that has insight into the three characteristics. This third
method, however, extends the comprehension to recognize that
there is also a mental process that is aware of the impermanence,
unsatisfactoriness, and not-self characteristics of the mental process that perceived matter. In this approach you would first contemplate the impermanence of matter in one of the incremental
stages of life, then contemplate the impermanence of each formation in the mental process that is aware of the impermanence of
that matter, and then contemplate that the mental process that
is aware of the impermanence of that previous mental process is
also impermanent. In order to contemplate ultimate reality and
not concepts it is essential to discern the specific consciousnesses
and associated mental factors at compose the cognitive series.
You will find that each component of this second mental process
is also impermanent, and so with the third and fourth mental
processes. In fact, every constituent of every mental process that
you find will be impermanent, but we don't just assume or deduce
this. For direct insight, we look carefully. Follow the contemplation through a series of four levels. At each level contemplate the
impermanence, unsatisfactoriness, and emptiness of the previous mental process with the aid of a subsequent mental process.
Practice in the same manner to contemplate the characteristic of
suffering, and then the characteristic of not-self regarding the all
material and mental components in these cognitive series.

Exercise 4. *Highlighting a Series of Ten Meditating Minds*
To further examine the meditating mind you may continue this
sequence of contemplating the meditating phenomena through
a series of ten perceptions. Although this procedure could continue without end, the *Visuddhimagga* recommends stopping at
ten because the mind may become too familiar with the practice
after excessive repetition and it will cease to have a disenchanting
effect.[292] The procedure is as follows:

1. Meditate on the impermanence of matter found in one interval of the life span.

2. Contemplate that the mental process (include twelve mental formations of the mind-door adverting consciousness, thirty-four mental formations of each impulsion consciousness, and thirty-four mental formations of the registration consciousnesses) that is aware of the impermanence of that matter (we may call this mind 1) is also impermanent.

3. Contemplate that the mental process (including all mental formations in each stage of the cognitive series) that just contemplated mind 1 (which we may call mind 2) is also impermanent.

4. Contemplate the impermanence of mind 2, by mind 3.

5. Contemplate the impermanence of mind 3, by mind 4.

6. Contemplate the impermanence of mind 4, by mind 5.

Thoroughly contemplate every component of the meditating mind as impermanent through a series of ten processes. Then perform the same sequence while perceiving the suffering characteristic. Finally, repeat the exercise perceiving phenomena as not-self.

The Removal of Wrong Views, Conceit, and Craving

After you have thoroughly contemplated all three characteristics of phenomena occurring in the five-door and mind-door cognitive processes, internally and externally, in the past, present, and future, according to the structure of mentality and materiality, the five aggregates, or the sense bases, then you may for a period of time emphasize each characteristic individually.

Exercise 5. *Highlighting the Removal of Wrong Views (diṭṭhi)*
For a discrete period of time—at least one sitting or perhaps each sitting for a few days—focus primarily on the contemplation of not-self. Notice the absence of any wrong view of self.

When you have thoroughly meditated on all the formations, material and mental, as not-self, wrong view will be removed.

Exercise 6. *Highlighting the Removal of Conceit (māna)*
Next, deeply contemplate the characteristic of impermanence for a discrete period of time. When you are contemplating impermanence, the conceit *I am* cannot arise. Conceit arises only when there is the perception of permanence. Observe the absence of conceit in that contemplating consciousness.

Exercise 7. *Highlighting the Removal of Craving (taṇhā)*
Similarly, focus for a discrete period of time on the characteristic of suffering and recognize the absence of craving when the characteristic of suffering is vivid. Craving can only arise when there is the erroneous perception that phenomena could serve as a suitable support for pleasure and happiness. Craving is abandoned through the insight into suffering.

Insight into the three characteristics has the immediate effect of removing the defilements that depend upon erroneous perceptions. This approach to training, however, cautions that defilements are not abandoned through the sole emphasis on a single characteristic. The combined force of insights into impermanence, suffering, and not-self generates the power that removes conceit, craving, and wrong views. The insight into impermanence has the ability to remove conceit only when it is supported by insights into suffering and not-self. The insight into suffering gains liberating power from insights into impermanence and not-self. Similarly, the insight into not-self effectively removes wrong views only when supported by insights into impermanence and suffering. Therefore, in this system of training you would meditate upon all three characteristics without neglecting any or favoring one. Allow the insight into the three characteristics to strengthen and mature so that together they transform the mind from a mode of ignorance to one of liberation. ←

CHAPTER 18

Release from the Bonds: Ten Fetters, Four Stages of Enlightenment, and Sixteen Knowledges

How did you cross the flood? By not halting and by not straining I crossed the flood.[293]
—SAMYUTTA NIKĀYA[294]

D O YOU EXPECT awakening to occur suddenly, like a lightning bolt that radically illuminates your life? Do you think of awakening as a gradual process that slowly transforms your life in the way that fine mist or fog slowly moistens cloth? The Buddhist practice offers a sure path for realization that includes the abandoning of unwholesome factors along with the cultivation of wholesome factors. The diligent practice of releasing the mind from the bondage of greed, hate, and ignorance develops virtue, concentration, and a clear understanding of things as they are and brings all causes of suffering to an end.

Long ago, two disciples of the Buddha, Venerables Sariputta and Punna Mantaniputta, compared Dhamma practice to a journey made by a king with relay chariots.[295] In those days, a king with urgent business in a distant province might use a system of relay chariots, taking the first chariot to a station where he would mount a new carriage with well-rested horses, leave the last one behind, and travel to a third station, where he would leave the second chariot behind and mount another chariot with fresh horses, continuing his journey stage by stage until he finally reached his destination. If he were asked upon arrival, "sir, did you come by this chariot," the king would answer "no." It was through the network of chariots, not an individual vehicle, that he accomplished the journey. Similarly, we develop many practices and attainments on our meditative journey—each skill, method, and stage of development carries us closer to our goal. The purpose of practice is not the perfection of techniques or the elevation of particular attainments. The step-by-step training creates a sequence of platforms; each accomplishment serves as the base for successive stages of progress. Venerable Punna Manta-niputta described the aim as the "practice for the sake of final nibbāna without clinging."[296]

Chapter 17 of this book includes instructions for an approach to insight meditation primarily derived from the traditional sources, thoroughly expounded in the *Visuddhimagga,* and taught by Venerable Pa-Auk Sayadaw. The present chapter places all these practices into the context of a series of traditional insight knowledges, as preserved in a standard progression of insight by Theravādan sources. The experience of this series produces an unmistakable and enduring sequence of inner transformations that culminate in a direct encounter with the deathless element—nibbāna.

1. *The knowledge of analyzing mentality and materiality.* This knowledge is accomplished by the type of clear discernment of material and mental phenomena discussed in detail in chapters 12, 13, and 16, in which you discern and analyze twenty-eight kinds of rūpas, fifty-two mental factors, cognitive processes, and the characteristics, functions, manifestations, and proximate causes of those factors. When this knowledge is attained, the mind is not habitually melding perceptions together into conceptual structures and narrative stories; it is able to tease out the distinctions, discriminate between the processes, and discern psychophysical elements as momentary events. You will be able to clearly distinguish the mental processes as distinct from material processes.

The Sixteen Knowledges

1. The knowledge of analyzing mentality and materiality
(*nāmarūpa-paricchedañāṇa*)

2. The knowledge of discerning cause and condition *(paccaya-
pariggahañāṇa)*

3. The knowledge of comprehension *(sammasanañāṇa)*

4. The knowledge of arising and passing away
(*udayabbayañāṇa*)

    (a) The tender knowledge of arising and passing away

    (b) The mature knowledge of arising and passing away

5. The knowledge of dissolution *(bhaṅgañāṇa)*

6. The knowledge of appearance as terror *(bhayañāṇa)*

7. The knowledge of danger *(adīnavañāṇa)*

8. The knowledge of disenchantment and dispassion
(*nibbidañāṇa*)

9. The knowledge of desire for deliverance
(*muncitukamyatañāṇa*)

10. The knowledge of reviewing the three characteristics
(*paṭisaṅkhārañāṇa*)

11. The knowledge of equanimity toward formations
(*saṅkhārupekkhāñāṇa*)

12. The knowledge of conformity with truth *(anulomañāṇa)*

13. The knowledge of change of lineage *(gotrabhuñāṇa)*

14. The path knowledge *(maggañāṇa)*

15. The fruition knowledge *(phalañāṇa)*

16. The knowledge of reviewing *(paccavekkhaṇañāṇa)*

You may notice that when you take a step and walk, an intention arises and then a movement follows—interactions of mental and material conditions arise together and produce an effect. Phenomena neither exist before arising nor persist after passing away. Mentality is not waiting for an object, and objects are not waiting for mentality. The removal of the illusion of continuity is a distinguishing feature of this insight; mental and material processes are illuminated exactly as they actually occur—as processes of distinct momentary events.

At this stage it will be evident that only mental and material phenomena are occurring. This insight makes it shockingly clear that there is just this experience and the knowing of it—there is no one to whom the meditation is happening, there is no soul, no being, no creator, and no one who can control or claim experience as their own. All perceptions are directly seen to be devoid of constructed concepts. All ephemeral and conditioned events are perceived as pure characteristics—not beings, entities, structures, stories, or concepts. It is an immediate, vivid, and direct knowledge that requires no explanation or thought. Through this stage of insight the impurity of the wrong view of an I, soul, being, or entity is removed. Although concentration is strong, this first knowledge designates only a preliminary phase of insight. At this stage, perception is not yet quick enough to discern the beginning, middle, and end of every process completely.

2. *The knowledge of discerning cause and condition.* With this knowledge you vividly see the dependently arisen nature of the five aggregates—materiality, feeling, perception, formations, and consciousness. This is accomplished by successfully contemplating causes and effects throughout past, present, and future lifetimes as explained in chapter 15. Through carefully analyzing causes and effects, you will discover the patterns that condition your life and learn how they sustain the cycle of suffering.

You will investigate the mechanisms that generate the mind and body, and see how events unfold due to causes and conditions. It will become clear, for instance, that eye-consciousness arises dependent upon the eye and visual objects, and that contact conditions feeling. This meditative practice illuminates the basic understanding that actions lead to results; causes condition existence. With the first knowledge *(knowledge of analyzing mentality and materiality)* you will have discerned each material element and mental factor with their distinct properties and functions. With the development of this second knowledge *(knowledge of discerning cause and condition)* you begin to understand the causal interrelationship of material and mental processes. It is through this examination that you will understand that events do not conform to your plans, are not determined by fate, and are not the design of a creator god.

To comprehend the interaction of mind and matter you may become aware of how an intention to lift the foot *causes* the lifting of the foot, how an intention to stretch the arm *causes* the stretching of the arm, yet no person is causing the lifting and stretching; no being is there stretching or lifting. It is merely a lawful interplay of causally related events. Intellectual understanding does not remove the false view of self. It is the power of direct knowledge that dispels the distortion of I-formations.

Through this meditative training you will observe a moment of sensory contact and find only interrelated causally related processes. Contact occurs dependent on the six sense bases (eye, ear, nose, tongue, body, and mind); feelings arise dependent on contact; feelings condition craving; craving conditions clinging; clinging propels the mind toward a formation of becoming; becoming gives rise to the birth of the sense of self. Finally, the conditionality of the psychophysical processes is carefully discerned. Recognize experience as an effect formed through a chain of causes.

Although people may cling to the five aggregates or attribute substantiality to mind and body, you will see that in fact birth arises when the past causes of craving, ignorance, and grasping conspire to produce continued existence. This insight knowledge reveals three phases of the round of becoming: (1) the cycle of defilements *(kilesavaṭṭa)*, (2) the cycle of actions *(kammavaṭṭa)*, and (3) the cycle of results *(vipākavaṭṭa)*. The cycle of defilements is the interaction of ignorance, craving, grasping, and wrong views that perpetuate future existence.

The cycle of action is the functional aspect of those defilements; it is represented by the kamma force produced by both wholesome and unwholesome actions. The cycle of results is the pleasant and painful results of those actions.

At this stage of the practice, your concentration and clarity will be strong enough to clearly discern many things while engaged in vipassanā meditation. However, perceptions may be disappearing so quickly that it might be difficult to see their endings. Meditators may be acutely aware of the arising and standing stage of both mental and material objects, but often the subsequent arising phenomena seem to come so quickly that you have not noticed the ending of the previous perception before you are drawn toward the arising of the new one. Some meditators feel overwhelmed by the plethora of perceptions that arise at this stage. The challenges at this stage are balanced by the understanding that ignorance, craving, and grasping produce painful effects, and also, relinquishment, compassion, and mindfulness produce profitable effects.[297] Your practice will bear fruit; your skillful actions will bring a desired result.

Informed by a strong taste of the conditioned nature of all experience and empowered by the deepening faith in the effectiveness of the path, this investigation gradually unfolds through the next few stages.

3. *The knowledge of comprehension.* This stage involves perceiving the impermanent, unsatisfactory, and not-self characteristic of all mental and material phenomena and their causes—internally, externally, near, far, gross, subtle, across past lives, throughout current existence, and into the future. The *knowledge of comprehension* is developed by contemplating groupings such as the five aggregates or twelve bases, and also by contemplating individual material or mental factors one by one. It encompasses the recognition of everything in the infinite universe as impermanent, unsatisfactory, and not-self. When you develop the *knowledge of comprehension* through the sustained explorations of the vipassanā exercises in chapter 17, you will know unequivocally that three characteristics apply to all conditioned phenomena—nothing

is apart, excluded, or spared. Impermanence is comprehended; suffering is comprehended; not-self is comprehended.

Now, every type of matter, mental constituent, causal relation, and cognitive process (including sense-sphere, jhāna, wholesome, and unwholesome processes) must be contemplated as impermanent, unsatisfactory, and not-self. The exhaustive contemplations characteristic of this stage can be time consuming, but they are invaluable. Variations in the exercises that were introduced in chapter 17 prevent stagnation and weariness, and demand that attention genuinely discern phenomena as *not I, not mine*, and *not myself*. It is important that the examination of phenomena be comprehensive—internal, external, near, far, gross, subtle, past, present, and future—and includes all materiality, mentality, and causal relationships. If you only examined preferred perceptions, only looked internally, or only discerned present causes, you might dismiss the universal and liberating truth that all formations whatsoever, mental or material, past, present, and future, for all existences—everyone, everywhere—are impermanent, unsatisfactory, and not-self. The vast and far-reaching comprehension of impermanence, suffering, and selflessness distinguishes this insight knowledge.

When your vipassanā practice has reached this stage of development, you'll find that you will be able to perform the detailed insight meditation practices described in chapter 17 without difficulty, but meditation may still require a great deal of energy. You may need to refresh attention with periodic "dips" into jhāna or concentration practice. Now you will successfully observe the beginning, middle, and end of mental and material processes more easily than in previous stages, but the discernment is not complete and the contemplation may feel a bit clumsy. Phenomena will still arise and pass more rapidly than your attention can perceive, so you may tend to see things as groups or concepts, rather than refined and meticulous perceptions. The contemplation is only partial and inconsistent at this stage. Sometimes characteristics are vividly clear, other times they are not so clear; sometimes arising is clear; other times the perishing is more clear. The traditional illustration of this stage portrays a man who uses a cane or walking stick to support his stride. The amount of ground that the walking stick or cane touches is small compared to the areas where it does not make contact. Similarly, although the meditator genuinely discerns some arising and passing of phenomena, there are many gaps in attention.

This can be a tumultuous stage for some meditators. The intensity of the insight practice can cause agitation if they think about their personal past causes or future possibilities. An overwhelming perception of impermanence and suffering can lead to boredom, withdrawal, or exhaustion. The heightened sensitivity may make some meditators prone to overreact to minor inconveniences, or to tumble into a cascading profusion of aversion or fear. However, as the *knowledge of comprehension* matures, a pervasive perception of impermanence, unsatisfactoriness, and emptiness brings the poignant realization that everything arises and dissolves; nothing is enduring, controllable, or possessable.

4. *The knowledge of arising and passing away.* There are two parts to this stage, the *tender knowledge of arising and passing away* and the *mature knowledge of arising and passing away.*

4a. *The tender knowledge of arising and passing away.* This fourth knowledge reveals the characteristics of the arising and passing away of phenomena intensely, clearly, and distinctly. Now the meditator will be able to perceive ultimate materiality and ultimate mentality arising and perishing, without falling back on course perceptions and compact concepts, groupings, or states. The truth of impermanence, unsatisfactoriness, and not-self becomes evident in every perception— you see it everywhere you look. When your perception is informed by insight, you will have a vivid "with your own eyes" type of experience, and know with certain knowledge that "only what is subject to falling arises, and to be arisen necessitates fall."[298]

At this stage the meditator contemplates the *causal* and *momentary* arising and perishing, and both the arising and perishing of causes and effects as described in Meditation Instructions 18.1 and 18.2. The *tender knowledge of arising and perishing* is attained when two aspects of direct knowledge reveal that it is only through the cessation of causes that effects will cease.

▸ *Insight regarding causal arising and perishing.* The insight into *causal arising* occurs with the direct insight that causes create the conditions for every birth into a new existence. The insight into *causal perishing* occurs with the direct insight that due to the cessation of those causes, the cycle of successive arising and the round of rebirths ends. This insight highlights the profound mark of an *arahant*—with the eradication of defilement and the complete cessation of the five causes (ignorance, craving, clinging, volitional formations, and kamma potency), the five aggregates end with the death of the *arahant* and do not produce any future arising.

▸ *Insight regarding momentary arising and perishing.* This insight highlights the successive arising and ceasing of mental and material processes, moment-by-moment, lifetime after lifetime. It reveals the incessant flow of rapidly changing causes, conditions, and effects that constitute life experiences.

⤳ MEDITATION INSTRUCTION 18.1

Contemplating the Arising and Perishing of Causes and Effects According to the Fifth Method

1. Establish concentration. To contemplate *causal arising and perishing*, discern (according to meditation instruction 15.1 steps 10 and 11, 15.4, and 15.5) your past and future existences until they come to an end.

   Recognize *causal arising* by observing that every mentality and materiality occurs due to five past causes—the supporting causes of ignorance, craving, and clinging, plus the productive causes of volitional formations and kamma potency. Systematically observe that, because of the arising of past causes, mentality and materiality arise.

   Recognize *causal perishing* by seeing that the powerful insight of the *arahant path* that occurs during your final existence destroys the subtle defilements of ignorance, craving, and attachment. Without these supporting causes, the production of a new birth cannot occur. Systematically confirm that because of the cessation of ignorance, craving, and clinging, neither mentality nor materiality is produced after the death of the *arahant*. Recognize the cessation of the round of rebirths by thoroughly contemplating the final cessation of causes and effects. For example contemplate that, because of the arising of ignorance, feeling/perception/volitional formations/consciousness arises; because of the complete cessation of ignorance, feeling/ perception/volitional formations/consciousness ceases without remainder with the death of the *arahant*.

2. Contemplate *momentary arising and perishing* to see that all formations, including causes and effects, arise and perish, moment by moment. For example, see that both the cause (ignorance) and the effect (alternately discern feeling, perception, volitional formations, and consciousness) perish as soon as they arise. Observe sense-door or mind-door cognitive processes during the course of each lifetime and systematically contemplate the successive arising and perishing of mental and material processes throughout past, present, and future lives. Every aggregate, element, and formation that you will find in every cognitive process perishes as soon as it arises.

   Through a careful examination of the *causal and momentary arising and perishing* of past, present, and future phenomena, you will recognize the two kinds of cessation: 1) cessation in which subsequent arising continues to occur, and 2) cessation in which there is no further arising.

3. To contemplate *the causal and momentary arising and perishing of causes and effects with insight* repeat the sequence linking causes and effects from your earliest past life through to your final existence, but this time contemplate:
   ▶ Because of the arising of causes, effects arise.
   ▶ Because of the cessation of causes, effects cease.
   ▶ The causes are impermanent, suffering, and not-self.

▶ The effects are impermanent, suffering, and not-self.

In each case you would identify the specific phenomena and causal relationship that you are observing, precisely discern the relevant mental factors and material elements, and alternately contemplate them as impermanent, suffering, and not-self. For example, when contemplating the arising and ceasing of ignorance you would discern twelve mental formations in the mind-door adverting moment, usually twenty mental formations in the impulsion mind-moments, and if a registration mind-moment occurs, see its eleven to thirty-four formations (see tables 13.8, 13.9, and 13.10). Then contemplate each component as impermanent, suffering, and not-self.

This is a systematic and exhaustive contemplation that encompasses every kind of formation involved in the production of a new life, and every phase in sense-door and mind-door cognitive processes that can occur during the course of each lifetime. Presenting every possible discernment here would require many pages and be boring to read, so a few simple illustrations of the contemplation will suffice. Practitioners may refer to the Visuddhimagga for more details, and seek guidance from qualified teachers.[299]

Illustration 1: Because of the arising of ignorance, kamma-produced materiality arises. Because of the cessation of ignorance, kamma-produced materiality ceases. Ignorance is impermanent. Kamma-produced materiality is impermanent.

Illustration 2: Because of the arising of object, perception arises. Because of the cessation of object, perception ceases. Object is suffering. Perception is suffering.

Illustration 3: Because of the arising of eye-contact, feeling born of eye-contact arises. Because of the cessation of eye-contact, feeling born of eye-contact ceases. Eye-contact is not-self. Feeling born of eye-contact is not-self. ↩

→ **MEDITATION INSTRUCTION 18.2**
*Contemplating the Arising and Perishing of Causes and Effects
According to the First Method*

You may also use the First Method for exploring dependent arising
(explained in meditation instruction 15. 6) to attain insight into the
arising and perishing of causes and effects. The progression is similar to the foregoing instructions for the Fifth Method.

a) To meditate on *arising*, review the sequence of meditation
   instructions in 15.6 and begin the discernment as follows:
   because of the arising of ignorance, volitional formations arise;
   because of the arising of volitional formations, consciousness
   arises...

b) To meditate on *perishing*, follow the sequence in meditation
   instruction 15.6 beginning the discernment as follows: because
   of the cessation of ignorance, volitional formations cease;
   because of the cessation of volitional formations, consciousness
   ceases...

c) To gain insight into the *arising and perishing of causes and effects*
   begin the discernment as follows: because of the arising of ignorance, volitional formations arise; because of the cessation of
   ignorance, volitional formations cease; ignorance is impermanent [suffering, not-self]; volitional formations are impermanent
   [suffering, not-self].

Thoroughly meditate on the causal factors that characterize each
link in the chain of dependent arising, meditating on phenomena
internally and externally, past, present, and future, throughout
successive lifetimes. Link causes and effects, and then alternately
contemplate each cause and each effect as impermanent, suffering,
and not-self. ←

In this stage the meditator will continue to thoroughly contemplate
mental and material phenomena as impermanent, unsatisfactory, and

not-self; as "this is not I, this is not mine, this is not myself"; or in the forty ways described in chapter 17.[300] As the vipassanā exercises are practiced, the mind grows increasingly light, quick, and pure. Now the meditator is able to observe the rapidly arising and passing phases clearly. Although many things occur together—materiality, mentality, causal arising, contemplation, knowledge—consciousness is efficient, sharp, and pliant enough to observe these subtle and rapidly arising and passing formations and see that "all formations are impermanent, all formations are subject to suffering, and all things are not-self."[301]

As the vivid recognition of impermanence, unsatisfactoriness, and emptiness makes an impression on consciousness, the meditator might experience a heightened enthusiasm for the Buddha's teaching and the power of this practice that could lead to visions of grandeur, the fantasy of becoming a great teacher, or zealous proselytizing. However, at this stage meditators are still subject to ten corruptions, impediments, or imperfections of insight that can cause agitation, distraction, complacency, or sidetrack the unwary meditator.[302] These imperfections are not unwholesome; they arise with vipassana meditation and are tied to insight. The experiences themselves are not errors, but they can impede the progress of insight if you delight in them, become seduced through craving or pride, or construct a view of self based on these meditative experiences. It would be a trap to feel special because of your attainments; it would be a mistake to consider the experiences associated with concentration and insight to be a possession that you deserve. Your hard-won accomplishments become corruptions if you cling to them. These experiences too must be contemplated as impermanent, unsatisfactory, and not-self until you deeply understand that they are not the liberating path.

Meditators can review their practice and consider if any of these ten imperfections *(upakkilesa)* are inhibiting progress.

(a) *Illumination.* The brightness of consciousness during vipassanā practice can surpass anything previously known, even in jhāna practice. It may manifest as a bright light in the mind like a spot light, headlight, or torch, or appear as radiant light emitting from the body. This illumination may be perceived with eyes open or closed, and appear to fill the room, the mind, or the whole world. If you become interested in this illumination or attribute much significance to it, this intense luminosity might be mistaken for a greater accomplishment than in fact it represents.

(b) *Knowledge.* The direct knowledge of mentality and materiality is keen, incisive, and sharp at this stage of vipassanā practice. You may comprehend the teachings you have learned from books or discourses more deeply than ever before. What you have read about is now vividly clear in your direct perception. This confirmation of knowledge creates enormous enthusiasm for the Dhamma and could inspire preaching or proselytizing that would detract from your meditative pursuits. This clear and vivid knowledge should not be mistaken for the goal.

(c) *Rapturous happiness.* Your body and mind may be filled with rapture. Buoyancy might become so intense that you could feel as though you are floating, flying, or rising into the air. Intensely happy feelings can foster attachment; therefore focus on the impermanence, unsatisfactoriness, and emptiness of happy feelings in order to diligently protect the mind from potential attachment.

(d) *Tranquility.* The tranquility *(passaddhi)* of body and mind arises together with a set of factors that includes lightness *(lahutā)*, malleability *(mudutā)*, workability *(kammaññatā)*, proficiency *(pāguññatā)*, and uprightness *(ujukatā)*. These six conditions will enable you to sit without fatigue, heaviness, or discomfort. The lightness brings a lively, buoyant, dynamic quality to the mind that enables your attention to move quickly and easily between objects. The malleability contributes a soft, flexible, pliant, and gentle quality that dispels rigidity and coarseness, and allows consciousness to adapt well to changing circumstances. The quality of workability introduces a healthy and capable quality to your practice, which counters fatigue, stiffness, pain, or distraction. Proficiency is expressed in a strong, efficient, and effective functioning of the mind that proceeds without hesitation, procrastination, or sluggishness. And the upright quality manifests by honest and straightforward engagement with phenomena free of hypocrisy or deceit.

Although pleasant, these experiences should not become a reason for pride, attachment, or satisfaction to fester. Meditators who do not identify this imperfection may fritter away precious time attempting to recreate pleasant meditations only to find that their practice stagnates.

(e) *Bliss and pleasure.* A sublime pleasure may fill consciousness; pain and distress are quelled. A traditional simile warns that a man who wishes to live and not die will avoid knowingly drinking poison from a cup, even if it has a pleasing taste.[303] Remain cautious, and do not be seduced by these happy states.

(f) *Resolution or decision.* The intensification of faith, confidence, and powerful resolution can inspire overwhelming adoration of the Buddha or teacher and extreme enthusiasm for the teachings. Ecstatic devotion can sometimes lead to emotional attachments, arrogant and overconfident opinions, or tearful outbursts that disrupt the forward movement of practice. A skillful meditator will recognize the imperfection in excessive fervor and the imbalance in captivating states, and then he or she will restore equilibrium through the mindful development of insight.

(g) *Exertion.* Balanced energy, neither lax nor strained, will dominate this stage of *the knowledge of arising and passing away.* You may discover that you can sit for many hours and function brilliantly with very little sleep. The vast energy resources that are tapped through strong concentration and insight practice must be carefully channeled toward further development or the power of this energy might become a basis for arrogance or pride.

(h) *Assurance or mindfulness.* Whatever object you direct your attention to will be known effortlessly with mindfulness. Mindfulness will be sturdy, established, and automatically arise in conjunction with each perception. Mindfulness, although an essential and faultless attribute, is not an appropriate cause for attachment. Mindfulness should not be distorted into serving as a feature of personality or personal asset.

(i) *Equanimity.* Equanimity arises as neutrality toward formations—if neutrality is excessive, it might degenerate into a superficially

Contemplating the Ten Corruptions of Insight

Examine the ten imperfections if and when they arise. Review the list and dutifully watch out for them. If you recognize any corruption, acknowledge both its advantages and limitations. Then, contemplate it as impermanent, unsatisfactory, and not-self. Recognize that imperfections are neither a sign of awakening nor the liberating path.

detached attitude. Attachment to the quietly peaceful feeling of equanimity can inhibit the production of the intense urgency that is needed for genuine awakening. The Buddha warns that if "he delights in that equanimity, welcomes it, and remains holding to it...[then] his consciousness becomes dependent on it and clings to it. A bhikkhu...who is affected by clinging does not attain Nibbāna."[304] When equanimity is present, concentration and insight develop easily. Like a well-balanced wheel that is already turning, the meditator will enjoy a smooth unfolding of insight, fueled by the momentum of equanimity. Be careful, however, to not mistake this adroitness with enlightenment or confuse the conditioned quality of equanimity with the realization of the unconditioned.

(j) *Attachment.* Subtle attachment to pleasant accomplishments might halt further development. The imperfection of attachment is latent in all the previous imperfections, and it might arise through the modes of craving, conceit, or wrong view. Notice when attachment is evident; bring mindfulness to even the subtle tendency to be impressed by your own insight knowledge. Even after genuine attainments, you may be vulnerable to these corruptions; therefore, the Buddha warned, "do not become intoxicated with that attainment...laud yourself or disparage others...fall into negligence...and stop short with that."[305] You may discover many wonderful things about reality, and experience authentic and sublime attainments, yet a genuine purification of mind demands that you "do not be proud of yourself on that account."[306]

Beyond the ten corruptions. Not every meditator will experience the full configuration of these ten corruptions of insight. You may discover that certain imperfections captivate your mind, while other imperfections never manifest. To make real progress, it is essential that you eliminate those impediments that do occur. Confront these corruptions with mindfulness whenever they appear.

This phase of the *tender knowledge of arising and passing away* requires intense effort—it is still a struggle to see the arising and passing of things, and the mind periodically falls prey to the ten corruptions.[307] Through a continuity of wise, gentle, and diligent practice, you will become confident that these flimsy imperfections cannot seduce you. The surmounting of these corruptions marks the completion of *the tender knowledge of arising and passing away.*

⤳ **Meditation Instruction 18.3**
Contemplating Insight Knowledge

As the perception of the arising and passing of phenomena becomes clear and quick, you may incorporate the contemplation of the impermanent, unsatisfactory, and not-self characteristics of the consciousness and cognitive processes associated with insight knowledge as explained in meditation instruction 17.11. Recognize that insight knowledge is also impermanent, unsatisfactory, and not-self. For instance, when you are meditating on the impermanence of a sound, consciousness arises in conjunction with a cognitive series that is not just hearing the sound; it is knowing the impermanence of the sound. The cognitive process of insight knowledge is a mind-door process; it is distinct from the sense-door cognitive process that hears the sound. Contemplating the impermanent, unsatisfactory, and not-self characteristics of the meditating consciousness extends the comprehensive arena for contemplation and breaks down the compactness of object as described in chapter 11. ←

4b. The mature knowledge of arising and passing away. The initial knowledges that comprise stages 1–4a bring forth a pervasive recognition of specific attributes of phenomena, including causation, characteristics, and imperfections. The *mature knowledge of arising and passing away* occurs when the imperfections are overcome and insight into the three characteristics is sharp. This stage will further dismantle any misperceptions that could distort the clear seeing of reality. In the mature phase, with the absence of the corruptions, attention will be keen, agile, and steadfast. The arising phase with the cause of arising, and the ending phase with the cause of ending, will be evident. Insight into the changing, unsatisfactory, and not-self characteristics of any formation will be proficient and the contemplation of all phenomena can continue unrestrained. The mind that is now unimpeded by any of the ten imperfections is "free from imperfections and steady in its course";[308] it is capable of penetrating to the source of attachment.

5. The knowledge of dissolution. Now the instructions change slightly. Stop giving attention to the arising and existence phases of mental or material phenomena; focus primarily on the dissolution, falling, or perishing phase of formations. This shift in emphasis may occur naturally or it may be an intentional choice. Don't bother to notice particular details about each formation. Focus only on the dissolution, falling, perishing, disappearing, vanishing. Insight will be sharp at this stage, and the incessant ceasing of phenomena will be vivid. Contemplate all things as *perishing, perishing.* The traditional analogy is of fragile pottery being smashed, or of fine dust being dispersed by a wind, in that, "He sees only their break up."[309] Direct your attention to exclusively perceive the passing phase of all formations. This awareness is likened to the view of a man who watches the surface of a pond during a heavy rainstorm and sees large bubbles break up as soon as they appear.[310] Consciousness and object perish simultaneously.

Contemplate both phenomena and insight knowledge as impermanent, unsatisfactory, and not-self while you observe the stream of perishing phenomena within cognitive processes. You may still see the
arising and standing stages, but an emphasis on dissolution at this
critical juncture will generate a powerful inclination that can propel
the mind through the remaining sequence of insights.

When stages 1–4 are practiced thoroughly, then the next several
stages (5–11) happen very quickly. The knowledges from stage 5 and
beyond often occur so quickly and fluidly that meditators might not
recognize them all as distinct stages. When conditions are favorable,
they may occur within the course of a few days, a few sittings, or even
a single sitting. The final five knowledges in this sequence (stages
12–16) will occupy only a few moments. Therefore, don't rush these
early stages. The mind must be able to discern the perishing of all
things with lightening speed, develop a strong momentum through
persistent insight, and maintain an undeterrable inclination toward
release.

6. *The knowledge of appearance as terror.* Now you are perched on the
   brink of a startling discovery. At this stage, you will witness the perishing of all phenomena so completely that you will see everything
   that you have relied upon for your sense of self dissolving with each
   passing moment. You will lose the familiar illusion of security that
   is habitually gained through self constructions. Grief, fear, or terror
   might arise with the loss of all cherished worldly experiences. This will
   not be a dramatic manifestation of emotional sorrow, personalized
   dread, or chronic anxiety; instead it manifests as an acute awareness
   that everything that arises is also dying, dissolving, and disappearing.
   The *Visuddhimagga* describes it as "simply the mere judgment that
   past formations have ceased, present ones are ceasing, and future ones
   will cease."[311]

   The *knowledge of appearance as terror* has a dramatic name; it arises
   out of the realization that all formations are perishing. Don't let fear
   or grief dissuade you from your pursuit of truth. Be mindful, and
   earnestly continue the practice of contemplating all phenomena as

impermanent, unsatisfactory, and not-self. Fear and grief will soon fade and be replaced by unshakable wisdom, clarity, and confidence.

7. *The knowledge of danger.* When you realize that your grief, fear, and suffering arise because of clinging to the five aggregates, you will view this clinging process as a danger. The stage of *knowledge of danger* is intimately aligned with the previous stage, appearance as terror. When you see everything perishing, you find no secure refuge in any configuration of past, present, or future material and mental formations. You realize that within the entire gamut of existence, no material and mental experience is capable of providing a stable resting place for identity. This recognition fosters a subtle and transformative repulsion toward impermanent perceptions.

Now you will see both the danger of attachment to formations and recognize that an escape from that danger is possible. This stage is not burdened by a feeling of fear; you have already comprehended the implications of the previous fear response. Now, you comprehend that the five aggregates pose a continuous danger as a basis for attachment. The *Visuddhimagga* states that when seeing formations as danger, one "takes no delight in the manifold field of formations."[312] This is not an aversive reaction to experience, but a profound understanding that clinging to the five aggregates of experience is keeping you bound to repeatedly bring consciousness into being and to fuel the cycle of suffering. The understanding of the ungraspable and unsatisfactory characteristic of all conditioned things is deep. The five aggregates are now exposed as a dangerous trap.

8. *The knowledge of disenchantment and dispassion.* When the mind is fortified by wisdom and equanimity, and unseduced by mental and material processes, profound disenchantment arises. This is a dispassionate stance toward phenomena; it is not aversion. The knowledges of terror (no. 6), danger (no. 7), and disenchantment and dispassion (no. 8) can occur for some meditators as distinct stages each having a noticeable duration. In fact, although they are listed as separate knowledges, they may occur in such rapid succession that they

appear to be aspects of the same perception. The knowledges of terror, danger, and dispassion may be considered "one in meaning, only the letter is different,"[313] because when appearance as terror occurs, you will naturally recognize the inherent danger and will experience dispassion toward those same formations. If you have done the exhaustive preparations associated with the tender and mature knowledges of arising and passing away (nos. 4a and 4b), you may discover that the stages of terror, danger, and disenchantment happen remarkably quickly and fluidly.

Persistence is needed to prevent the stalling of momentum. For now, even things that previously interested you, such as personal growth, sensual pleasures, meditative attainments, and heavenly potentials, will not appeal to the mind so infused with disenchantment and dispassion. Some meditators may also lose interest in the meditation practice, or find their commitments derailed by finding fault with food, housing, or teaching styles. Suspend all complaints. Strive to sever attachment. Remember your aim. Continue with diligence. And let nothing deter you from your search for peace.

The *Visuddhimagga* compares disenchantment toward phenomena to the preferences of a golden swan or a powerful lion. This swan loves the expansive great lakes of spacious Himalayan foothills and does not seek satisfaction in a filthy mud hole at the outskirts of a village; the lion loves to roam freely and would not enjoy a gilded cage. Similarly, the meditator finds no pleasure in formations and inclines only toward the contemplation of the characteristics that will lead to freedom. When your mind stops seeking sensual entertainments and pleasures, it may incline only toward the peace of nibbāna.[314]

Consistent meditation on the ubiquitous characteristics of impermanence, suffering, and not-self will culminate in the desire for deathless liberation. You don't need to conjure up the desire; it arises as a natural consequence of the systematic unfolding of insight. By this point in the progression, you will have done many exercises and contemplated many mental and material objects in light of those characteristics. Although you might long to be finished with the exercises, the deeper and genuine yearning is to be freed from formations that continually oppress the mind. Burdened by the ceaseless bending of mind toward matter and the continuous death of all that arises, a poignant realization occurs—it is utterly useless to reach toward sensory experience for happiness. It boils down to the insight that nothing is permanent, and so nothing is worth getting attached to. You may have experienced similar understandings previously in this training, but at this stage, empowered by the momentum of concentration and insight, the dispassion causes a cascading series of transformations. Deeply wearied and disgusted with all transitory phenomena, your mind will seek release.

9. *The knowledge of desire for deliverance.* When disenchantment is strong through the maturation of the previous stage, the mind yearns for freedom; it wants only to be delivered. Just as an animal that is caught in a trap will have a consuming wish to be released, you will experience a profound desire to escape from the trap of conditioned formations. The *Visuddhimagga* describes it this way: "Just as a fish in a net, a frog in a snake's jaws, a jungle fowl shut into a cage, a deer fallen into the clutches of a strong snare, a snake in the hands of a snake charmer, an elephant stuck fast in a great bog, . . . a man encircled by enemies, etc., . . . just as these are desirous of being delivered, of finding an escape from these things, so too this meditator's mind is desirous of being delivered from the whole field of formations and escaping from it."[315] No temporary pleasure, no material comfort, no personal accomplishment will dissuade you from this deep and earnest need for deliverance from the bonds of suffering. You will sense the profound truth of Venerable Sariputta's exclamation, "To be reborn is suffering; not to be reborn is happiness."[316] You will understand the necessity and power of relinquishment, as the Buddha taught, "Not apart from enlightenment and austerity, not apart from restraint of the sense faculties, not apart from relinquishing all, do I see any safety for living beings."[317]

10. *The knowledge of reviewing the three characteristics.* At this stage mindfulness is strong, the capacity for discerning subtle conditions

is highly refined, insight is sharp, and the mind is exceedingly quick, light, agile, concentrated, and stable. Invigorated by the desire for freedom, you will be earnestly committed to the contemplation of formations as impermanent, unsatisfactory, and not-self. You may emphasize whichever contemplations produce the greatest calm and clarity—build momentum through your strongest abilities. If you prefer to contemplate materiality, then emphasize the contemplation of matter; if you prefer to contemplate dependent arising, then contemplate the cycle of causality. Although all the characteristics should, to some extent, still be included in the meditations, you may highlight impermanence, unsatisfactoriness, or emptiness. If you have mastered the jhānas, emphasizing the mental factors associated with jhāna as either impermanent, unsatisfactory, or not-self can build powerful momentum.

This stage does not require a great deal of time; it is not labored. Inspired by the desire for deliverance, you will zealously recognize phenomena as they are actually occurring and discover a remarkably equanimous response toward all things. The sequence of these knowledges is illustrated by the story of a fisherman who reaches into his net to grab a fish that he has caught, when, to his horror, discovers that he has actually grabbed a huge snake. As soon as he sees it, he is frightened, recognizes the danger, is repulsed by the experience, and feels no enchantment toward the snake—he desires only release from it. Motivated to safely free himself from the grip of this dangerous and disagreeable beast, he carefully unwinds the coils from his arm and systematically weakens it by rapidly circling it above his head a few times before flinging it away. Similarly, a meditator will view psychophysical experience as a fearful and dangerous ground that breeds attachment. Systematic contemplation of the three characteristics is likened to the whirling of the snake overhead; it weakens the arising of formations and renders them incapable of appearing as permanent, satisfying, and self-existing.[318] Essentially, you are preparing the mind to effectively remove the source of suffering.

11. The knowledge of equanimity toward formations. Now, having thoroughly discerned the three characteristics inherent to all formations, both terror and delight will disappear and you will discover a pervasive neutrality toward formations. You will see everything as a mere cluster of causally related mental and material processes, and you will remain utterly unimpressed by phenomena. The mind will remain composed while observing the rapidly appearing and disappearing mental and material formations. Practice will be effortless now, and you will sail through the meditative exercises without struggle; it may seem like the practice has all come together and flows easily. Each subtle perception will appear as unadorned functions and characteristics. Practice will be pleasant and dominated by joy and calmness. You'll engage with an impartial and equanimous view toward all formations while you effortlessly continue the vipassanā meditations. This stage can be quite a relief after the intensity and turmoil of preceding stages.

If you delight in this equanimity though, and enjoy the smoothness of the endeavor, a false sense of pride or subtle attachment might arise along with such corrupting thoughts as, "It is going so well now, I must be doing it right." It is important to maintain a consistent contemplation of the impermanence, suffering, and emptiness of phenomena to prevent psychophysical processes from becoming a support for concepts of *I, me,* or *mine.* With the development of the *knowledge of equanimity toward formations,* all aggregates are known as void of self. You will know that there is no "myself" and nothing belonging to "myself"; there is no "another self" and nothing belonging to "another self."[319]

Contemplate all phenomena until this stage matures. You may emphasize the phenomena that are easiest for your mind to contemplate, but sometimes meditate on impermanence, sometimes unsatisfactoriness, and sometimes selflessness; sometimes meditate on matter, sometimes mental formations; sometimes contemplate phenomena that is internal, sometimes external; sometimes recognize causes, sometimes effects; and also include past, present, and future formations. If you have mastery of jhānas, you can build greater momentum by emphasizing the thirty-one to thirty-five mental formations associated with jhāna states as preferred vipassanā objects. You will enjoy a calm and composed facility with practice now—but this is not nibbāna. Don't stop with mere equanimity!

The *knowledge of equanimity toward formations* seems to be a stage in which even diligent meditators can get stuck—there is comfort, calmness, clarity, and balanced attention, so no obvious hindrance is apparent. But the experience of equanimity might become a foundation for clinging.[320] Subtle errors can hide attachment and prevent progress. The meditator may not even be aware that a great opportunity is present for full awakening. You may need a teacher to point you beyond the peaceful but limited stage of *equanimity toward formations*.

Eventually, a moment comes when material and mental formations seem to disappear or fade. Sometimes materiality vanishes first and only mental phenomena are seen perishing; continue to meditate upon that perishing mentality. In a short time, all material and mental phenomena will seem to cease. This is the critical moment when the mind must accept only the authentic experience of nibbāna as the object, free of all conceptual configurations.

When fascination with impermanent things ends, a great spaciousness opens where the unconditioned may reveal itself. At this juncture, a critical shift may occur, beyond all possible manipulations and efforts. Now there is nothing familiar to hold on to, nothing to cling to. Even the activities related to these meditative procedures cease. In this moment of cessation, insight knowledge may naturally turn toward the deathless element and see nibbāna as peaceful. The mind may enter the experience of nibbāna—the unformed, unfabricated, deathless element. This difficult-to-describe transition is illustrated with the simile of a land-finding crow that accompanied seafaring ships. The crow will be released while the ship is at sea. If it sees land, it will fly directly toward the shore; if it does not see land it will return to the crow's nest on the mast of the ship.[321] Similarly, at this stage, the mind is released from clinging to the aggregates of experience. If the mind turns toward the deathless element and sees it as peaceful, it will not turn back. If the mind does not see nibbāna, or perceive nibbāna as peaceful, it will turn back to the stage of *equanimity toward formations.* This may occur repeatedly, and the meditator may coast along calmly perceiving formations pass away, unaware of being stuck.[322]

By this stage the process is unfolding out of the momentum of dispassion. You must let go of all attachment; do not cling to either equanimity or meditative exercises. Allow the inclination of your practice to carry you to the peace of nibbāna.

12. The knowledge of conformity with truth. The *knowledge of conformity with truth* coincides with the maturity of the *knowledge of equanimity toward formations* and lasts for a duration of three impulsion consciousness moments (see Table 18.2). This spontaneous transitional phase is so brief that meditators rarely can recognize it as a distinctive stage. Conformity knowledge describes an automatic series of mind-moments through which the mind adapts itself to the new object. It functions as a bridge between the consciousness that has taken mental and material formations as the object and the consciousness that is about to arise with nibbāna as object. This stage of conformity can be illustrated by the technique used by relay racers who match the speed of the previous runner even before the baton is passed. The moment of conformity prevents an abrupt shift between the previous stages that took the five aggregates as object, to the succeeding stages that will take nibbāna as object.

Now, one of the three characteristics may become predominant and serve as the doorway to nibbāna. If impermanence comes to the fore, then the realization that follows is classified as the "signless liberation of mind." If the characteristic of suffering is dominant, the realization will be called the "desireless liberation of mind." If not-self is emphasized, the realization is classified as the "voidness liberation of mind." Any of the three characteristics can be a gateway to the deathless. Each door can be a portal to the same supramundane knowledge: a glimpse of what lies beyond mundane mental and material processes. Each designation—signless, desireless, voidness—reflects the particular contemplation that impelled the final release.

13. The knowledge of change of lineage. This knowledge represents the fourth impulsion consciousness in the cognitive process that takes nibbāna as object. Although this insight has nibbāna as object, it does not destroy defilements. It is immediately followed by the path knowledge which has an inherently purifying effect. The *Visuddhimagga* explains, "Conformity is able to dispel the murk of defilements that conceal the truth, but is unable to make nibbāna its object. Change of lineage is only able to make nibbāna its object, but is unable to dispel the murk that conceals the truth."[323] This series of knowledges is amazingly quick—just a matter of a few mind-moments that occur in the process of perceiving nibbāna and constitute the cognitive series of the path. Although incredibly brief, each is listed as a distinct knowledge in order to highlight its specific function in this significant transformation that marks the change of lineage from an ordinary person to a noble one (see Table 18.2).

Now the mind has turned away from all material and mental processes; it has opened to another reality—the unconditioned, unborn, deathless, nibbāna. Ultimate reality is not a concept. Nibbāna is not a place or a thing. Nibbāna contains no materiality and includes no mentality. It includes no space or properties. There is a total absence of characteristics of diversity or changing factors that would create instability. It is void of all conditioned formations. It is described as:

> Consciousness without feature, without end,
> Luminous all around:
> Here water, earth, fire, and wind have no footing;
> Here long and short, course and fine,
> Fair and foul, mentality and materiality
> Are all brought to an end.
> With the stopping of consciousness,
> Each is here brought to an end.[324]

14. The path knowledge. Although you may earnestly and consistently cultivate the eightfold path, it is not designated as a "noble path" until a significant realization has occurred. The entrance to the noble

TABLE 18.1
Four Stages of Enlightenment

Stages/Paths	Fetters Removed or Reduced	Rebirth Potentials
Stream-enterer	*Removes:* 1. the erroneous view of self 2. doubt regarding the efficacy of Buddha's teaching 3. belief that purification comes through performing rites and rituals	Maximum of seven more rebirths in sensory realms
Once-returner	Does not cut off any fetters completely, but greatly reduces sensual desires and ill will	Maximum of one more rebirth in sensory realms
Nonreturner	Completely cuts off sensual desire and ill will	No further sense-sphere births, but may have further existences in nonsensory realms
Arahant	*Removes the remaining five fetters:* 1. desire for existence in the fine-material sphere 2. desire for existence in the immaterial spheres 3. conceit 4. restlessness 5. ignorance	No further existence in either sensory or nonsensory realms

path is the moment when both consciousness and object are supramundane. This realization encompasses a perfection of right view of the peaceful state, right thought of nibbāna, right mindfulness of nibbāna, right effort toward nibbāna, right concentration on nibbāna as object, and also the three abstinences regarding speech, action, and livelihood; hence, it is equated with the fulfillment and realization of the noble eightfold path.

Although the consciousness that realized nibbāna operates with the five aggregates, nibbāna does not reflect any diverse attributes. Nibbāna is causeless and without feature. The realization of nibbāna, however, is temporal and transient. Nibbāna may be described as "coolness" since the *realization* of nibbāna cools, quenches, and extinguishes the fires of greed, hate, and delusion. Attempts to describe this encounter with unconditioned reality embrace many words: *unformed, taintless, truth, other shore, subtle, undiversified, peace, deathless, supreme goal, safety, exhaustion of craving, wonderful, freedom, shelter, refuge, beyond.*[325] Since it is impossible to reduce to language, many meditators prefer to express this profound cessation of greed, hatred, and delusion with the Pali term *nibbāna.* Likened to the ocean that possesses a uniform flavor of salt, nibbāna is of one taste—the taste of liberation.[326]

Path knowledge, as a potent encounter with nibbāna, follows inevitably after *the knowledge of change of lineage,* lasts for merely one moment of consciousness, and will be immediately followed by *fruition knowledge.* More precisely, *path knowledge* is the fifth impulsion consciousness in the cognitive process that takes nibbāna as object (see Table 18.2). *Path knowledge* has an immediate effect—it results in the radical weakening or complete destruction of defilements. This is the moment of triumph—the profitable moment that eradicates defilements and cleanses the mind. In this moment, suffering has been fully understood, craving has been abandoned, the mind has plunged into nibbāna, the eightfold path has been developed, and the maturation of liberating insight is ensured.[327] As described in the *Visuddhimagga,* "The path follows upon [the knowledge of change of lineage] in uninterrupted continuity, and as it comes into being it pierces and explodes the mass of greed, the mass of hate, and the mass of delusion never pierced and exploded before."[328] It is traditionally believed that once path knowledge has been attained, one will never fall away from this realization; it assures one of progress and closes the door to woeful states.

The four paths: Four distinct stages of *path knowledge* mark four significant moments when fetters are weakened or destroyed. In conjunction with the direct experience of nibbāna, four supramundane paths can occur, commonly called the *four paths* or *four supramundane paths*. They may occur in rapid succession, although more often they are separated by days, years, or lifetimes of practice. Although stories are told of meditators who experience rapid or sudden realization, most people relinquish these defilements gradually over the course of years or lifetimes of practice. Whenever it occurs, the moment of *path knowledge* is significant—it radically weakens or completely uproots these binding forces and enables the mind to realize its liberation from the defilement. The four paths identify the state of the meditator and mark the moment of paramount significance when the mind sheds its attachment to predictable defilements.[329] Each path moment is similar in that each takes nibbāna as object and is the result of non-clinging to mental and material phenomena. Each path moment differs by the particular fetters that it weakens or removes. Complete enlightenment is realized when the greed, hatred, and delusion that bind beings to the wheel of existence are completely eradicated.

With the attainment of the first path of entering the stream *(sotāpattimagga)*, three fetters *(saṃyojana)* are removed: personality view *(sakkāyadiṭṭhi)*, which maintains the belief that self is the five aggregates, skeptical doubt about the efficacy of Buddha's teachings *(vicikicchā)*, and the erroneous belief that rites and rituals will purify the mind *(sīlabbataparāmāsa)*. With this attainment the meditator is assured that liberation will occur in the course of, at most, seven lifetimes. When the second path is reached with the stage of once-returner *(sakadāgāmimagga)*, the fetters of sensual lust *(kāmarāga)* and ill will *(vyāpāda)* are attenuated, but not eradicated, and the meditator may return to the sense-sphere of human existence for at most one more lifetime. The third path attainment eradicates sensual lust and ill will. Someone at the stage of nonreturner *(anāgāmimagga)* can never again be reborn in the sense-sphere because there is no desire that could pull one into a sensory realm. A nonreturner may be reborn in heavenly abodes and is assured of sequentially higher births until final nibbāna is attained. The fourth path attainment, referred to as the *arahant path (arahattamagga)*, is the final and complete cessation of all suffering in which the remaining five fetters are abandoned: (1)

desire for fine material existence *(rūpa-rāga)* including attachment to jhāna states; (2) desire for immaterial existence *(arūpa-rāga)*, which refers to attachment to the immaterial states; (3) conceit *(māna)*, which is the subtle formation of a self concept often fueled by comparing things as better, worse, or equal; (4) restlessness *(uddhacca)* that continues to seek for more satisfying experiences; and (5) ignorance *(avijjā)* regarding the ultimate nature of things.

Without ignorance there can be no further becoming. When all defilements are removed, the five aggregates will continue to function through the current life span only as long as they are supported by previous kamma. An *arahant* who performs action without attachment creates no causes that could produce future results. Like a flame that is extinguished when the support of the wick burns away and the wax is spent, when the fuel of defilement has ended with the arhant path, there is no support for continued becoming.

15. The fruition knowledge. Immediately following the impulsion consciousness of *path knowledge* comes *fruition knowledge,* which spans the sixth and seventh impulsion consciousnesses that have taken nibbāna as the object. This is the moment when one experiences the taste of this peace. Nibbāna is an ultrasubtle realization; it is so refined that in comparison even the highest immaterial jhānas appear unbearably gross. The mind inclines toward it and prefers it to all other objects. The Buddha explained that "One directly knows Nibbāna as Nibbāna. One does not conceive of oneself as one with Nibbāna. One does not conceive of oneself as in Nibbāna. One does not conceive of oneself apart from Nibbāna. Why is that? So that one may fully understand it."[330]

Whereas each of the four path knowledges is experienced only once,[331] the fruition knowledges can be repeated many times. Meditators practice to reenter and remain absorbed in states that have nibbāna as the object. Just as a meditator can develop mastery with mundane jhānas, the fruition attainment can also be repeated, mastered, and maintained for a long time. These attainments, called supramundane jhānas, provide extraordinarily pure resting states for consciousness.

TABLE 18.2
Cognitive Process that Takes Nibbāna as Object

Consciousness Moment	Mind-Door Adverting	First Impulsion (Javana)	Second Impulsion (Javana)	Third Impulsion (Javana)	Fourth Impulsion (Javana)	Fifth Impulsion (Javana)	Sixth Impulsion (Javana)	Seventh Impulsion (Javana)	Life-Continuum (Bhavaṅga)
Object	Impermanence/suffering/not-self characteristic of mentality/materiality				The Signless, the Unformed, Cessation, Nibbāna				Previous life's near-death object
Knowledges		Conformity with Truth			Change of Lineage	Path	Fruition		
	Mundane				Supramundane				Mundane

16. *The knowledge of reviewing.* The mind will emerge from the fruition attainment, reflect upon it, and analyze the mental factors of the realizing consciousness. This reflection is not an analysis of nibbāna itself; this reflection reviews the cognitive process that realized nibbāna. It is a natural reviewing process that spontaneously follows the path and fruition moments as the mind tries to comprehend this unusual event. It may be as basic as the reflexive inquiry: What was that? The mind knows that what just occurred was not of the same order as anything previously experienced in the realm of mind and matter, and therefore it will naturally reflect. But minutes, hours, or even days after the path and fruition knowledges were attained a meditator with knowledge of the process might use a systematic structure to review the experience in five ways.

(a) Review the *path knowledge*. Review the process that led to the cessation of conditioned formations and consciousness.

TABLE 18.3
Schedule of the Removal of Defilements

Defilement	Stages of Enlightenment	Stream-entry	Once-returning	Nonreturning	Arhantship
Delusion					■
Shamelessness of wrongdoing					■
Fearlessness of wrongdoing					■
Restlessness					■
Greed (sensual)				■	
Greed (nonsensual)					■
Wrong view		■			
Conceit					■
Hatred				■	
Envy		■			
Possessiveness		■			
Worry				■	
Sloth					■
Torpor					■
Doubt		■			
Total		4	0	3	8

(b) Review the *fruition knowledge.* Review the bliss and peace experienced in association with the attainment; recognize that this is an experience of freedom. Specifically, you should review the mental factors that arose in association with the consciousness of realization. If cessation occurred while contemplating sensory phenomena, there will be thirty-seven mental factors (thirty-four wholesome factors involved in sensory processes plus the three factors of abstinence in the noble path—right speech, right action, and right livelihood). If cessation occurred while contemplating jhāna factors, the number will vary depending upon the relevant jhāna (this will include mental factors present during jhāna, plus the three factors of abstinence in the noble path—right speech, right action, and right livelihood). Follow the same procedures discussed in chapter 13 to discern mind-door cognitive processes.

(c) Review nibbāna. Gain the certainty that this was not an imaginative, conceptual, or speculative knowledge. It was not a thought about nibbāna, concept of nibbāna, or desire for nibbāna. Instead, consciousness released its habitual reliance upon conditioned psychophysical processes and directly realized nibbāna.

(d) Review the defilements that have been destroyed.

(e) Review the defilements that have yet to be destroyed. The review of defilements that have been destroyed and have yet to be destroyed can be accomplished by reviewing the unwholesome mental factors as discerned in meditation instruction 13.5. After a genuine path attainment, certain unwholesome factors will cease to arise in the meditator's consciousness. The mind will not conjure them, not even when prompted. Then, throughout your daily life, continue to notice the defilements that still arise and which ones never again trouble you. Know what requires further purification.

WHAT TO DO NEXT?

After an authentic cessation experience, you may wonder what to do next. Do you just continue to meditate the same way as though nothing happened? You will have a few choices to make.

For some meditators, both jhāna and insight practices feel dreadfully coarse now, and there is no wish to engage in them until the experience of nibbāna is repeated or the sublime bliss subsides. During this period, you may gain mastery in this supramundane experience. Apply specific resolves to remain in the fruition attainment for one hour, two hours, or longer. Thoroughly and repeatedly experience the fruition attainment of stream-entry. Although jhāna-like, the realization of nibbāna is not a concentration state. Supramundane attainments are the result of vipassanā and occur through dispassion toward arising and passing phenomena, not fixation upon a chosen object.

During the Buddha's life, there was an occasion when many monastics confidently declared their realization of liberation. This caused a stir in the nearby town; people did not know if they were boasting false attainments, deluding themselves, or expressing genuine realization.[332] The Buddha acknowledged that some monastics had indeed realized final liberation and that others had not, but either way, the meditator should practice to be sure that no lust, hatred, or delusion enters the mind. He likened practice to the care that a man would give to a wound inflicted by a poison arrow. After the arrow had been removed and the poisonous humor expelled by a surgeon, the man must take good care of his health, eat suitable food, wash and anoint the wound, and avoid contamination from dust and dirt that could cause infection. In short, he should take care of the wound so that it will thoroughly heal. Likewise, if you believe that you have had a profound experience of nibbāna and that the arrow of suffering has been removed, it is essential to be diligent and maintain your practice. If you don't maintain your concentration and protect the wisdom, then any remaining lust, hatred, or ignorance might invade your mind. Even after powerful insight, enlightenment experiences, or profound transformations, we diligently protect the mind with mindfulness.

ASPIRING FOR FURTHER ATTAINMENTS

After the attainment of stream-entry you may wish to commit to further your practice and wear away the fetters of greed and hatred. With a strong resolve to realize the second stage of enlightenment, continue to contemplate mental and material processes as impermanent, unsatisfactory, and not-self. Practice vipassanā in the various ways presented in chapter 17. The quality of attention might fall back to the third or fourth knowledge, in which primarily the middle of the objects is perceived. You may feel as though your ability to see phenomena is no longer sharp; the arising and perishing phases may not appear as crisply nuanced now. Although lingering qualities of joy, buoyancy, and energy may suffuse your mind and body with a sense of well-being, practice can feel coarse. By contemplating the impermanent, suffering, and not-self characteristics again and again, the momentum of dispassion will gradually increase until it draws the mind through the same sequence of insight knowledges. Although they will be generally the same insights into impermanence, unsatisfactoriness, and not-self, dispassion will deepen and the path moment purifies the mind at a deeper level. When a second path experience occurs, it radically weakens the fetters of greed and hatred such that these defilements can hardly arise again; only the underlying tendencies toward desire and ill will remain.

Similarly, when aspiring for the third and fourth stages of enlightenment, deeper insight into the impermanent, unsatisfactory, and selfless nature of all conditioned things will heighten dispassion and propel the mind yet again through the sequence of knowledges. Each level of path attainment will uproot the corresponding fetters and purify the mind.

The sequential training in virtue, concentration, and wisdom expressed through these sixteen knowledges, ten fetters, and four stages of enlightenment may inspire, humble, or intimidate readers. If the progression appears daunting, don't worry about memorizing every detailed list, sequence, and formula. Attainment occurs with the ending of the fetters, and peace is known through a purity of release. Enjoy the direct and precise nature of this practice. It will guide you to an intimate and unmistakable encounter with reality. This training has been undertaken by generations of meditators, and it leads directly to a sublime, peaceful, and ultimate awakening.

CHAPTER 19

Of Lasting Benefit: Practice in the Midst of Daily Life

Lose the greed for pleasure.
See how letting go of the world is peacefulness.
There is nothing that you need to hold on to,
And there is nothing that you need push away.
—SUTTA NIPĀTA[333]

T HE TELEPHONE RANG. An eager salesman was promising me that I would gain "the peace of mind I deserve" if I just purchased an extended warranty for my car today. We might wish that peace could be so easily acquired, but peace won't be found through insurance policies, wealth, or relationships. Until you know and trust an effective route to authentic happiness and peace you may spend a vast amount of your life indulging in serial joys and momentary comforts. You might seek beautiful sights to store in memory for later review or cultivate an array of friendships in order to feel warmly loved throughout your life. Even though you know that attachment to changing phenomena is suffering, you might still find yourself spellbound when the first tulips open in your springtime garden, swooning over the taste of buttered mashed potato, or racing to capture a spectacular sunset view on film. Most people seek security and satisfaction by consuming, possessing, and preserving beauty and pleasure.

The Buddhist tradition recognizes the deeply conditioned character-istic of craving, and it also demands that we take responsibility for our perpetuation of it. There was an instance when a diligent disciple of the Buddha, though living a virtuous meditative life, distracted himself by admiring and smelling the blooming lotus flowers in a nearby pond. A celestial being *(deva),* endeavoring to steer the monk from this lingering attachment to sensory pleasure, admonished him to refine his restraint. Realizing that even innocuous pleasures such as smelling flowers can perpetuate craving and clinging, the monk welcomed the deva's repri-mand and invited him to intervene anytime. But the deva refused to watch over him to correct his faults, insisting that the monk must take responsibility for himself.[334] Likewise, we must each take responsibility for our own desires, for the hindrances that obsess our minds, for the restlessness and distraction that plague attention, and for the conse-quences of our actions. It is not that sensual pleasures are evil; they sim-ply do not have the capacity to satisfy us. Genuine peace occurs when we relinquish every conceivable attachment. As the Buddha taught, "Dry up the remains of the past, and have nothing for the future. If you do not cling to the present, you shall go from place to place in peace."[335]

PRACTICE AT HOME

Some readers might wonder how this methodical approach could relate to the struggles of daily life and may doubt if it is even possible for lay-people to do this practice. Actually it is quite possible and, surprisingly, not so very difficult. But it does require consistent effort, clear intention, and conducive conditions. Decide that you really can take time for prac-tice, then sit down and begin. Turn off the radio, silence your phone, log off the internet, and get your buttocks on the cushion and your atten-tion in the present moment. Just as the hen sits on her eggs until the chicks are ready to break out from the shell, you must diligently cultivate concentration and insight until you experience the fruit of release.

When I was first introduced to this systematic meditative training, replete with detailed exercises and explanatory charts, I felt overwhelmed. Only after slowly engaging with the practices, in multiple retreats over the course of several years, did the path appear welcoming, like a series of well-placed steppingstones and bridges, a trail that others have traveled before me. It is a method that is both economical and elegant—a direct path to nibbāna. The liberating teachings are practical—they work—and are worth the effort and diligence needed to maintain them.

Any sequential system, defined by stages and levels, holds the danger of triggering ambition for success, fear of failure, or unrealistic expectations. Although I frequently hear meditators blame the systematic nature of the practice for their perceived lack of progress, the fault is not inherent to a structured approach. The problem usually lies in the defilements. Meditators must unravel any unwholesome tendencies toward conceit, impatience, anger, arrogance, indolence, or doubt. If you fail to attain jhāna after reading this book and trying these exercises, don't despair—most people need an intensive retreat that is specifically dedicated to jhāna training. If the nuances of the ultimate realities bewilder you, don't worry—most people need the guidance of teachers who are trained in these rigorous practice methods. If you have not clearly discerned causal links between lifetimes, don't give up—many people need to deepen concentration again and again in order to successfully discern these subtle processes.

The stages that are presented in a linear format in this book are often practiced in alternation. You might apply concentration to insight, for instance, and then use insight to inform deeper concentration. If worldly responsibilities prevent you from establishing the seclusion needed for absorption, don't be discouraged—with or without the seclusion of jhāna, great benefits accrue through this meditation practice. It is, however, a rigorous training that will require renunciation, diligence, and dedication.

If you are concerned that undertaking a systematic approach will cramp your personal style, understand that I deliberately emphasized an exhaustively methodical approach in this manual in order to present a thorough training guide, to encourage the establishment of a strong foundation, and to articulate a clear path of awakening. Although the rigorous systematic style can be annoying at times, it is simply an attempt to curtail the common tendencies to indulge personal idiosyncrasies, preferences, conceit, or laziness. A sloppy training can thwart success. You will not, however, be stuck doing systematic exercises for the rest of your life. Once you have established deep concentration, discerned ultimate realities, and tasted the liberating potential of insight, you will be well endowed with the skills to playfully and intuitively moderate and explore life according to the needs, conditions, and interests of the moment.

How successfully you progress through a systematic method and how well you maintain the practice in daily life will depend upon the way that you choose to live. A frequently recited Buddhist verse encapsulates the most basic instructions: "Do no evil, engage in what is wholesome, and purify your mind; this is the teaching of the Buddhas."[336] Throughout each day, innumerable opportunities invite compassionate, skillful, and wise action; your life provides many occasions to abandon harmful attitudes and actions, and to cultivate wholesome states. Every moment presents an opportunity to bring mindfulness and wisdom into your responses to living. How you engage with your daily life will affect your quality of attention and facility with meditation.

You can create a lifestyle that supports your interest in concentration and insight. Notice what your attention is drawn to while driving, eating, waiting, or relaxing. Do you find ease in tranquility and calmness or do you fill the quiet moments with entertainments and fantasies? If you are often seduced by television and movies, or become frantic with work and relationship dramas, it may be difficult to quiet the mind and see clearly. If you come home tired and crave the passive entertainment of a TV movie, you might encourage your discipline by recalling the disciple of the Buddha who pined away an entire night of meditation lamenting that he was missing a festival.[337] Although the Buddha's generation did not contend with video games, television, telephones, or computers, they too had to overcome the temptation of sensual pleasures and the fruitless quest for comfort. Every single day you make choices about how to spend your time, how to direct your mind, and how to live. If you value clarity, don't drink. If you value truth, don't lie. If you value peace, don't intend harm to others. Whatever your family, work, economic, and social responsibilities may be, you have an enormous influence over

How Did I Spend Today?

For many years I asked myself a simple but explicit question each night before I went to sleep: Did I spend today well? Gradually and consistently bring your life into full alignment with your deepest values by sparking a daily inquiry into how you are living. Some days the inquiry may stimulate considerations of virtue, morality, and precepts as you ponder the ethical implications of choices you made. Sometimes the reflection may bring joy when recalling spontaneous acts of compassion and generosity. Sometimes urgency will arise, with resolve to not waste this precious life with the trivial accumulation of temporary comfort, social status, or the laziness that permits the mind to wander into fruitless worry or daydreams. Sometimes the question will invite hidden lessons and valuable insights to emerge. By asking a general reflective question, you steer the course of your development; then, you won't look back disappointed at the time of your inevitable death wondering, "What did I do with this life?"

how you engage with your own life's conditions. What kind of life are you creating for yourself? Is it the life that you want to live?

Every endeavor demands some sacrifice—by choosing one item on a restaurant menu, you implicitly abandon all the other delicious dishes. Although many meditators can successfully attain jhāna in a retreat structure, fewer people are willing to alter their daily lifestyle to permit regular absorption. Even after attaining deep states on retreat, most people need some basic conditions to maintain access to jhāna in daily life, including virtuous action, honesty, avoiding television and agitating entertainments, a minimum of two hours a day in meditation (preferably

⁀) Daily Insight

Although it can be challenging to consistently see the subtleties of mind and matter during active daily life, you can certainly carry much of what you have learned through intensive meditation into your awareness of activities, choices, emotions, thoughts, and events. You can experiment with integrating the understandings and practices gleaned from your in-depth explorations into your life.

Suggestion 1: Each week choose an activity to examine, for example, bathing. Bring mindful attention to the mind and body engaged in that pursuit. Each time that you bathe, contemplate the impermanent, unsatisfactory, not-self, or repulsive qualities to whatever elements you may perceive. It could be as simple as observing the material element of temperature changing during the course of your bath.

Suggestion 2: Resolve to clear your mind of obstructive states and refuse to fuel the reproduction of unwholesome states. For example, when you become aware that your mind is entertaining a stream of judging thoughts, mindfully examine the formation called judging. It will probably be composed of the eighteen or twenty mental formations associated with states of hatred. Once you make the decision to not condition hatred, direct your attention in a wholesome way in the next moment. In all likelihood the energy that supports chronic judging will have dissipated through wise examination. Contemplate how rapidly mental states change. If you find your mind wandering into daydreams, analyze the restless drifting mind to recognize the sixteen mental formations that compose general restlessness or the nineteen to twenty-two mental formations that compose conceit. Sense the unwholesome roots of delusion that are inherent in fantasy. Recognize the danger of shamelessness and fearlessness of wrongdoing that arise in conjunction with restlessness. Choose how you will direct your attention in the next moment of experience.

Suggestion 3: Learn how you can live your life continuing to nurture both calmness and clarity. Sensory restraint and basic mindfulness training are essential. Approach your daily meditation practice with the aim of supporting both concentration and insight. You may choose to practice with various objects, stick with just the breath, or integrate many of the exercises gleaned from this book. You might emphasize concentration or the four elements meditation. There is no single correct way to approach your daily meditation. Make a choice as to how you will direct your attention and then notice what your effort produces. Wise reflection will allow you to steer your practice continuously toward liberation.

more), and the genuine desire to sojourn, from time to time, in the bliss of seclusion. This requires a considerable degree of commitment and effort, but it is a remarkably small sacrifice to make for the fruits that this practice provides.

Although it is certainly possible to sustain jhāna, discern ultimate materiality and mentality, and develop a rigorous insight practice in the context of a contemporary lay lifestyle, most people seem to maintain a daily meditation practice that strengthens mindfulness, concentration, and insight in general ways, and then periodically intensify their practice before, during, and after periodic retreats. A practice that integrates consistent daily sitting, thoughtful contemplation of the Buddha's teachings, impeccable attention to virtue, joyful engagement with meritorious actions like giving and serving, and periodic intensive retreats will nurture your quest for the deepest happiness and peace of a liberated mind.

Practice can become an ongoing source of joy; it is not a burdensome chore. Whether practice is pleasant and easy or a challenging struggle, don't let negligence creep into your days. Every moment of your life is a precious opportunity for developing the mind. Is this moment of existence incorporated into your practice of awakening? Every day you can find opportunities to apply the insights that you have gleaned, strengthen mindfulness, and enhance the consistency of wise attention.

The training does not end with a great insight, the accomplishment of jhāna, or even the realization of nibbāna. On one occasion, the Buddha praised Venerable Sariputta's attainment and remarked that if someone should wish:

> "May I often abide in voidness," he should consider thus: "On the path by which I went to the village for alms, or in the place where I wandered for alms, or on the path by which I returned from alms round, was there any desire, lust, hate, delusion, or aversion in my mind regarding forms cognizable by the eye?"
>
> If by so reviewing, he knows...there was desire, lust, hate, delusion, or aversion in [his] mind regarding forms cognizable by the eye, then he should make an effort to abandon those evil unwholesome states.
>
> But if, by reviewing he knows...there was no desire, lust, hate, delusion, or aversion in [his] mind regarding forms cognizable by the eye, then he can abide happy and glad, training day and night in wholesome states.[338]

The Buddha encouraged Venerable Sariputta to observe his daily reactions and uproot any residual defilements that might linger. Even after astounding accomplishments, he continued to reflect. You can heed the same advice by observing your mind as you drive to work in the morning, walk to the office, eat lunch, answer the telephone, greet colleagues and clients, pay your taxes, cook dinner, care for a sick friend, launder your clothing, exercise at the park, and meditate. If you uncover unwholesome factors, deal wisely with them. If you recognize wholesome states, be glad, and enjoy the continued cultivation of the pure mind.

Developing a daily life practice is more comprehensive than just sitting in meditation. Skillful practice is embedded in how you relate to life. Through mindfully reviewing the state of your experience, sometimes with meticulous precision in meditation, and sometimes more generally in daily activities, you will gradually purify your mind and transform your life. Like a skilled sailor who adjusts the sails of his boat in order to propel his journey, use your engagement with every activity to develop your path.

May you realize the supreme happiness of nibbāna.

Notes

CITATIONS

D   sutta: verse within designated sutta

A   numerical collection (chapter): sutta within designated chapter

M   sutta: verse within designated sutta

S   thematic collection (Saṃyutta): sutta number within designated Saṃyutta, (periodically includes verse reference)

Ud   chapter: sutta within designated chapter

It   chapter: sutta numbered from beginning of It

Sn   chapter: sutta within designated chapter, (verse numbered from beginning of Sn)

Dhp   verse numbered from beginning of Dhp

Vism   chapter: verse within designated chapter

Vimm   fascicle, chapter, section: subsection

Sam   chapter: paragraph numbered from beginning of Sam

INTRODUCTION: APPROACHING DEEP CALM AND INSIGHT

1 It. 3:87
2 S. 35:99; S. 35:160; S. 22:5; S. 56:1
3 A. IV:162; A. X:29
4 M. 99:12 Subha Sutta: To Subha
5 A. V:176
6 The Pa-Auk Monastery in Burma (Myanmar) has many qualified teachers in residence year round and welcomes practitioners from around the world. For information regarding retreats and courses led by Shaila Catherine (mostly in the USA) see www.imsb.org.
7 Currently Venerable Pa-Auk Sayadaw's publications *Knowing and Seeing* and *Workings of Karma* are available online. See www.dhammaweb.net.
8 *The Middle Length Discourses of the Buddha (Majjhima Nikāya), The Connected Discourses of the Buddha (Samyutta Nikāya), The Path of Purification (Visuddhimagga),* and *A Comprehensive Manual of Abhidhamma (Abhidhammattha Sangaha)* are important sources that will support this training.
9 M. 107 Gaṇakamoggallāna Sutta: To Gaṇakamoggallāna

CHAPTER 1: CLEARING THE PATH: OVERCOMING
THE FIVE HINDRANCES

10 S. 46:31, S. 46:32
11 Vism. VIII:200
12 The *Visuddhimagga* suggests a few methods of counting as a preliminary practice to bring the attention into connection with the meditation subject of the breath. See Vism. VIII:190–196.
13 Ud. 4.3
14 It. 4:111
15 D. 22:13 Mahāsatipaṭṭhāna Sutta: The Greater Discourse on the Foundations of Mindfulness
16 A. V:77
17 A. V:193
18 S. 23:2
19 A. VI:63
20 M. 91:14 Brahmāyu Sutta: Brahmāyu
21 M. 145 Punnovada Sutta: Advice to Punna
22 M. 102:17 Pañcattaya Sutta: The Five and Three
23 Vism. IX:38
24 Vism. XIV:167
25 Sn. 4:15(942) Attadaṇḍa Sutta
26 Vism. VIII:153
27 M. 19:8 Dvedhāvitakka Sutta: Two Kinds of Thought
28 S. 9:11(787–788)
29 Sn. 3:8(588) Salla Sutta: The Dart
30 Ud. 4:1
31 M. 32:9 Mahāgosinga Sutta: The Greater Discourse in Gosinga
32 M. 20:7 Vitakkasaṇṭhāna Sutta: The Removal of Distracting Thoughts

33 S. 5:5(532–535)
34 S. 46:2
35 M. 15:8 Anumāna Sutta: Inference
36 D. 2:69–74 Sāmaññaphala Sutta: The Fruits of the Homeless Life
37 D. 2:75 Sāmaññaphala Sutta: The Fruits of the Homeless Life

CHAPTER 2: LEADING THE WAY: ENHANCING FIVE CONTROLLING FACULTIES

38 Sn. 3:1(424) Pabbajja Sutta: The Going Forth
39 A. VIII:63; Thanissāro Bhikkhu, trans. *Handful of Leaves* (San Diego: Mettā Forest Monastery, 2002)
40 A. VII:67
41 D. 16 Mahāparinibbāna: The Great Passing
42 Joanne Lauck, *The Voice of the Infinite in The Small* (Mill Spring: Swan-Raven & Co., 1998, p. 224)
43 A. VI:55
44 Vism. IV:67–73
45 Vism. IV:67–73
46 Vism. XXII:39–40
47 Vism. IV:34
48 A. X:15
49 A. II, i, 5
50 M. 111 Anupada Sutta: One by One as They Occurred
51 A. IV:117
52 See Bhikkhu Bodhi's introduction to vol. 2 of *The Saṃyutta Nikāya* (Boston: Wisdom Publications, p. 1507).
53 A. III:30
54 M. 149 Mahasalayatanika Sutta: The Great Sixfold Base
55 M. 117:3 Mahācattārīsaka Sutta: The Great Forty
56 For a fuller discussion of this point, see Analayo, *Satipaṭṭhāna: The Direct Path to Realization* (Birmingham: Windhorse Publications, 2004, p. 74).
57 Vism. XVI:96–98
58 The Pali term kusala may be translated as profitable, wholesome, or skillful. It refers to conditions that lead to the production of meritorious action.
59 S. 48:10
60 M. 19 Dvedhāvitakka Sutta: Two Kinds of Thought
61 M. 19:6 Dvedhāvitakka Sutta: Two Kinds of Thought
62 M.19.8 Dvedhāvitakka Sutta: Two Kinds of Thought
63 Vism. IV:45–49
64 S. 48:52

CHAPTER 3: ELEVEN SUPPORTS FOR DEVELOPING CONCENTRATION

65 S. 1(59–60)
66 Vism. IV:42–66. Here the list of ten skills for absorption is described. Chapter IV, paragraph 61, contains a similar list for the development of the enlightenment factor

of concentration that adds one additional item—the reflection on the peaceful attainments. Hence, combining the lists, I have presented eleven supports for concentration. A similar list is included in Vimm. Fascicle IV, chap. VIII, sect. 1.

67 Vimm. Fascicle IV, chap. VIII, sect. 1: *Ten Ways* and *Simile of the Horse Chariot*
68 Vimm. Fascicle IV, chap. VIII, sect. 1
69 The *Visuddhimagga* (IV:51–56) offers multiple strategies for arousing the enlightenment factors of investigation, energy, and rapture.
70 The *Visuddhimagga* (IV:57–62) offers multiple strategies for arousing the enlightenment factors of tranquility, concentration, and equanimity.
71 Vism. IV:64

CHAPTER 4: BEYOND DISTRACTION: ESTABLISHING JHĀNA THROUGH MINDFULNESS WITH BREATHING

72 It. 4:110; It. 4:111; A. IV:11
73 Vism. IV:92
74 Vimm. Fascicle IV, chap. VIII, sect. 1: *Simile of Chariot and Army*
75 Vism. IV:88–91
76 Vism. IV:88–91
77 Vism. IV:90; Vimm. Fascicle IV, chap. VIII, sect. 1
78 Vism. IV:90
79 Vimm. Fascicle IV, chap. VIII, sect. 1
80 Vism. VIII:214–315
81 Vism. VII:212–213
82 Vism. VIII:208
83 M. 148:29–33 Chachakka Sutta: The Six Sets of Six
84 Vism. IV:33
85 See Bhikkhu Bodhi, ed., *A Comprehensive Manual of Abhidhamma: The Abhidhammattha Sangaha of Acariya Anuruddha* (Seattle: Buddhist Publication Society, 2000, p. 331).
86 Vimm. Fascicle IV, chap. VIII, sect. 1: *Fixed Meditation-Jhāna*
87 S. 28:1
88 D. 2:75–76 Sāmaññaphala Sutta: The Fruits of the Homeless Life
89 Vism. IV:129
90 M. 66 Laṭukikopama Sutta: Simile of the Quail
91 A. IX:35
92 S. 28:2
93 D. 2:78 Sāmaññaphala Sutta: The Fruits of the Homeless Life
94 For reflections on disadvantages and advantages of each jhāna, see the *Vimuttimagga*, Fascicle V, chap. VIII, sect. 2: *Entrance into the Second Meditation; The Third Meditation, Jhāna; The Fourth Meditation, Jhāna; The Sphere of Infinite Space;* and so on.
95 S. 28:3
96 D. 2:80 Sāmaññaphala Sutta: The Fruits of the Homeless Life
97 S. 28:4
98 D. 2:82 Sāmaññaphala Sutta: The Fruits of the Homeless Life
99 D. 2:97 Sāmaññaphala Sutta: The Fruits of the Homeless Life

INTRODUCTION TO SECTION II:
CONCENTRATION BEYOND THE BREATH

100 M. 101:44 Devadaha Sutta: At Devadaha
101 Vism. VIII:155
102 Commentary to Dhammapada verse 285

CHAPTER 5: EMBODYING YOUR WORLD:
CONTEMPLATING THIRTY-TWO PARTS OF THE BODY

103 Ud. 3:5
104 *Dispeller of Delusion* (I:1053–1212) includes forty-four pages of detailed descriptions and instructions for this meditation practice.
105 Color of the body part can be used to generate four jhānas with color kasiṇas; the repulsive perception can cultivate the first jhāna, and the discernment of space leads to the meditation on material elements. See Vimm. Fascicle VII, chap. VIII, sect. IV: *Thirty-Two Parts of the Body.*
106 The body parts are listed in M. 10:10 Satipatthana Sutta: Foundations of Mindfulness; A. X:60; and M. 286 Mahāhatthipadopama Sutta: The Greater Discourse on the Simile of the Elephant's Footprint.
107 M. 10:10 Satipatthana Sutta: Foundations of Mindfulness
108 I have chosen to follow Bhikkhu Bodhi's use of the term *diaphragm.* Alternatives include *membrane* and *pleura,* which may be more accurate translations, but more difficult for many people to visualize or recognize.
109 Some lists of body parts found in the suttas do not include the brain. The brain appears to be a later addition to the list of thirty-two parts of the body.
110 This method makes great use of the mental light that arises in conjunction with concentration and insight meditation. Brief references to the light of wisdom can be found in the A. IV:141–145. This brief discourse mentions four lights: the light of the moon, sun, fire, and wisdom.
111 Vimm. Fascicle VII, chap. VIII, sect. IV
112 Vism. VIII:140
113 Sam. 7:1198

CHAPTER 6: EXPANDED PERCEPTIONS: TEN KASIṆA CIRCLES

114 A. III:100(1–10)
115 Vimm. Fascicle IV, chap. VIII, sect. 1: *Meaning of Kasiṇa*
116 D. 33 sect. 3.1(10–11) Sangīti Sutta: The Chanting Together
117 Vimm. Fascicle IV, chap. VIII, sect. 1
118 This color has been interpreted differently by various teachers and texts. *The Visuddhimagga* uses the term *blue* to describe it (V:12). The *Vimuttimagga* uses the term *blue-green* (Fascicle V, chap. VIII, sect. II: *The Blue-Green Kasiṇa*). When I was given the instruction, the word *black* was used.
119 The *Vimuttimagga* (Fascicle V, chap. VIII, section II: *The Air Kasiṇa*) mentions that the air kasiṇa can be grasped either through sight or through touch.

120   Vism. IV:30
121   Vism. XII:2–7

CHAPTER 7: INFINITE PERCEPTIONS: FOUR IMMATERIAL JHĀNAS

122   Sn. 3:12(736–737) Dvayatānupassanā Sutta: Origination and Cessation
123   D. 9:14 Poṭṭhapāda Sutta: About Poṭṭhapāda. Translated by John Kelly. I have modi-
       fied the translator's use of the term "forms" to "materiality" in order to conform with
       Venerable Pa-Auk Sayadaw's use of terminology and maintain consistency throughout
       this book.
124   D. 9:15 Poṭṭhapāda Sutta: About Poṭṭhapāda. Translated by John Kelly
125   D. 9:16 Poṭṭhapāda Sutta: About Poṭṭhapāda. Translated by John Kelly
126   Vism. X:46
127   Vism. X:51
128   Vism. X:54
129   M. 106:11 Āneñjasappāya Sutta: The Way to the Imperturbable

CHAPTER 8: BOUNDLESS HEART: LOVING-KINDNESS, COMPASSION, APPRECIATIVE JOY, AND EQUANIMITY

130   Sn. 1:8(143–151) Mettā Sutta: Loving-Kindness
131   Sn. 1:8(143–151) Mettā Sutta: Loving-Kindness
132   M. 127 Anuruddha Sutta: Anuruddha; S. 46:54
133   M. 52 Aṭṭhakanāgara Sutta: The Man From Aṭṭhakanāgara. This is one of the rare dis-
       courses in which the divine abidings are explicitly presented as a basis for insight.
134   A. 1:vi(3–5)
135   Vism. IX:2
136   Vism. IX:1
137   Vism. IX:2
138   Vism. IX:23
139   A. III:99
140   Sn. 1:8(143–152) Mettā Sutta: Loving-Kindness
141   Vism. IX:9–10
142   Vism. IX:102
143   Vism. IX:102
144   Vism. IX:111
145   Sam. 13:1881–1904
146   Vism. 9:103
147   Vism. IX:104
148   A. V:57
149   Vism. IX:111

CHAPTER 9: REFLECTIONS ON DEATH: CONTEMPLATING THE CORPSE

150   A. VIII:73
151   S. 48:41

152 A. V:77–78
153 Sn. 3:8(578) Salla Sutta: The Dart
154 A. VII:70
155 Dhp. verse 41
156 A. VIII:74
157 A. VIII:74; A. VI:19
158 A. V:57
159 A. X:48
160 A. VIII:73
161 A. IV:113
162 A. VIII:73
163 S. 36.7
164 S. 36.7
165 S. 36.7
166 M. 10:14 Satipaṭṭhāna Sutta: Foundations of Mindfulness; M. 119 Kāyagatāsati Sutta: Mindfulness of the Body
167 A. V:57
168 A. V:57

CHAPTER 10: ELEVEN SKILLS FOR JHĀNA MEDITATION

169 A. V:57
170 S. 34
171 S. 46.33

CHAPTER 11: CONCEPTS AND REALITY: PENETRATING THE ILLUSION OF COMPACTNESS

172 It. 3:63
173 M. 113 Sappurisa Sutta: The True Man
174 M. 140 Dhātuvibhanga Sutta: The Exposition on the Elements
175 See Pa-Auk Sayadaw's *The Workings of Kamma*, chapter III. Page 93 includes a description of dissolving the compactness of materiality, and page 105 contains a description of dissolving the compactness of mentality.
176 S. 22:102
177 S. 5:10
178 S. 28:1
179 Ud. 6:6
180 Vism. XXI:4, note 3

CHAPTER 12: EXPLORATIONS OF MATTER: FOUR ELEMENTS MEDITATION

181 Ud. 3:5
182 Vimm. Fascicle VIII, chap. VIII, sect. V: *The Determining of the Four Elements*

183 An excellent description of the discernment of ultimate materiality can be found in Pa-Auk Sayadaw's *The Workings of Kamma,* chapter III, pp. 90–102.

184 This list of twenty-eight materialities may be expanded to thirty with the addition of the material quality of torpor and the integration of matter; see Vimm. Fascicle X, chap. XI, sect. I: *Sense Organ of Body*

185 Vimm. Fascicle VIII, chap. VIII, sect. V: *Four Ways of Grasping the Element of Fire* and *Six Ways of Grasping the Element of Air*

186 M. 28:6 Mahāhatthipadopama Sutta: The Greater Discourse on the Simile of the Elephant's Footprint

187 M. 28:11 Mahāhatthipadopama Sutta: The Greater Discourse on the Simile of the Elephant's Footprint

188 M. 28:16 Mahāhatthipadopama Sutta: The Greater Discourse on the Simile of the Elephant's Footprint

189 M. 28:21 Mahāhatthipadopama Sutta: The Greater Discourse on the Simile of the Elephant's Footprint

190 It. 3:61. This brief discourse identifies three types of eyes: fleshy eye, divine eye, and wisdom eye.

191 D. 2:84 Sāmaññaphala Sutta: The Fruits of the Homeless Life

192 References to the space element are found in M. 62:12 Mahārāhulavāda: The Greater Discourse of Advice to Rāhula, and in M. 140:8–18 Dhātuvibhanga Sutta: The Exposition of the Elements

193 Vimm. Fascicle VII, chap. VIII, sect. IV: *Thirty-Two Parts of the Body*

194 Vism. XI: 117; Vimm. Fascicle VIII, chap. VIII, sect. V, *The Determining of the Four Elements*

195 Pa-Auk Sayadaw's *The Workings of Kamma,* chapter III, p. 90

196 Definitions of these twenty-eight materialities *(rūpas)* can be found in the Vism. XIV:34–80

197 Serious practioners of this method will find Pa-Auk Tawya Sayadaw's *Knowing and Seeing* to be a valuable resource for practical and detailed instructions.

198 Vism. XX:70

199 Pa-Auk Tawya Sayadaw's *Knowing and Seeing,* revised edition II, p. 134–137

200 Vism. XI:115

201 Vism. XIV:226

CHAPTER 13: NATURE OF MIND: DISCERNING
ULTIMATE MENTALITY

202 A. I,v,8

203 *The Dispensation's Usage,* Pa-Auk Sayadaw, unpublished manuscript, p. 143

204 For further study, see Bhikkhu Bodhi, ed., *A Comprehensive Manual of Abhidhamma: The Abhidhammattha Sangaha of Acariya Anuruddha* (Seattle: Buddhist Publication Society, 2000).

205 *A Comprehensive Manual of Abhidhamma,* p. 76

206 Sam. 1:114

CHAPTER 14: A MAGIC SHOW: EMPTINESS OF THE FIVE AGGREGATES

207 S. III:140. In order to keep a consistent usage of the primary terms throughout this book, I have substituted "materiality" or "matter" for *rūpa*, rather than the translator's original choice of "forms."

208 *The Dispeller of Delusion (Sammohavinodanī)* includes chapters on each of these categories.

209 As an alternative to the five aggregate model, to practice according to the element model, you may follow the same instructions, but organize phenomena into the following five categories: (1) materiality, which would include all the rūpas in each sense door, e.g., the sixty-three rūpas of the eye-door; (2) object, e.g., color; (3) consciousness, e.g., eye-consciousness; (4) contact, e.g., eye-contact; (5) feeling, and along with feeling see the whole cognitive process with all the present mental factors. See S. 18 Rāhulasaṃyutta, and M. 147 Cūḷarāhulovāda Sutta: The Shorter Discourse of Advice to Rāhula.

210 Vism. XIV:224

211 Vism. XIV:224

212 Sam. 1:145–152

213 Vism. XIV:224

214 Sam. 1:145–152

215 Vism. XIV:224

216 Sam. 1:145–152

217 M. 38:8 The Mahātaṇhāsankhaya Sutta: The Greater Discourse on the Destruction of Craving

218 Vism. XIV:224

219 Sam. 1:145–152

220 M. 22:40 Alagaddūpama Sutta: The Simile of the Snake

221 S. 35:152; S. 45:5

222 M. 28:28 Mahāhatthipadopama Sutta: The Greater Discourse on the Simile of the Elephant's Footprint

CHAPTER 15: CAUSES AND EFFECTS: TWELVE LINKS OF DEPENDENT ARISING

223 M. 98:61 Vāseṭṭha Sutta: To Vāseṭṭha

224 A. VI:63

225 A. V:57

226 A. VI:39; S. 14:12; M. 9 Sammādiṭṭhi Sutta: Right View

227 D. 15 Mahānidāna Sutta: The Great Discourse on Origination

228 M. 115:11 Bahudhātuka Sutta: The Many Kinds of Elements

229 Miln. abridged edition: part II, question 21, The Chicken and the Egg; Pali Text Society, Horner edition reference: III,ii.

230 A. X:61–62

231 Thānissaro Bhikkhu, *The Shape of Suffering* (Metta Forest Monastery, 2008)

232 S. 38:9

233 A. X:61–62

234 Vimm. Fascicle XI, chap. VII, section I: *Differences between Name and Form*
235 Sam. 6:917
236 M. 38:40 Mahātaṇhasankhaya Sutta: The Greater Discourse on the Destruction of Craving
237 Sam. 6:917
238 Sam. 6:917
239 M. 87 Piyajātika Sutta: Born from Those Who Are Dear
240 A. IV:77
241 For an examination of causation, see Noa Ronkin, *Early Buddhist Metaphysics: The Making of a Philosophical Tradition* (London: Routledge Curzon Press, 2005, p. 193).
242 Sam. 6:749 ff.
243 *Abhidhammattha Sangaha*, p. 303
244 M. 38 The Mahātaṇhāsankhaya Sutta: The Greater Discourse on the Destruction of Craving includes most of these alternative methods. I have relied upon Venerable Pa-Auk Sayadaw's unpublished training worksheets for the specifics and structure of these exercises.
245 Sam. 6:743
246 Sam. 6:743
247 Discern two aspects of contact as causes for five-door adverting consciousness: (1) since the arising of five-door adverting consciousness depends upon the ceasing of the previous mind-moment, discern the thirty-two to thirty-four mental factors associated with the preceding life-continuum consciousness; and (2) discern the eleven mental factors that compose the five-door adverting consciousness.
248 Discern two aspects of contact as causes for receiving consciousness: (1) since the arising of receiving consciousness depends upon the ceasing of the previous mind-moment, discern the eight mental factors associated with the preceding sense-door consciousness; and (2) discern the eleven mental factors that compose the receiving consciousness.
    Discern three aspects of contact as causes for investigating consciousness: (1) since the arising of investigating consciousness depends upon the ceasing of receiving consciousness, discern the eleven mental factors associated with the preceding receiving consciousness; (2) discern the eight mental factors associated with the sense door; and (3) discern the eleven or twelve mental factors that compose the investigating consciousness.
249 Discern two aspects of contact as causes for the first impulsion consciousness: (1) the eight mental factors associated with the sense door, and (2) the appropriate quantity of mental factors that compose the impulsion consciousness that you are meditating upon. Note that the preceding mind-moment will be discerned when considering attention as a cause.
    Discern three aspects of contact as causes for the second through seventh impulsion consciousnesses: (1) since the arising of each impulsion consciousness depends upon the ceasing of the previous mind-moment, discern the quantity of mental factors associated with the preceding impulsion consciousness; (2) discern the eight mental factors associated with the sense door; and (3) discern the appropriate quantity of mental factors that compose the impulsion consciousness that you are meditating upon.
250 Determining consciousnesses have three present causes (material base, object, and contact). Include three aspects of contact: (1) eight mental factors associated with the

sense-door, (2) eleven or twelve mental factors associated with the preceding investigating consciousness, and (3) the twelve mental factors associated with that determining consciousness.

Registration consciousnesses have five past causes and three present causes. Include three aspects of contact: (1) eight mental factors associated with the sense-door, (2) the appropriate quantity of mental factors associated with the preceding mind-moment, and (3) the appropriate quantity of mental factors associated with that registration consciousness.

Mind-door adverting consciousness arising dependent upon a sense object has three present causes (material base, object, and contact). Here, contact includes three aspects: (1) eight mental factors associated with the sense-door, (2) thirty-two to thirty-four mental factors associated with the preceding life-continuum consciousness, and (3) twelve mental factors associated with that mind-door adverting consciousness.

Impulsion consciousnesses that arise within a mind-door process yet are dependent upon a sense object, have four present causes (material base, object, contact, and attention). Include three aspects of contact as causes for the arising of the first impulsion consciousness: (1) eight mental factors associated with the sense-door, (2) thirty-two to thirty-four mental factors associated with the previous life-continuum consciousness, and (3) the appropriate quantity of mental factors arising with this first impulsion consciousness. Discern four aspects of contact as causes for the arising of the second through seventh impulsion consciousnesses: (1) eight mental factors associated with the sense-door, (2) thirty-two to thirty-four mental factors associated with the previous life-continuum consciousness, (3) the appropriate quantity of mental factors arising with the preceding impulsion consciousness, and (4) the appropriate quantity of mental factors arising with impulsion consciousness that you are examining. To examine attention as a cause, discern the twelve mental factors in the preceding mind-door adverting moment.

251 Discern two aspects of contact as causes for mind-door adverting consciousness: (1) since the arising of mind-door adverting consciousness depends upon the ceasing of the previous mind-moment, discern the thirty-two to thirty-four mental factors associated with the life-continuum consciousness; and (2) discern the twelve mental factors that compose the mind-door adverting consciousness.

252 Discern two aspects of contact as causes for the first impulsion consciousness in mind-door processes: (1) thirty-two to thirty-four mental factors associated with the previous life-continuum consciousness; and (2) the appropriate quantity of mental factors arising in this first impulsion consciousness. Note that the twelve factors of the preceding mind-adverting moment are discerned when examining attention as a cause.

Discern three aspects of contact as causes for each subsequent impulsion consciousness in a mind-door process: (1) the appropriate quantity of mental factors arising in the preceding impulsion consciousness, (2) thirty-two to thirty-four mental factors associated with the life-continuum consciousness, and (3) the appropriate quantity of mental factors arising in the impulsion consciousness that you are examining. Note that mind-door is included as a cause for every impulsion consciousness through the discernment of life-continuum consciousness.

253 The meditation instructions are a simplified version extracted from the training exercises that Pa-Auk Sayadaw guided me through in 2008. More details about these traditional methods can be found in *Dispeller of Delusion* (Sam. 6:635 ff.).

CHAPTER 16: A THOROUGH EXAMINATION:
RECOGNIZING THE CHARACTERISTIC, FUNCTION, MANIFESTATION,
AND PROXIMATE CAUSE

254 Sn 5:3(1048) Puṇṇakamānavapucchā: Puṇṇaka's Questions
255 See chapter II of the *Abhidhammattha Sangaha* for succinct and traditional descriptions.
256 Consciousness has the singular characteristic of cognizing an object yet it may manifest in multiple ways and serve various functions. Table 16.2 includes the types of
consciousnesses that are examined in this book. The *Abhidhamma Piṭaka* includes
a more comprehensive classification scheme in which the consciousness aggregate
is initially categorized by mundane and supramundane processes, then divided into
sense-sphere, material-sphere, or immaterial processes, further distinguished by wholesome, unwholesome, resultant, or functional attributes, and still further classified as
prompted or unprompted. In this way consciousness is analyzed into 89 or 121 types.
This degree of detail is beyond the scope of this introduction; readers may find further
elaboration in the *Abhidhammattha Sangaha*.
257 S. 35:99–100; S. 35:160–161; S. 22:5–6; S. 56:1–2
258 S. 35:99–100; S. 35:160–161; S. 22:5–6; S. 56:1–2

CHAPTER 17: LIBERATING INSIGHT: CONTEMPLATING
THREE UNIVERSAL CHARACTERISTICS

259 A fourth characteristic, that of repulsiveness *(asubha)* can be included with these contemplations. I have chosen to focus on the primary three characteristics to simplify
what might already appear to be a rather complex methodology. Meditators who are
adept at this process may add the perception of repulsiveness to the practices, thereby
contemplating four characteristics as explained at the end of this chapter.
260 Dhp., verses 277–279
261 M. 106:5 Āneñjasappāya Sutta: The Way to the Imperturbable
262 S. 35:93
263 Dhp., verse 112
264 A. IX:20
265 Sam. 1:24
266 S. 22:102
267 S. 1:11
268 Sam. 2:237–240
269 Sam. 2:241
270 A. IV:49
271 Sn. 3:12(727) Dvayatānupassanā Sutta: Origination and Cessation
272 M.147:9 Cūḷarāhulovāda Sutta: The Shorter Discourse of Advice to Rāhula. A similar
sequence is explored with ear and hearing, nose and smelling, tongue and tasting, body
and tactile feelings, mind and thinking. In short, the Buddha taught that we should
abandon desire for whatever is impermanent, suffering, and not-self. To conform to
Venerable Pa-Auk Sayadaw's careful usage of terms designating ultimate realities, I have
slightly altered Venerable Ñāṇamoli's and Venerable Bodhi's translation by changing
their word "forms" to Pa-Auk Sayadaw's preferred rendering, "color." See also S. 35:
162–164 and S. 18.

273 M. 140 Dhātuvibhanga Sutta: The Exposition of the Elements, and M. 28:6 Mahā-
     hatthipadopama Sutta: The Greater Discourse on the Simile of the Elephant's
     Footprint
274 M. 74.12 Dīghanakha Sutta: To Dīghanakha
275 Ajahn Chah, *Food for the Heart* (Boston: Wisdom Publications, 2002), p. 348
276 S. 22:122
277 S. 35:6
278 A. VII:46
279 Sn. 3:12(757–758) Dvayatānupassanā Sutta: Origination and Cessation
280 Eighteen elements are classified as concrete or real rūpas: earth, water, fire, wind ele-
     ments; the sensitivity of the eye, ear, nose, tongue, and body; color, sound, odor, and
     flavor; nutritive essence, life faculty, heart-base materiality; and sex-determining mate-
     rial elements. See chapter 12.
281 The ten nonconcrete or unreal aspects of matter include space, bodily intimation, ver-
     bal intimation, the lightness, pliancy, wieldiness, growth, continuity, aging, and imper-
     manence of the real material. See chapter 12.
282 S. 18 Rāhulasaṃyutta; and M. 147 Cūḷarāhulovāda Sutta: The Shorter Discourse of
     Advice to Rāhula
283 Vism. XX:18–20
284 Vism. XX:18–20
285 Vism. XX:46–92
286 Vism. XX:61–67
287 Vism. XX:68
288 Vism. XX:69
289 Vism. XX:71–72
290 Vism. XX:73
291 Vism. XX:76–88
292 Vism. XX:81

CHAPTER 18: RELEASE FROM THE BONDS: TEN FETTERS, FOUR STAGES
OF ENLIGHTENMENT, AND SIXTEEN KNOWLEDGES

293 "Flood" is a metaphor for the four floods *(asavas)* that keep beings bound to the cycle
     of existence: floods of craving for sensory pleasures, craving for existence, ignorance,
     and wrong view
294 S. 1:1
295 M. 24 Rathavinīta Sutta: The Relay Chariots
296 M. 24:10 Rathavinīta Sutta: The Relay Chariots
297 S. 14:12
298 Vism. XX:104
299 Vism. XX:93–104
300 Vism. XX:18–20
301 A. III:134
302 Vism. XX:105–130
303 M. 105 Sunakkatta: To Sunakkatta
304 M. 106:10 Āneñjasappāya Sutta: The Way to the Imperturbable
305 M. 29 Mahāsāropama Sutta: The Greater Discourse on the Simile of the Heartwood

306 A. IX:14
307 Vism. XXI:1
308 Vism. XXI:9
309 Vism. XXI:27
310 Vism. XXI:27
311 Vism. XXI:32
312 Vism. XXI:43
313 Vism. XXI:44
314 Vism. XXI:43
315 Vism. XXI:45–46
316 A. X:65
317 S. 2:17
318 Vism. XXI:82
319 Matara Sri Ñāṇārāma Mahāthera, *The Seven Stages of Purification and the Insight Knowledges* (Kandy, Sri Lanka: Buddhist Publication Society, 1983), p. 51.
320 M. 106:10 Āneñjasappāya Sutta: The Way to the Imperturbable
321 Vism. XXI:65
322 Vism. XXI:64
323 Vism. XXII:9
324 D. 11:85 Kevaddha Sutta: About Kevaddha. I have modified the translator's use of the phrase "name and form" to "mentality and materiality" in order to conform with Venerable Pa-Auk Sayadaw's use of terminology and maintain consistency throughout this book.
325 S. 43:14–43
326 Ud. 5:5
327 Vism. XXII:14
328 Vism. XXII:11
329 S. 55:24
330 M. 1 Mūlapariyāya Sutta: The Root of all Things
331 Sn. 3:11(714) Nālaka Sutta: Nālaka
332 M. 105 Sunakkhatta Sutta: To Sunakkhatta

Chapter 19: Of Lasting Benefit: Practice in the Midst of Daily Life

333 Sn 5:11(1098) Jatukaṇṇīmānavapuccha: Jatukaṇṇis's Question
334 S. 9:14(795–801)
335 Sn. 5:11(1099) Jatukaṇṇīmānavapuccha: Jatukaṇṇi's Question
336 Dhp. verse 183
337 S. 9:9(783–784)
338 M. 151:2 Pindapataparisuddhi Sutta: The Purification of Almsfood

Bibliography

PRIMARY SOURCES

Pa-Auk Tawya Sayadaw. *Knowing and Seeing,* revised edition, Kuala Lumpur: WAVE Publications, 2003.

———. *The Workings of Kamma,* Singapore: Pa-Auk Meditation Centre, 2008.

TRANSLATIONS OF PALI CANON AND ANCIENT BUDDHIST COMMENTARY

Bodhi, Bhikkhu, ed. *Abhidhammattha Sangaha: A Comprehensive Manual of Abhidhamma,* Pariyatti edition, Seattle: Buddhist Publication Society, 2000.

———, trans. *The Connected Discourses of the Buddha: A Translation of the Saṃyutta Nikāya,* Boston: Wisdom Publications, 2000.

Ehara, N. R. M., Soma Thera, and Kheminda Thera, trans. *The Vimuttimagga: The Path of Freedom by Arahant Upatissā,* Kandy: Buddhist Publications Society, 1977.

Fronsdal, Gil, trans. *The Dhammapada: A New Translation of the Buddhist Classic,* Boston: Shambhala Publications, 2005.

Ireland, John D., trans. *The Udana and the Itivuttaka: Inspired Utterances of the Buddha and the Buddha's Sayings,* Kandy: Buddhist Publication Society, 1997.

Ñāṇamoli, Bhikkhu, trans. *Visuddhimagga: The Path of Purification: The Classic Manual of Buddhist Doctrine and Meditation, by*

Bhadantācariya Buddhaghosa, Kandy: Buddhist Publications Society, 1991.

———. *The Dispeller of Delusion: Sammohavinodanī Parts I and II,* Oxford: Pali Text Society, 1996.

———. *The Middle Length Discourses of the Buddha: A Translation of the Majjhima Nikāya* (ed. and rev. Bhikkhu Bodhi), Boston: Wisdom Publications, 1995.

Nyanaponika Thera and Bhikkhu Bodhi, trans. and ed. *Numerical Discourses of the Buddha: An Anthology of Suttas from the Aṅguttara Nikāya,* Walnut Creek: Alta Mira Press, 1999.

Mendis, N. K. G., *The Questions of King Milinda: An Abridgement of the Milindapañha,* Kandy: Buddhist Publications Society, 2001.

Saddhātissā, H., trans. *Sutta Nipāta,* London: Curzon Press, 1994.

Thanissāro, Bhikkhu, trans. *Handful of Leaves, Vols. 1–4,* San Diego: Mettā Forest Monastery, 2002–2003.

Walshe, Maurice, trans. *The Long Discourses of the Buddha: A Translation of the Dīgha Nikāya,* Boston: Wisdom Publications, 1995.

CONTEMPORARY TEACHINGS

Analayo. *Satipaṭṭhāna: The Direct Path To Realization,* Burmingham: Windhorse Publications, 2004.

Buddhadasa, Bhikkhu. *Handbook for Mankind,* Bangplad: Dhammasapa, 1998.

Catherine, Shaila. *Focused and Fearless: A Meditator's Guide to States of Deep Joy, Calm, and Clarity,* Boston: Wisdom Publications, 2008.

Flickstein, Mathew. *Swallowing the River Ganges: A Practice Guide to the Path of Purification* (reprinted in 2007 as *The Meditator's Atlas*), Boston: Wisdom Publications, 2001.

Matara Sri Ñāṇārāma Mahāthera. *The Seven Stages of Purification and the Insight Knowledges,* Kandy, Sri Lanka: Buddhist Publication Society, 1983.

Ñāṇamoli, Bhikkhu. *Life of the Buddha According to the Pali Canon,* Kandy, Sri Lanka: Buddhist Publications Society, 1992.

Poonja, H. W. L. *The Truth Is,* San Anselmo, CA: VidyaSagar Publications, 1998.

Ronkin, Noa. *Early Buddhist Metaphysics: The Making of a Philosophical Tradition,* London: Routledge Curzon Press, 2005.

Thānissaro, Bhikkhu. *The Shape of Suffering,* Valley Center, CA: Metta Forest Monastery, 2008

U Jotika, Sayādaw. *A Map of The Journey,* Yangon, Myanmar: Waterfall Publishing House, 2004.

Glossary of Pali Terms and Buddhist Concepts

Abhidhamma	A comprehensive analysis of empirical reality. The "third basket" (piṭaka) or group of texts in the Buddhist canon which emphasizes an analytical consideration of dhammas.
Abhidhammattha Saṅgaha	The Comprehensive Manual of Abhidhamma, literally translated as "a compendium of things contained in the Abhidhamma," was probably composed by Ācariya Anuruddha sometime between the tenth and twelfth centuries in Sri Lanka. It has become the most widely used introduction to the Abhidhamma.
abhinīhāra kusala	Skill in resolution.
adhimokkha	Decision, conviction.
adosa	Nonhatred.
āhāraja ojaṭṭhamaka kalāpa	Eight-factored material kalāpa that contains nutritive essence as the eighth factor, and is produced by nutriment.
ahirika	Shamelessness of wrongdoing. A willingness to do evil actions based on an absence of self-respect.
ājīva	Livelihood.
ākāsa	Space. The aspect of materiality that defines the borders, gaps, and apertures surrounding other material phenomena. Can also refer to spatial concepts that point to areas void of perceptible matter.
akusala	Unwholesome, unskillful, unprofitable.
alobha	Nongreed.

amoha	Nondelusion. Seeing things as they actually are, free from misperception. Often used synonymously with paññā, ñāṇa, and vijjā.
anāgāmī	Nonreturner. One who has attained the third stage of enlightenment. An anāgāmī has uprooted the defilements of greed for sense desires and anger. This person will experience no more rebirths in sensual realms.
ānāpānasati	Mindfulness with breathing.
anattā	Not-self. The absence of inherent or independent self existence; the lack of self-essence. The third of three characteristics common to all conditioned phenomena. The recognition of anattā is dependent upon anicca and dukkha.
Aṅguttara Nikāya	The Incremental Discourses or The Numerical Discourses. A canonical collection of Buddhist discourses that are organized by numerical list.
anicca	Impermanence. The first of three characteristics common to all conditioned phenomena.
anipphannarūpa	Nonconcrete or unreal materiality. Refers to ten qualities or modes of corporeality.
anottappa	Fearlessness of wrongdoing. A willingness to do evil actions based on an absence of respect for others.
anusaya	Underlying tendencies, tendencies toward.
anussati	Recollection.
āpo	Water.
arahant	Fully enlightened being. One who has uprooted all the defilements and experiences no more mental suffering. Having attained the fourth and final stage of enlightenment, he or she will not be reborn.
ārammaṇa	Object, basis, condition, ground, cause, support. Refers to the various meditation objects included in this training, but more broadly, it refers to any object that consciousness arises in dependence upon.
ārammaṇa kusala	Skill in the object.
ārammaṇaghana	Compactness of object.
ariya	Noble, noble one.

ariyamagga	Noble path consciousness. The culmination and goal of vipassanā practice. The experience of the cessation of matter and mind, that is, the temporary cessation of all conditioned experience. There are four levels of noble path consciousness, each one uproots particular defilements.
ariyaphala	Fruition, noble fruit. Refers to the consciousness moments that follow a noble path consciousness. In this state the mind experiences the peaceful cessation of mental and material constructions and may dwell with nibbāna as the object for an extended period of time.
arūpa	Immaterial.
āsava	Taint, corruption, influx, outflow. Refers to four defilements that obstruct liberation: 1) taint of sensual desire, 2) taint of desiring existence, 3) taint of ignorance, 4) taint of wrong view.
asubha	Repulsive. Lit. "not beautiful."
avijjā	Ignorance. Not seeing what is true—namely, the impermanence, unsatisfactoriness, and not-self characteristics of things; and seeing what is not true—namely, the erroneous assumption that objects and experiences possess permanence, happiness, and self-nature.
bhava	Becoming, existence.
bhāva	Nature. Refers to sexual characteristics of the body. A commentarial term that refers to the material faculties of femininity and masculinity.
bhāva dasaka kalāpa	Ten-factored material kalāpas that contain sex-determining materiality as the tenth factor.
bhāvanā	Mental development.
bhavaṅgacitta	Life-continuum consciousness. A kamma resultant type of consciousness that functions to link cognitive processes.
bhikkhu	Full male renunciate. A male monk in the Buddhist order who keeps the 227 rules of the Vinaya, shaves his head, wears robes, and lives dependent on alms. Sometimes refers to both lay and ordained practitioners who keep away from the dangers of worldly life to seek release from samsaric existence.
bhikkhunī	Full female renunciate. A female nun in the Buddhist order

	who observes the Vinaya for women, shaves her head, wears robes, and lives dependent on alms.
bodhi	Awakening, enlightenment.
brahmaloka	A type of divine realm. A brahma is a denizen of that realm.
brahmavihāra	Divine abode. Refers to four qualities or boundless states: loving-kindness, compassion, appreciative joy, equanimity.
Buddha	One who is awakened. The historical Buddha lived in northern India between the fourth and fifth centuries BCE.
Buddhānussati	Recollection of the virtues of the Buddha.
cakkhu	Eye.
cetanā	Intention, volition.
cetasika	Mental factor. Refers to the mental factors that are associated with any moment of consciousness.
cakkhu dasaka kalāpa	Ten-factored material kalāpas that contain eye-sensitivity materiality as the tenth factor.
chanda	Desire. The willingness to act. This can be toward wholesome or unwholesome pursuits.
citta	Mind, consciousness, mental state. Sometimes used synonymously with manas or viññāṇa.
cittaja ojaṭṭhamaka kalāpa	Eight-factored material kalāpa that contains nutritive essence as the eighth factor, and is produced by mind.
cuticitta	Death consciousness. This is a process-freed type of consciousness that occurs at the moment of death.
dāna	Generosity, giving, donation, offering. Considered a fundamental practice for those who want to diminish the force of craving.
deva	Celestial being, radiant being, angel, deity.
dhamma	The nature of things, natural law, or fundamental truth. The teaching of the Buddha, the practice of virtue, meditation, and wisdom, the liberating path. (Sanskrit: Dharma)
Dhammapada	Verses on the teaching. A canonical compilation of brief teachings that are quoted as popular sayings of the Buddha.
dhammas (dhammā)	Objects, natural phenomena, qualities. A philosophical word that refers to any conditioned mental or material

object or the unconditioned. In the early Discourses of the Buddha, the singular form (dhamma) was primarily used to refer to the doctrine of the Buddha's teachings. With the development of Abhidhamma theory, the plural form (Pali, dhammā; English-Pali fusion, dhammas) was used to refer to all experiential phenomena.

dhātu	Element. May refer to material or immaterial elements.
Dīgha Nikāya	The Long Discourses. A collection of Discourses of the Buddha that are comparatively long.
diṭṭhi	View, opinion. Often refers to the wrong view that takes something to be substantial and permanent when in fact it is impermanent and not-self.
domanassa	Grief. Refers to mental pain.
dosa	Hatred, aversion, anger, animosity, hostility, not-wanting. The state of mind that turns away from a painful experience. Along with lobha and moha, one of the three forces that perpetuate suffering.
dukkha	Unsatisfactoriness, suffering, pain, stress. The second of three characteristics common to all conditioned phenomena. Results from impermanence and craving.
dvāra	Door. Refers to the sense doors of eye, ear, nose, tongue, body, and mind.
ekaggatā	One-pointedness of mind that unifies consciousness with a single object.
gandha	Odor.
ghana	Mass, compact, solid, thick, dense.
ghāna	Nose.
gocara	Range, domain, resort, pasture, arena, field.
gocara kusala	Skill in the range.
hadaya dasaka kalāpa	Ten-factored material kalāpas that contain heart-base materiality as the tenth factor.
hadayarūpa	The material heart.
hadayavatthu	Heart base. Material basis for consciousness. Theravāda tradition believes that mind processes arise dependent upon sensitivities within blood in a chamber of the heart.

hetu	Cause, reason, condition. Often used in conjunction with mūla, which means root.
hiri	Shame of wrongdoing that is based on self-respect.
iddhi	Success, power. Refers to accomplishments in concentration and insight, or psychic powers.
indriya	Faculty.
issā	Envy, jealousy. The wish that others not experience happiness or success.
itthibhāva indriya	Femininity faculty. The material element that determines the features, signs, and ways of the female.
jarā	Aging, decay.
jāti	Birth.
javana	Impulsion. Refers to the phase of the cognitive process in which consciousness experiences the object most vividly.
jhāna	Meditative absorption in which the mind is single-pointedly unified with a single perception. Four primary jhānas are emphasized in this book, each of which is defined by specific mental factors.
jīva	Life.
jivhā	Tongue.
jīvita navaka kalāpa	Nine-factored material kalāpa that contains life faculty as the ninth factor. Functions as "digestive fire."
jīvitindriya; jīvita	Life faculty, vitality. The factor responsible for maintaining the existence of other material elements and mental factors.
kalāpa	Group, unit, cluster.
kallitā kusala	Skill in pliancy.
kāma	Sensuality, desire for sense objects.
kāmacchanda	Sensual desire. The term for the first hindrance.
kāmarāga	Sensuous lust.
kamma	Action. Wholesome or unwholesome action that leads to results. (Sanskrit: karma)
kamma vipāka	The results of action.

kammaññatā	Workability, wieldiness. A feature of material elements and mental states expressed by pliancy, strength, and adaptability.
kammanta	Action. Right action refers to restraint from killing, stealing, and sexual misconduct.
kammasatti	Force of action, potency, potential. Refers to the potential for causes to bring results.
kammaṭṭhāna	Lit. "working-ground." The term refers to the various subjects of meditation such as breath, color, space, compassion, repulsive corpse, etc.
kammavaṭṭa	Kamma round. Refers to the kamma force produced by both wholesome and unwholesome actions.
karuṇā	Compassion. The wish that beings not suffer. The second of the four brahmavihāras.
kasiṇa	Lit. complete or whole. Refers to the ten expanded concentration subjects that include four colors and six elements.
kāya	Body. May refer to the anatomical body or to a grouping of either material or immaterial things as we might refer to "a body of water," or "a body of knowledge." In this book I render *kāya* sometimes literally as "body" and other times more descriptively as "mental body" or "associated mental factors."
kāya dasaka kalāpa	Ten-factored material kalāpas that contain body-sensitivity as the tenth factor.
kāyaviññatti	Bodily intimation. The material property that manifests as a bodily display of intention such as through gestures and movement.
khandha	Aggregate. The five aggregates that constitute a being include: materiality, feeling tone, perception, formations, and consciousness.
kiccaghana	Compactness of function.
kilesa	Defilement. A torment of mind.
kilesavaṭṭa	Defilement round. Refers to the ignorance, craving, grasping, and wrong views that perpetuate future existence.
kukkucca	Worry, remorse.
kusala	Wholesome, skillful, profitable.

lahutā	Lightness. A feature of material elements and mental states expressed by quickness, agility, and mobility.
lakkhaṇa	Characteristic. The salient quality of the phenomenon. The three characteristics of existence include: anicca, dukkha, anattā.
lobha	Greed, attachment. The mind's grasping on to a pleasant experience. Along with dosa and moha, one of the three forces that perpetuate suffering.
loka	World.
macchariya	Possessiveness, avarice, stinginess, miserliness. The wish not to see others as happy as one is oneself; manifests in the unwillingness to share.
magga	Path. Word for the productive moment of enlightenment when the mind takes nibbāna as the object and defilements are uprooted.
Majjhima Nikāya	The Middle Length Discourses. A collection of Discourses of the Buddha that are primarily presented in narrative structures and are of moderate length.
māna	Conceit, pride. Often manifests through comparisons of better, worse, or equal to.
manas (mano)	Mind, consciousness. May be used synonymously with citta or viññāṇa.
manasikāra	Attention.
manodvāravajjana	Mind-door adverting consciousness. Functions to receive and recognize the impact of mental data. In a mind-door cognitive process this functions similar to the votthabbanacitta in a sense-door process.
māra	A metaphorical figure in Buddhist scripture that personifies the hindrances that obstruct concentration or insight. The lord of all conditioned realms who attempts to keep beings tied to sensual existence. Is sometimes called the evil one, the tempter, king of death. Derived from maraṇa, the Pāli term for "death."
maraṇa	Death.
mettā	Loving-kindness, friendliness. The wish that other beings should enjoy internal and external safety, mental and physi-

cal happiness, and ease of well-being. The first of the four brahmavihāras.

micchādiṭṭhi	Wrong view. Unwise or erroneous interpretation of things.
middha	Torpor. Constricted, dull, unworkable state of consciousness.
moha	Delusion. Not knowing the ultimate characteristics of things. Along with dosa and lobha, one of the three forces that perpetuate suffering.
muditā	Appreciative joy. Rejoicing in the accomplishment and good fortune of others. Also called sympathetic, empathetic, or altruistic joy. The third of the four brahmavihāras.
mudutā	Malleability. A feature of material elements and mental states expressed by responsiveness, nonresistance, gentleness, and the absence of rigidity or stiffness.
nāma	Mentality, name.
ñāṇa	Knowledge. Often used synonymously with amoha, paññā, and vijjā.
ñāṇadassana	Knowledge and vision.
nibbāna	The unconditioned, deathless, unborn element. Perfectly undefiled state that is neither mind nor matter. Coolness, peace, extinguished, cessation. (Sanskrit: nirvāna)
nikāya	Group, body. Term used for the major collections of Buddhist texts.
nīla	A dark color, sometimes described as green, blue, black, or brown, which can be used to develop a colored kasiṇa.
nimitta	Mark, sign, image, condition. The term nimitta has many meanings and can be applied to coarse as well as subtle stages in the development of the meditation object. The term often refers to a subtle mental perception or counterpart sign of the meditation object.
nipphannarūpa	Concrete or real materiality. Refers to the eighteen material elements.
nīvaraṇa	Hindrance. A mental state that obstructs meditation. There are five classic hindrances: sensual desire, aversion, sloth and torpor, restlessness and worry, and doubt.
ojā	Nutriment.

ottappa	Fear or dread of wrongdoing that is based on respect for others. The wish to refrain from immoral actions because one considers the consequences, including the opinions of wise persons.
paccavekkhan-ṇañāṇato	Reviewing knowledge or retrospective knowledge. Refers to the insight that arises with the reviewing of a fruition attainment.
paccaya	Condition. Something upon which something else depends.
paccupaṭṭhāna	Manifestation. Refers to how something presents itself in lived experience.
padaṭṭhāna	Proximate cause. Refers to the immediately preceding conditions that permit something to occur.
pāguññatā	Proficiency. A feature of mental states expressed by effectiveness and health.
Pāli	The language of the Theravāda scriptures. A language that is closely related to Magadhi, which is thought to be the language spoken by the Buddha and his disciples.
pañcadvāravajjana	Five-door adverting consciousness. The consciousness that turns the mind toward the sense door.
paññā	Understanding, wisdom, knowledge. Often used synonymously with amoha, ñāṇa, and vijjā.
paññāloka	Light of wisdom. Refers to the luminosity of mind that accrues through concentration and insight practice.
papañca	Proliferation of thought, projections, conceptual diversification, mental associations.
paramattha	Ultimate. Supreme, truth, highest, intrinsic, irreducible.
paramattha dhamma	Abhidhamma theory identifies the ultimate constituents of mind and matter as irreducible, nonconceptual, and nonconventional elements, properties, or functions that can be directly perceived without the mediation of concepts. The ultimate realities include: consciousness, material phenomena, mental phenomena, and nibbāna.
pāramī	Perfection, completion, fulfillment. Often used to refer to the potency of past accomplishments that support meditation practice and successful attainments.

pasāda	Refers to the sensitivity of the material elements that register the impact of sensory objects.
passaddhi	Tranquility.
passati	To see, observe. Related to vision.
paṭhavī	Earth.
paṭiccasamuppāda	Dependent arising. Refers to the conditional relations that govern material and mental processes. Often formulated into a doctrine of twelve causally related links.
paṭisandhicitta	Rebirth-linking consciousness. It is a kamma resultant type of consciousness that arises at the moment of conception with the formation of a new life.
phala	Fruition, fruit.
phassa	Contact. A mental factor that arises when consciousness is impacted by sensory or mental data. Contact occurs with the meeting of the sense base, sense object, and sense consciousness.
piṭaka	Basket. Refers to the primary canonical collections: Vinaya Piṭaka, Sutta Piṭaka, Abhidhamma Piṭaka.
pīti	Rapture, delight, pleasure, enthusiasm, and happiness that refreshes attention. Physical and mental lightness and agility resulting from purity of mind; a delighted interest in what is happening.
puggala	Person.
purisabhāva indriya	Masculinity faculty. The material element that determines the features, signs, and ways of the male.
rāga	Lust, passion.
rasa	Taste.
rūpa	Materiality, form, matter.
sacca	Truth.
sadda	Sound.
saddhā	Faith, confidence, trust, conviction.
sakadāgāmī	Once-returner. Refers to the person who has attained the second stage of enlightenment with the weakening of the fetters of greed and hatred.

sakkaccakāri kusala	Skill in thoroughness.
sakkāyadiṭṭhi	Personality belief. The belief that there is a self that is the same as or is the owner of the mind and body. This is the first of the ten fetters and is eradicated with the first stage of enlightenment.
saḷāyatana	Six-fold sense base. Includes eye, ear, nose, tongue, body, and mind.
samādhi	Meditative concentration, unification of mind.
samādhi kusala	Skill in concentration.
samāpatti	Attainment. Refers to the eight attainments that include the four material jhānas and four immaterial absorptions.
samāpatti kusala	Skill in attainment.
samatha	Calmness of mind due to concentration.
sammā	Right. Lit. "the fulfillment of." This term is used to refer to the factors of the noble eightfold path and describes each factor as right understanding, right intention, right speech, right action, right livelihood, right effort, right mindfulness, and right concentration.
sammasana	Comprehension, determining, mastering, grasping, understanding.
sampajañña	Clear comprehension, full awareness.
sampaṭicchanacitta	Receiving consciousness. The consciousness in the cognitive series that immediately follows a sense-door consciousness and receives the impact of the sensory object in the mind.
sampatti rasa	Functioning through the achievement of a goal.
saṃsāra	Wandering from one thing or experience to another, repeated cycles. The cycle of craving and suffering caused by ignorance of ultimate truth that leads to repeated rebirths.
samūhaghana	Compactness of mass.
saṃyojana	Fetter.
Saṃyutta Nikāya	The Kindred Sayings or The Connected Discourses. A collection of Discourses of the Buddha that are organized according to theme.

saṅgha	Community. A gathering of realized ones or those dedicated to the liberating practices.
saṅkhārā	Volitional formations. Thoughts, intentions, and actions that accumulate kamma.
saññā	Perception, recognition, conceptualization.
santatighana	Compactness of continuity.
santīraṇacitta	Investigating consciousness. The mind-moment in the cognitive series that immediately follows the occurrence of receiving consciousness and is responsible for examining the mental data.
sappāya kusala	Skill in suitability.
sāsana	Teachings. Lit. "message." Used to refer to the teachings of the Buddha.
sātacca kusala	Skill in persistence.
sati	Mindfulness, awareness. The observing power of the mind, which clearly experiences an object without reacting to it. Includes a component of remembering and recollection.
satipaṭṭhāna	Foundations of mindfulness.
sayadaw	Burmese word meaning respectable or honorable teacher. It is a customary and respectful way for students to address a monastic teacher.
sīla	Virtue, ethics, morality.
sīlabbataparāmāsa	The erroneous belief that rites and rituals will purify the mind.
somanassa	Joy, bliss, happiness. Refers to mental pleasure.
sota	Ear. Stream (of the Dhamma).
sotāpanna	Stream-enterer. One who has attained the first stage of enlightenment by experiencing nibbāna. Such a person uproots the illusion of self, ends doubt in the efficacy of the dhamma teachings, and ceases to believe that any rite or ritual can bring about liberation. A sotāpanna cannot be reborn as an animal or in hell due to the weakening of his or her defilements and is assured of continued development toward full awakening.

sukha	Happiness, joy, contentment. May refer to mental or physical pleasure.
suññatā	Emptiness. The recognition of not-self as the absence of substantial or eternal existence.
sutta	Discourse or dialog. Lit "thread or string." The suttas form the "second basket" of Buddhist texts and are composed of collections of discourses given by the Buddha and great disciples.
Sutta Nipāta	A text of brief and pithy teachings of the Buddha.
Sutta Piṭaka	The "second basket" (piṭaka) or group of texts in the Buddhist canon, which includes the discourses of the Buddha and the great disciples.
tadārammaṇacitta	Registration consciousness. The concluding mind-moments in cognitive processes that savor the mental data. This registration, or savoring of the mental data, occurs after the impulsions have experienced the cognition and before the life-continuum mind-moments.
tanhā	Desire, craving, wanting.
Tathāgata	One who has thus gone beyond. Refers to the Buddha. Is a common way that the Buddha refers to himself in the discourses.
tatramajjhattatā	Evenness of mind, mental balance, neutrality, or equilibrium. Lit. "standing in the middle." An aspect of equanimity that is expressed by evenly distributed mental factors, impartiality, and the avoidance of extremes.
tejo	Fire, heat.
Theravāda	Teaching of the Elders. Lit. "the speech of the elders." Refers to a school of Buddhism that survives to this day and is commonly found in Sri Lanka, Thailand, and Burma (Myanmar).
thīna	Sloth, sleepiness, mental dullness.
thīnamiddha	Sloth and torpor. These two mental factors always arise together. The term for the third hindrance.
ṭhiti kusala	Skill in stability.
tiratana	Three Jewels. These are Buddha, Dhamma, and Saṅgha.
Udāna	The Inspired Utterances. A collection of brief discourses of the Buddha that include poetic verses.

udayabbaya	Rise and fall.
uddhacca	Restlessness.
uddhaccakukkucca	Restlessness and worry. The term for the fourth hindrance.
ujukatā	Uprightness, rectitude. Made straight, direct, honest. A quality of mental states that is characterized by honesty and straightforwardness and is opposed to hypocrisy, crookedness, and deception.
upacāra samādhi	Neighborhood concentration, access concentration. Refers to the conditions that precede jhāna or simulate jhāna-like conditions.
upacaya	Production, growth, appearance. Refers to the emergence of material or mental phenomena.
upādāna	Clinging, attachment, grasping. The mind's grasping on to an object and refusing to let go.
upakkilesa	Imperfection, impurity, corruption. May refer to the ten imperfections of insight that must be surmounted in vipassanā practice.
upekkhā	Equanimity, impartiality, even-mindedness. Lit. "onlooking from above." The quality of mind that remains centered without inclining toward extremes. The term implies an observational attitude that supports balance. Also, the fourth of the four brahmavihāras.
utuja ojaṭṭhamaka kalāpa	Eight-factored material kalāpa that contains nutritive essence as the eighth factor, and is produced by temperature.
vācā	Speech.
vacīviññatti	Verbal intimation. The material property that manifests in the verbal display of intention such as speech and vocalization.
vaṇṇa	Color, visible data, visible object.
vaṭṭa	Round. Refers to the round of rebirths. The cycle of dependent arising is sometimes divided into three rounds: the rounds of action, defilement, and results.
vatthu	Physical base. The six material organs upon which mental processes and cognition depend.
vāyo	Wind, air.

vedanā	Feeling tone. Experience of pleasant, unpleasant, or neutral feelings produced through contact with material or mental phenomena.
vicāra	Sustained attention, sustained application of the mind. The aspect of concentration consisting of the mind's sustained attention on the object. In some contexts vicāra may be translated with more active terms such as pondering, investigation, reflection, or examination.
vicikicchā	Doubt, skeptical criticism. The exhaustion of mind that comes about through excessive conjecture. The term for the fifth hindrance.
vijjā	Knowledge. Often used synonymously with amoha, ñāṇa, and paññā.
vimokkha	Deliverance, liberation.
vimutti	Freedom, deliverance.
vinaya	Discipline. Usually used to refer to the "first basket" (piṭaka) or group of texts in Buddhism, which records the rules and teaching stories related to monastic protocol and training.
viññāṇa	Consciousness. The mental state that cognizes an object. Sometimes used synonymously with citta or manas.
vipāka	Result. Particularly the result of kamma. Conditions that arise due to past actions.
vipariṇāma	Change.
vipassanā	Insight, clear seeing. Lit. seeing through various modes. The energetic observation of mental and physical objects in their aspect of impermanence, unsatisfactoriness, and lack of an inherent, independent essence or self.
virāga	Without lust, dispassion.
virati	Abstinence. Refers to the practice of refraining from wrong action in body, speech, and thought.
viriya	Effort, energy, strength. The energy or effort expended to direct the mind continuously toward the object. Derived from the word for hero.
visuddhi	Purification.

Visuddhimagga	The Path of Purification. An important and exhaustive instructive text written in the fifth century C.E. by Buddhaghosa in Sri Lanka. It appears to be an elaboration based on the first century text titled *Vimuttimagga,* but contains more specific instructions for the development of virtue, concentration, and insight. It is a widely used manual for meditators throughout the Theravādan world.
vitakka	Initial application of the mind. Applied attention or thought. Directed attention toward the object of meditation.
viveka	Seclusion, detachment, solitude. Descriptive term for the calm state that occurs when the mind is undisturbed by defilements.
voṭṭhabbanacitta	Determining consciousness. The mind-moment in the cognitive series that follows an investigating consciousness and recognizes the impact of the mental data.
vuṭṭhāna kusala	Skill in emergence or ascent.
vyāpāda	Aversion, ill will. The term for the second hindrance. Also spelled byāpāda.
yogi	One who practices meditation.

Index

A

abandonment
  of cravings, 18
  factors abandoned, the four jhānas
    and, 90
  the four aspects of perception, 138
  hindrances, 12
  lesser happiness to attain greater
    happiness, 17
  obstacles, 26
  of pleasure and pain, 49, 87
  thoughts, 21
  unwholesome states and wrong
    attention, 14, 38, 40, 429, 468
Abhidhamma
  Abhidhamma theory, 216–17, 255
  becoming, as defined in, 321
  on conditionality, 327
  on the distillation of phenomena
    into constituent parts, 265
  on the earth element, 222
  on the fire element, 223–24
  on ignorance, 315
  on life-continuum consciousness,
    73
  model of consciousness and mental
    factors, 255
  in this manual, 1, 3, 4
  on the water element, 223
  on the wind element, 224

abodes, divine. *See* divine abodes
  (brahmavihāras)
absence
  the concept of, 139–40
  of hindrances, 62
  of the perception of matter, 133, 136
absorption
  approaching, signs of, 62–63
  depth of absorption in jhāna,
    74–77
  and discernment, shifting between,
    263, 269
  lay lifestyle and, 469, 471
  peace of, reflection on, 59
  repulsiveness element and, 110, 113,
    114
  skillful effort and, 37
  skill in ability, 193–94
  skill in attainment, 192
  skill in concentration, 192–93
  stability of, 121
  See also jhāna; *specific jhānas*
abstinence or restraint, the three
  aspects of, 258, 379, 456, 462
access concentration. *See* neighborhood concentration *(upacāra
  samādhi)*
access to jhāna. *See* neighborhood concentration *(upacāra
  samādhi)*

five past causes, 338
past and present causes, 337
past lives
  discernment of causes from previous lifetimes, 324–26
  last object of consciousness, in previous lifetimes, 333–34
  meditation instruction, further back in time, 346–47
path knowledge
  four paths, 457–59
  reviewing, 460
  in the sixteen knowledges, 455–59
paṭicca-samuppāda. See dependent arising *(paṭiccasamuppāda)*
patience
  for discerning precise mental moments, 265
  equanimity and, 158
  of the tiger, 35–36
  as wholesome state, 14
perception *(saññā)*
  base of neither-perception-nor-nonperception, 140–43
  bhavaṅga state and, 73–74
  characteristic, function, manifestation, and proximate cause of, 371
  contemplating the faults of, 141
  faults of, and the *nimitta*, 71–72
  mindfulness and, 42
  as one of the five aggregates, 298–99
perishing. *See* arising and passing away; death
persistence, skill in *(sātacca kusala)*, 198–99
personality wrong view, 458
phenomena
  the concrete materialities, table of, 221
  meditation instruction contemplating phenomena one by one, 401–2

defining phenomena by characteristic, function, manifestation, and proximate cause, 356–58
  forty ways of viewing phenomena with the three characteristics, 408–11
  reflection on the ephemeral nature of, 423–24
  See also specific phenomena
phrases
  for *karuṇā* practice, 170
  for *mettā* practice, 150–51, 160, 163–65, 167–69
  for *muditā* practice, 172
  for *upekkhā* practice, 174–75
pīti (rapture)
  characteristic, function, manifestation, and proximate cause of, 373
  fading of, in the third jhāna, 86
  as one of the ten imperfections, 442
  third jhāna factor, joyous interest in the breath, 64–65, 67
pity, 155, 177
  See also aversion *(vyāpāda)*
planning, the habit of, 22–23, 207
pleasure *(sukha)*
  associated with body consciousness or mental objects, and the characteristic, function, manifestation, and proximate causes of, 369
  of the first jhāna, 77
  as one of the ten imperfections, 443
  two categories of, 17
pliancy, skill in *(kallitā kusala)*, 194–95
Poonja, H. W. L., 23
possessiveness *(macchariya)*, 256, 257, 276, 302, 303, 304, 382, 461
posture
  avoiding sloth and torpor, 38, 41
  in the *bhavaṅga* state, 74

wisdom, light of. *See* light of wisdom
    (paññāloka)
workability *(kammaññatā)*
    arising with tranquility, 442–43
    of associated mental factors, the
        characteristic, function, mani-
        festation, and proximate causes
        of, 377
    characteristic, function, manifesta-
        tion, and proximate causes of,
        363
    of consciousness, the characteristic,
        function, manifestation, and
        proximate causes of, 377
    as mental factor, 256, 258, 283, 286,
        291, 377
    as mental formation, 262, 273, 281
    as nonconcrete materiality, 221,
        363

worry *(kukkucca)*, 21, 27, 256, 276,
    383, 461
    See also restlessness and worry
        (uddhaccakukkucca)
wrongdoing
    shamelessness of wrongdoing
        (ahirika), 256, 257, 276, 380, 461
    shame of wrongdoing *(hiri)*, 256,
        262, 272, 280, 283, 286, 374, 379
wrong views *(diṭṭhi)*
    characteristic, function, manifesta-
        tion, and proximate cause of, 381
    removing, meditative exercise for,
        427–28
    role of, in exploring dependent aris-
        ing, 328

Y
yellow *kasiṇa*, 122–23, 131

About the Author

SHAILA CATHERINE began her meditation practice in 1980 and has accumulated eight years of intensive silent retreat experience. For nearly a decade, Shaila studied with masters in India, Nepal, and Thailand. Since 2003, she has focused on using the deep concentration of jhāna as the basis for insight, and since 2006, her practice has been guided by the teachings of Venerable Pa-Auk Tawya Sayadaw of Burma (Myanmar). Shaila has taught meditation since 1996, and in 2006 she founded Insight Meditation South Bay, a Buddhist meditation center in Mountain View, California. She authored *Focused and Fearless: A Meditator's Guide to States of Deep Joy, Calm, and Clarity* (2008), and she leads retreats and courses on the cultivation of concentration and mindfulness-based insight practices internationally.

Insight Meditation South Bay
www.imsb.org

About Wisdom Publications

WISDOM PUBLICATIONS is dedicated to offering works relating to and inspired by Buddhist traditions.

To learn more about us or to explore our other books, please visit our website at www.wisdompubs.org.

You can subscribe to our e-newsletter or request our print catalog online, or by writing to:

Wisdom Publications
199 Elm Street
Somerville, Massachusetts 02144 USA

You can also contact us at 617-776-7416, or info@wisdompubs.org.

Wisdom is a nonprofit, charitable 501(c)(3) organization and donations in support of our mission are tax deductible.